Electronic Payment Systems

Law and Emerging Technologies

Edward A. Morse

AMERICAN BAR ASSOCIATION
Business Law Section

Cover design by Catherine Zaccarine/ABA Publishing

Printed in the United States of America.

21   5 4 3

Library of Congress Cataloging-in-Publication Data

Names: Morse, Edward A., 1962- editor. ǀ American Bar Association. Section of
    Business Law, sponsoring body.
Title: Electronic Payment Systems: Law and Emerging Technologies / edited by Edward A. Morse.
Description: First edition. ǀ Chicago : American Bar Association, 2017. ǀ
    Includes index.
Identifiers: LCCN 2017052417 ǀ ISBN 9781634259620 (print)
Subjects: LCSH: Electronic funds transfers—Law and legislation—United
    States. ǀ Payment—United States—Data processing. ǀ Electronic
    commerce—Law and legislation—United States.
Classification: LCC KF1030.E4 E424 2017 ǀ DDC 332.1/788—dc23
LC record available at https://lccn.loc.gov/2017052417

Table of Contents

PART II: THE NEXT GENERATION

PART III: LEGAL AND POLICY INSIGHTS IN THE PAYMENTS ENVIRONMENT

Contributors

Jacqueline Allen is currently general counsel at American First Finance. She was previously an associate at Dykema Cox Smith where she advised banks, credit unions, fintech companies, money transmitters, nondepository lenders, mobile wallet providers, payment processors, and other technology companies. Jacqueline's practice focuses on compliance and regulatory matters, with a particular emphasis on consumer protection, anti-money laundering, e-commerce, privacy, and data security. She previously worked at the Federal Deposit Insurance Corporation (FDIC) and Federal Trade Commission (FTC). She is also a certified information privacy professional with a concentration in U.S. law (CIPP-US), a certified regulatory compliance manager (CRCM), and a certified anti-money laundering specialist (CAMS). Jacqueline may be contacted at jacquelineconleyallen@gmail.com.

Jessie Cheng is presently deputy general counsel at Ripple, where she advises on regulatory and commercial matters with respect to cross-border payments and banking, distributed financial technology, and digital currencies. Previously, Jessie was counsel and officer in the Legal Group of the Federal Reserve Bank of New York, providing legal advice to the financial services areas of the bank, including funds transfer services, international currency distribution, and central bank and international account services. Before joining the bank, she practiced law as an associate at the New York law firm Wachtell, Lipton, Rosen & Katz. A member of the American Bar Association (ABA), Jessie currently serves as vice chair of the Payments Subcommittee of the ABA Business Law Section's Uniform Commercial Code Committee. She holds a B.A. from Yale University and a J.D. from Columbia School of Law.

Mark Dabertin is a special counsel at Pepper Hamilton LLP. Before joining Pepper, Mark spent nearly 20 years working at major payment card firms, including Discover Card, JPMorgan Chase & Co., and Citibank. His experience at those companies spanned both card issuance and merchant acquiring, and included managing the compliance team that supported the U.S. and global acquiring activities of Chase

Paymentech. Mark was also the first person to serve as the legal officer and head of compliance of a retailer-owned and managed nationwide credit card program. He began his career as a financial services lawyer at the U.S. Office of the Comptroller of the Currency (OCC) and received his J.D. (cum laude) from the Indiana University Maurer School of Law.

Grayson J. Derrick is a partner in the Technology and Intellectual Property Section at Baird Holm LLP in Omaha, Neb. He focuses his practice on assisting financial services clients, specifically in the prepaid card industry, with regulatory matters, including money transmitter/money service business licensing issues, change in control issues, privacy and security issues, and anti-money laundering compliance programs. Gray assists clients with negotiating agreements for on all forms of information technology matters. He handles a wide range of matters relating to various aspects of intellectual property law, including domestic and international trademark prosecution, copyright prosecution and resolving domain name and other Internet related conflicts. Gray received a Juris Doctor, with distinction, in 2001 from the University of Nebraska College of Law. He received a Bachelor of Arts in Political Science, with Honors, from the University of Florida in 1997.

Malcolm Dowden is a legal director with Womble Bond Dickinson (UK) LLP. He has extensive experience with electronic communications regulation in the United Kingdom and also in the Gulf Cooperation Council region, India, and Southeast Asia. Through that work, Malcolm developed a particular interest in the development and regulation of online and mobile payment systems and their implications for joint ventures and other contractual relationships between electronic communications networks and payment and financial service providers.

Jay A. Dubow is a partner with Pepper Hamilton LLP, resident in the Philadelphia office. He is a member of the firm's White Collar Litigation and Investigations and its Commercial Litigation Practice Groups and co-chair of its Securities and Financial Services Enforcement Group. Jay focuses his practice on complex business litigation, with a special emphasis on defending against derivative and securities class action litigation and representing clients involved in investigations by the U.S. Securities and Exchange Commission, the Pennsylvania Department of Banking and Securities, and various self-regulatory organizations, including stock exchanges and the Financial Industry Regulatory Authority, Inc. He also conducts internal investigations on behalf of clients. In 2008, he joined a client, Advanta Corp., as senior vice president, general counsel, and chief administrative officer. He began his career as a branch chief in the Division of Enforcement of the U.S. Securities and Exchange Commission in Washington, D.C. Active in local and national bar associations, Jay is a leader in the ABA's Business Law Section and currently serves as chair of its Securities Litigation Subcommittee.

Erin Fonte is a member and financial services, payments, and fintech lawyer with Dykema Gossett PLLC. She is head of Dykema's Financial Services Regulatory and Compliance Group and the Fintech, Payments, and Digital Commerce Industry Group. Her practice includes advising fintech companies, financial institutions, alternative payments providers, vendors, and retailers regarding financial services, regulatory, and payment systems laws. She regularly advises regarding mobile banking, mobile payments, and mobile wallet products and services. Erin also advises advertisers, marketers, and retailers/companies regarding add-on mobile products such as mobile loyalty/rewards and geolocation advertising/coupons/offers. Erin has experience with a broad range of matters related to financial technology, banking and financial services, digital commerce, technology/Internet products, privacy and data protection laws, and general corporate matters. She frequently writes and speaks on payments, mobile payments, and privacy/data security issues, and is a member of the Federal Reserve's Faster Payments Task Force. She holds a B.A. from the University of Texas at Austin, and received her J.D. (with distinction) from Stanford Law School. Erin may be reached at efonte@dykema.com, and followed on Twitter at @PaymentsLawyer.

Jillian Friedman is Senior Digital Banking & Fintech Legal Counsel at the National Bank of Canada. In this capacity she advises bank partners on legal and regulatory issues related to virtual currency, blockchain, and new technology in financial services. She is also a leader in National Bank's blockchain initiative. Previously, Jillian acted as counsel to Montreal's Bitcoin Embassy, the first such "embassy" in the world. She has also made representations before the Senate Committee on Banking, Trade and Commerce's digital currency investigation. She regularly speaks at conferences and she has been recognized for her views on technology law issues in numerous legal, academic and news media, and co-authored the first legal book on virtual currency, The Law of Bitcoin. She holds a B.A. from McGill University and an LL.B. and J.D. from University of Montreal.

Julian Hamblin is a senior partner in Womble Bond Dickinson (UK) LLP's technology law team. His main areas of practice include advising on strategic outsourcing programs, digital innovation, online services including payment services, and data protection. He is an officer of the IBA Technology Law committee and currently serves as vice-chair of its Internet Business sub-committee. Particularly known for his work on retail information technology systems, Julian also advises extensively in the regulated financial services sector. Clients include major retailers, government bodies, and financial institutions.

Crystal Kaldjob is an associate in the Financial Services Practice Group at Morrison Foerster, where she advises financial services clients on a wide range of issues in regulatory and transactional contexts, including advising on strategic partnerships, loan portfolio sales and acquisitions, and other agreements related to consumer products, as well as compliance with consumer and retail banking laws, including laws related to the offering and operation of products and services such as credit and debit cards and payment products and lending.

Elizabeth A. Khalil is a partner at Dykema Gossett PLLC, resident in the firm's Chicago and Washington, D.C., offices. She advises financial institutions and other clients in the financial services space on a wide range of regulatory compliance and risk management matters, including with regard to privacy and data security. She previously held positions at the OCC and the Federal Deposit Insurance Corporation (FDIC) in Washington, D.C., and was a senior associate in the Financial Institutions and Privacy Groups of Hogan Lovells US LLP (formerly Hogan & Hartson). She holds a B.S. (cum laude) from Georgetown University and a J.D. from the University of Michigan Law School. She may be reached at ekhalil@dykema.com.

Paul Lanois is an attorney admitted to the bars of the District of Columbia (DC-USA), New York (NY-USA), and the Supreme Court of the United States (SCOTUS). He regularly publishes articles on technology law and is frequently invited to speak on such topics. Paul has spoken at conferences in the United States and across Europe. His views have been noted in diverse publications and media outlets in relation to privacy, data protection, and technology-related matters. He was named a "Cybersecurity & Data Privacy Trailblazer" by the *National Law Journal* and an "Innovative Corporate Counsel" by Law360. Paul was also recognized as a leading lawyer in the Legal 500's GC Powerlist and received the second annual Advocacy Award from the Association of Corporate Counsel (ACC). He has been recognized as a fellow of information privacy (FIP) by the International Association of Privacy Professionals (IAPP) and is a certified information privacy professional, with concentrations in Asian law (CIPP/A), U.S. law (CIPP/US), European law (CIPP/E), and Canadian law (CIPP/C). He is also a certified information privacy manager (CIPM) and a certified information privacy technologist (CIPT). He was an associate professor at the University of Cergy-Pontoise in France and an associate at major international law firms (Simpson Thacher & Bartlett, Allen & Overy and Linklaters). Paul graduated from the University of Paris-Sorbonne with a master's degree in business law and a postgraduate degree in private and public economic law. He also holds an LL.M. degree from the University of Pennsylvania Law School and a Certificate in Business and Public Policy from the Wharton School at the University of Pennsylvania.

Yafit Lev-Aretz is a postdoctoral research fellow at the Information Law Institute and an adjunct professor at the Media, Culture, and Communications Department at New York University. Yafit studies self-regulatory regimes set by private entities and the legal vacuum they create. She is especially interested in the growing use of algorithmic decision-making, choice architecture in the age of big data, and the ethical challenges posed by machine learning and artificially intelligent systems. Her research also highlights the legal treatment of beneficial uses of data, such as data philanthropy and the data for good movement, striving to strike a delicate balance between privacy protection and competing values. Previously, Yafit was an intellectual property fellow at the

Kernochan Center for the Law, Media, and the Arts at Columbia University, where she analyzed online practices from copyright and trademark law perspectives. Yafit holds an S.J.D. from the University of Pennsylvania Law School, an LL.M from Columbia Law School, and an LL.B from Bar-Ilan University in Israel.

Eileen Lyon is the General Counsel and Chief Compliance Officer for Kik Interactive Inc., a leading innovator in the online chat space and which conducted a token distribution of Kin, a cryptocurrency, in 2017. Ms. Lyon has also represented numerous financial institutions as general counsel, most recently Citizens Business Bank, and as external counsel for regulatory matters, including compliance with the Bank Secrecy Act. She is a graduate of the Gould School of Law at the University of Southern California Law Center and is a member of the California State Bar Association's Financial Institutions Committee.

Nizan Geslevich Packin is an assistant professor of law at Baruch College, City University of New York, an affiliated faculty at Indiana University's Cybersecurity and Internet Governance Center, and an adjunct professor at New York University. Nizan has an LL.M from Columbia University Law School and an S.J.D. from the University of Pennsylvania Law School. Prior to entering legal academia, Nizan practiced corporate law at Skadden Arps, externed in the Eastern District of New York, interned at the Federal Trade Commission, and clerked in the Israeli Supreme Court.

Emma Radmore is a legal director in the financial services regulatory team at Womble Bond Dickinson (UK) LLP. She has more than 20 years' experience of advising banks, payment service providers, and other financial institutions on their obligations under relevant regulatory requirements, including financial crime prevention requirements. Emma is also on the editorial boards of several UK financial services and financial crime prevention industry journals. She has won several awards for her legal and training skills.

Eli A. Rosenberg is a payments attorney at Baird Holm LLP in Omaha, Neb. Eli provides counsel to financial institutions and other financial services businesses with respect to their electronic banking, merchant-acquiring, electronic funds transfer, credit card, debit card, and prepaid card businesses. He also assists financial institutions and money service businesses with state and federal regulatory compliance and other regulatory matters including money transmitter/money service business licensing issues. In addition, Eli assists money service businesses in contracting with service providers and their agents, and he regularly negotiates services agreements and independent sales organization, BIN, agent bank, and association contracts. Eli serves as regulatory counsel to the Network Branded Prepaid Card Association. Eli received his Juris Doctor from the University of Kansas School of Law in 2012, where he served as a member of the Moot Court Council and as Note and Comment Editor of the Kansas Law Review. He is a recipient of the James P. Mize Trial Advocacy Award and the Faculty Award for Outstanding Achievement.

Sean Ruff is an attorney in the Financial Services Practice Group at Morrison & Foerster, LLP. His practice focuses on advising clients from the rapidly developing FinTech sector. He represents both emerging and established FinTech organizations, including non-bank and traditional banking institutions, with respect to complex regulatory and transactional matters. He has particular experience with funds transmission and related compliance initiatives, Bank Secrecy Act/Anti-Money Laundering regulation, alternative lending structures, traditional and non-traditional electronic payments and payment cards and consumer financial services.

Jonathan J. Wegner is a partner and corporate section chair at Baird Holm LLP in Omaha, Neb. He regularly advises financial institutions and non-bank financial service providers in connection with e-commerce, electronic payment systems, mobile wallets, mobile banking, and credit, debit and prepaid card programs. He assists financial institutions and financial service providers with a wide range of regulatory and compliance matters, including consumer protection compliance programs, BSA/AML compliance, Regulation II compliance, CFPB inquiries, privacy and security issues and third party service provider oversight. He serves as antitrust counsel to the Debit Network Alliance, a consortium of U.S. debit card networks formed to address technical standards for debit card transactions throughout the United States. Jonathan received his law degree, summa cum laude, from Creighton University School of Law. Prior to joining the firm, he worked as a business reporter for the Omaha World-Herald, Business Week Online and Consumer Reports. He studied British Literature at Oxford University and holds a Masters in Science of Journalism from Northwestern University.

George M. Williams jr is senior counsel in the New York office of Arnold & Porter Kaye Scholer LLP. His practice currently involves issues of financial regulation and the structuring of financial transactions. Prior to practicing law, he taught theoretical linguistics.

Jane K. Winn is a professor at University of Washington School of Law in Seattle, Washington, and a faculty director of the Center for Advanced Study & Research on Innovation Policy. Her teaching and research interests are in the area of commercial law, with a focus on how globalization and technological innovation are transforming national legal systems. Jane is co-author of *The Law of Electronic Commerce* (4th ed. Supp. 2017); many of her other publications are available from ssrn. com/author=334081. A graduate of Queen Mary College, University of London, and Harvard University, she is a member of the American Law Institute and received Fulbright research grants in 2008 and 2016 to study the rise of e-commerce in Greater China. Jane has been a visiting faculty member at University of California-Berkeley; Peking University, Tsinghua University, and Guanghua Law School at Zhejiang University in China; Sciences Po and Université Jean Moulin Lyon III in France; Melbourne University and Monash University in Australia; Chulalongkorn University in Thailand; and National Law University-Odisha in India.

About the Editor

Edward A. Morse is a professor of law at Creighton University School of Law in Omaha, Nebraska, where he holds the McGrath North Mullin & Kratz Endowed Chair in Business Law. He also currently serves as president of the university faculty. His research interests include taxation, regulation, and the intersection of law and technology, often involving interdisciplinary collaboration with colleagues in accounting, economics, and finance. His publications include more than forty articles, book chapters, books, and studies. He is a member of the bar in Nebraska (active) and Georgia (currently inactive), and he is a CPA in Iowa. He is a frequent speaker and presenter in professional and academic contexts, and he also consults regularly in areas that relate to his expertise. He is a longtime member of the ABA Tax Section and the Business Law Section, where he has served in various leadership roles. Recently, he served as the co-chair of the Electronic Payments subcommittee of the Cyberspace Law committee. Ed and his wife, Susan, have six children. Together, they operate a family cattle farm in rural Iowa, www.morsebeef.com.

Introduction

Technological innovations have impacted the structure and form of payment systems, increasing their variety as well as their ubiquity in modern society. This book explores these innovations and the legal and technological questions that they present.

Tapping into the experience and insights of lawyers and academics throughout the ABA Business Law Section, this book presents a topical discussion of the principal electronic payment systems utilized today. Chapters 1 through 3 discuss the primary modern payment systems, which form the "rails" for significant innovation. Legacy systems based on banks, credit cards, and non-bank money transmitters have relatively long histories and well-developed legal frameworks designed to meet demands for practical, efficient, and effective means of facilitating payments. While new technologies have also affected these systems, they have continued to benefit from their leading market position and widespread usage.

As the dynamics of competition affect the payments marketplace, legacy systems have progressed while new systems have emerged to challenge their hegemony. Chapters 4 through 6 discuss this next generation of payments technologies, which are seeking to deliver greater efficiency, convenience, and utility for businesses and consumers. Some of these new payment systems innovate by utilizing existing "rails" in new applications. For example, mobile wallet technologies frequently use credit cards and some peer-to-peer technologies utilize credit cards and ACH transactions. However, others are using new technologies, including distributed ledger technology used in cryptocurrencies, which potentially allow participants to avoid existing intermediaries and regulatory structures.

Regulatory frameworks serve multiple functions. Rules to resolve conflicts and enhance trust among the participants may be instrumental in helping a system to develop and flourish, but other relevant social norms play a significant role. Governments seeking to address problems of crime and terrorism face new challenges in globally functional electronic payment systems that can potentially circumvent their oversight. Chapters 7 through 8 discuss some important regulatory concerns, including money laundering, tax enforcement, and sanctions regimes, with chapter 7 focusing on U.S. approaches and chapter 8 focusing on European approaches and developments in cross-border payments outside the U.S. Chapter 9 provides a broad tour of the EU regulatory environment, while chapter 10 provides illustrations of some practical challenges for compliance by firms in the United Kingdom after Brexit.

Finally, chapters 11 through 13 provide current reflections and forward-looking thoughts on issues and concerns presented by technologies that are closely related to electronic payments. As the Internet of Things continues to expand its scope and impact on our daily lives, how are payment systems likely to adapt to these changes? And while we often extoll the benefits of technology, laws and regulations are also informed by critical examination of related social impacts. How does this movement toward electronic payment systems impact the poor and socially disadvantaged? As the digital revolution creates unprecedented volumes of data that are easily accessible and amenable to analysis, how does the emerging application of data analytics impact credit terms, privacy, and other social norms? How do these changes affect governmental regulation of the safety and soundness of systems, including banking and monetary policies? The authors in the final three chapters boldly address these and other topics.

This book is a cooperative venture that has benefitted from insights from many members of the Committee on Cyberspace Law. I am particularly grateful to our Committee Chair, Theodore Claypoole, my co-chair in the Electronic Payments subcommittee, Steven Middlebrook, as well as Sarah Jane Hughes, Candace Jones, and Denny Rice, each of whom has made important contributions that have shaped the structure and content of this work. The broad range of authors in this work, who are based in the U.S., Canada, Switzerland, and the U.K., reflects the global networks, connections, and friendships that emerge from work within the Business Law Section. These relationships enrich our lives and equip us to better serve our clients in an increasingly mobile and interconnected world.

Edward A. Morse

PART I

Legacy Payment Systems

The "Rails"

Chapter 1

Bank Systems

Jonathan J. Wegner, Eli A. Rosenberg,
and Grayson J. Derrick

In payments, it is easy to focus on the dollars and cents, the pounds and pence. But it is important to remember that, at its most essential, each payment begins with an obligation—an obligation to give over the value you have for the value you want. The payment is the act that discharges this obligation.

In ancient civilizations, this took place by direct exchange or barter of goods and services. However, the exchange of value has evolved progressively over centuries, first with government-issued currencies that represented stores of value and enabled trade among merchants and much later with banking institutions that served as payment intermediaries in the communities they served.

In the United States, a community banking model emerged in the late 1830s as "free banks" were allowed to form under state laws to provide basic but essential intermediary services.[1] These first banks enabled payment by local bank notes that were capable of being exchanged for legal tender (originally gold or silver coins, which later were supplanted by modern paper fiat currency). The system was far from uniform, with unique bank notes being issued by each institution, the value of which largely depended on the proximity of the holder to the issuing bank. After fits and starts at creating a uniform currency in the United States, Congress established the Federal Reserve System in 1913,[2] giving rise to the modern paper currency with which we are all familiar today—and which we use less and less frequently in modern commerce.

The Federal Reserve System is responsible for much of the physical infrastructure and legal framework underlying many of today's major bank payment systems: checks, Automated Clearing House (ACH) transfers, and wires. These systems

---

1. Federal Reserve Bank of Minneapolis, *A History of Central Banking in the United States*, https://www.minneapolisfed.org/community/student-resources/central-bank-history/history-of-central-banking (last visited May 19, 2017).
2. *Id.*

represent a significant but diminishing segment of U.S. payment volumes, although such payments still represent the vast majority of the notional value (i.e., actual dollar value) of all U.S. funds transfers due to the use of wire transfer services for most high-value fund transfers.[3]

More important for payments professionals, the legal underpinnings of these systems serve as the model upon which most other emerging payment systems have been designed. And aside from the card networks described in Chapter 2 and public ledgers or "blockchains" detailed in Chapter 5, there really is no other way to move money today—unless you own an armored car.

I. CHECKS

It is hard to understand how modern payment systems work without some understanding of how checks are cleared and settled. Both the modern ACH system and wire transfer services evolved from the systems (or contortions) bankers have made use of over the centuries to route, authenticate, clear, and settle checks.

The check, as a method of payment, has been documented as far back as the 11th century, when a tourist witnessed an Iranian trader present a written order in Basra for his account to be debited for payment.[4] Such orders have proliferated over the centuries as legal systems evolved to make them enforceable, negotiable, and, in certain cases, irrevocable. Today, these instruments are governed by articles 3 and 4 of the Uniform Commercial Code (U.C.C.), as modified and interpreted by each state adopting those uniform laws.

Checks are basically payment orders issued by the owner of an account to the financial institution that holds the owner's funds, instructing the financial institution to pay the owner's funds over to a third party. Under article 3, the issuer of this payment order is referred to as the drawer, and the person who accepts the check for payment of an obligation is a payee and becomes its holder. An unbelievable number of things can happen to the check between the time it is issued and the time it is presented for payment at the account owner's financial institution.[5] However, until the check is presented to the drawer's financial institution for payment and actually paid, the legal obligation of the drawer to satisfy the payment order embodied in the check is not discharged.

---

3. Fedwire transfers in 2015 totaled more than $834 trillion. *See* Board of Governors of the Federal Reserve System, *Fedwire Funds Services—Annual Statistics*, https://www.federalreserve.gov/payment systems/fedfunds_ann.htm (last visited May 19, 2017). By comparison, the notional value of 2015 ACH funds transfers totaled less than $50 trillion. *See* The Electronic Payments Association (NACHA), *History and Network Statistics*, https://www.nacha.org/ach-network/timeline (last visited May 19, 2017).

4. Stephen Quinn & William Roberds, *The Evolution of the Check as a Means of Payment: A Historical Survey*, 93 Fed. Res. Bank Atlanta: Econ. Rev. 4 (2008), *available at* https://www.frbatlanta.org/-/media/Documents/research/publications/economic-review/2008/vol93no4_quinn_roberds.pdf.

5. For example, articles 3 and 4 govern who bears the risk of loss whenever a check is sold, transferred, lost, stolen, destroyed, altered, canceled, or issued without valid authority.

While the check can be presented for payment at the same bank upon which it was drawn, the true utility of the check lies in the ability of its holder to submit the check for collection via his or her own financial institution (the depository bank).[6] Article 4 sets forth the legal framework for transmitting a check presented for payment at one bank for collection at the drawer's financial institution. For purposes of understanding modern payment systems, the key lesson to be learned from checks is this process of clearing and settlement by the network of banks[7] that connect the bank of first deposit with the bank on which the check is drawn.

This system evolved over centuries. For many years, bankers cleared and settled checks bilaterally, carrying checks from one office to another to present them for payment in currency or coin.[8] As might be expected, this caused long delays between issuance, presentment, and settlement.[9] It also created risks, such as risks of insufficient funds by the time the check was presented or theft as bankers lugged settlement funds in the form of currency and coin from one institution to another.

To address these issues, bankers created clearing houses. The first was the London Clearing House, formed in 1773 by 31 banks. It was a place at which bankers from each institution met to exchange and settle checks in a single location. By 1841, this clearing house had developed processes for netting obligations from multiple sources in a multilateral fashion, and net settlement via settlement accounts at the Bank of England had emerged by 1854, eliminating the carriage of physical currency and coin from one bank to another.

Regional clearing houses began to develop in U.S. money centers as early as 1853,[10] but the sheer physical size of the country frustrated efforts to develop an efficient, nationwide check-clearing system. However, the financial panic of 1907 prompted Congress to bring more order to the balkanized check system that had evolved as the nation sprawled following the expansions facilitated by railroads and sovereign land grants. During the 1907 financial crisis, certain banks refused to clear checks drawn on other banks, causing the insolvency of a number of otherwise sound financial institutions.[11] In response, Congress empowered the Federal Reserve System to establish a nationwide check-clearing system to which all banks ultimately would be afforded uniform access.[12]

---

6. The body of law surrounding checks is by far the most thorough and well-developed of any extant payment system, and the law governing the checking system is extensively covered in other publications, including the American Bar Association's *The ABCs of the UCC Article 3: Negotiable Instruments, and Article 4: Bank Deposits and Collections and Other Modern Systems.*

7. Article 4 includes definitions for the depository bank, payor bank, intermediary bank, collecting bank, and presenting bank, and an individual financial institution may qualify as one or more of these depending on where the check is in the process of collection.

8. Quinn & Roberds, *supra* note 4.

9. Today, many banks continue to clear checks bilaterally using imaging standards set by the Electronic Check Clearing House Organization.

10. The first clearing house in the United States was established in New York City in 1853. Federal Reserve, *History of the Federal Reserve*, https://www.federalreserveeducation.org/about-the-fed/history (last visited July 21, 2017).

11. *Id.*

12. *Id.*

Over the next century, this system rapidly expanded and continued to improve. First, Congress prohibited banks that utilized the Federal Reserve System for clearing checks from charging presentment fees, a practice that had resulted in payees receiving less than full value for the checks they presented for payment. To avoid such fees, collecting banks would engage in a practice known as "circuitous routing," which was designed to avoid such charges but also routinely resulted in substantial delays in the clearing and settlement of checks.[13] Later, in the late 1950s and early 1960s, the emergence of transit routing numbers and magnetic ink character recognition (MICR) encoding facilitated bulk automated sorting of checks on a much broader scale.[14] More recently, advances in check imaging technology coupled with the adoption of Check 21[15] has made it possible to use electronic imaging technology to eliminate the expense and delay of transporting physical checks across the country for clearing and settlement.[16]

In each step of this evolution, the physical handling of the payment instrument has become less labor-intensive and less integral to its clearance and settlement. However, as our late partner and payments law pioneer Terrence P. Maher was fond of saying, "We've spent our entire careers trying to eliminate parchment from payments."

That day may finally be dawning.

II. ACH SYSTEM

The ACH system was developed in the 1970s not long after the development of MICR encoding on checks. The addition of MICR encoding to checks significantly expedited processing and dramatically increased check volumes. This, coupled with advances in computing technology, led bankers to the realization that transactions could be cleared and settled by the exchange of data in lieu of physical check presentment. Implementation of such systems occurred gradually through regional clearing house associations. The first clearing house for the exchange of paperless debit entries emerged in California, followed quickly by Georgia and then regional efforts in the upper Midwest and New England.[17] Ultimately, these efforts coalesced in the late 1970s in the creation of what is now known as the ACH system.

Today, this system is one of the largest payment networks in the United States. More than 24 billion ACH transactions were processed in 2015, which were fairly

---

13. *Id.*

14. MICR Education Center, *What Is MICR?*, http://www.whatismicr.com/MICR_education_center.html (last visited May 19, 2017).

15. 12 U.S.C. §§ 5001–5018 (2016).

16. On Sept. 11, 2001, planes were grounded for days and check float—the value of checks in the process of transportation and collection—rose to $47 billion (about eight times the normal daily level), creating an impetus for Congress to adopt Check 21. *See* David B. Humphrey & Robert Hunt, Federal Reserve Bank of Philadelphia, Getting Rid of Paper: Savings from Check 21 (May 2012), *available at* https://philadelphiafed.org/research-and-data/publications/working-papers/2012/wp12-12.pdf.

17. *See* NACHA Operating Rules app. A, History of the ACH System.

evenly divided between credit and debit entries.[18] Most U.S. demand deposit accounts are connected to the ACH system, which not only is commonly used to facilitate recurring transactions but also powers most bill-pay platforms utilized by demand deposit accounts and many mobile wallets.

A. Basics of the ACH System

Transactions via the ACH system have their own nomenclature, reflective of the manner in which the system operates.[19] Each transaction is referred to as an "entry," which is a debit or credit entry to the originator's account. The party that initiates the transaction is the "originator" and the party that receives the entry is the "receiver." An originator initiates an entry via an "originating depository financial institution" (ODFI) (i.e., its bank, thrift, or credit union). The ODFI transmits the entry to an ACH operator (e.g., the Federal Reserve System or a private correspondent bank or private ACH operator, like the Electronic Payments Network (EPN)[20]). The ACH operator switches the transaction to a "receiving depository financial institution" (RDFI) (i.e., the receiver's bank). The ODFI and RDFI debit or credit their respective customer's accounts based on whether the originator sent funds to or pulled funds from the receiver's account.

Each day, the ACH operator calculates the net settlement amounts of all ACH files and entries processed by its ODFIs, which are then settled via the Federal Reserve's Net Settlement Service.[21] This results in a net credit or net debit to each financial institution's settlement account, which is maintained at the Federal Reserve Banks. Private-sector ACH operators settle their ODFIs' transactions via a similar arrangement with the Federal Reserve.

Historically, settlement of ACH transfers generally has occurred within one to two business days. Under current Electronic Payment Association (formerly the National Automated Clearing House Association (NACHA)) Operating Rules, ACH credits settle in one to two business days and ACH debits settle on the next business day.[22] Recently adopted changes to the NACHA Operating Rules will require that same-day ACH entries be available in coming years. Furthermore, the Federal Reserve's Faster Payments Task Force is presently in the process of identifying ways to make real-time payments a reality in the United States.

The ACH system is unique among payment systems in that it permits origination of both credit and debit entries to an account.[23] As such, the originator of an ACH entry can both send a payment to a third party and pull funds from a third party's account (subject, of course, to having obtained previously written authorization from the accountholder to do so). The ACH system originally was used for services

---

18. *See* NACHA, *History and Network Statistics, supra* note 3.
19. *See* NACHA Operating Rules art. 8, Definitions of Terms Used in These Rules.
20. EPN is owned by the Clearing House, a consortium of the 30 largest banks in the United States.
21. *See* NACHA Operating Rules OG 5–6.
22. *See id.* at OG 6.
23. *See id.* at OG 1–4, 7.

that are still in high demand today, like direct deposit of payroll and automatic pay-ment of recurring bills (e.g., mortgage and utility payments). More recently, it has evolved to handle a variety of commercial bill payments, check conversion transac-tions, and one-time consumer payments for online or telephone purchases.

The ACH system is probably the most cost-effective way to transfer funds from one U.S. deposit account to another U.S. deposit account, with individual transac-tions typically completed for pennies.[24] As discussed in Chapter 2, transactions pro-cessed on the card networks are subject to merchant discount fees that include interchange fees, which are deducted from the payment received by the merchant. The merchant discount fee represents a payment for services provided by the card network, the issuing bank, and the acquiring bank and offsets some of the losses incurred as a result of fraudulent or unauthorized transactions.[25] Given the signifi-cantly lower cost of using the ACH system, many of the financial technology com-panies described elsewhere in this book (including PayPal and Dwolla) utilize the ACH system as the backbone of their services, making their banking partners critical vendors for their financial service offerings.

NACHA is a nonprofit organization that promulgates the rules governing use of the ACH system. The members of NACHA are financial institutions, and there are multiple classes of membership, with member rights and obligations determined by the NACHA bylaws. NACHA establishes the rules and standards for the processing and settlement of entries and undertakes to ensure they conform to U.S. laws, which differ significantly depending on whether the funds transfer is classified as a com-mercial transaction or consumer transaction.

B. Liability—Commercial Transactions

Commercial funds transfer transactions take as a given that the counterparties are sophisticated commercial participants. Chains of contract govern the parties' rights and relationships, with certain important gaps filled by state laws.

To access the ACH system, ODFIs and RDFIs must enter into contracts with an ACH operator. These contracts require each ODFI and RDFI to comply with the NACHA Operating Rules.[26] The ODFI is responsible for warranties included in the Operating Rules and indemnifies ACH network participants against breach of such warranties.[27] These include warranties concerning the entry's valid and continu-ing authorization from the originator and receiver of the entry, the entry's com-pliance with the Operating Rules, the completeness of the entry with respect to

---

24. For example, Chase Bank N.A. imposes an incremental ACH transfer fee of 15 cents per trans-action. *See, e.g.*, Chase, *ACH Payments*, https://www.chase.com/business-banking/online-banking/ach-payments (last visited May 19, 2017).

25. These fees can vary widely, depending on whether the card is a "regulated" debit card, an unreg-ulated debit card, or a credit card, subject to negotiated discounts for high-volume merchants.

26. ACH operators may have their own rules that supplement the NACHA Operating Rules. For example, the Federal Reserve's Operating Circular 4 applies to ACH entries processed by the Federal Reserve as ACH operator.

27. *See* NACHA Operating Rules OG 29–30, Warranties and Indemnifications.

required information, the entry's timeliness, and the entry's compliance with NACHA security procedures.[28] In addition to these general warranties, the NACHA Operating Rules also impose on ODFIs additional warranties with respect to specific transaction types (often related to check conversion or remotely created entries).

The rules also include strong indemnities from the ODFI to the RDFI and other ACH network participants, including indemnities against damages for breach of any warranty or for any damages that result from an RDFI's failure to comply with the Consumer Financial Protection Bureau's (CFPB's) Regulation E, discussed in Part II.C below. Additional indemnities apply to international ACH entries originated by an ODFI, as well as certain person-to-person entries. Because these indemnities are extremely broad and not limited by time, only the statute of limitations for breach of contract claims cuts off an ODFI's liability for breach of these warranties, which in some states may expose an ODFI for liability up to seven years after a transaction occurs.[29]

In light of the important role of the ODFI as gatekeeper for the ACH network, ODFIs require that each originator enter into a contractual agreement before using the system both to establish the originator's obligations under the Operating Rules and to shield the ODFI from the originator's acts or omissions. The Operating Rules actually contain minimum requirements for such agreements, which must bind the originator to the NACHA Operating Rules, authorize the ODFI to originate entries to receivers, require that the originator comply with applicable law, include termination rights for violations, and permit the ODFI to audit the originator's compliance with the Operating Rules.[30] These agreements also typically include mirror indemnification rights with respect to breach of warranty claims that may be brought against an ODFI under the Operating Rules as a result of an originator's breach of its ODFI agreement.

While this contractual and rules-based framework provides the procedures for initiating and receiving entries via the ACH system, article 4A of the U.C.C. governs allocation of liability for unauthorized transfers and erroneous transfers.[31] U.C.C. 4A covers a number of other matters not addressed in the NACHA Operating Rules, such as allocation of risk among the participants in the electronic funds transfer and when transactions are final under state law.[32] These rules strongly favor financial institutions in light of the extremely low fees charged to commercial users of the service. In general, if a security procedure provided by the bank and adopted by the customer is "commercially reasonable," the risk of loss is allocated to the

---

28. *See id.* § 2.4.1.

29. *See* NACHA Operating Rules OG 29, Relationships with Originators, Third-Party Senders, or Sending Points.

30. *See id.* § 2.2.2.

31. U.C.C. art. 4A has been adopted by all 50 states and the District of Columbia; however, the NACHA Operating Rules provide that U.C.C. 4A as adopted by the state of New York is controlling in the absence of agreements to the contrary.

32. U.C.C. § 4A-108.

customer.[33] In the event of payment error, damages generally are limited to an interest credit and recovery of certain costs that may be incurred by the originator or receiver of the entry. Other direct and consequential damages generally are prohibited unless otherwise agreed in writing by the financial institution.[34]

C. Liability—Consumer Transactions

The Electronic Funds Transfer Act (EFTA) as implemented by the CFPB's Regulation E[35] establishes the rights of consumers and obligations of financial institutions that maintain consumer asset accounts, which can be used to effectuate electronic funds transfers. It covers consumer asset accounts, payroll accounts, and prepaid accounts held directly or indirectly by a financial institution and established primarily for personal, family, or household purposes.[36]

Regulation E sets forth requirements for electronic funds transfers, including preauthorized transfers, remittance transfers, and overdraft protection plans. It sets forth differing initial and periodic disclosure requirements and error resolution procedures depending on the type of account and type of funds transfer. Most important, it includes frameworks for error resolution and allocating liability between financial institutions and consumers—and it generally allocates risk of loss to the financial institution.

For purposes of the ACH system and the emerging payments environment that is the subject of this volume, the question of whether an "access device" is implicated in an electronic fund transfer is a threshold question for purposes of determining the rules for allocating liability. Under Regulation E, an "access device" is defined as a "a card, code, or other means of access to a consumer's account, or any combination thereof, that may be used by the consumer to initiate electronic fund transfers."[37] If an access device is implicated in the electronic funds transfer, the consumer must notify the issuer of the access device within two business days of discovering it is lost or stolen in order to qualify for $50 limited liability.[38] If the consumer fails to provide timely notice with respect to the loss of the access device, consumer liability with respect to the unauthorized transfers is limited to the lesser of $500 or the actual losses.[39] In the event an access device is not implicated in the electronic fund transfer, the consumer has 60 days from the date he or she receives a periodic statement setting forth the unauthorized or erroneous transfer to dispute its authenticity. Failure to do so results in consumer liability for those losses incurred after the close of the 60 days and before notice to the institution.[40] In each

33. See the discussion *infra* Part III concerning wire transfer services for detailed information concerning allocation of risk and limitation of liability.
34. U.C.C. § 4A-305.
35. 12 C.F.R. § 1005.1–.20 (2016).
36. *Id.* § 1005.1.
37. *Id.* § 1005.2.
38. *Id.* § 1005.6(b)(1).
39. *Id.* § 1005.6(b)(2).
40. *Id.* § 1005.6(b)(3).

instance, the burden of proof is on the financial institution to show that it would not have incurred the losses had the consumer notified the institution within the applicable notice period.[41]

These rules apply generally to consumer asset accounts and payroll card accounts. However, prepaid accounts also are subject to a new prior registration requirement in order to be eligible for the error resolution and limitations on liability set forth in Regulation E. Because certain types of prepaid accounts may be acquired and used by an accountholder prior to completion of customer due diligence and other standard account opening procedures, it may not be possible to know sufficient identifying information with respect to the customer alleging an error or unauthorized transfer in order to properly complete a reasonable investigation. The registration process also is designed to protect financial institutions against "first-party fraud," in which a customer fraudulently alleges an error has occurred to obtain funds from a financial institution, which typically is required to comply with the provisional credit requirements of Regulation E in order to be able to meet the required resolution time frames.

D. Liability—Federal Government Transactions

Although the NACHA Operating Rules govern most forms of ACH transfer, a separate set of rules cover funds transfers via the ACH system by the federal government. These rules[42] are promulgated by the Bureau of the Fiscal Service of the U.S. Department of the Treasury and compiled and distributed in what is commonly referred as the "Green Book."[43]

The Green Book is designed to deal primarily with exceptions or issues unique to federal government operations. It constitutes a comprehensive guide for financial institutions that receive ACH payments from and send payments to the federal government. Familiarity with the Green Book is important for financial institutions, as most federal payments, with few exceptions, are made through the ACH system. The Green Book includes information on enrollment options for federal payments, the processing cycles for federal payments such as Social Security benefits, scenarios in which a financial institution is obligated to return a federal payment, how to deal with alleged nonreceipt of a payment from a beneficiary, and notifications of changes. In addition, the Green Book also contains relevant contact information for federal agencies and, where applicable, website addresses.

E. International ACH Transfers

The ACH system operates in the United States only, but ACH operators maintain links to other nations' payment systems and facilitate such transactions via the

---

41. *Id.* § 1005.6(b)(2)–(3).
42. 31 C.F.R. pt. 210 (2016).
43. Bureau of the Fiscal Service, *Green Book—Guide to Federal ACH Payments*, https://www.fiscal.treasury.gov/fsreports/ref/greenBook/greenBook_home.htm (last visited May 19, 2017).

International ACH (IAT) Entry class. Such transfers initially were used to facilitate pension payments to retirees living overseas, but use has expanded to include cross-border payments to suppliers. These electronic funds transfers are fraught with complexity due to the lack of an international ACH operator and the need to connect two national payment systems. As such, risks abound with respect to timing, settlement, and foreign currency exchange. Simple discrepancies, like formatting requirements and different local bank holidays, also create challenges.

F. Common Types of ACH Transfers

The ACH system features common and recurring transaction types, many of which involve payments from and payments to consumers. In addition, business-to-business transactions (e.g., for supplies, benefits, or other payments) often are effected via ACH transfer. Such transactions are classified by Standard Entry Class (SEC) Codes, which are included in the entry data with each transaction.

- Prearranged Payment and Deposit (PPD) Entry. PPD Entries were the first type of entry made available via the ACH network and are used for transactions between a consumer and a business. They most commonly are used for recurring bill payments from consumers. They also may be used for recurring payments to consumers, such as payroll, benefit, or pension payments. In each case, consumer authorization must be given before the transaction is effectuated.

- Corporate Credit or Debit (CCD) Entry. CCD Entries provide the backbone of many bank treasury services platforms and are routinely used for business-to-business transactions. They can be initiated by purchasers or, less frequently, authorized vendors to make regular trade payments. Companies also use CCD Entries to consolidate funds within a corporate family to a central deposit account for purposes of cash management.[44] The one challenge to utilization of CCD when making supplier payments is the need for the buyer to maintain records with respect to the routing and account numbers for the account to which each payment is made—something not required when making direct payment by check.

- Check Conversion. A variety of SEC Codes have been established for transactions involving checks that are intended to expedite the payment process. As a general proposition, the check is scanned, data from the check is converted into an ACH entry, the original check is removed from the payment stream, and the party converting the check must warrant that the original check will not be presented for payment.[45] The ACH entry debits the check-writer's bank account, with the rights of the participants

---

44. NACHA Operating Rules OG 150.
45. *See id.* § 2.5.1.

governed by NACHA rules instead of articles 3 and 4 of the U.C.C. These SEC Codes include:

- Accounts Receivable Conversion (ARC) Entry. An ARC Entry is a single-entry ACH transaction created from information obtained on a check that is received via mail, dropbox, delivery service, or in person for a bill payment. In lieu of an express written authorization, authorization for the transaction is deemed to have been given when the receiver proceeds with a transaction after being given conspicuous notice that the payment may be presented as an electronic funds transfer.
- Back Office Conversion (BOC) Entry. Like ARC Entries, BOC Entries are deemed to have authorization given via notice at the point of purchase. As the name implies, checks are later processed in the merchant's "back office." Additional warranties regarding the originator must be given for these entries, including that the originator uses commercially reasonable methods to verify the receiver's identity and that a customer service phone number is maintained and answered during normal business hours.[46]
- Point of Purchase (POP) Entry. POP Entries are immediately converted to an electronic funds transfer from a consumer check at a merchant's point of purchase. The check must be voided immediately and returned to the consumer, and detailed information concerning the electronic funds transfer must be included in the receipt.[47]
- Represented Check (RCK) Entry. When a consumer check is returned for non-sufficient funds or uncollectable funds, a merchant may re-present the check for payment as an RCK Entry.[48] This enables the payee to save check processing costs and determine the exact timing of the payment submission. Any non-sufficient funds fee charged to the consumer's account must be presented as a separate entry.[49]
- Direct Consumer Payments. Whereas PPD Entries most commonly facilitate recurring payments to or from consumers, the WEB, TEL, and CIE Entry classes typically are used to permit one-time transfers from a consumer account.
- Telephone-Initiated (TEL) Entry. TEL Entries permit a business to debit the account of a consumer via an oral authorization given over the telephone.[50] Either the business initiating the entry must have a preexisting

---

46. *See id.* § 2.5.2, OR 13.

47. *See id.* § 2.5.10, OR 17–18.

48. An RCK Entry is deemed to be a presentment notice for purposes of U.C.C. art. 4. The receipt of the RCK Entry constitutes presentment of the check under U.C.C. § 4-110, and a return is deemed a notice of dishonor under U.C.C. § 4-301. This presentment framework is deemed a contractual modification of the Federal Reserve's Regulation CC as permitted under 12 C.F.R. pt. 229.37.

49. NACHA Operating Rules § 2.5.13, OR 19–20.

50. *See id.* at OG 230–35.

relationship with the consumer or the consumer must have initiated the call in which the authorization is given. Furthermore, the business must comply with a number of risk-management obligations, including verification of the consumer's identity and bank routing number, audio recording of authorizations followed by written notice of receipt of the authorization to the consumer, and recordkeeping requirements. For purposes of obtaining valid authorizations to a TEL fund transfer, compliance with the Electronic Signatures in Global and National Commerce (E-SIGN) Act's requirements for electronic disclosures and authentication also may apply.

- Internet-Initiated/Mobile (WEB) Entry.[51] When a consumer gives an authorization over the Internet or wireless network, a WEB Entry may be initiated. These may be debits initiated by businesses or credits initiated by other consumers for things like bill payments or online purchases. The consumer provides account and routing numbers to enable initiation of the entry. Due to the anonymity afforded users on the internet, the NACHA rules require originators to adopt commercially reasonable procedures for WEB Entries, such as use of secure internet protocols, methods to authenticate the receiver's identity, routing number validation, and systems that can detect fraudulent transaction patterns.

G. ACH System Access and Security

The NACHA Operating Rules establish minimum data security requirements that apply to ACH data, and state and federal laws also establish security rules that apply to certain types of data, such as consumers' personally identifiable information.[52]

All commercial (nonconsumer) participants in the ACH network are required to establish and maintain security policies and procedures for the initiation, processing, and storage of data related to or contained in entries. These policies and procedures must protect the confidentiality and integrity of consumers' nonpublic personal information and defend against anticipated threats and unauthorized use of such information.[53] Financial institutions and third-party service providers (discussed in Part II.H below) are required to conduct annual self-assessments of these security requirements as part of their mandatory annual ACH compliance audit.

The NACHA Operating Rules require that ACH entry information must be sent via a secure session or encrypted using information security technology that is commercially reasonable and complies with regulatory requirements. Encryption

---

51. *See id.* at OG 236–50.
52. *See* 15 U.S.C. §§ 6801–6809 (2016); *see also* Federal Financial Institutions Examination Council (FFIEC) Information Technology Examination Handbook InfoBase, *IT Booklets,* http://ithandbook.ffiec .gov/it-booklets.aspx (last visited May 19, 2017).
53. NACHA Operating Rules OG 24.

standards continuously evolve and are generally described in materials regularly updated by the Federal Financial Institutions Examination Council (FFIEC) in its Information Technology Booklet on Information Security.[54] Commercial reasonableness is the standard by which the adequacy of security procedures is evaluated in the event a security breach or unauthorized transaction occurs. Like encryption standards, the standards for commercial reasonableness may evolve over time, although the burden of proving that the security used in a transaction was not commercially reasonable falls on the user of the system (i.e., the customer). However, recent case law[55] has caused many financial institutions to look beyond the FFIEC guidance with respect to security procedures to other sources of security standards, such as National Institute of Standards and Technology (NIST) guidelines, to ensure ongoing compliance.[56]

Some consumer-initiated ACH entry classes, like WEB Entries, have much higher fraud risk. With such entries, a consumer could erroneously or fraudulently enter another person's account number. Due to the up-to-30-day lag between a transaction and the issuance of a monthly statement, coupled with the application of Regulation E's 60-day rule for reporting unauthorized transactions, a bank may be liable for unauthorized transactions up to 90 days after they occur. When frauds occur in an anonymous, online environment, the odds of successfully recovering a consumer's misappropriated funds are very, very slim.

The risk is heightened still further in payment systems, like PayPal, where the payment system may serve as an intermediary between a buyer and seller. For example, to enable a real-time payment, the payment system may cause its own funds to be paid to a seller and simultaneously initiate a WEB Entry to pull funds from a consumer's account. If the consumer did not authorize the transaction, the payment system bears the risk of loss. To mitigate this risk, systems like PayPal often use a "micro-deposit" scheme, where two small deposits are made to the consumer's account. The amount of each micro-deposit then must be reported by the consumer to the payment system to validate the ownership of the account. Many online payment providers have adopted this tactic to reduce the risk of originating unauthorized WEB Entries.

H. Third-Party Senders

One additional participant in the ACH system is worthy of special mention in a book devoted to emerging payment systems: third-party senders. These service providers enter into relationships with ODFIs to initiate and process entries on behalf of originators with whom the ODFI does not have a direct contractual relationship.[57] These

---

54. FFIEC, *supra* note 52.

55. *See* Patco Constr. Co. v. People's United Bank, No. 11-2031, 2012 U.S. App. Lexis 13617 (1st Cir. July 3, 2012) (finding that bank's security procedures were not commercially reasonable as a matter of law even though bank complied with then-current FFIEC standards).

56. NACHA Operating Rules OG 25–26.

57. *Id.* at OG 254.

nonbank entities are able to leverage the ACH system to create services that add value to the general payment intermediation services that banks provide. As non-bank participants in payment services, complex issues often arise involving whether or not state money transmission licensure obligations apply to a company that may be deemed a third-party sender.

The lack of a direct contractual relationship between the ODFI and the originator increases credit risk to the ODFI since it does not have a direct contractual relationship with the originator of the entry.[58] As such, ODFIs contractually obligate third-party senders to take on the obligations of the ODFI under the NACHA Operating Rules and require third-party senders to enter into agreements with originators that bind them to the NACHA rules. ODFIs also are expected to conduct thorough customer due diligence and to establish financial limits on batches and files submitted by third-party senders to mitigate risk.

I. Continued Evolution of the ACH System

Since its development in the 1970s, the ACH system has continued to evolve to better fit and meet the needs of a changing payments environment. NACHA implemented revisions to the NACHA Operating Rules, effective September 23, 2016, to provide the capability for moving payments faster and to enable same-day processing for nearly any ACH entry, also known as "Same Day ACH."[59]

Same Day ACH gives ODFIs the ability to offer Same Day ACH products and services by submitting files through two clearing windows provided by the ACH operators. RDFIs are then required to accept "same day" credit entries from the ODFI and to make funds available to their depositors by the end of their processing day.

Same Day ACH offers a number of potential benefits and significant use cases, as compared with current ACH processing times. For example, Same Day ACH may be used to process payroll payments and provide flexibility for late and emergency payrolls or missed deadlines. Similarly, Same Day ACH can assist consumers in making bill payments by enabling them to make more on-time payments on a bill's due date. Same Day ACH is applicable to nearly every type of ACH payment, with the exception of international transactions or high-dollar transactions for amounts more than $25,000. Further, while Same Day ACH is initially applicable only to credit entries, future phases already are set for implementation on September 15, 2017, and March 16, 2018, respectively. These phases will first extend Same Day ACH to debit entries in addition to credit entries, and then will ensure funds availability by 5:00 p.m. at the RDFI's local time.

---

58. *Id.* at OG 259.
59. NACHA, *Same Day ACH: Moving Payments Faster*, https://www.nacha.org/rules/same-day-ach-moving-payments-faster (last visited May 19, 2017).

III. WIRE TRANSFER SYSTEMS

Wire transfer systems are designed to effect same-day, high-value funds transfers. They are known as "real-time, gross-settlement" systems, in contrast to the net settlement processes used in the ACH system and by card networks.[60] This means that each wire transfer transaction is settled and cleared individually as it occurs instead of in batches of netted transactions a few times a day. These systems typically are used by commercial entities and financial institutions for payments that are time-sensitive (such as the closing of a merger or a trade of securities) or required to be fully guaranteed.

In many countries, there is only one wire transfer system, but the United States has two—Fedwire and the Clearing House Interbank Payment System (CHIPS). Fedwire is maintained and operated by the Federal Reserve and accessible to any institution that maintains a clearing account at the Federal Reserve. By contrast, CHIPS is owned by the Clearing House, a consortium of the 30 largest U.S. financial institutions, which are the primary users of CHIPS. While Fedwire is a bona fide real-time gross settlement system, CHIPS permits its participants to engage in multilateral netting of payments but still processes payments in real time.

The Fedwire system has existed for almost 100 years.[61] As noted above, settlement of funds transfers prior to the implementation of the Federal Reserve System was highly fragmented and involved exchange of physical bullion, currency, and coin. In 1918, the Federal Reserve Banks introduced a funds transfer system using Morse code, which enabled member banks to transfer balances held at the Federal Reserve using a secure communications network. The system adopted improvements in technology over the ensuing decades, including telex systems, computer systems, and today's proprietary communications systems.

Wire transfers are far less numerous than ACH or card network funds transfers, but the dollar value of such transfers far exceeds that of any other payment method. Wire transfers averaged more than $3.2 trillion transferred each day in 2015. The 2015 average transfer amount was about $6 million, with an average daily volume of 566,496 wire transfers.[62] In short, the wire transfer system is not heavily used when compared to the transaction count for other payment systems, but it does most of the heavy lifting.[63]

The gross settlement process helps protect participants in the system from insolvency risk that would arise from bank failures given the huge sums transferred via the system. When a customer initiates a typical wire transfer, the sending bank debits its customer's account and sends the payment order to Fedwire. The Federal

---

60. Federal Reserve Bank Services, *Fedwire Funds Services*, https://www.frbservices.org/service offerings/fedwire/fedwire_funds_service.html (last visited May 19, 2017).

61. THE FEDERAL RESERVE, THE FEDWIRE FUNDS SERVICE: ASSESSMENT OF COMPLIANCE WITH THE CORE PRINCIPLES FOR SYSTEMICALLY IMPORTANT PAYMENT SYSTEMS (July 2014), *available at* http://www.federalreserve.gov/payment systems/files/fedfunds_coreprinciples.pdf.

62. *Fedwire Funds Services—Annual Statistics*, *supra* note 3.

63. See *supra* note 3 for transaction and volume data for ACH and wire transfers.

Reserve Bank at which the sender's bank maintains its master account then debits that account and credits the master account of the receiving bank. The receiving bank then credits the receiver's bank account.[64] While simple to describe, the risk of each transfer cannot be overstated. If a customer does not have good funds available when the wire transfer is initiated, or if the sending bank's master account has insufficient available funds for the Federal Reserve Bank to credit the receiving bank's account, an overdraft (i.e., a loan) will occur if the transaction is permitted to go through. While a bank may permit a daylight overdraft for certain customers with the expectation that good funds will be on hand by the close of the business day, the bank assumes credit risk in doing so and may not be able to recover funds from its customer if it is unable to pay.

Corporate account takeovers and initiation of fraudulent transfers by unauthorized persons therefore present a major risk to a financial institution and its customers. Financial institutions assume a certain amount of fraud risk in ACH and card network payments, and losses associated with fraudulent transactions are either expected to be minimal given the nature of the transaction (e.g., PPD Entries for direct deposit of payroll) or are intended to be compensated for and absorbed via merchant discount fees (e.g., interchange fees in debit card EFTs). However, with a typical fee for a wire transfer of less than $50, a financial institution could never be compensated adequately for even a single unauthorized multimillion-dollar wire transfer loss.

With such high stakes involved but such comparatively low fees, the legal framework governing the wire transfer system strongly favors financial institutions and shifts risk to their customers, provided that a financial institution makes significant investments in developing and maintaining robust security procedures. As noted above, article 4A allocates risk of loss with respect to unauthorized funds transfers to the sender of the payment order if the financial institution initiating the payment order has made available "commercially reasonable" security procedures. Article 4A does not define what constitutes "commercially reasonable" security procedures. Such matters are a question of law to be determined based on a number of factors, such as industry practice, the circumstances of the customer's use of the payment systems (e.g., the size, type, and frequency of payment orders), the customer's wishes, and the alternative security procedures made available by the financial institution to its customer.[65]

Article 4A includes a presumption in favor of the bank that a security procedure is commercially reasonable if the customer expressly agrees in writing to be bound by any payment order accepted by the bank in compliance with the security procedure chosen by the customer and if the customer had been offered a security

---

64. For rules governing and detailed information concerning the rights and obligations of the participants in the wire transfer process, see subpt. B of the Federal Reserve's Regulation J (12 C.F.R. pt. 210.25 *et seq.*) and the Federal Reserve Bank's OPERATING CIRCULAR NO. 6: FUNDS TRANSFER THROUGH THE FEDWIRE FUNDS SERVICE (2016), *available at* https://www.frbservices.org/files/regulations/pdf/operating_circular_6_06302016.pdf.

65. U.C.C. § 4A-202(c).

procedure that was, in fact, commercially reasonable.[66] For that reason, most commercial wire transfer agreements contain a customer representation that the customer agrees the chosen security procedure was commercially reasonable.

IV. FASTER PAYMENTS

Improvement to the legacy payment systems is ongoing. In 2015, the Federal Reserve published a whitepaper, "Strategies for Improving the U.S. Payment System,"[67] which called for the development of improved payment systems that feature secure, real-time, and cross-border payments capable of rapid clearing and settlement with finality. This led to the formation of the Faster Payments Task Force, a group of more than 300 representatives from leading payments system operators and participants.

The goals of the task force are ambitious and represent an attempt to bring balance to the uneven development of new and faster payment systems and the proliferation of technologies and standards to effectuate clearing and settlement. The stated goal of the task force is to assess proposals to cultivate a safe, ubiquitous faster payments solution.[68] The criteria established for evaluation of proposals focus on ubiquity, efficiency, safety, security, and speed.[69] Appropriate legal and governance frameworks for the implementation of the standards also are under consideration.

The submission process for proposed solutions to establish such a system in the United States is ongoing, and the development of such a system may take significant time and investment. The task force received 19 proposals, which are in the process of being reviewed. None appear to be comprehensive or to satisfy all of the effectiveness criteria, but each represents a step toward realizing the task force's goals. The fragmentation of the proposals suggests that compromises on the evaluation criteria likely will be made.

Even when a faster payments system ultimately emerges, it is almost a certainty that the legacy systems will continue to serve financial institutions for a long, long time. After all, even today, checks are still one of the most common forms of payment. Assuming that legacy systems will continue to satisfy the needs of most payors and payees, such compromises are likely to be acceptable to the marketplace, especially if the work efforts of the task force result in standardization that enable the market to realize interoperable, ubiquitous faster payment solutions.

---

66. *Id.*

67. U.S. FEDERAL RESERVE SYSTEM, STRATEGIES FOR IMPROVING THE U.S. PAYMENT SYSTEM (Jan. 26, 2015), *available at* https://fedpaymentsimprovement.org/wp-content/uploads/strategies-improving-us-payment-system .pdf.

68. The Federal Reserve, *Faster Payments Effectiveness Criteria*, https://fedpaymentsimprovement .org/faster-payments/effectiveness-criteria/ (last visited May 19, 2017).

69. *Id.*

Chapter 2

Charging Ahead—from Innovation to Industry

Mark Dabertin and Jay Dubow[1]

Near magical ease of use, such as the tapping of a mobile phone or the waving of a credit card, has become expected in the fiercely competitive payment card industry. Yet the apparent simplicity and fleeting duration of a card transaction— often mere seconds transpire between the card's presentment and confirmation of payment—belie its true complexity. A consumer's use of his or her payment card, whether it is a credit, debit, or prepaid card, triggers a financial transaction involving a myriad of contractual obligations, operational interdependencies, and regulatory requirements. As will be explored in this chapter, the seamlessness experienced by the consumer in using his or her card depends on close coordination among multiple parties that is primarily achieved through industry self-regulation.

Describing what happens in a payment card transaction is akin to describing a complex football play that resulted in a touchdown (i.e., the fact of the touchdown is obvious, but many of the play's most important attributes will be missed by a casual "armchair" fan). Knowing something more about the game, the rules, and the players is necessary for deeper understanding. Following a brief summary of the history of payment cards, this chapter first introduces the key "players" in a card transaction and then discusses their respective roles as the transaction proceeds. Next, the chapter reviews the primary types of payment card products and the legal requirements that govern them. The chapter then concludes with a discussion of newer payment technologies and the extent to which the device used to initiate the transaction, such as a mobile phone versus a plastic card, affects the applicable risks.

---

1. Mark Dabertin and Jay Dubow are with Pepper Hamilton LLP.

I. HOW IT BEGAN

A. New Industry Arises in Post-WWII America

The card payment industry began in 1950 with the introduction of the world's first multi-use payment card, the Diners Club® Card. This product was the brainchild of a businessman named Frank McNamara, who recognized the potential mass appeal of a convenient means of paying that could be used anywhere, as opposed to the single-merchant payment cards that were available at the time. Diners Club was an immediate success, attracting 10,000 cardholders in its first year on the market, and grew steadily throughout the financially prosperous 1950s.[2] In 1959, American Express followed suit by issuing its own, destined to be enormously successful, charge card.[3]

In 1958, the first nationwide credit card, as opposed to a charge card, the BankAmericard® issued by Bank of America, made its debut. The popularity of credit cards, which allow consumers to pay over time using borrowed funds, versus merely postpone lump sum payment of the full purchase amount, quickly eclipsed that of charge cards; albeit, both products continue to be offered today.[4]

In 1966, Bank of America began granting licenses to other banks to issue BankAmericards. Four years later, in 1970, Bank of America transferred control of the BankAmericard program to a group of its licensees. Those licensees, in turn, established National BankAmericard Inc. (NBI), which assumed the responsibility for managing, promoting, and developing the BankAmericard system from Bank of America. In 1976, NBI was renamed Visa®.[5]

In 1966, a group of financial institutions created the Interbank Card Association (ICA) to compete head-to-head with the BankAmericard. The ensuing products marketed and supported by ICA met with success and, in 1969, ICA began doing business as MasterCharge®. As in the case of Visa, ICA's new name caught on quickly with the public; MasterCharge was tweaked to MasterCard in 1979, in recognition of the fact that charge cards were no longer the predominate payment card product.[6]

In addition to competing for broad acceptance by merchants, Visa and MasterCard compete with each other by offering card benefits to issuers as part of their respective product-brand offerings (e.g., zero liability for lost/stolen and travel-related services).[7] Such benefits allow issuers to offer more attractive products

---

2. Diners Club International, *The Story behind the Card*, https://www.dinersclubus.com/home/about/dinersclub/story?nav=left (last visited May 20, 2017).

3. AMERICAN EXPRESS, OUR STORY, *available at* https://secure.cmax.americanexpress.com/Internet/GlobalCareers/Staffing/Shared/Files/our_story_3.pdf.

4. A number of leading issuers currently offer card products that combine charge and credit features. Such "two in one" products pose legal challenges with respect to providing consumers readily understandable disclosures of the applicable terms and conditions.

5. Wikipedia, *Visa Inc.*, https://en.wikipedia.org/wiki/Visa_Inc (last edited May 15, 2017).

6. Mastercard, *We've Been Making History for 50 Years*, https://www.mastercard.us/en-us/about-mastercard/who-we-are/history.html (last visited May 20, 2017).

7. *See, e.g.*, Visa, *Visa Traditional Credit Card Benefits*, https://usa.visa.com/support/consumer/card-benefits.html (last visited May 20, 2017).

and services while having a significant portion of the attendant costs and expenses, including marketing costs, borne by the association. Indeed, the development of Visa and MasterCard during the 1960s, which is discussed in the following section, spurred the adoption of many popular card features that are now standard.

II. CARD INDUSTRY KEY PLAYERS

A. Card Associations

The four largest card associations (i.e., Visa, American Express, MasterCard, and Discover[8]) comprise the collective heart of the payment card industry. Together with the applicable legal requirements, the associations set the rules governing: (1) proof and verification of customer identity; (2) data elements collected and transmitted for any card transaction; (3) safeguarding customer information against theft and intrusion; and (4) processes for investigating and resolving contested card transactions. The associations also establish the rules for "acquiring" (i.e., signing up and enabling) merchants to accept card payments, and the processing and settlement of card transactions. Lastly, the associations play a critical role in maintaining industrywide compliance utilizing monetary fines to induce conformity. In sum, returning to our earlier football analogy, the card associations establish the rules of the game, maintain the field of play, referee the action, and collectively function as the league commissioner.

As reported by CreditCards.com, Visa is the largest of the four major card associations by a wide margin. In 2014, U.S. credit purchase volume for Visa was $1.2 trillion, up from $1.1 trillion in 2013. As of September 2014, there were 304 million Visa credit cards in circulation in the United States and 545 million Visa credit cards in circulation outside of the United States. The chart below, which was prepared by CreditCards.com, shows the respective purchase volume of each of the four largest card associations.[9]

Purchase Volume by Card Network

	Visa		American Express		MasterCard		Discover	
	2013	2014	2013	2014	2013	2014	2013	2014
$ Billions	$1,100	$1,200	$637	$668	$560	$607	$123	$129

---

8. Discover Card® was launched by Dean Witter in 1986, which was then part of Sears. The card was heavily marketed to Sears shoppers and became the only credit card Sears accepted. In1993, Dean Witter became a separate entity and in 1997 Dean Witter merged with Morgan Stanley. The latter spun off the Discover Card division in 2007 as a separate public company. Like American Express, Discover established and continues to maintain its own payment network, which was originally named the NOVUS payment network. CreditCardForum, *The History of the Discover Credit Card*, http://creditcardforum.com /blog/the-history-of-the-discover-credit-card/ (last visited May 20, 2017).

9. Tamara E. Holmes, *Credit Card Market Share Statistics*, CREDITCARDS.COM, June 22, 2016; http://www .creditcards.com/credit-card-news/market-share-statistics.php.

The market dominance and resulting power of Visa and MasterCard has attracted, and continues to attract, close scrutiny for purposes of federal antitrust laws. To this end, until 2004, when the U.S. Supreme Court declined to consider the appeal of a Second Circuit Court of Appeals judgment in favor of the U.S. Department of Justice in an antitrust lawsuit against Visa and MasterCard, those associations had contractually barred their respective members from issuing American Express Cards or Discover Cards. In June 2016, the Second Circuit rejected the adequacy of a $7.25 billion settlement of an antitrust case against Visa and MasterCard brought by major retailers alleging price-fixing by those associations in setting debit and credit card fees, finding that all potential claimants were not adequately represented.[10] Hence, the ultimate amount of the settlement will be even larger. In short, the enormous power wielded by the associations inherently presents anti-competitive risks. Yet, one can argue that such concentrated power was necessary to develop the consistent and largely self-regulated card payment industry that exists today.

1. Obligations of Card Association Members

By agreeing to the terms and conditions of membership, each member commits to both the card association and other members that it will abide by the association's bylaws, operating regulations, and standards. As a result, in addition to accepting responsibility for monetary fines that may be assessed by the association for non-compliance, each member makes binding contractual commitments to other members that could be enforced through a breach of contract lawsuit.[11] For example, each member agrees to establish and maintain operational controls that conform to the association's requirements for preventing money laundering. In addition, the card associations require members to complete periodic questionnaires that address material deficiencies in those operational controls based on independent testing or self-assessments. Through their respective responses, each member attests to the accuracy and completeness of its responses to both the association and other members, which entails potential liability risks.

In addition to facing the possibility of lawsuits from other members, card association members face the risk of lawsuits from nonmembers claiming status as third-party beneficiaries of association requirements. This is what Fifth Third Bank experienced following the massive information security breach of cardholder

---

10. *In re* Payment Card Interchange Fee & Merch. Disc. Antitrust Litig., 827 F.3d 223, 2016-2 Trade Cas. (CCH) ¶ 79,680 (2d Cir. 2016).

11. Because association membership is a multilateral contract by and between the association's respective members, it is important for a bank contemplating membership in a new card association to have a complete and accurate understanding of the association's rules and its willingness and ability to enforce them. The need for such diligence is likely to increase in the future as Internet-based "fintech" firms seek to compete with the established card associations by establishing their own payment networks.

data incurred by the BJ's Wholesale Club retail chain in 2004.[12] In order to be able to accept card payments, BJ's had to contract with card association members. Accordingly, BJ's entered into a merchant processing agreement with Fifth Third, the acquisitioning bank, and a member of Visa. Following BJ's information security breach, credit card issuer Sovereign Bank sued Fifth Third, alleging that Fifth Third's failure to satisfy the requirements of the Visa Operating Regulations for safeguarding customer information contributed to its losses. Sovereign Bank asserted that as an issuer of Visa-branded cards, it was an intended beneficiary of Fifth Third's membership agreement with Visa. Similar lawsuits by parties claiming third-party beneficiary status were brought against other card association members following the major breach of cardholder information that Target Corporation incurred in 2013.[13]

2. Association Requirements and Applicable Law

Card association requirements often dovetail with and augment requirements of applicable law. For example, the Member Alert to Control High Risk (MATCH) List must be consulted whenever a new merchant is acquired, and it must be monitored throughout the ensuing merchant relationship. Another example is the Payment Card Industry Security Standards (PCI), which are issued by the Payment Card Industry Security Council.[14]

A merchant's inclusion on the MATCH List indicates that the merchant has an unacceptably high rate of charge-backs (i.e., reversed payments) and may be engaging in fraudulent or unlawful activities. A merchant may be reported for inclusion on the MATCH List by card issuers, acquiring banks, or payment processors. Whenever a new merchant is added to the MATCH List, the applicable card association sends an alert to all card processors. Pursuant to applicable card association rules, an acquiring bank must contact the reporting party to learn the underlying reasons for the listing. The MATCH List thus compliments anti-money laundering laws, including the "know your customer" rules discussed in Part IV.B.4. Furthermore, together with the screening of merchants against government-issued sanctions lists required by law, including the Office of Foreign Assets Control (OFAC) list, the MATCH List helps to prevent the card payment systems from being misused as vehicles to perpetrate crimes.

The PCI standards are designed to ensure that all participants in the payment card industry maintain effective information security policies, technologies, and processes for protecting cardholder data against unauthorized intrusion and theft.

---

12. *Sovereign Bank v. BJ's Wholesale Club, Inc.*, 533 F.3d 162, 51 A.L.R. 6th 657 (3d Cir. 2008).

13. *In re* Target Corp. Customer Data Sec. Breach Litig., 66 F. Supp. 3d 1154 (D. Minn. 2014).

14. The council was jointly established and continues to be supported by Visa, MasterCard, American Express, Discover, and JCB International (a leading Japan-based credit card company). Although the council issues the PCI standards, their implementation is the individual responsibility of each of those entities.

Although the Payment Card Industry Security Council is responsible for issuing the standards, each card association is responsible for implementing them with its membership. The associations' requirements for PCI compliance substantially dovetail with legal requirements for safeguarding the nonpublic personal information of consumers.

The card associations enforce compliance with the PCI standards by levying monetary penalties against acquiring banks (i.e., noncompliance by a merchant will result in its acquiring banks being fined). The acquiring bank, in turn, will pursue its own penalty or take other actions against the noncompliant merchant under the terms of the merchant processing agreement between those parties. For example, the acquiring bank may suspend the merchant's ability to accept card payments until the merchant has implemented appropriate remedial actions.

Persistent failures by an acquiring bank to enforce PCI compliance effectively with its merchants could result in that bank's suspension or ultimate expulsion from the applicable card association.

B. Acquiring Banks

As noted earlier in this chapter, card associations restrict membership to banks. Hence, the activities that collectively comprise the business of merchant processing are closely associated with "acquiring" banks that regularly contract with merchants to accept card transactions.[15] An acquiring bank may enter into agreements with merchants directly or indirectly, through an independent third-party sales organization (ISO). In this regard, the acquiring bank owns the unique identification number that is issued by the card association to be used in processing and settling card transactions. For Visa, the number is the bank identification number (BIN); for MasterCard it is the ICA number.

1. Outsourcing of Activities

In order to control costs and take advantage of externally available resources and expertise, acquiring banks commonly outsource certain functions to third parties. For example, using ISOs to acquire merchants is a standard industry practice. An acquiring bank may also rely on ISOs or other merchant service providers (MSPs) to perform application intake and processing, purchase authorization, payment processing, charge-back processing, fraud detection, accounting, and the sale and lease of electronics terminals.[16] Outsourcing acquiring banks continue to bear the risk of noncompliance, including contractual responsibility for monetary penalties

---

15. OFFICE OF THE COMPTROLLER OF THE CURRENCY, SAFETY AND SOUNDNESS HANDBOOK—MERCHANT PROCESSING (Aug. 2014) [hereinafter OCC HANDBOOK] (contains a detailed discussion of acquiring banks and the legal and business risks that are associated with merchant processing), *available at* https://www.occ.gov /publications/publications-by-type/comptrollers-handbook/pub-ch-merchant-processing.pdf.

16. *Id.* at 3–4.

that may be assessed by the card associations from third-party conduct. According to the Office of the Comptroller of the Currency (OCC), the third parties offering such services to acquiring banks number in the hundreds.[17] As of March 2016, the five largest U.S. payment processing firms ranked by total annual purchase transactions volume were as follows: (1) First Data Corp., (2) Vantiv Technology Co., (3) Chase Paymentech Co., (4) Bank of America, and (5) Heartland Payment Systems Inc.[18]

"Rent-a-BIN" is a card industry term that refers to an arrangement in which the acquiring bank permits an ISO or MSP to settle card transactions using the bank's card association number (i.e., BIN or ICA) with minimal involvement by the bank. In such cases, the acquiring bank retains all risk of loss and remains responsible for settling transactions with the card association. The effective oversight of Rent-a-BIN relationships is extremely important. Note that Rent-a-BIN relationships are a common industry practice and if properly managed, are not disfavored by bank regulators.[19]

2. Adding New Merchants

Acquiring banks and their agents act as gatekeepers to the card payment systems for merchants and have strong economic incentives for ensuring that every prospective merchant is rigorously vetted. As noted earlier, the card associations may levy monetary fines against the acquiring bank and the acquiring bank may face costly lawsuits from other members if its acquired merchants fail to comply with PCI standards. In addition, under each association's operating rules, an acquiring bank is required to make an issuing bank financially whole if a consumer successfully challenges a card transaction (e.g., based on fraud or dissatisfaction with the purchased item) and the affected merchant fails to reverse the transaction and disgorge the funds received. This contingent liability for charge-backs is one of the primary economic risks for acquiring banks.

After a prospective merchant satisfies the acquiring bank's requirements for the verification of its identity (including the nature and location of its business activities) and assuming the merchant is not included on the MATCH List or government-issued sanctions lists (e.g., the OFAC list), the merchant will be evaluated for compliance with PCI standards. Once the merchant is approved to accept card payments, the acquiring bank will establish a risk profile for the merchant based on industry type and specific business attributes, which is informed by the bank's prior experience dealing with similar entities.

---

17. *Id.* at 4.
18. The Nilson Report, *Charts and Graphs Archive—Top Acquirers in the U.S. 2015*, https://www.nilsonreport.com/publication_chart_and_graphs_archive.php?1=1&year=2016 (last visited July 22, 2017).
19. OCC Handbook at 5.

To protect itself against the risk of loss, the acquiring bank (or its MSP)[20] will require an approved merchant to establish a reserve account to offset potential losses. The acquiring bank will typically establish an expected pattern and range of card transactions based on a combination of factors, including the nature of the merchant's business, and its size, location, number of years in business, and, if available, its historical volume, frequency, and size of card transactions. The resulting transaction expectations and tolerances will be used by the acquiring bank in setting the amount of the merchant's reserve. In addition, throughout the parties' relationship, the acquiring bank will monitor the merchant's performance against its expectations and investigate variances to determine their cause. For example, a marked increase in payment volume could be the result of business expansion or the merchant's misuse of its account for unlawful purposes. Depending on the results of its investigation, the acquiring bank may increase the merchant's reserve requirement, modify the merchant's existing risk and transaction profiles, or seek to terminate the relationship.

C. Card Issuers

1. Legal Requirements

As further discussed in this chapter, the activities of card issuers are governed by a comprehensive scheme of federal and state laws and regulations covering all aspects of the card product or service (i.e., in the case of credit cards, from the point of the marketing offer; through account opening, servicing, and account termination; and up to collection of the final amount owed).

2. Association Rules

In addition, card issuers must comply with the terms and conditions of their agreement with the card association with whom they issue card products and services, which may overlap with the applicable legal requirements. For example, section 1.4.3.1 of the Visa Core Rules requires an issuer to include language in its cardholder agreement stating that "the Card must not be used for any unlawful purpose, including the purchase of goods or services prohibited by applicable laws or regulations."[21] Other sections of the Visa Core Rules address the protection of customer information and the risk of identity theft; for example, section 1.4.4.2 of the Visa Core Rules establishes requirements for the issuance of personal identification numbers (PINs), and section 4.1.11.3, in turn, states requirements for the protection of PINs against misappropriation.[22]

---

20. As noted above, it is very common for acquiring banks to outsource activities. Thus, it is likely that most if not all of the activities described in this paragraph would be performed by an MSP.

21. Visa, Visa Core Rules and Visa Product and Service Rules (2015), *available at* https://usa.visa.com /dam/VCOM/download/about-visa/15-April-2015-Visa-Rules-Public.pdf.

22. *Id.*

III. PAYMENT PROCESSING

A. Transaction Authorization

Having introduced the key players, it is time to consider how a card payment transaction occurs. The following illustration of the authorization process is reproduced from the OCC's Handbook for Merchant Processing.[23]

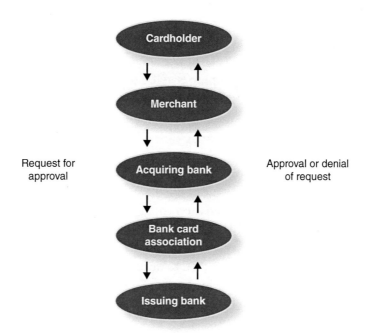

The methodology employed for accepting a credit card in a payment transaction initiated at point-of-sale (POS) has evolved over the years from carbon paper-based imprinting devices, to electronic terminals that read information contained in a magnetic strip by swiping the card, and, more recently, to terminals that read a microchip embedded in the card and employ nearfield communication technology to accept transactions from mobile phone-based payment applications. In addition, the percentage of no-card-present transactions initiated online continues to mushroom. Regardless of the method used to initiate a card payment transaction, however, the authorization process shown above has remained unchanged over the years (i.e., once a given transaction is in the card payment system, how it got there has no material effect on what happens next).

As noted previously, the U.S. card payment industry has experienced multiple massive data security breaches of cardholder information within the past several years. In response to those breaches, the four major card associations have pushed for the universal adoption of cards equipped with an embedded Europay,

---

23. OCC HANDBOOK, *supra* note 14, at 8 (Fig. 1).

MasterCard, and Visa (EMV) chip, which is a prevalent form of card in Europe. As of October 1, 2015, under the respective rules of each of those associations, the financial responsibility for fraud occurring in a card-present transaction rests with any party that failed to promote the use of EMV chip cards. Thus, if a card issuer issues EMV chip-equipped cards and a merchant has not upgraded its POS terminals to be able to read such cards, the merchant would be liable for associated card-present fraud. Conversely, the card issuer would be liable if it continues to only issue cards with magnetic stripes and the merchant has upgraded its POS terminals.

According to a 2016 survey of credit card customers conducted by CreditCards .com, approximately 70 percent of new credit cards issued to consumers included an EMV chip. In reporting the results of the survey, CreditCards.com noted that the ability of merchants to accept such cards was lagging behind by a wide margin, with industry estimates of the acceptance rate ranging between 22 percent and 37 percent.[24]

Clearing is the process of delivering final transaction data from acquiring banks to card issuers for posting to the cardholder's account. Settlement, in turn, is the process of transmitting sales information to card issuers for collection from cardholders and the payment of funds to merchants, and is also the point at which the "interchange" fees charged by card issuers and the card associations are deducted. The following illustration from the OCC's Merchant Processing Handbook shows the respective parties involved in the clearing and settlement of a card transaction together with the flow of funds.[25]

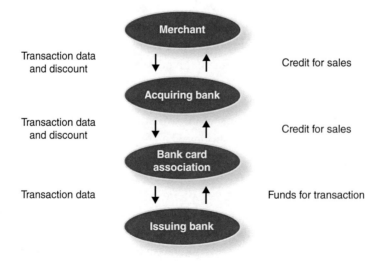

---

24. Sienna Kossman, *Poll: 70 Percent of Consumers Now Have EMV Chip Cards*, CREDITCARDS.COM, Apr. 6, 2016, http://www.creditcards.com/credit-card-news/emv-chip-cards-arrive-poll.php.

25. OCC HANDBOOK, *supra* note 14, at 9.

As noted earlier, it is common for acquiring banks to outsource activities to MSPs. Thus, the above illustration is simplified in that it does not show the third-party payment processors that are likely to be involved.

Card issuers typically pay the settlement bank of the applicable card association using Fedwire, which is a real-time (i.e., near instantaneous) funds transfer system. In order to have access to Fedwire, the card issuer must maintain an account at the Federal Reserve Bank from which funds will be sent. The settlement bank that receives the funds from the card issuer likely will also utilize Fedwire in paying the acquiring bank.[26] Lastly, acquiring banks typically pay merchants using the Automated Clearing House (ACH) electronic network for financial transactions.[27]

B. Charge-Backs

Charge-backs are a common occurrence in the card payment industry. Although, as noted earlier, a high rate of charge-backs may indicate fraud or possible money laundering—and must always be investigated for that reason—charge-backs also occur in the ordinary course for legitimate reasons. The OCC's Merchant Processing Handbook identifies the following most common causes:

- Technical: expired authorization [for the transaction], insufficient funds, or bank processing error
- Clerical: duplicate billing, incorrect amount billed, or refund never issued
- Quality: consumer claims to have never received the goods as promised at the time of purchase
- Fraud: consumer claims not to have authorized the purchase, or identity theft[28]

The charge-back process is governed by the rules of the applicable card association together with applicable law. As is shown below in an illustration of the charge-back process reproduced from the OCC's Merchant Processing Handbook,[29] when a customer disputes a transaction, the card issuer gives the customer provisional (i.e., conditional) credit in the amount of the transaction. The card issuer, in turn, receives provisional credit in that amount from the acquiring bank. If, upon investigation, the reason for the charge-back is determined to be valid (e.g., nondelivery of the purchased goods or services) the acquiring bank will recover the amount of the transaction from the merchant and the card issuer will make permanent the provisional credit that it gave the customer. However, if the charge-back is for valid reasons and the merchant fails to refund the transaction amount back to the acquiring bank (e.g., due to the merchant's financial failure), then the acquiring bank suffers a loss. This contingent liability for charge-backs poses a significant economic risk

---

26. *Id.* at 10.
27. *Id.*
28. *Id.* at 11.
29. *Id.* at 12.

for an acquiring bank (i.e., given the possibility of a subsequent nonrecoverable charge-back, an acquiring bank's payment to a merchant is roughly analogous to an extension of credit).

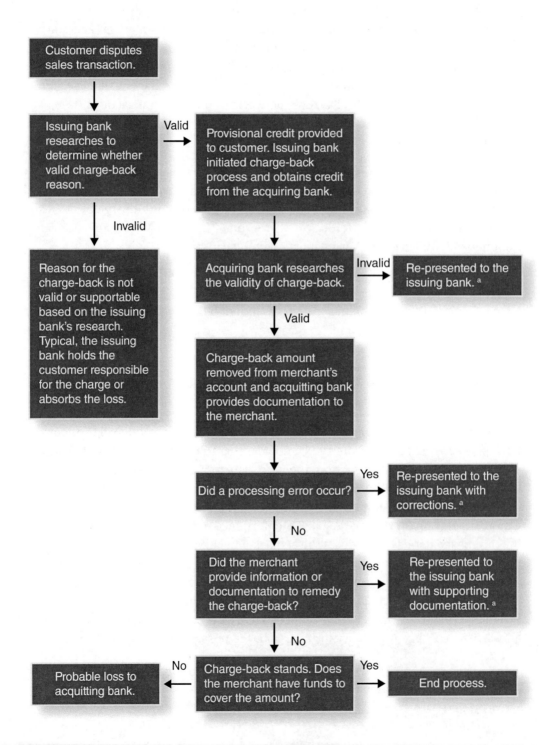

As noted above, the card associations act as a payment clearinghouse between the card issuer and the acquiring bank. Furthermore, at each stage in the charge-back process the rules of the card association both establish the parties' respective obligations and determine which party bears the associated economic risks.

IV. CARD PRODUCTS AND APPLICABLE LAW

Payment card products are subject to legal requirements imposed at both the federal and state levels. In this section, we first review the types of laws that apply to each of the most common types of payment cards and then take a closer look at particular legal requirements.

A. Types of Card Products

1. Charge Cards

These products typically allow the cardholder to delay payment-in-full of purchase transactions until month-end.

Applicable requirements include:

- No unfair, deceptive, or abusive acts or practices
- E-signature requirements
- Credit reporting requirements
- Privacy and safeguarding of consumer nonpublic personal information
- Anti-money laundering and sanctions screening
- Collections requirements

2. Credit Cards

These products allow the cardholder to: (1) finance purchase transactions by drawing on an open-end revolving line of credit, and (2) repay amounts borrowed over the course of time by making monthly payments in at least the contractually specified minimum payment amount.

Applicable requirements include:

- No unfair, deceptive, or abusive acts or practices
- Specific requirements for advertising and disclosures
- E-signature requirements
- Rate and fee restrictions
- Antidiscrimination "fair lending" laws
- Debt protection product requirements
- Credit reporting requirements
- Privacy and safeguarding of consumers' nonpublic personal information
- Anti-money laundering and sanctions screening
- Collections requirements

3. Debit Cards

These products allow the cardholder to pay using an access device that draws funds directly from his or her checking account. A debit card issued in connection with a branding relationship between the card issuer and a major card association (e.g., Visa or MasterCard) offers the same capacity for general use as a credit card.

Applicable requirements include:

- No unfair, deceptive, or abusive acts or practices
- Requirements for advertising and disclosures
- E-signature requirements
- Requirements for electronic funds transfers
- Fee restrictions (e.g., overdraft and returned checks fees)
- Specific disclosure requirements if cardholders are allowed to overdraw their accounts
- Privacy and safeguarding of consumers' nonpublic personal information
- Anti-money laundering and sanctions screening

4. General Use Prepaid Cards

These products allow the cardholder to pay using funds that were paid to the card issuer in advance (i.e., "preloaded") for future use in card payment transactions. A prepaid card issued in connection with a branding relationship between the card issuer and a major card association (e.g., Visa or MasterCard) offers the same capacity for general use as a credit card. Prepaid cards may be sold in specific non-reloadable amounts (e.g., $50.00) or may be reloadable by the cardholder.

Applicable requirements include:

- No unfair, deceptive, or abusive acts or practices
- Specific requirements for advertising and disclosures
- E-signature requirements
- Specific requirements for electronic funds transfers
- Fee restrictions
- Antidiscrimination "fair lending" laws (if cardholders are allowed to over-spend the prepaid amount and use credit to make or complete transactions)
- Privacy and safeguarding of consumers' nonpublic personal information
- Anti-money laundering and sanctions screening

5. Gift Cards

These products are typically sold in non-reloadable specific amounts and may only be used in payment transactions with a single merchant or a particular group of merchants.

Applicable requirements include:

- No unfair, deceptive, or abusive acts or practices
- Specific requirements for advertising and disclosures
- Fee restrictions

B. Key Laws

1. Unfair, Deceptive, or Abusive Acts or Practices

Section 5(a) of the Federal Trade Commission Act prohibits "unfair or deceptive acts or practices in or affecting commerce" (UDAP).[30] This prohibition applies to all card issuers and encompasses all types of card payment products. Section 5 has historically been primarily enforced by the Federal Trade Commission (FTC).[31] However, for those card issuers that are banks, section 5 is enforced by the applicable federal banking agency responsible for supervising and examining the issuer.

In 2000, the OCC issued a cease and desist order entered into by consent (i.e., consent order) against Providian National Bank in connection with its consumer credit card products that broke new ground by being based entirely on alleged UDAP violations. Although section 5 has existed in its current form since the mid-1930s, prior to the Providian consent order, it had never been used by a bank agency as the only basis for taking formal enforcement action. The UDAP violations alleged against Providian by the OCC included: (1) failure to adequately disclose to consumers significant limitations in the benefits of a debt protection program; (2) deceptive advertising of a balance transfer offer that for many of the consumers who accepted the offer resulted in higher interest rates than what they had been paying prior to the transfer; and (3) deceptive advertising of a "no annual fee card" that required consumers to pay a $156 annual fee for their mandatory participation in the aforementioned debt protection program.[32] As a result of this consent order, Providian incurred financial costs that totaled a then-record $300 million for civil penalties and mandatory customer reimbursements.

In 2010, the Dodd-Frank Wall Street Reform and Consumer Protection Act established new federal law prohibitions against "unfair, deceptive, or abusive acts or practices" (UDAAP) committed in connection with a "consumer financial product or service."[33] These prohibitions are interpreted and enforced by the

---

30. 15 U.S.C. § 45(a).

31. For example, in 2008, the FTC filed a lawsuit against CompuCredit alleging numerous violations of the UDAP prohibitions of section 5 in connection with CompuCredit's marketing of high-cost credit card products to economically disadvantaged "subprime" borrowers. CompuCredit and the FTC eventually entered into a $114 million settlement. This action is notable for several reasons. First, CompuCredit was not the issuer of the subject card products. Rather, CompuCredit designed, marketed, and serviced the products, which were issued by a Federal Deposit Insurance Corp. (FDIC)-regulated bank under the terms of a joint venture between those parties. In addition, the fact that the cards were marketed to subprime consumers was an important factor because what constitutes a deceptive practice under section 5 is determined based on how a reasonable member of the class of consumers that was specifically targeted would have viewed the subject marketing offer. *See* Press Release, FTC, FTC Sues Subprime Credit Card Marketing Company and Debt Collector for Deceptive Credit Card Marketing (June 10, 2008), *available at* https://www.ftc.gov/news-events/press-releases/2008/06/ftc-sues-subprime-credit-card-marketing-company-debt-collector.

32. Press Release, OCC, Providian to Cease Unfair Practices, Pay Consumers Minimum of $300 Million under Settlement with OCC and San Francisco District Attorney (June 28, 2000), *available at* https://www.occ.gov/static/news-issuances/news-releases/2000/nr-occ-2000-49.pdf.

33. 12 U.S.C. §§ 5481, 5531, 5536(a).

Consumer Financial Protection Bureau (CFPB), an independent federal agency that was established under the Dodd Frank Act. The mission of the CFPB is targeted to protecting consumers throughout all stages of the "product or service lifecycle" (i.e., sale, servicing, or collection) of any consumer financial product or service.[34] In addition to granting the CFPB the authority to interpret and enforce the UDAAP prohibitions, the Dodd-Frank Act transferred the responsibility for interpreting a total of 14 existing federal consumer protection statutes to the CFPB.

As a matter of policy, the CFPB is supposed to interpret the unfair and deceptive prongs of UDAAP consistently with how the FTC and the federal banking agencies have historically interpreted those terms for purposes of UDAP.[35] However, the CFPB has chosen to interpret and apply the abusive standard on an ad hoc basis in enforcement actions.[36] According to numerous industry critics of the CFPB, the expectations for the covered party described in a resulting consent order have been applied routinely as "rules" in subsequent CFPB investigations of unrelated providers. Unlike formal rulemaking, which guarantees advance notice and opportunities to comment, such "quasi-rulemaking" provides no opportunity to anticipate and adapt to forthcoming material changes in supervisory expectations or influence future standards.

In June 2012, the CFPB issued a consent order against Capital One for alleged unfair and deceptive practices committed in connection with sales of credit card "add on" debt protection products.[37] This order against Capital One wound up being the first in a stream of similar consent orders targeting the credit card add on product sales practices of banks. The order issued against Citibank in June 2015 resulted in civil penalties and customer reimbursements totaling $700 million.[38]

Note that the above-described federal prohibitions against unfair, deceptive, and abusive acts or practices do not preempt the requirements of state laws. In this regard, all states maintain consumer protection statutes and those laws may impose more rigorous standards than what is required under federal law.

---

34. Press Release, CFPB, Consumer Financial Protection Bureau Outlines Bank Supervision Approach (July 12, 2011), *available at* http://www.consumerfinance.gov/about-us/newsroom/consumer-financial -protection-bureau-outlines-bank-supervision-approach/.

35. CFPB, CFPB Supervision and Examination Manual UDAAP 1 (Oct. 2012), *available at* http://files .consumerfinance.gov/f/201210_cfpb_supervision-and-examination-manual-v2.pdf.

36. For an explanation of the rationale for this approach, see CFPB Director Richard Cordray, Remarks at the Consumer Bankers Association (Mar. 9, 2016), http://www.consumerfinance.gov /about-us/newsroom/prepared-remarks-of-cfpb-director-richard-cordray-at-the-consumer-bankers -association/.

37. Administrative Proceeding, *In the Matter of* Capital One Bank (July 16, 2012) (No. 2012-CFPB-0001), http://files.consumerfinance.gov/f/201207_cfpb_consent_order_0001.pdf.

38. Press Release, CFPB, CFPB Orders Citibank to Pay $700 Million in Consumer Relief for Illegal Credit Card Practices (July 21, 2015), *available at* http://www.consumerfinance.gov/about-us/newsroom /cfpb-orders-citibank-to-pay-700-million-in-consumer-relief-for-illegal-credit-card-practices/.

2. Truth-in-Lending Act and Regulation Z

Credit card products are subject to the requirements of the Truth-in-Lending Act (TILA)[39] and Regulation Z,[40] through which the TILA is implemented. These requirements affect virtually every aspect of credit card lending, including:

- Advertising
- Underwriting
- Interest rates
- Fees
- Card issuance and replacement
- Disclosures
- Periodic statements
- Payments
- Billing error resolution
- Changes in terms
- Forbearance programs

The TILA was enacted on May 29, 1968, as title I of the Consumer Credit Protection Act.[41] In its original form, the core purpose of the TILA was to enable consumers to compare loans offered by different lenders by requiring the full and uniform disclosure of terms and conditions. In this regard, Regulation Z defines "finance charge" as "any charge payable directly or indirectly by the consumer and imposed directly or indirectly by the creditor as an incident to or a condition of the extension of credit" and states precise rules of calculation, including which costs must be included or excluded. In addition, card issuers must disclose the "annual percentage rate" (APR) in their advertising and other disclosures of terms and conditions, which represent the actual cost of credit expressed as a yearly rate. To this end, the stated APR must be accurate within one-eighth of one percentage point above or below the rate determined using the rules of calculation specified in Regulation Z.[42] Furthermore, the disclosure requirements of Regulation Z are very precise and dictate the font size, location, and format of certain disclosures. For example, in their marketing solicitations and applications, card issuers are required to disclose the finance charge, the APR, and other information regarding costs and fees using the following tabular format.[43]

---

39. 15 U.S.C. § 1601 *et seq.*
40. 12 C.F.R. § 1026. Regulation Z received its name from the naming convention that the Federal Reserve Board employs for regulations issued by that agency (i.e., Regulation A is first, followed by Regulation B, and so forth). Until the Dodd Frank Act was enacted in 2010, the Federal Reserve Board issued Regulation Z, which is now issued by the CFPB.
41. Pub. L. No. 90-321, 82 Stat. 146.
42. 12 C.F.R. § 1026.14(a).
43. The tabular disclosure is commonly referred to within the card payment industry as the "Shumer Box" in reference to Charles Schumer, the then-New York congressman and now-U.S. senator, who sponsored federal legislation requiring that terms of credit cards be clearly outlined in any promotional material.

G-10 (A) Applications and Solicitation Model Form (Credit Cards)

Interest Rates and Interest Charges	
Annual Percentage Rate (APR) for Purchases	[Purchase rate] [Description that rate varies and how it is determines, if applicable]
APR for Balance Transfers	[Balance transfer rate] [Description that rate varies and how it is determined, is applicable]
APR for Cash Advances	[Cash advance rate] [Description that rate varies and how it is determined, is applicable]
Penalty APR and When it Applies	[Penalty rate] [Description of events that may result in the penalty rate] [Description of how long penalty rate may apply]
[How to Avoid Paying Interest on Purchases/ Charge]	[Description of grace period for purchases or statement that no grace period applies]
Minimum Interest Charge]/ Minimum Charge]	[Description of minimum interest charge or minimum charge]
For Credit Card Tips from the Consumer Financial Protection Bureau	[Reference to the Bureau's Website]

Interest Rates and Interest Charges	
[Annual Fee]/ [Set-up and Maintenance Fees]	[Notice of available credit, if applicable] [Description of fees for availability or issuance of credit, such as an annual fee, if applicable]
Transaction Fees • Balance Transfer • Cash Advance • Foreign Transaction	[Description of balance transfer fee] [Description of cash advance fee] [Description of foreign transaction fee]

Interest Rates and Interest Charges	
Penalty Fees • Late Payment • Over-the-Credit Limit • Returned Payment	[Description of late payment fee] [Description of Over-the-credit limit fee] [Description of returned payment fee]
Other Fees • Required [insert name of required insurance, or debit cancellation or suspension coverage]	[Description of cost insurance, or debt cancellation or suspension plans] [Cross reference to additional information, if applicable]

How We Will Calculate Your Balance   [Description of balance commutation method]

Loss of Introductory APR   [Circumstances in which introductory rate may be revoked and rate is revoked, if applicable]

[Description that rate applies after introductory rate is revoked varies and how it is determined, if applicable]

Over the years, the TILA has evolved from its original purpose to provide a broader range of protections to consumers. For example, the TILA and Regulation Z give consumers a "right of rescission," which allows them three days to reconsider their decision to enter into a loan agreement and back out without losing money.[44] And, the billing error resolution provisions require issuers to provide a consumer provisional credit pending the outcome of an investigation where the consumer timely reports suspected fraud or billing inaccuracies, or exercises his or her right to refuse payment based on dissatisfaction with the quality of the good or services acquired using his or her card.[45] In this regard, if the card issuer fails to conclude its investigation within the maximum allowable time period specified in Regulation Z, the issuer must decide the dispute in the consumer's favor by making the provisional credit permanent.[46]

On May 22, 2009, President Obama signed the Credit Card Accountability Responsibility and Disclosure (CARD) Act into law. The CARD Act was prompted by practices that had become commonplace in the credit card industry that were widely viewed as unfair to consumers. Those practices included "universal default," pursuant to which a consumer's interest rate could be increased by the card issuer based on failure to pay an unrelated loan obtained from a different lender. The act also targets "two-cycle billing," pursuant to which card issuers applied interest charges to two full cycles of card balances rather than the most recent billing cycle's balance, thereby eliminating the grace period for consumers who paid off their entire balance in one month but who carried a balance the following month. In addition, the act targeted "fee harvester" credit card products, which were typically targeted to economically disadvantaged consumers, required the upfront payment of application fees that were disproportionately large in comparison to the amount of credit available, and primarily relied upon the aggressive assessment of late fees and other charges to generate a profit for the issuer.

As a result of the CARD Act, Regulation Z was amended to include "Special Rules Applicable to Credit Card Accounts and Open-End Credit Offered to College Students" addressing the following areas:

- Ability to pay
- Limitations on fees
- Allocations of payments
- Limitations on the imposition of finance charges
- Limitations on increasing annual percentage rates, fees, and charges
- Requirements for over-the-limit transactions
- Reporting and marketing rules for college student open-end credit
- Internet posting of credit card agreements
- Reevaluation of rate increases
- Credit and charge card solicitations[47]

---

44. 12 C.F.R. § 1026.15.
45. *Id.* § 1026.13.
46. *Id.* § 1026.13(d)(3) and 15 U.S.C. § 1666(e).
47. 12 C.F.R. § 1026.51–.61.

Pursuant to the ability to pay requirements of the Special Rules, a card issuer cannot open a credit card account for a consumer unless and until the card issuer has considered the consumer's ability to make the required minimum periodic payments based on the consumer's income or assets and the consumer's current obligations.[48] Moreover, for consumers under the age of 21, the issuer must either: (1) obtain financial information demonstrating the consumer has an "independent ability" to make the required minimum periodic payments; or (2) obtain a signed agreement from a cosigner, guarantor, or joint applicant who is at least 21 years old who agrees to be jointly liable with the under-aged consumer for any debt on the account.[49]

The fee restrictions imposed by the Special Rules generally limit the total amount of fees a consumer can be required to pay during the first year after account opening to no more than 25 percent of the credit limit in effect when the account was opened. In addition, fees assessed against consumers for violating the terms of accounts must either be justified by evidence of the resulting costs incurred by the issuer or capped at specified "safe harbor" amounts.[50]

The payment allocation provisions of the Special Rules generally require that any payments made in excess of the minimum amount due must be applied first to the balance with the highest APR and then to other balances in descending order based on the applicable APR.[51] For accounts with balances subject to deferred interest or a similar program, such excess payments must be applied differently during the last two billing cycles prior to expiration of the deferred period. Specifically, the issuer must allocate the excess amounts first to the balance subject to the deferred interest and then to other balances from highest to lowest APR, as described above.[52]

The finance charge limitations of the Special Rules prohibit issuers from engaging in two-cycle billing (see above). Specifically, an issuer must not impose finance charges as a result of the loss of a grace period on a credit card account if those finance charges are based on: (1) balances for days in billing cycles that precede the most recent billing cycle; or (2) any portion of a balance subject to a grace period that was repaid prior to the expiration of the grace period.[53]

The limitations on increasing APRs, fees, and charges contained in the Special Rules prohibit any increases subject to certain specified exceptions. Those exceptions are: (1) "Temporary rate, fee, or charge exception," which allows an increase, subject to certain conditions, to a specified amount upon expiration of a six-month

---

48. *Id.* § 1026.51(a).

49. *Id.* § 1026.51(b).

50. The safe harbor amounts are adjusted from time to time. The current amounts are $27.00 for the first occurrence and $38.00 for a subsequent occurrence, or 3 percent of the delinquent balance on a charge card account that requires payment of outstanding balances in full at the end of each billing cycle if the card issuer has not received the required payment for two or more consecutive billing cycles. *Id.* § 1026.52(b)(1).

51. *Id.* § 1026.53(a).

52. *Id.* § 1026.53(b).

53. *Id.* § 1026.54(a).

period or longer; (2) "Advance notice exception," which allows the issuer to increase the rates, fees, or charges at a later date with advance notice of the future increase, subject to prohibitions on increasing the APR during the first year after the account is opened, while the account is closed, or while the card issuer does not permit the consumer to use the account for new transactions; (3) "Delinquency exception," which allows the issuer to increase a rate, fee, or charge due to the consumer's nonpayment subject to certain conditions; (4) "Workout and temporary hardship exception," which allows the issuer to return a rate, fee, or charge to the original amount following a temporary reduction made due to financial hardship, subject to requirements for giving advance notice; and (5) "Servicemembers Civil Relief Act exception," which allows the issuer to return the APR to the original amount following a temporary reduction made as the result of the consumer's active military duty.

3. Electronic Fund Transfers Act

Debit cards and gift cards are subject to the requirements of the Electronic Fund Transfers Act (EFTA), which is intended to protect individual consumers engaging in electronic fund transfers. The EFTA is implemented through Regulation E. The full range of services covered by the EFTA include transfers conducted through automated teller machines, POS terminals, automated clearing house systems, telephone bill-payment plans, and remote banking programs. In this regard, Regulation E defines the term "electronic funds transfer" to include:

- POS transfers
- Automated teller machine transfers
- Direct deposits or withdrawals of funds
- Transfers initiated by telephone
- Transfers resulting from debit card transactions, whether or not initiated through an electronic terminal

Regulation E establishes requirements for both persons that issue an "access device" and persons that initiate electronic fund transfers. The term "access device" is broadly defined in the regulation as "a card, code, or other means of access to a consumer's account, or any combination thereof, that may be used by the consumer to initiate electronic fund transfers."[54]

The requirements of Regulation E only apply to transfers from an "account," which is defined as "a demand deposit (checking), savings, or other consumer asset account (other than an occasional or incidental credit balance in a credit plan) held directly or indirectly by a financial institution and established primarily for personal, family, or household purposes." Hence, a consumer's receipt of a credit card cash advance, which involves borrowed funds versus funds deposited in an asset account, would not be a covered transaction.

---

54. *Id.* § 1005.2(a)(1).

Regulation E requires that disclosures of terms and conditions "be clear and readily understandable, in writing, and in a form the consumer may keep, except as otherwise provided in this part."[55] Although Regulation E includes certain model disclosures, it is generally less prescriptive than Regulation Z. For example, Regulation E provides that recurring automatic electronic fund transfers can be authorized "only by a writing signed or similarly authenticated by the consumer,"[56] but does not address the precise content or the form of such authorization. On the other hand, the requirements of Regulation E for overdraft services, which were added in 2009, are prescriptive in a manner similar to Regulation Z. Briefly, a consumer must provide affirmative "opt-in" consent to overdraft services after having received notice of the applicable terms and conditions, and model disclosures for such purposes are stated in the appendix to the regulation.[57]

As in the case of Regulation Z, Regulation E establishes requirements for resolving alleged errors and requires that provisional credit be provided to the consumer pending the outcome of the issuer's investigation. Notice of unauthorized transactions must be reported within 60 days of the consumer's receipt of his or her periodic statement, and notice may be given in person, by telephone, or in writing.[58]

If a consumer's access device is lost or stolen, Regulation E requires the consumer to report the loss or theft within two business days after learning of the loss. If the consumer's report is timely, the regulation caps the maximum liability for unauthorized transactions at $50.00. Furthermore, if the report is made beyond two business days, the consumer's maximum liability is capped at $500.00 unless the issuer is able to demonstrate that earlier notification would have prevented the unauthorized transfers from occurring.

Creditors are prohibited by Regulation E from making a consumer loan subject to the condition that the consumer repay via automatically recurring electronic fund transfers.[59] It is permissible, however, to offer a monetary incentive, such as a reduced interest rate, for the purpose of encouraging the consumer to choose that form of repayment.[60]

Finally, Regulation E includes separate requirements for gift cards, gift certificates, and general-use prepaid cards. These requirements restrict the ability of the issuer to assess fees for dormancy, inactivity, or service fees to no more than one fee per month, and require disclosures regarding the amount of such fees.[61] In addition, the sale of cards with an expiration date is prohibited unless certain conditions are

---

55. *Id.* § 1005.4(a)(1).
56. *Id.* § 1005.10(b).
57. *Id.* § 1005.17; app. A-9 (Model Consent Form for Overdraft Services).
58. In contrast, Regulation Z requires such notice to be provided in writing; albeit, most card issuers allow consumers to report unauthorized transactions via phone.
59. 12 C.F.R. § 1005.10(e).
60. Supplement I to 12 C.F.R. pt. 1005, § 1005.10(e), ¶ 1.
61. 12 C.F.R. § 1005.20(d).

met, including the requirement that the card must have at least five years remaining prior to expiration at the time of sale.[62]

4. Anti-Money Laundering and Sanctions Screening

The Bank Secrecy Act (BSA),[63] as amended by the USA PATRIOT Act,[64] requires card associations, acquiring banks, and card issuers to establish and maintain a written anti-money laundering program. As is further discussed below, the expectations for such programs vary based on the nature of a covered party's business activities and the associated risks of money laundering. To this end, debit and prepaid cards pose higher risks than credit cards.

As an operator of a credit card system, each card association is required to maintain a written anti-money laundering program which is reasonably designed to prevent the card system from being used to facilitate money laundering or the financing of terrorist activities.[65] At a minimum, the program must include policies, procedures, and internal controls designed to ensure that the operator does not authorize, or maintain authorization for, any person to serve as an issuing or acquiring institution without the operator taking appropriate steps, based upon the operator's risk assessment for money laundering and terrorist financing threats, to guard against that person issuing the operator's credit card or acquiring merchants who accept the operator's credit card in circumstances that facilitate money laundering or the financing of terrorist activities.[66]

All financial institutions are required to maintain a written anti-money laundering program. The primary components of a given institution's anti-money laundering program will address: (1) customer identification performed at the time of account opening; (2) "know your customer" ongoing monitoring; and (3) the investigation and timely reporting of suspicious activities.

The anti-money laundering programs of acquiring banks rely heavily on sophisticated automated monitoring systems to identify potential suspicious activity. As noted earlier in this chapter, "normal" transaction parameters (e.g., size, volume, and frequency) are established for each new merchant at the time of on-boarding and subsequent material variances from those parameters are promptly investigated. Modern monitoring systems, as opposed to rules-based systems, employ "machine learning" to identify emerging patterns of potentially suspicious activities and apply that learning across all similar merchants. Furthermore, ongoing monitoring necessarily includes knowledge of any new additions to the MATCH List and appropriate follow-up. In addition to conducting ongoing monitoring, acquiring banks perform periodic due diligence that may range in scope, depending on the subject merchant's risk level and the extent of ongoing monitoring, from full scale

---

62. *Id.* § 1005.20(e).
63. 31 U.S.C. § 5311 *et seq.*
64. Pub. L. No. 107-56, 115 Stat. 272 (2001).
65. 31 C.F.R. § 103.135.
66. *Id.* § 103.135(c).

reperformance of the diligence that was performed at the time of on-boarding to requiring completion of a written questionnaire.

The anti-money laundering program of a card issuer will vary depending on the type of card products offered. In general, the risks of money laundering presented by credit cards are considered relatively low both because no asset account is involved and a detailed record is generated for each transaction.[67] Furthermore, the immense volume of credit card transactions poses huge challenges for ongoing monitoring and consumer concerns over privacy make such monitoring extremely challenging and controversial. As a result, the anti-money laundering program of a credit card issuer typically centers on identifying customers at the time of account opening, consistent with the requirements of applicable law.[68] The anti-money laundering program of an issuer of debit cards or re-loadable prepaid cards, on the other hand, will emphasize both customer identification at the time of account opening and the ongoing monitoring of funds moving in and out of the consumer's asset account. In this regard, all forms of asset accounts have a higher inherent risk of money laundering because the account may be used as a repository for, and to conceal the true nature of, the proceeds of criminal activities.

In addition to satisfying the requirements of the BSA, card issuers are required by the Fair Credit Reporting Act to establish and maintain a written anti-identity theft program,[69] which may be combined with the institution's anti-money laundering program, and must comply with the identify theft "Red Flags Rule."[70] This rule seeks to ensure that financial institutions and creditors are aware of signs or indicators that an identity thief is actively misusing another individual's sensitive data, typically to obtain products or services from the institution or creditor. The Red Flags Rule requires that written policies and procedures be maintained for purposes of (1) identifying patterns, practices, or activities that indicate the possible existence of identity theft; (2) detecting whether identity theft may be occurring in connection with the opening of a covered account or an existing covered account; and (3) appropriately responding to signs of possible identity theft. The Red Flags Rule includes special requirements for the handling of requests for a replacement or an additional card received from a debit or credit card customer following a recent change of that customer's address.[71]

---

67. *See* U.S. General Accounting Office, Money Laundering: Extent of Money Laundering through Credit Cards Is Unknown (July 2002) (GAO-02-670), *available at* http://www.gao.gov/assets/240/235231.pdf.

68. *See* 31 C.F.R. § 103.121.

69. 15 U.S.C. § 1681m.

70. 12 C.F.R. § 41 (OCC); *id.* § 222 (Federal Reserve Banks); *id.* §§ 334 and 364 (FDIC).

71. In such cases, the card issuer may not issue an additional or replacement card until, in accordance with its reasonable policies and procedures and for the purpose of assessing the validity of the change of address, the card issuer notifies the cardholder of the request at the cardholder's former address or by any other means of communication that the card issuer and the cardholder have previously agreed to use, and the cardholder is given a reasonable means of promptly reporting incorrect address changes, or the card issuer otherwise assesses the validity of the change of address in accordance with its policies and procedures for such purposes. *Id.* § 334.91(c).

Lastly, a critical component of each and every card issuer's anti-money laundering program is its policies, procedures, and operational practices for ensuring that a Suspicious Activity Report is prepared and submitted to the Financial Crimes Enforcement Network (FinCEN) of the U.S. Department of the Treasury whenever the issuer detects a known or suspected criminal violation of federal law or a suspicious transaction related to a money laundering activity or a violation of the BSA.[72]

V. NEW CARD PAYMENT TECHNOLOGIES

Over the past several years, mobile phone-based card payment services have become increasing commonplace. Such services typically employ a combination of near-field communication, tokenization (i.e., the substitution of proxy number in place of the actual credit or debit card number), and data encryption. Moreover, while some phone-based services utilize a secure microchip that is embedded in the phone, others involve cloud-based applications. The primary risk associated with these services is the potential for data security breaches, which the services are each designed to minimize. None of the phone-based services introduced to date alter the underlying card transaction (i.e., the only material difference is how the card transaction gets communicated to the card associations). Thus, from a legal standpoint, phone-based payments do not give rise to increased risks—save with respect to the data security risks presented by newer and relatively untested technologies.

If a future card payment service (whether phone-based or otherwise) were to be based on a new, non-card association payment system, the attendant business *and* legal risks would be greater unless and until the new system proved reliable in terms of both its business performance and its ability to ensure compliance with applicable laws.

---

72. *See id.* § 353.

Chapter 3

Nonbank Money Transmitters

Jacqueline Allen and Elizabeth Khalil[1]

I. INTRODUCTION

The movement of money by entities other than banks has been common for centuries, at one time conducted by stagecoach and by riders on horseback. Today, nonbank money transmission often takes place electronically. Yet the legal framework has not been updated to specifically cover electronic money transmission. Rather, any time that an activity involves moving funds from one place to another, whether physically or electronically, there is a chance that one or more state money transmitter laws—and accompanying licensing requirements—will be triggered, as well as certain federal laws.

The current regulatory landscape covering money transmission consists of a mix of state and federal law, with no single preemptive federal regime that defines or regulates all money transmission activities. State-by-state licensing is required, with no single uniform set of definitions, standards, or application requirements. This inconsistent state-based framework may seem counterintuitive for an activity that has become national, or even international, by its nature, but to date, no preemptive federal scheme has been established.

II. TYPES OF MONEY TRANSMISSION

Federal and state statutory definitions of money transmission tend to be broad and generally cover any entity that receives and transfers money. Traditional forms of money transmission involve providing physical currency in person to an entity to

---

1. Jacqueline Allen can be reached at jacquelineconleyallen@gmail.com, and Elizabeth Khalil can be reached at ekhalil@dykema.com.

transfer to a designated recipient or convert to some form of payment instrument. Newer forms of money transmission have evolved in online and mobile channels that provide greater flexibility by allowing customers to send money without providing physical currency or visiting a brick-and-mortar location. While traditional types of money transmission typically require the sender and/or recipient to pay a fee, newer types of money transmission more often pass the expense along to the merchant or other participants in the system besides the sender and/or recipient.

A. Traditional Money Transmission Businesses

Money transmission has traditionally included entities that offer wire and remittance transfers, provide bill payment services, sell money orders, sell stored-value cards, and/or offer delivery services. Customers typically pay a fee to utilize these services to send money.

To use traditional wire transfer services, customers provide funds in person at a physical location to be delivered to another person designated by the customer at another physical location, usually another city, state, or country. The designated recipient must provide a reference number to pick up the money. The physical pickup location is typically an agent of a major provider in the wire transfer business, such as Western Union or MoneyGram. In exchange for the money transfer service, the customer pays a fee to the business. This type of service clearly falls within the scope of federal and state regulation of money transmission.

Customers can also initiate money transfers over the phone or Internet. These channels make it possible to send money at any time and without having to visit a physical location. Instead, the customer can provide bank account, debit card, or credit card information to a money transfer business and the business will electronically transfer the value of the transaction to the customer's designated recipient. Western Union and MoneyGram provide these services in addition to their in-person transfer services. As with transfers from physical locations, customers pay a fee to the money transfer business for these types of services.

Another example of a traditional type of money transmission is a bill payment service, in which a customer provides the customer's payment information and the service provider sends the customer's money to a third-party payee (the biller). Bill payment services purport to allow customers to pay bills in less time than it would usually take the customer to mail in a bill payment to the biller. The customer typically pays the bill payment provider a nominal fee, which is typically less than a late payment fee the customer might be required to pay to the biller if the customer were to pay the bill late. As with other money transfers made over the phone or Internet, bill payments can be sent at any time and without having to visit a physical location, although some bill payment providers also offer bill payment services at physical locations. As discussed later in this chapter, federal and some state laws exempt bill payment service providers from regulation if the provider is acting as an agent of the biller, while some states take the position that such activity is regulated.

Money orders provide customers an alternative to using cash or writing checks. For a fee, a customer can purchase a money order in a specific amount and make the money order out to a payee. Money orders can be appealing for customers who do not have checking accounts and cannot write checks, but still want to have a paper trail and receipt in connection with a payment to a recipient. Western Union and MoneyGram are two entities that sell money orders in addition to wire transfer services. The U.S. Postal Service (USPS) also sells money orders.

"Stored-value" or "prepaid" products function to transmit the value of money between the participants in a payment transaction. First, a customer purchases a prepaid card or other type of stored-value device and provides money to the issuer or an agent of the issuer, such as a cashier in a retail store. The customer may pay by cash, check, debit card, credit card, or any other form of payment the issuer accepts. After the customer purchases the stored-value product, the purchased amount is associated with that stored-value device. When the customer makes a purchase of goods or services with the stored-value device, the issuer transfers the amount of the purchase, up to the value associated with that device, to the merchant who sold the goods or services to the customer. As discussed later in this chapter, some states exempt certain "closed loop" stored-value products from money transmission regulation.

Delivery services are another traditional type of money transmission business; they provide delivery services to customers, which may include the physical delivery of money. As such, entities including the USPS, Federal Express, and United Parcel Service can each implicate money transmission laws. Most states exempt USPS, but not necessarily other delivery services, from regulation.

B. New and Emerging Forms of Money Transmission

As the payments industry has shifted away from a paper-based system to an electronic system, innovators have introduced a number of services that facilitate payments outside traditional depository institution channels. The processing of transactions and movement of funds now commonly takes place through mobile channels, including through mobile wallets and mobile applications (apps). Whether that constitutes "money transmission" requires a case-by-case look at the structure of the transactions and the flow of funds.

Many services are available through Internet-based channels as well as through mobile services. Chase QuickPay is one type of mobile payment service that functions through both Internet and mobile interfaces. This service allows customers to make person-to-person (P2P) payments through the Chase website or mobile app to any other user who is registered with Chase QuickPay. Another P2P service, clearXchange, allows people and businesses to use online or mobile app channels to send money to anyone with a U.S. bank account. The service facilitates the transfer of funds from the sender's bank account to the bank account of the recipient.

A mobile wallet can be "loaded" with certain forms of payment, such as credit and debit cards, accepted by the wallet provider. Customers can then use the mobile wallet to pay at participating merchants. Android Pay, Apple Pay, PayPal, and Samsung Pay are each examples of mobile wallets. The use of mobile wallets is typically free of charge for the end user—the person using the mobile wallet to make a payment—but may impose costs on issuers of the payment methods drawn on by the mobile wallet and on the merchants accepting payment through the mobile wallet.

Mobile card readers can make it easier for merchants to accept payments "on the go" at locations merchants might not traditionally have been able to accept payments. For instance, taxi drivers can now accept credit and debit card payments by using a Square Reader that plugs into the taxi driver's phone. Customers can provide their debit or credit cards to the taxi driver to scan through the Square Reader. Many of the mobile card readers are used to make mobile devices into "point-of-sale" terminals, and, as such, do not constitute "money transmission" under federal or state law definitions if they conduct transactions in the same manner as traditional in-store point-of-sale hardware and software. Payments in the mobile channel (including P2P payments) are discussed in more detail in Chapter 4.

Payment processing may also fall within federal and state law definitions of "money transmission" based upon the structure of the transaction and the flow of funds involved. Payment processors typically facilitate the receipt of payments by merchants, and they may operate in physical, Internet, or mobile channels. However, payment processors may also act on behalf of customers who are sending the payment. Typically, a payment processor has a contractual relationship with either the merchant recipient or customer payor and acts on that party's behalf. As with bill payment service providers, federal and most state laws exempt from regulation payment processors acting on behalf of the merchant or recipient. However, regulators in some states, such as Washington and Pennsylvania, recently began treating payment processors as conducting regulated money transmission.

III. LEGAL AND REGULATORY FRAMEWORKS

Money transmission is regulated at both the federal and state levels. Federal laws that regulate "money services businesses" (MSBs), which is defined to include "money transmitters,"[2] impose anti-money laundering requirements by extending certain provisions of the Bank Secrecy Act (BSA) to MSBs. As a result, MSBs, including money transmitters, must register with the Financial Crimes Enforcement Network (FinCEN) and comply with certain BSA requirements.

While federal regulation of MSBs focuses on objectives such as preventing money laundering, state laws generally focus on ensuring the safety and soundness of nonbank money transmitters—in other words, to decrease the likelihood that

---

2. 31 C.F.R. § 1010.100(ff)(5) (2016).

the money transmitter will fail and leave users unable to access their funds. These laws typically require nonexempt entities to obtain a license from the state agency that regulates money transmission and extend consumer protections for individuals who transmit money. Banks and credit unions are generally exempt from licensing requirements because they are already chartered, insured, and supervised for safety and soundness by federal and/or state regulators.

A. Federal Regulation

At the federal level, money transmission by MSBs is supervised and enforced by FinCEN, a bureau of the U.S. Department of the Treasury. MSBs are governed by title 31, parts 1010 and 1022 of the Code of Federal Regulations.

1. Definition of Money Transmission

Under FinCEN regulations, a "money transmitter" is a "person that provides money transmission services" or "[a]ny other person engaged in the transfer of funds."[3] "Money transmission services" means "the acceptance of currency, funds, or other value that substitutes for currency from one person *and* the transmission of currency, funds or other value that substitutes for currency to another location or person by any means."[4] "Any means" includes, but is not limited to, "through a finance agency or institution; a Federal Reserve Bank or other facility or one or more Federal Reserve Banks; the Board of Governors of the Federal Reserve System, or both; an electronic funds transfer network; or an information value transfer system."[5] In other words, money transmission involves the movement of funds from Person A to the money transmitter, and then from the money transmitter to Person B.

2. Exemptions under Federal Law

a. Generally

The FinCEN rules exempt certain types of persons from the definition of a "money transmitter." Payment processors and providers of prepaid access will not be considered money transmitters if they only conduct the following activities and no others:

1. Provide the delivery, communication, or network access services used by a money transmitter to support money transmission services
2. Act as a payment processor to facilitate the purchase of, or payment of a bill for, a good or service through a clearance and settlement system by agreement with the creditor or seller (i.e., the merchant/retailer)

---

3. *Id.* § 1010.100(ff)(5)(i)(A).
4. *Id.* (emphasis added).
5. *Id.*

3. Operate a clearance and settlement system or otherwise act as an intermediary solely between BSA-regulated institutions. This includes but is not limited to the Fedwire system, electronic funds transfer networks, certain registered clearing agencies regulated by the U.S. Securities and Exchange Commission (SEC), and derivatives clearing organizations, or other clearing house arrangements established by a financial agency or institution

4. Physically transport currency, other monetary instruments, other commercial paper, or other value that substitutes for currency as a person primarily engaged in such business, such as an armored car, from one person to the same person at another location or to an account belonging to the same person at a financial institution, provided that the person engaged in physical transportation has no more than a custodial interest in the currency, other monetary instruments, other commercial paper, or other value at any point during the transportation

5. Provide prepaid access

6. Accept and transmit funds only integral to the sale of goods or the provision of services, other than money transmission services, by the person who is accepting and transmitting the funds[6]

b. Payment Processors

As noted above, a person is excluded from the definition of a "money transmitter" if that person "[a]cts as a payment processor to facilitate the purchase of, or payment of a bill for, a good or service through a clearance and settlement system by agreement with the creditor or seller."[7] This is commonly referred to as the "processor exemption" to the MSB registration requirement.

FinCEN has elaborated on the processor exemption in various rulings, concluding that a merchant payment processor who processes payments from consumers "as an agent of the merchant to whom the consumers owe money—rather than on behalf of the consumers themselves—is not a money transmitter by virtue of such activities."[8] In another ruling, FinCEN explained that the transfer of funds through the Automatic Clearing House (ACH) system from consumers to merchants as payment for goods or services purchased from those merchants constitutes payment processing and not money transmission.[9] The processing, settlement, and clearing of funds services that payment processors may provide is deemed to be ancillary to such processors' primary business of coordinating payments from a purchaser to a merchant, for example.[10] It is not possible for a processing entity to coordinate

---

6. *Id.* § 1010.100(ff)(5)(ii)(A)–(F).

7. *Id.* § 1010.100(ff)(5)(ii)(B).

8. Whether an Authorized Agent for the Receipt of Utility Payments Is a Money Transmitter, FIN-2008-R006 (May 21, 2008).

9. Definition of Money Transmitter (Merchant Payment Processor), FIN-2003-8 (Nov. 19, 2003).

10. Bank Secrecy Act Regulations; Definitions and Other Regulations Relating to Money Services Businesses Rule, 76 Fed. Reg. 43,593 (July 21, 2011) (to be codified at 31 C.F.R. pts. 1010, 1021, and 1022).

such payments without providing ancillary processing, settlement, and clearing of funds services.[11] The exemption applies only to processing, settlement, and clearing of funds services by payment processors on behalf of the creditor/seller and not to such services by payment processors on behalf of the debtor/buyer.[12] Many processors only facilitate payment transaction instructions whereby money is transferred from the customer's account (demand deposit, credit card, or stored-value account) to the merchant's "settlement" account. Accordingly, those processors are never in the "flow of funds" because no funds are deposited in an account that the processor owns or controls.

c. Prepaid Access Providers

A person is also excluded from the definition of "money transmitter" if the person only provides prepaid access.[13] However, a prepaid access provider is still an MSB and must comply with separate requirements applicable to MSBs under the FinCEN rules in title 31, chapter X of the Code of Federal Regulations.[14] Certain sellers of prepaid access are also MSBs and must comply with certain requirements under those rules.[15]

On July 29, 2011, FinCEN issued a final rule (the Prepaid Access Rule) amending its regulations applicable to MSBs with regard to "prepaid access" (formerly known as "stored value").[16] The rule became effective September 27, 2011, and modified 31 C.F.R. parts 1010 and 1022.[17] The purpose of the Prepaid Access Rule is to bring prepaid card issuers within the scope of the BSA, which requires "financial institutions," MSBs, and other providers of various money-related services to take appropriate actions to prevent their services from being used for money laundering or terrorist financing.[18]

The rule defines "prepaid access" as "[a]ccess to funds or the value of funds that have been paid in advance and can be retrieved or transferred at some point in the future through an electronic device or vehicle, such as a card, code, electronic serial number, mobile identification number, or personal identification number."[19] Closed-loop prepaid access—prepaid access that can be used only for transactions involving a defined merchant, location, or set of merchants or locations—is included within this definition.[20] A "prepaid program" is "an arrangement under which one or more persons acting together provide(s) prepaid access."[21]

---

11. *Id.*
12. *Id.*
13. 31 C.F.R. § 1010.100(ff)(5)(ii)(E).
14. *Id.* § 1010.100(ff)(4).
15. *Id.* § 1010.100(ff)(7).
16. Bank Secrecy Act Regulations—Definitions and Other Regulations Relating to Prepaid Access, 76 Fed. Reg. 45,403 (July 29, 2011) (to be codified at 31 C.F.R. pts. 1010 and 1022).
17. *Id.*
18. *Id.*
19. 31 C.F.R. § 1010.100(ww).
20. *Id.* § 1010.100(kkk).
21. *Id.* § 1010.100(ff)(4)(iii).

Under the Prepaid Access Rule, certain arrangements that are deemed to present a low risk of money laundering or other illicit behavior will not be deemed a prepaid program. For example, "closed-loop prepaid access to funds not to exceed a $2,000 maximum value that can be associated with a prepaid access device or vehicle on any day" is excluded.[22] The $2,000 limit is per device or vehicle and does not require aggregation of all purchases of separate prepaid cards by an individual in a single day.[23]

An arrangement that provides prepaid access only to "[f]unds not to exceed $1,000 maximum value and from which no more than $1,000 maximum value can be initially or subsequently loaded, used, or withdrawn on any day through a device or vehicle" is also excluded from the definition of a "prepaid program."[24] This exclusion is not limited to closed-loop arrangements. Thus, a person could avoid falling within the definition of a "prepaid program" by limiting the value of the funds and the amount of funds that may be loaded, used, or withdrawn on any device or vehicle up to $1,000 on any one day (e.g., an open-loop stored-value card that can be used anywhere Visa or MasterCard is accepted).

The participants in a prepaid program must designate one participant to serve as the provider of prepaid access.[25] If the participants do not designate a provider, the provider will be the participant in the program with principal oversight and control over the program.[26] Five factors will be considered in determining whether a participant has principal oversight and control:

1. Organizing the prepaid program
2. Setting the terms and conditions of the prepaid program and determining that the terms have not been exceeded
3. Determining the other businesses that will participate, which may include the issuing bank, payment processor, or distributor
4. Controlling or directing the appropriate party to initiate, freeze, or terminate prepaid access
5. Engaging in activity that demonstrates oversight and control of the prepaid program[27]

Even if a person would not be considered a "provider" of prepaid access, regulators will also evaluate whether the person could be considered a "seller" of prepaid access because certain sellers of prepaid access are MSBs.[28] An entity is a "seller" of prepaid access if it receives funds or the value of funds in exchange for an initial or subsequent loading of prepaid access and the entity

---

22. *Id.* § 1010.100(ff)(4)(iii)(A).
23. *Id.*
24. *Id.* § 1010.100(ff)(4)(iii)(D)(1)(ii).
25. *Id.* § 1010.100(ff)(4)(i).
26. *Id.* § 1010.100(4)(ii).
27. *Id.*
28. *Id.* § 1010.100(ff)(7).

1. sells prepaid access offered under a prepaid program that can be used before verification of customer identification, or
2. sells prepaid access (including closed-loop prepaid access) to funds that exceed $10,000 to any person during any one day, and has not implemented policies and procedures reasonably adapted to prevent such a sale.[29]

In other words, there is also a $10,000-per-day, per-person limit. A person can be deemed a "seller of prepaid access" and then fall within the Prepaid Access Rule if it "[s]ells prepaid access (including closed-loop prepaid access) to funds that exceed $10,000 to any person during any one day, and has not implemented policies and procedures reasonably adapted to prevent such a sale."[30] FinCEN has clarified that a one-off situation where funds exceeding $10,000 were inadvertently sold to a single person during any one day will not necessarily bring that person under the rule.[31] Rather, the key question is whether that person had implemented policies and procedures reasonably adapted to prevent such a sale.[32]

The same federal laws regarding prepaid access described above will apply to any gift card program, because a gift card is a form of prepaid access. Thus, issuers and sellers of gift cards, other than closed-loop gift cards for which funds cannot exceed $2,000, must register as a federal MSB unless they qualify for an exception.

3. Compliance Requirements under Federal Law

The compliance requirements that FinCEN imposes apply to MSBs, which are defined in the FinCEN rules to include: (1) dealers in foreign currency; (2) check cashers; (3) issuers or sellers of traveler's checks or money orders; (4) providers of prepaid access; (5) money transmitters; (6) the USPS; and (7) sellers of prepaid access.[33] The definition of MSB does not include: (1) banks; (2) foreign banks; (3) entities registered with or examined by the SEC or the U.S. Commodity Futures Trading Commission; or (4) natural persons who would otherwise be considered dealers in foreign currency, check cashers, issuers or sellers of traveler's checks or money orders, providers of prepaid access, or money transmitters except for the fact that they engage in these activities on an infrequent basis and not for gain or profit.[34] Accordingly, the rules applicable to MSBs apply to both money transmitters and certain providers and sellers of prepaid access, even though such providers and sellers are not money transmitters.

MSBs must comply with requirements under the BSA generally applicable to "financial institutions," as well as with requirements specific to MSBs. First, each

---

29. *Id.*
30. *See id.*
31. FinCEN, Frequently Asked Questions: Final Rule—Definitions and Other Regulations Relating to Prepaid Access (Nov. 2, 2011), https://www.fincen.gov/news_room/nr/html/20111102.html.
32. *Id.*
33. 31 C.F.R. § 1010.100(ff).
34. *Id.* § 1010.100(ff)(8).

MSB must register with FinCEN within 180 days after becoming an MSB, counting from the day after the date the MSB is established.[35] In addition to initial registration, each MSB must renew its registration every two years.[36]

An MSB must also maintain a list of agents, if any, for the preceding calendar year.[37] An agent is "a business that an issuer authorizes, through written agreement or otherwise, to sell its instruments or, in the case of funds transmission, to sell its send and receive transfer services."[38] The issuer is the business ultimately responsible for the payment of money orders or traveler's checks, or a money transmitter that has the obligation to guarantee payment of a money transfer.[39] A person who is an agent of an MSB, but not otherwise acting as an MSB, is not required to register with FinCEN.[40]

Each MSB must also develop, implement, and maintain an effective anti-money laundering (AML) program.[41] The AML program must be in writing and include the following components:

1. Policies, procedures, and internal controls to comply with BSA requirements
2. Designation of a person who will have day-to-day responsibility for compliance with the AML program and the BSA requirements
3. AML training for appropriate employees
4. An annual independent review of the MSB's compliance with its AML program[42]

An MSB must file a Suspicious Activity Report (SAR) with FinCEN if it detects any suspicious activity in connection with a transaction that the MSB believes may be relevant to a possible violation of law or regulation.[43] The MSB must file each SAR within 30 calendar days after the date the MSB initially detects facts that may provide a basis for filing a SAR.[44]

Specifically, an MSB *must* file a SAR if both of the following occur: (1) A transaction or series of transactions involve or aggregate funds or other assets of $2,000 or more, and (2) the MSB knows, suspects, or reasonably suspects the transaction, or pattern of transactions, falls into one or more of the following categories: (a) involves funds derived from illegal activity, is intended or conducted in order to hide or disguise funds or assets derived from illegal activity as part of a plan to violate or evade any federal law or regulation or to avoid any reporting requirement

35. *Id.* § 1022.380 (2016); FinCEN, Answers to Frequently Asked Questions (FAQs) for Money Services Businesses (MSBs) (Aug. 1, 2003), https://www.fincen.gov/financial_institutions/msb/pdf/msbfaqs.pdf.

36. 31 C.F.R. § 1022.380(b)(2).

37. *Id.* §§ 1022.380(a)(1), 1022.380(d); FinCEN, *supra* note 34.

38. FinCEN, *supra* note 8.

39. *Id.*

40. *Id.* § 1022.380(a)(3).

41. *Id.* §§ 1022.210 (2016), 1022.320 (2016).

42. *Id.* §§ 1022.210(c), 1022.210(d).

43. *Id.* § 1022.320(a)(1).

44. *Id.* § 1022.320(b)(3).

under federal law or regulation; (b) is designed to evade any BSA regulations; (c) has no business or apparent lawful purpose or is not the sort in which the particular customer would normally be expected to engage, and the MSB has no reasonable explanation for the transaction after examining the available facts, including the background and possible purpose of the transaction; or (d) involves the use of the MSB to facilitate criminal activity.[45] MSBs must also file a Currency Transaction Report (CTR) for each currency transaction of *more than* $10,000.[46]

Further resources for MSBs on federal BSA/AML compliance include, for instance, FinCEN's *Bank Secrecy Act/Anti-Money Laundering Examination Manual for Money Services Businesses*, which provides additional information for money transmitters to reference to ensure compliance with federal laws that FinCEN enforces.[47] In December 2014, the Federal Financial Institutions Examination Council (FFIEC) updated its *Bank Secrecy Act/Anti-Money Laundering Examination Manual*, which includes a section on nonbank financial institutions.[48]

In addition to BSA/AML obligations, MSBs have certain obligations under sanctions programs administered by the U.S. Department of the Treasury's Office of Foreign Assets Control (OFAC). OFAC administers and enforces economic sanctions programs primarily against countries and groups of individuals, such as terrorists and narcotics traffickers. The sanctions prohibit U.S. persons from engaging in certain trade or financial transactions and other dealings, unless authorized by OFAC or expressly exempted by statute. There may be broad prohibitions on dealings with countries, and also against specific individuals and entities named in OFAC's list of Specially Designated Nationals (SDNs) and Blocked Persons (collectively, the SDN List). In addition, OFAC maintains other sanctions lists that may have different prohibitions associated with them.

U.S. persons—including all U.S. citizens, U.S. incorporated entities, and their foreign branches—are prohibited from dealing with SDNs wherever they are located and must comply with OFAC regulations. U.S. persons are expected to exercise due diligence in determining whether any such persons are involved in a proposed transaction. The penalties for violations can be substantial. MSBs must exercise due diligence in determining whether any blocked persons are involved in a proposed transaction. Because OFAC's programs are dynamic, it is important to check OFAC's website on a regular basis to have the most updated information regarding the latest restrictions affecting countries and parties with which a money transmitter might do business. Either the MSB itself, or a third-party vendor, may conduct this "OFAC screening" function.

---

45. *Id.* § 1022.320(a)(2).
46. *Id.* §§ 1022.311 (2016), 1010.311 (2016).
47. FinCEN, Bank Secrecy Act/Anti-Money Laundering Examination Manual for Money Services Businesses (Dec. 2008), *available at* https://www.fincen.gov/news_room/rp/files/MSB_Exam_Manual.pdf.
48. FFIEC, *Bank Secrecy Act/Anti-Money Laundering Examination Manual*, https://www.ffiec.gov /bsa_aml_infobase/pages_manual/manual_online.htm (last visited May 20, 2017).

Federal consumer protection laws and regulations also apply to money trans-mitters and MSBs as well as to banks and other financial institutions. In particular, the Electronic Fund Transfer Act (EFTA), as implemented by the Consumer Financial Protection Bureau's (CFPB's) Regulation E, sets forth requirements related to "elec-tronic fund transfers" (EFTs) to or from consumer accounts.[49] The CFPB has also issued Regulation E rules specifically covering "remittance transfers," to give certain rights to consumers who send money electronically to foreign countries.[50] The rules apply to most remittance transfers if they are: (1) more than $15; (2) made by a con-sumer in the United States; and (3) sent to a person or company in a foreign country. This includes many types of fund transfers, including wire transfers. The rules apply to money transmitters as well as to other entities such as banks and credit unions. The rules do not apply to providers that consistently provide 100 or fewer remit-tance transfers each year. The rules require remittance transfer providers to supply certain disclosures to consumers regarding matters such as exchange rates and fees and to secure consumer rights to cancel a transaction and to have errors resolved.

B. State Regulation

Forty-nine states and the District of Columbia currently require a license to conduct "money transmission." South Carolina and New Mexico are the latest states to enact money transmission licensing requirements.[51] Both states passed legislation in 2016; New Mexico's law became effective in 2017 and South Carolina's will become effec-tive after implementing regulations are issued. Montana is the only state that does not currently license money transmission.

States use various names to refer to money transmission, such as "sale of checks" or "money services"; determining whether and how a given money trans-mission activity is covered is not always simple. The analysis will also include whether any exclusions apply. For example, some states exclude payment proces-sors to the extent such entities provide processing, clearing, or settlement services between entities exempt from the state's money transmitter laws.[52] Other states exclude money transmissions that are incidental to, and a necessary part of, certain businesses.[53]

Entities that meet the definition of a money transmitter, and that are not other-wise exempt from licensure, must generally obtain a license from the state agency that regulates money transmission. To obtain a license, the entity must meet certain requirements, which vary by state.

---

49. 12 C.F.R. pt. 1005.
50. *Id.* subpt. B.
51. A. 266, R. 305, H. 4554, 121st Gen. Assem. (S.C. 2016); H.R. 250, 52nd Leg., 2d Sess. (N.M. 2016).
52. *See, e.g.*, Okla. Stat. Ann. tit. 6, § 1512(6) (West 2016); Okla. Admin. Code § 85:15-1-3(9) (2016); Iowa Code Ann. § 533C.103 (2016); Mich. Comp. Laws Ann. § 487.1004(i) (West 2016); Wash. Rev. Code Ann. § 19.230.020(9) (West 2016).
53. *See, e.g.*, Kan. Stat. Ann. § 9-511 (West 2016).

I. Definitions of Money Transmission

Of the states that require a money transmitter license, almost all define "money transmission" as involving the sale or issuance of some type of payment instrument. For instance, under California law, "money transmission" means any of the following:

1. Selling or issuing payment instruments
2. Selling or issuing stored value
3. Receiving money for transmission[54]

Under Illinois law, a "money transmitter" is a person located in, or doing business in, Illinois and who directly, or through authorized sellers (i.e., agents), engages in one or more of the following activities:

1. Sells or issues payment instruments
2. Engages in the business of receiving money for transmission or transmitting money
3. Engages in the business of exchanging, for compensation, money of the U.S. government or a foreign government to or from money of another government[55]

"Transmitting money" in Illinois means the transmission of money by any means, including transmissions to or from locations within the United States or to and from locations outside of the United States by payment instrument, facsimile or electronic transfer, or otherwise, and includes bill payment services.[56]

In Texas, "money transmission" is "the receipt of money or monetary value by any means in exchange for a promise to make the money or monetary value available at a later time or different location."[57] Money transmission includes "receiving money or monetary value for transmission, including by payment instrument, wire, facsimile, electronic transfer, or ACH debit," but does not include "the provision solely of online or telecommunication services or connection services to the Internet."[58]

These are just a few examples of how states and the District of Columbia define "money transmission" and "money transmitter," and an analysis of all potentially applicable state laws and District of Columbia laws is highly recommended for an entity to determine whether or not it is required to obtain a money transmitter license in one or more states or the District of Columbia.

a. Prepaid Access

As is evident from California's definition of money transmission, some states consider entities that sell or issue stored value to be conducting money transmission.[59]

---

54. CAL. FIN. CODE § 2003(q) (West 2016).
55. 205 ILL. COMP. STAT. 657/5 (2016).
56. *Id.*
57. TEX. FIN. CODE ANN. § 151.301(b)(4) (West 2016).
58. *Id.* § 151.301(b)(4)(A)(iii), (b)(4)(B).
59. *See, e.g.,* CAL. FIN. CODE § 2003(o)(2).

As noted later, however, some states do not consider such activities to be money transmission, and some states carve out closed-loop prepaid access from the definition of "payment instrument."[60]

b. Virtual Currencies

Several states consider virtual and digital currencies to be money transmission. Washington, for instance, has formally added virtual currency to its money transmitter law.[61] The New York Department of Financial Services started licensing virtual currency in 2015. Under New York's virtual currency rules, any person engaging in "Virtual Currency Business Activity" must become licensed.[62] "Virtual Currency Business Activity" is defined broadly and includes, but is not limited to, buying and selling virtual currency as a customer business as well as storing, holding, or maintaining custody or control of virtual currency on behalf of others.[63]

Several states have, however, specifically stated that virtual or digital currency activities only constitute money transmission under certain circumstances. For example, Texas has taken the position that money transmission does not occur when a person receives cryptocurrency in exchange for a promise to make it available at a later time or a different location because cryptocurrency is not money under the Texas Money Services Act.[64] In contrast, the exchange of cryptocurrency for sovereign currency through a third-party exchange is generally considered money transmission because the person exchanging the currencies receives the buyer's sovereign currency in exchange for a promise to make it available to the seller.[65] Similarly, exchange of cryptocurrency for sovereign currency through an automated machine (e.g., a bitcoin ATM) can be money transmission.[66]

Virtual currency issues are discussed in more detail in Chapter 5.

2. Exemptions under State Law

Looking beyond the definition of "money transmission," each state lists certain entities that are expressly exempt from all of that state's money transmitter statutes and regulations. Typical entities that are exempt include banks, credit unions, savings and loan associations, the United States and any federal agencies, the USPS, and the state itself, as well as any of the state's agencies.[67] Certain agents of individuals conducting money transmission may also be exempt,[68] but states vary as to whether they exempt only agents of licensed money transmitters or also agents of entities

---

60. *See, e.g.*, ALASKA STAT. ANN. § 06.05.990 (West 2016).
61. S.B. 5031, 65th Leg. (Wash. 2017).
62. N.Y. COMP. CODES R. & REGS. tit. 13, § 200.3(a) (2016).
63. *Id.* § 200.2(q).
64. Texas Department of Banking Supervisory Memorandum-1037, Regulatory Treatment of Virtual Currencies under the Texas Money Services Act (Apr. 3, 2014).
65. *Id.*
66. *Id.*
67. *See, e.g.*, 205 ILL. COMP. STAT. 657/15 (2016).
68. *See, e.g., id.* 657/10 (exempting authorized sellers of licensees).

that are exempt from money transmission licensing themselves (such as agents of banks). Payment processors may also be exempt, but states vary as to whether the exemption is expressly provided for by statute or regulatory interpretation.[69] Some states also reserve the right to exempt additional entities, as needed.[70]

a. Agents

Certain states provide an express agency exemption. In California, a person who provides money transmission in the state on behalf of a licensed entity, but is not licensed as a money transmitter, will be considered an "agent" so long as the licensed entity "becomes liable for the money transmission from the time money or monetary value is received by that person."[71]

Texas's agency exemption provides that a person is exempt if it

> acts as an intermediary on behalf of and at the direction of a license holder in the process by which the license holder, after receiving money or monetary value from a purchaser, either directly or through an authorized delegate, transmits the money or monetary value to the purchaser's designated recipient, provided that the license holder is liable for satisfying the obligation owed to the purchaser.[72]

A person acting as the agent of a person already exempted (e.g., a federally insured financial institution) is also exempt so long as: (1) the exempt entity is liable for satisfying the money services obligation owed to the purchaser on the agent's receipt of the purchaser's money, and (2) the exempt entity and agent enter into a written contract appointing the agent as the exempt entity's agent and the agent acts only within the scope of authority outlined in the contract.[73]

b. Prepaid Access

At least two states, Washington and West Virginia, also expressly exempt entities that issue or sell stored-value cards from money transmitter licensing requirements. The state of Washington excludes stored-value sellers and issuers from money transmitter statutes and regulations, if the funds are covered by federal deposit insurance immediately upon the sale or issuance of the stored value.[74] Similarly, West Virginia exempts the "issuance and sale of stored value cards or similar prepaid products which are intended to purchase items only from the issuer or seller of the stored value card."[75]

---

69. *See, e.g.*, Cal. Fin. Code § 2010(h) (West 2016) (providing an express, statutory exemption).

70. *See, e.g.*, Tex. Fin. Code § 151.302(c)(3) (West 2016) (providing the Texas Department of Banking commissioner the right to exempt a person who "does not charge a fee to transmit money or transmits money without a fee as an inducement for customer participation in the person's primary business").

71. Cal. Fin. Code § 2003(b).

72. Tex. Fin. Code § 151.003(7) (West 2016).

73. *Id.* § 151.003(5).

74. Wash. Rev. Code Ann. § 19.230.020(14) (West 2016).

75. W. Va. Code Ann. § 32A-2-3(c) (West 2016).

The majority of the states that do not expressly exempt entities that issue or sell stored-value cards from money transmission licensure requirements carve out from the definition of "payment instrument" any instruments that are sold and issued by the same party. For instance, Alaska's Uniform Money Service Act states that the term "payment instrument" "does not include an instrument that is redeemable by the issuer in merchandise or service, a credit card voucher or a letter of credit."[76] In other words, closed-loop gift cards are generally exempt from the definition of money transmission in most states.

States that do not expressly carve out stored value from "payment instrument" may have interpretive letters on point. New York has issued an interpretation of its statute, concluding that a certain closed-loop gift card program was exempt from licensing requirements.[77]

In Texas, stored value means "monetary value evidenced by an electronic record that is prefunded and for which value is reduced on each use" and includes prepaid access as defined in 31 C.F.R. § 1010.100(ww).[78] The term does not, however, include an electronic record that is "redeemable only for goods or services from a specified merchant or set of affiliated merchants, such as: (i) a specified retailer or retail chain; (ii) a set of affiliated companies under common ownership; (iii) a college campus; or (iv) a mass transportation system."[79] Thus, the Texas definition of stored value includes anything that would be considered prepaid access under federal law with the exception of closed-loop prepaid access.

The California Department of Business Oversight (California DBO) has published several opinion letters on this topic. In 2013, the California DBO published an opinion letter interpreting language in its statute to exclude closed-loop gift cards from the definition of "money transmission," rendering closed-loop gift cards exempt from money transmitter licensing in California.[80] The letter concluded that closed-loop stored value is not money transmission under the California Money Transmission Act. Thus, the sale or distribution of gift cards, e-cards, or other similar closed-loop stored-value products does not meet the definition of "money transmission" and such activity is not subject to money transmitter licensing under California state law.[81]

The Pennsylvania Department of Banking has also determined that a retailer who was both issuing and selling its own gift cards was not in the "business of receiving money for deposit or transmission" so as to require it to obtain a Pennsylvania

---

76. Alaska Stat. Ann. § 06.05.990 (West 2016).

77. New York State Department of Financial Services, Banking Interpretations 366, 640(3), 640(5), and 641(1) (Apr. 14, 2005).

78. Tex. Fin. Code § 151.301(8).

79. 31 C.F.R. § 1010.100(ww).

80. California Division of Financial Institutions, Commissioner's Op. No. 004 on Sale and/or Distribution of Gift Cards That Are Only Redeemable by the Issuer for Goods or Services Provided by the Issuer or Its Affiliate (May 28, 2013).

81. *Id.*

money transmitter license.[82] Massachusetts has taken an even broader position by declaring that the issuance of any type of stored value is exempt from money transmitter licensing.[83] The Massachusetts opinion did not, however, address the *sale* of stored value.

c. Payment Processors

There are several states in which the money transmitter statute or regulation provides an express exemption for certain types of payment processors. California, for instance, exempts

> [a]n operator of a payment system to the extent that it provides processing, clearing, or settlement services, between or among persons excluded by this section, in connection with wire transfers, credit card transactions, debit card transactions, stored value transactions, automated clearing house transfers, or similar funds transfers, to the extent of its operation as such a provider.[84]

Illinois provides an almost identical exemption.[85]

In some states that do not have an express processor exemption, regulators have issued legal and interpretive opinions recognizing a processor exemption. In 2014, the California DBO issued an opinion letter determining that a data processor was not required to obtain a money transmitter license under California state law.[86] The letter cited several factors in its determination. First, the data processor was submitting transaction data to a bank on behalf of merchants, while the bank was maintaining a settlement account in the bank's name for the benefit of the merchants.[87] The bank had sole ownership and control over the account and was using it to process merchant transactions and settle with merchants.[88] The bank had responsibility for processing transactions and settling with merchants via the settlement account.[89] The data processor was only batching all payment transaction requests and sending a settlement request to the bank each day, which included merchant identifications.[90] Also, the bank was debiting the data processor's account for charge-backs and other return-related issues, rather than taking that money from the bank's settlement account.[91]

82. Pennsylvania Department of Banking Interpretive Letter, Gift Cards Issued by Retail Stores (May 13, 2005).

83. Massachusetts Consumer Affairs and Business Regulation Selected Op. 04-100, Whether Prepaid Reloadable Stored Value Cards Trigger Licensure Statutes Relative to the Business of Selling, Issuing, or Registering Checks or Money Orders or Foreign Money Transmittal (Apr. 26, 2005).

84. Cal. Fin. Code § 2010(h) (West 2016).

85. 205 Ill. Comp. Stat. 657/15(6) (2016) (exempting "[a]n operator of a payment system to the extent that it provides processing, clearing, or settlement services between or among persons exempt under this Section in connection with wire transfers, credit card transactions, debit card transactions, stored value transactions, automated clearing house transfers, or similar funds transfers").

86. California DBO, Opinion Letter on Data Processor That Does Not Have Possession or Control of Money—Not Subject to MTA (May 20, 2014).

87. *Id.*

88. *Id.*

89. *Id.*

90. *Id.*

91. *Id.*

The bank was acting as an originating depository financial institution (ODFI) in providing ACH services to the merchants.[92] Finally, the processor's website and Terms of Service stated that the bank was responsible for conducting settlement activities and that the data processor did not actually or constructively receive, take possession of, or hold any money or monetary value for transmission.[93] The Terms of Service also stated that the data processor was not a money transmitter or a bank.[94] The California DBO particularly emphasized the fact that the bank was debiting the data processor's account for charge-backs and not using the funds in the settlement account allocated to one sub-merchant to pay off the obligations of another merchant.[95] The California DBO's standard seemed to focus on who has legal or constructive ownership, control, or possession of the merchant funds.[96]

In 2013, the California DBO came to a similar conclusion in a different opinion letter. It determined that an entity providing software and receiving only instructions, orders, or directions to transmit money or monetary value for transmission was not conducting money transmission.[97] The flow of funds worked in such a way that a customer would initiate a transaction and the funds would be transferred directly from the customer to an account at a bank for which the bank had sole custody and control of the funds.[98] The bank took title to the funds until it arranged for the funds to be moved to the receiver's account.[99] At no time did the software provider have any ownership or control of the account or of any funds transmitted.[100]

The Texas Department of Banking (Texas DOB), which regulates money transmission in Texas, has also taken the view that some payment processing activities do not constitute money transmission. The Texas DOB has issued three legal opinions, summarized below, addressing this issue.

In a 2003 letter, the Texas DOB determined a company that provided third-party ACH origination services was not required to obtain a money transmission license.[101] The company acted as an agent for merchants to initiate ACH entries by debiting and transferring funds from a consumer's account to credit a merchant's account. The company entered into service agreements with each of the merchants and each agreement provided that the company was the merchant's agent "with full power and authority to act on behalf of Merchant." The company had an operating account at a bank in which it temporarily held the consumer's funds before transferring the funds to the merchant. The company never took control of the consumer's funds for further transactions and held the funds only as the merchant's agent at the end

---

92. *Id.*
93. *Id.*
94. *Id.*
95. *Id.*
96. *Id.*
97. California Division of Financial Institutions, Opinion Letter on Software Company That Does Not Have Possession or Control of Money—Not Subject to Money Transmission Act (May 16, 2013).
98. *Id.*
99. *Id.*
100. *Id.*
101. *Id.*

of the settlement process, pursuant to agreements with the merchants. The Texas DOB found that the company was not "receiving currency or an instrument payable in currency to transmit the currency or its equivalent by . . . electronic means or through the use of a financial institution . . . or another funds transfer network."

In 2006, the Texas DOB was presented with a similar fact pattern and again found that a company acting as a payment processor for various merchants was not required to obtain a money transmitter license.[102] The company enabled merchants' customers to pay for purchases by direct debit from customers' bank accounts through ACH transactions. The company acted solely on behalf of the merchants and did not have any direct contact with merchants' customers. Nor did the company receive or hold the merchants' customers' funds or transfer funds or perform money transmission services on behalf of customers. The company did temporarily hold the merchants' funds in a company-controlled account at the end of the settlement process, but only as an agent of the merchants and pursuant to an agreement between the merchants and the company. The customers paid the merchants or received refunds from the merchants, and the company, on behalf of the merchants, facilitated settlement of the transactions through the ACH network. The company never took control of or held the merchants' customers' funds for further transmission or payment and so the company did not "receive money for transmission" under the Texas Money Services Act.

Most recently, in 2014, the Texas DOB concluded that a company providing bill payment services as an agent of a payee was not conducting money transmission and thus was not required to obtain a money transmitter license.[103] In order to utilize such a "payee agent model," a company must demonstrate that it has actual express authority, in the form of a written contract, to receive money on behalf of a biller. The Texas DOB emphasized that because it is difficult to discern whether a company has apparent authority, it will recognize the "payee agent model" exception only when a company has actual authority that is expressly granted in a written agreement when determining whether a money transmitter license is required. The agreement must, at a minimum, "appoint the agent to receive and process payments to the principal on behalf of the principal." Furthermore, the scope of the agency relationship delineated in the agreement "must include the receipt of money from customers from payment to the Biller" and "further confirm that the Biller is obligated to consider the receipt of funds by the Provider to be the same as receipt by the Biller itself, such that consumers are given credit by the Biller for having paid regardless of whether the Provider ever remits the money to the Biller."

The Texas DOB also adopted a new rule concerning payment processors in November 2015.[104] The new rule excludes two types of payment processors from Texas money transmission licensing requirements by expanding on two exclusions

---

102. Texas DBO, Op. No. 06-01 (2006).
103. Texas DBO, Op. No. 14-01 (2014).
104. 7 Tex. Admin. Code § 33.4.

that already exist under Texas law.[105] Under the Texas Finance Code, a person who acts as an intermediary on behalf of a licensed money transmitter to assist in transmitting funds after the licensee receives them is not required to obtain a license.[106] The new rule extends this exclusion further by including payment processors who act on behalf of non-licensed entities (e.g., banks) that have been excluded or exempted from licensing.[107]

The second new exclusion under the rule expands the Texas DOB's 2014 legal opinion to some situations in which there is no explicit agency appointment in a contract.[108] Specifically, an agent of a merchant may be exempt from money transmission licensing requirements, even without an express contractual appointment, if the merchant, upon receipt of funds from the agent, immediately either (1) provides the purchased goods and services to the consumer, or (2) credits the consumer for the full amount of the funds received by the agent, does not make the credit revocable, and evidences the credit in writing.[109] The merchant must also provide the purchased goods and services regardless of whether the agent transmits the funds.[110]

Other states have issued interpretations concluding that payment processors are covered by that state's money transmission laws and regulations. For instance, Washington has issued an interpretative statement stating that merchant payment processing constitutes money transmission under the Washington Uniform Money Services Act.[111] Thus, entities conducting payment processing in Washington must obtain a money transmission license and comply with other requirements under the Washington Uniform Money Services Act *unless* the Washington Department of Financial Institutions grants a waiver to the entity—meaning that the processor has to actively seek a waiver from the state of Washington or risk becoming an unlicensed money transmitter. And, of course, if the state of Washington does not grant the waiver, the processor would have to obtain a Washington money transmission license. Pennsylvania has also issued an interpretation, concluding that a person is conducting money transmission, and therefore must be licensed, if that person collects money from consumers and forwards it to charitable, religious, or other nonprofit organizations.[112]

3. Compliance Requirements under State Law

States that license money transmission generally prohibit a person from engaging in money transmission without first obtaining a license, unless that person is otherwise

---

105. *Id.*
106. Tex. Fin. Code § 151.003(7).
107. 7 Tex. Admin. Code § 33.4(c) (2016).
108. *Id.* § 33.4(d).
109. *Id.* § 33.4(d)(1).
110. *Id.* § 33.4(d)(2).
111. Washington Department of Financial Institutions, Interpretive Statement 2016-1: Payment Processors (Jan. 1, 2016).
112. Pennsylvania Department of Banking and Securities Memorandum, All Persons That Are Engaged in Money Transmission by Selling Services to Persons Including Non-profits, Religious Organizations, Charities, and Political Campaigns ("Third-Party Recipient") for the Movement of Money from a Donor's Bank Account or Credit Card to a Third-Party Recipient (Sept. 29, 2015).

exempt.[113] Most states now process money transmitter license applications through the National Multistate Licensing System (NMLS), though there currently is not a single application or license that gives reciprocal licensing in other states.

Currently, it can take up to two years to obtain a license in some states, and the fees to obtain licenses in each state can be significant. Licensing requirements vary widely among states, but they usually require a licensee to maintain a minimum net worth; to post security, such as a surety bond; and maintain certain permissible investments. States generally take one of five approaches to imposing net worth requirements on money transmitter licensees.

Several states simply require a flat net worth amount. The amounts range from as little as $1,000 in Hawaii[114] to as much as $1,000,000 in Utah.[115] Other states fall somewhere in the middle. For instance, Kentucky and Pennsylvania require net worth amounts of $500,000.[116]

Some states take a tiered approach to setting net worth requirements based on the licensee's number of locations and/or authorized delegates. For instance, Texas requires a net worth of $100,000 if there are four or fewer authorized delegate locations, or $500,000 if there are five or more authorized delegate locations.[117] Illinois requires a base net worth of $35,000 for a licensee's principal office, plus additional amounts based on the number of locations, up to as much as $500,000 if there are 25 or more locations.[118] Florida requires a minimum net worth of $100,000, plus $10,000 per location, up to $2,000,000 total.[119]

Other states take a tiered approach based on the volume of transactions. Washington requires a net worth of $10,000 for every $1,000,000 of money transmission volume, with a minimum of $10,000, but no maximum.[120] New Hampshire requires a net worth equal to the lesser of (1) $1,000,000, or (2) the average daily outstanding money transmissions in the prior calendar year.[121]

States such as California, Colorado, Maryland, and Texas have built-in regulator discretion in determining net worth based on certain statutorily specified factors. For example, California requires a net worth of $250,000–$500,000, depending on the following factors:

1. The nature and volume of the projected or established business
2. The number of locations at or through which money transmission is or will be conducted
3. The amount, nature, quality, and liquidity of its assets
4. The amount and nature of its liabilities

113. *See, e.g.*, 205 ILL. COMP. STAT. 657/10 (2016).
114. HAW. REV. STAT. § 489D-6 (2016).
115. UTAH CODE § 7-25-203(1)(a).
116. KY. REV. STAT. ANN. § 286.11-011 (2016); 7 PA. STAT. & CONS. STAT. ANN. § 6104 (2016).
117. TEX. FIN. CODE § 151.307 (2016).
118. 205 ILL. COMP. STAT. 657/20 (2016).
119. FLA. STAT. ANN. § 560.209 (2016).
120. WASH. REV. CODE ANN. § 19.230.060; WASH. ADMIN. CODE § 208-690-060 (2016).
121. N.H. REV. STAT. ANN. § 399-G:5 (2016).

5. The history of its operations and prospects for earning and retaining income
6. The quality of its operations
7. The quality of its management
8. The nature and quality of its principals
9. The nature and quality of the persons in control
10. The history of its compliance with applicable state and federal law
11. Any other factor the commissioner considers relevant[122]

Some states, such as Georgia, Massachusetts, and New York, have no net worth requirements; these states do have bond requirements, which can be substantial, in and of themselves, similar to the vast majority of states that also have net worth requirements.

Licensees must also pay initial application fees and recurring annual fees to maintain the license. States may also require background checks on principals of money transmitter license applicants. After a money transmitter license is issued, states will require regular transactional activity reports to the state regulator and may periodically audit money transmitter licensees.[123]

Some states also impose limitations around money transmitters' ability to appoint authorized delegates. Washington does not permit a money transmitter licensee to appoint an authorized delegate if the authorized delegate does not have a physical location in Washington.[124] Texas also sets forth specific requirements a licensee must meet to conduct business through an authorized delegate.[125]

C. State and Federal Penalties for Violations

State and/or federal sanctions can be issued for violations of any law applicable to money transmitters.

In particular, failure to comply with licensing requirements carries significant risk. The potential penalties for engaging in unlicensed money transmitter activities can be severe. Engaging in money transmission without obtaining a required state license may not only violate state law but also federal law, and may involve criminal sanctions. The licensing authority may also revoke a license under circumstances provided in the relevant state's laws.

Under federal criminal law, "Whoever knowingly conducts, controls, manages, supervises, directs, or owns all or part of an unlicensed money transmitting business, shall be fined in accordance with this title or imprisoned not more than 5 years, or both."[126] That statute defines "unlicensed money transmitting business" to mean

---

122. Cal. Fin. Code § 2040 (West 2016).
123. *See, e.g., id.* § 2039 (requiring money transmitter licensees to file certain annual reports) and *id.* § 2033 (permitting the California Department of Oversight to conduct examinations of money transmitter licensees).
124. Wash. Admin. Code § 208-690-035(5) (2016).
125. Tex. Fin. Code § 151.402(b) (2016).
126. 18 U.S.C. § 1960 (2016).

a money transmitting business which affects interstate or foreign commerce in any manner or degree and—(A) is operated without an appropriate money transmitting license in a State where such operation is punishable as a misdemeanor or a felony under State law, whether or not the defendant knew that the operation was required to be licensed or that the operation was so punishable; (B) fails to comply with the money transmitting business registration requirements under section 5330 of title 31, United States Code, or regulations prescribed under such section; or (C) otherwise involves the transportation or transmission of funds that are known to the defendant to have been derived from a criminal offense or are intended to be used to promote or support unlawful activity[.][127]

Failure to register with FinCEN as an MSB also can trigger civil money penalties (CMPs) as well as possible criminal prosecution. Under the BSA and its implementing rules, "Any person who fails to comply with any requirement of 31 U.S.C. 5330 or this section [31 C.F.R. 103.41] shall be liable for a civil penalty of $5,000 for each violation, in an amount up to $5,000 for each day a registration violation continues."[128] FinCEN maintains a list of enforcement actions initiated under these requirements on its website.[129]

State authorities may also bring civil and/or criminal actions under their own state laws for violations of their money transmitter requirements. For example, under Texas's Money Services Act, the state may enter into a consent order with a person to address violations of the act, including licensing requirements.[130] The states may also assess CMPs against a person that:

(1) has violated this chapter or a rule adopted or order issued under this chapter and has failed to correct the violation not later than the 30th day after the date the department sends written notice of the violation to the person; (2) if the person is a license holder, has engaged in conduct specified in Section 151.703 [conduct warranting revocation or suspension of license]; (3) has engaged in a pattern of violations; or (4) has demonstrated wilful disregard for the requirements of this chapter, the rules adopted under this chapter, or an order issued under this chapter.[131]

Texas may assess up to $5,000 for each violation or, in the case of a continuing violation, $5,000 for each day that the violation continues, with each transaction in violation of this chapter and each day that a violation continues considered a separate violation.[132]

The Texas Money Services Act also provides for criminal penalties where a person

(1) intentionally makes a false statement, misrepresentation, or certification in a record or application filed with the department or required to be maintained under

---

127. *Id.* § 1960(b).
128. 31 U.S.C. § 5330(e) (2016); 31 C.F.R. § 103.41(e) (2016).
129. FinCEN, *Enforcement Actions for Failure to Register as a Money Service Business*, https://www .fincen.gov/news_room/ea/ea.msb.html (last visited May 20, 2017).
130. Tex. Fin. Code § 151.706 (2016).
131. *Id.* § 151.707.
132. *Id.*

this chapter or a rule adopted or order issued under this chapter, or intentionally makes a false entry or omits a material entry in the record or application; or (2) knowingly engages in an activity for which a license is required under Subchapter D or F without being licensed under this chapter.[133]

If the banking commissioner of Texas has reason to believe that an unlicensed person has engaged, or is likely to engage, in activity for which a money transmitter license is required, the commissioner may order the person to cease and desist from the violation until the person is issued the license. The commissioner may issue an emergency cease and desist order in accordance with section 151.710 if the commissioner finds that the person's violation or likely violation threatens immediate and irreparable harm to the public.[134]

Section 151.703 of the Texas Money Services Act specifies the circumstances under which a licensee's license may be suspended or revoked. The Texas banking commissioner *must* revoke a license if the commissioner finds that: "(1) the net worth of the license holder is less than the amount required under this chapter; or (2) the license holder does not provide the security required under this chapter."[135] The commissioner *may* suspend or revoke a license or order a license holder to revoke the designation of an authorized delegate if the commissioner has reason to believe that:

> (1) the license holder has violated this chapter, a rule adopted or order issued under this chapter, a written agreement entered into with the department or commissioner, or any other state or federal law applicable to the license holder's money services business; (2) the license holder has refused to permit or has not cooperated with an examination or investigation authorized by this chapter; (3) the license holder has engaged in fraud, knowing misrepresentation, deceit, or gross negligence in connection with the operation of the license holder's money services business or any transaction subject to this chapter; (4) an authorized delegate of the license holder has knowingly violated this chapter, a rule adopted or order issued under this chapter, or a state or federal anti-money-laundering or terrorist funding law, and the license holder knows or should have known of the violation and has failed to make a reasonable effort to prevent or correct the violation; (5) the competence, experience, character, or general fitness of the license holder or an authorized delegate of the license holder, or a principal of, person in control of, or responsible person of a license holder or authorized delegate, indicates that it is not in the public interest to permit the license holder or authorized delegate to provide money services; (6) the license holder has engaged in an unsafe or unsound act or practice or has conducted business in an unsafe or unsound manner; (7) the license holder has suspended payment of the license holder's obligations, made a general assignment for the benefit of the license holder's creditors, or admitted in writing the license holder's inability to pay debts of

---

133. *Id.* § 151.708 (2016).
134. *Id.* § 151.702 (2016).
135. *Id.* § 151.703(a) (2016).

the license holder as they become due; (8) the license holder has failed to terminate the authority of an authorized delegate after the commissioner has issued and served on the license holder a final order finding that the authorized delegate has violated this chapter; (9) a fact or condition exists that, if it had been known at the time the license holder applied for the license, would have been grounds for denying the application; (10) the license holder has engaged in false, misleading, or deceptive advertising; (11) the license holder has failed to pay a judgment entered in favor of a claimant or creditor in an action arising out of the license holder's activities under this chapter not later than the 30th day after the date the judgment becomes final or not later than the 30th day after the date the stay of execution expires or is terminated, as applicable; (12) the license holder has knowingly made a material misstatement or has suppressed or withheld material information on an application, request for approval, report, or other document required to be filed with the department under this chapter; or (13) the license holder has committed a breach of trust or of a fiduciary duty.[136]

IV. PRIVACY AND DATA SECURITY

Nonbank money transmitters are subject to federal and state laws, regulations, and policies regarding the privacy and data security of consumer information. Many of these legal requirements are the same as those that apply to banks, but the supervisory framework through which compliance is evaluated and enforced differs from the framework applicable to banks. Banks are examined on an ongoing basis by federal and/or state bank examiners, who evaluate a bank's compliance with applicable laws and regulations, including those related to privacy and data security. Nonbank money transmitters are potentially subject to the jurisdiction of multiple agencies on the federal and state levels, but are not examined as banks are. State oversight of money transmitters varies greatly, not only as to whether examinations are conducted but also concerning their subject matter. Money transmitters might face federal enforcement actions related to privacy or data security by the CFPB or Federal Trade Commission (FTC), but typically only after a problem—such as a data breach—already has occurred and been detected. Only a minority of nonbank financial companies are subject to examination by the CFPB, and the FTC is an enforcement agency—it does not perform examinations of entities in the ordinary course of its supervision to check for ongoing compliance and concerns. Thus, nonbank money transmitters may face less scrutiny on an ongoing basis with regard to privacy and data security compliance.

A. Federal Law

The key federal law imposing privacy and data security requirements on money transmitters is the Gramm-Leach-Bliley Act of 1999 (GLBA).

---

136. *Id.* § 151.703(b).

1. Gramm-Leach-Bliley Act

The financial privacy and data security provisions of the federal GLBA apply to "financial institutions,"[137] a definition that is broad enough to include nonbank money transmitters. For these GLBA purposes, "financial institution" is defined as "any institution the business of which is engaging in financial activities as described in section 4(k) of the Bank Holding Company Act of 1956 (12 U.S.C. 1843(k)). An institution that is significantly engaged in financial activities is a financial institution."[138] In turn, the many examples of "financial activities" in section 4(k) of the Bank Holding Company Act include "transferring . . . money."[139]

The FTC has authority to enforce GLBA with respect to financial institutions that are not subject to the jurisdiction of the federal banking agencies, the SEC, the Commodity Futures Trading Commission, or state insurance authorities. Thus, nonbank money transmitters not subject to the jurisdiction of any of these agencies will be subject to the FTC's enforcement of the CFPB's GLBA Privacy Rule and the FTC's GLBA Safeguards Rule. These rules cover information collected about individual consumers, and do not cover information collected in business or commercial activities.

Under the Privacy Rule, a financial institution must provide consumers certain privacy notices regarding the ways that the financial institution may share the consumers' "nonpublic personal information" (NPPI), such as account numbers or account history, with anyone other than an affiliate of the financial institution.[140] Consumers have the right to opt out of certain types of sharing, and the notices must provide them with a reasonable way to do so. The financial institution must not share NPPI with nonaffiliates except as disclosed in such notices, and where the consumer has not opted out of the sharing, with certain exceptions, such as for sharing with law enforcement or sharing that is necessary to process or service a transaction the consumer has requested.[141]

Under the FTC's Safeguards Rule, financial institutions must develop a written information security program (WISP) that describes its plan to protect customer information. The plan must be appropriate to the financial institution's size and complexity, the nature and scope of its activities, and the sensitivity of the customer information it handles. As part of its plan, each company must designate one or more employees to coordinate its information security program; identify and assess the risks to customer information in each relevant area of operations, and evaluate the effectiveness of the current safeguards for controlling these risks; design and implement a safeguards program, and regularly monitor and test it; select service providers that can maintain appropriate safeguards, require them by contract to maintain safeguards, and properly oversee their activities; and evaluate and adjust

---

137.   15 U.S.C. § 6801(a)–(b) (2016).
138.   *See* 16 C.F.R. § 313.3(k) (2016).
139.   12 U.S.C. § 1843(k)(4)(A) (2016).
140.   16 C.F.R. §§ 313.4–.9 (2016).
141.   *Id.* §§ 313.13–.15 (2016).

the program in light of relevant circumstances, including changes in the financial institution's business or operations, or the results of security testing and monitoring.

The Safeguards Rule requires financial institutions to assess and address the risks to customer information in all areas of their operation, including with regard to employee management and training; information systems; and detecting and managing system failures.

In the event of a breach, the Safeguards Rule does not impose the types of prescriptive actions in response that many state data breach laws do. GLBA does not preempt more protective state laws, and thus money transmitters and other financial institutions must also comply with such state laws where applicable.

B. State Law

The states also have laws regarding data privacy, data security (regarding keeping information protected from unauthorized access, such as requirements to encrypt data), and notification of affected consumers in the event of data breaches. As with other types of state laws applicable to money transmitters, these laws vary by state in their provisions, application, and penalties for noncompliance. They generally do not specifically name money transmitters in their coverage, but rather apply broadly to businesses or other persons collecting or maintaining certain types of information of residents of that state.

In particular, state data breach laws often prescribe specific steps that persons covered by the laws must take in the event of a data breach involving certain types of information, including notification of affected persons. Forty-seven states, the District of Columbia, Guam, Puerto Rico, and the Virgin Islands have such laws.

C. Private Industry Standards

Money transmitters can also be subject to contractual standards established by private-sector authorities. In particular, for activities involving payment cards such as credit cards, the Payment Card Industry Security Standards Council (PCI SSC) has established a framework to promote the secure handling of cardholder information. A central component of that framework is the PCI Data Security Standard (PCI DSS), which sets forth standards and processes for prevention, detection, and appropriate responses to security incidents. The PCI standards cover "payment cards," defined to mean any payment card or device that bears the logo of the founding members of the PCI SSC—American Express, Discover Financial Services, JCB International, MasterCard Worldwide, and Visa, Inc.[142] Money transmitters that do not use or process payment card data—say, because they transmit funds using only bank account information—will not be subject to PCI DSS.

---

142. PCI Security Standards Council, Payment Card Industry (PCI) Data Security Standard (DSS) and Payment Application Data Security Standard (PA-DSS) Glossary of Terms, Abbreviations, and Acronyms v.3.2 (Apr. 2016).

V. LOOKING TO THE FUTURE

As money transmission methods continue to evolve, the need for modernization of the existing licensing and supervisory framework may also continue to evolve. On the most basic level, there may be an increased need to more consistently define who or what constitutes a "money transmitter" under federal and state laws, and what types of activities are covered or excluded from licensing and other requirements. As new payment innovations continue to emerge, it may grow increasingly difficult to analogize those innovations to legacy statutory definitions and regulator interpretations.

Also, there may be an increased demand for additional efficiency in the application and supervision process. The current reality consists of a patchwork of state laws and state-by-state licensing application requirements, imposing delay and expense, as well as the need to ensure that a money transmitter operating in more than one state understands and complies with all the nuances of the laws of every such state. Because money transmission is typically inherently interstate in nature, obtaining a license in only one state, or complying with the laws of only one state, would likely not be effective or practical. In addition, for any entity operating on the Internet or in the mobile channel, that entity is automatically operating in all 50 states and the District of Columbia based on the potential location of customers. States currently do not grant reciprocity for licensees from other states, nor is there a single common application form or process to use to apply for licensing in multiple states. Even though most states now process money transmitter license applications through the NMLS platform, the requirements for such licensing remain a state-by-state matter.

The Conference of State Bank Supervisors and the Money Transmitter Regulators Association have made efforts to promote the modernization and streamlining of how money transmission is regulated. This includes increasing consistency in supervision of money transmitters. The Office of the Comptroller of the Currency (OCC) also is considering creating a new type of bank charter designed for financial technology (fintech) companies. Currently, the charter is envisioned to amount to a limited-purpose national bank charter, which would allow chartered fintech companies to comply with federal laws rather than a state-by-state set of laws, as national banks currently are able to do through their OCC charters. As of this writing, it is unclear when, or if, such a charter will in fact be offered, but one of the motivating factors in the OCC's evaluation of such a limited-purpose fintech charter is numerous complaints from innovators in the fintech space that the multistate money transmission licensing regime is too costly, time intensive, and byzantine for fintech start-ups, and is often a substantial barrier to timely launching of a product on a limited budget.

PART II

The Next Generation

Innovators and/or Disruptors

Chapter 4

Mobile Wallets/ Mobile Payments and Peer-to-Peer Payments

Erin Fonte

I. INTRODUCTION

One of the buzz words in financial services is "fintech" (i.e., "financial technology"). Numerous start-ups and venture capital/private equity entities are investing in developing new technologies that seek to "disrupt and disintermediate" traditional financial services. One of the first beachheads in the current fintech invasion is mobile payments.

Mobile payments technology is poised to create a globally dramatic shift in how individuals pay for goods and services, track spending, interact with retailers, and even manage personal finances. Mobile payments are also becoming big business for nonfinancial institution (non-FI) alternative payments providers. Many of these services offered by non-FIs seek to "disintermediate" traditional banking relationships, creating a fundamental shift in how individuals conduct day-to-day purchasing and interact with their finances.

It was anticipated that there would be more than 4.8 billion individuals using a mobile phone by the end of 2016. A recent report noted that 39 percent of all mobile users in the United States had made a mobile payment in 2015, up from 14 percent in 2014; usage could reach the 70 percent range by 2017.[1] Currently, these payments are happening in a variety of manners using a variety of technologies.

Here is a brief timeline of how the "electronification" of payments over the past 35 years has lead to the expansive future potential for mobile payments technology.

---

1. John Rampton, *The Evolution of the Mobile Payment*, TECHCRUNCH, June 17, 2016, https://techcrunch.com/2016/06/17/the-evolution-of-the-mobile-payment/.

1983: David Chaum, an American cryptographer, starts work on creating digital cash by inventing "the blinding formula, which is an extension of the RSA algorithm still used in the web's encryption." This is the beginning of cryptocurrencies.

1994: Although this is disputed, some believe that the first online purchase, a pepperoni and mushroom pizza from Pizza Hut, occurred in this year.

1998: PayPal is founded.

1999: Thanks to Ericsson and Telnor Mobil, mobile phones could be used to purchase movie tickets.

2003: 95 million cell phone users worldwide made a purchase via their mobile device.

2007: Both the iPhone and the Android operating system (OS) are released.

2008: Bitcoin is invented.

2011: Google Wallet is released.

2014: Apple Pay is launched, followed a year later by Android and Samsung Pay.

2017: $60 billion in mobile payment sales will be reached.

2020: 90 percent of smartphone users will have made a mobile payment.[2]

Mobile payments have the potential to dramatically affect the world of retailing. These digital wallets, such as Apple Pay and Android Pay, are "smart" payment devices that can integrate payments with two-way, real-time communications of any type of data. Integration of payments with real-time communications holds out tremendous promise for retailers: the combination in a single platform of search, advertising, payment, shipping, customer service, and loyalty programs. Such an integrated retail platform offers brick-and-mortar retailers a potentially superior ability to identify, attract, and retain customers, bringing e-commerce-type platforms into the brick-and-mortar environment.[3]

At the same time, however, mobile payments present materially different risks for merchants than traditional plastic card payments precisely because of their "smart" nature. Some mobile payments products and services can also reallocate flows of consumer data from merchants to FIs, depriving merchants of valuable customer information used for anti-fraud, advertising, loyalty, and customer service purposes.[4]

Part II below discusses mobile wallets, mobile payments, and person-to-person (P2P) mobile transfers, including a description of the various mobile payments types, mobile payments products, and how mobile payments technology changes traditional payments transactions. Part III discusses potential risks involved with mobile wallets/mobile payments. Part IV provides a detailed overview of the regulatory

---

2. *Id.*

3. Adam J. Levitin, *Pandora's Digital Box: The Promise and Perils of Digital Wallets*, 166 U. Pa. L. Rev. (2017), *available at* https://papers.ssrn.com/sol3/papers.cfm?abstract_id=2899104.

4. *Id.*

framework that currently governs mobile payments in the United States. Finally, the chapter concludes with current policy questions and considerations regarding mobile wallets/mobile payments. This chapter does not touch upon the current and emerging cutting-edge technologies of wearables and connected Internet of Things devices that are being used for payment functionality. Those technologies are also developing at a rapid pace, but in many ways the resulting payment applications are being built upon the "new rails" of mobile payments products and systems discussed in this chapter.

II. MOBILE WALLETS, MOBILE PAYMENTS, AND P2P TRANSFERS

A. Mobile Banking v. Mobile Wallets/Mobile Payments

The novelty of mobile technology and payment services provided by non-FIs understandably contributes to confusion about the differences between mobile banking and mobile payments. Many FIs offer some combination of the online banking services via mobile devices, initially by short messaging service (SMS) that older model "feature" phones use, but now primarily through either a truncated mobile website that operates in a mobile browser or by a native on-device mobile application (mobile app).[5] Common mobile banking services now include the following traditional online banking functions, along with some new features:

- Account balance inquiries and statement information
- Bill payment services
- Traditional funds transfer services (i.e., between accounts)
- Branch and automated teller machine (ATM) location services
- Transaction alerts based on dollar thresholds or other user-established parameters
- Mobile remote deposit check capture services (i.e., "check deposit by phone")[6]

By contrast, we may refer to mobile payments as a term that includes payments services and products offered not just by FIs, but also by emerging and alternative non-FI payments providers as well, such as PayPal (offering a non-FI account that processes and settles transactions between buyers and sellers), Boku (allowing payment for goods and services by charging to a mobile phone bill, which the customer chooses how to settle and pay), or Square (alternative credit/debit card processing service and technology using a mobile device to process payments for small merchants).[7]

---

5. Erin F. Fonte, *Overview of Mobile Payments in the United States*, 32 BANKING & FIN. SERVICES POL'Y REP. 2 (2013).
6. *Id.*
7. *Id.* at 3.

Traditional FIs are also innovating in the mobile banking space, as some FIs like JPMorgan Chase (Chase Pay) and Capital One (Capital One Wallet) are offering mobile wallet products. However, non-FIs are leading the development and introduction of myriad other new products in the mobile payments space.

B. Mobile Payment Types and Products

There are currently three basic types of mobile payments transactions:

- Mobile commerce transactions utilize a mobile internet browser to perform standard e-commerce transactions.
- Mobile payments transactions use either some unique technology form factor (such as near-field communication (NFC) or barcode technology like the Starbucks mobile app), or in-app payment functionality (like a "buy" button) to initiate authorization and payment.
- Mobile wallets seek to replace an individual's full "wallet" of payment options by storing payment card and payment account credentials and then leveraging one of the various technological form factors to initiate authorization and payment.[8]

This chapter will not address mobile commerce transactions in depth, nor will it address "in-app" transactions in depth. Instead, it will focus on mobile payments transactions and mobile wallet services, along with other P2P transactions that utilize various technology form factors (such as QR codes or NFC technology) and various payment rails (such as Automated Clearing House (ACH), debit, or credit card rails) to process and settle. Although a variety of terms sometimes are used with regard to mobile wallet/mobile payments and related technologies, the following discussion will use these general categories.

The majority of mobile payments conducted today that are not mobile commerce (i.e., just web commerce conducted via mobile device browser) fall into three types of mobile payments services.

I. Digital Wallets

A "digital wallet" typically refers to a payment service that provides

1. a smartphone app for making financial transactions at a merchant's physical point of sale; and/or
2. a desktop app for making credit/debit/ACH purchases online. It eliminates entering shipping, billing, and credit card data when a purchase is made at a website. The data either resides in the cloud or is encrypted on the user's computer, and the wallet's digital certificate identifies the cardholder/accountholder. A digital wallet may also store insurance and

---

8. *Id.*

loyalty cards, drivers' licenses, identification cards, and site passwords. Some wallet apps let users enter additional data.[9]

An example of a single merchant digital wallet that can be used only on e-commerce or mobile commerce via the Internet would be the digital wallet of Amazon. An example of a general-use digital wallet that can be used in both an e-commerce/mobile commerce via the Internet, or via physical point-of-sale systems is MasterCard's Masterpass or Visa's Visa Anywhere.

2. Mobile Wallets

A "mobile wallet" typically refers to a service that enables payment at a physical point of sale via mobile device. A smartphone wallet app typically is capable of storing multiple payment account credentials (e.g., credit card, debit card, prepaid card, ACH) and employs various user authentication methods and technology to initiate payment transactions. As of the writing of this chapter, Apple Pay, Android Pay, and Samsung Pay are mobile wallet services currently operating in the United States.

3. P2P Transfers

Mobile P2P transfers are a type of mobile payment that is also a subset of "account-to-account" transfers, whereby transfers are made directly between the sender's and receiver's bank accounts (as opposed to using credit, debit, or prepaid card accounts). In most cases, mobile P2P transfers use existing retail payment systems (such as the debit card rails or the ACH rails) to deposit and withdraw funds. The simplest case is when the payor and the payee maintain accounts at the same FI. This type of payment is called an "on-us" or "book" transaction. These transactions are settled by posting accounting entries on the books of one FI. P2P transfers also may occur between individuals at different FIs, which typically settle either via ACH or debit card rails. As technology advances, the transfer of funds through the use of proximity devices, such as mobile devices, is increasing.[10] Examples of current P2P products within the United States are Venmo (owned by PayPal), Zelle (owned by Early Warning and involving major U.S. banks), Dwolla, and Square's Square Cash feature supporting mobile P2P payments.

---

9. PCMagazine Encyclopedia, *Definition of Digital Wallet*, http://www.pcmag.com/encyclopedia/term/41399/digital-wallet (last visited May 20, 2017).

10. *See* Federal Financial Institutions Examination Council (FFIEC) IT Examination Handbook Infobase, *Online Person-to-Person (P2P), Account-to-Account (A2A) Payments and Electronic Cash*, http://ithandbook.ffiec.gov/it-booklets/retail-payment-systems/payment-instruments,-clearing,-and-settlement/card-based-electronic-payments/online-person-to-person-(p2p),-account-to-account-(a2a)-payments-and-electronic-cash.aspx (last visited May 20, 2017).

C. What Mobile Wallet/Mobile Payments Technologies Change in Traditional Payments Transactions

The way that mobile wallets/mobile payments change traditional payments transactions is that instead of having to use a physical plastic credit, debit, or prepaid card (either magnetic stripe or Europay, MasterCard, and Visa (EMV) chip), the payment credentials for the underlying credit, debit, or prepaid card or bank account are stored and transmitted either by the user's digital wallet (with payment credentials typically securely stored in the cloud) or from the user's mobile device (where payment credentials are stored in encrypted form, often using proxy tokens or some other form of tokenization of underlying payment account information). For physical point-of-sale mobile payments, payment credentials are transmitted from consumers to merchants at the point of sale using a variety of different technologies. Several of the technologies described below implement measures to take the payment credential account number (often referred to in the industry as the "primary account number" or PAN) out of the payment initiation, authorization, and settlement process to make payment credentials more secure by never giving fraudsters the ability to hack and capture "live" or actionable payment account information. Without full payment account information, it is much more difficult for fraudsters to either fully clone a payment account or to use the underlying payment account and associated personal information to commit identity theft.

For example, several NFC-based mobile wallet/mobile payments products utilize proxy tokens that do not contain full payment account information, but can be utilized by a trusted third party to "re-associate" the low-value proxy token (i.e., one with no "live" payment account information) with the user's actual payment account information. This is essentially how Apple Pay works. When a user provisions his or her payment account to Apple Pay and then uses Apple Pay at the physical point of sale, the information stored in the "secure element" within the iPhone is not actual payment account data, but rather is a "device primary account number" (DPAN) issued by the card network for that particular card to Apple.

When the DPAN is presented at the merchant's NFC-enabled device at the point of sale, the merchant sends the DPAN to the card network (e.g., MasterCard or Visa), and the card network then "re-associates" the DPAN with the actual PAN for the payment card, sends the authorization request to the card issuing FI for authorization, and then transmits an approved authorization request back to the merchant. The merchant never has the PAN, and the issuing bank never has the DPAN—the card networks as the "tokenizers" are the only entity able to associate the DPAN proxy with the actual PAN on the payment account.

The issue of tokenization and the various approaches and technologies around security of payment account information could easily fill another chapter of this book, but suffice it to say that for purposes of understanding mobile wallet/mobile payments technology, one of the key selling points to issuing banks, merchants, and consumers is that, in theory, mobile payments technologies should be able to significantly reduce, if not altogether eliminate, the instances when "live" payment account information is present (in either encrypted or unencrypted form) at every stage of transaction initiation, authorization, and settlement.

1. Method of Transmission of Payment Authorization Data from Consumers to Merchants in Mobile Payments Technologies

a. NFC

NFC is a wireless transmission protocol that allows for encrypted exchange of payment credentials and other data at close range whereby a point-of-sale device "reads" the payment account credentials when the user either swipes or taps his or her NFC-equipped mobile device on the NFC reader present on the NFC-enabled point-of-sale device. NFC utilizes a "secure element" to store the consumer's payment credentials on the consumer's mobile device for access and use at the physical point of sale. Examples of mobile wallets/mobile payments that use NFC technology include Apple Pay, Android Pay, and Samsung Pay.[11]

In the United States, there are currently three models that leverage NFC technology to support contactless mobile wallets:

- NFC with secure element (SE)[12]
- NFC with host card emulation (HCE)[13] software that replaces the SE in the mobile device to enable the NFC wallet app to perform card emulation. Payment tokens are downloaded from a cloud server and stored in the mobile OS.
- NFC with a trusted execution environment (TEE), a secure area of the main processor in the mobile device that stores a payment token[14]

---

11. Rampton, *supra* note 1.

12. *See* Susan Pandy, Marianne Crowe & Brian Russell, Federal Reserve Bank of Boston Payment Strategies, Understanding the Role of Host Card Emulation in Mobile Wallets (May 10, 2016) ("GlobalPlatform defines a secure element ('SE') as a tamper-resistant one-chip secure microcontroller capable of securely hosting applications and their confidential and cryptographic data (e.g. key management). In payment applications, the SE controls interactions between trusted sources (bank) and trusted applications (mobile payments app) stored on the SE and third parties (merchant the user is paying). The secure domain protects the user's credentials and processes the payment transaction in a trusted environment. There are three types of SE's—Subscriber Identity Module (SIM)/Universal Integrated Circuit Card (UICC), micro SD, and embedded secure element (eSE)."), *available at* https://www.bostonfed.org/publications/payment -strategies/understanding-the-role-of-host-card-emulation-in-mobile-wallets.aspx.

13. *See id.* ("The term 'host card emulation' ('HCE') was introduced in 2012 by SimplyTapp to describe the ability for a mobile wallet app to communicate through the NFC controller to a contactless NFC-enabled POS terminal/reader to pass payment card credentials (or payment token), eliminating the need for a physical SE managed by the mobile network operator (MNO). Research in Motion (RIM) had previously implemented a similar process on its Blackberry Bold 990 device in 2011, referring to it as 'virtual target emulation.'").

14. *Id.* at 1. The term "payment tokens" refers to tokens as defined under the *EMV Payment Tokenization Specification* (http://www.emvco.com/specifications.aspx?id=263.) Also, for more information about the tokenization and the difference between security (acquirer/processor) and payment tokenization (network/issuer), see Marianne Crowe et al., Federal Reserve Bank of Atlanta & Federal Reserve Bank of Boston, Is Payment Tokenization Ready for Primetime? Perspectives from Industry Stakeholders on the Tokenization Landscape (June 2015), *available at* http://www.bostonfed.org/bankinfo/payments-strategies/publications/2015 /tokenization-prime-time.pdf.

Of the three primary NFC mobile wallet/mobile payments solutions available in the United States today, Apple Pay stores payment tokens in the SE in the mobile device (first model described above), Android Pay uses HCE to store tokens in the Android KitKat v4.4 (or higher) mobile OS (second model described above), and Samsung Pay uses NFC and HCE, but stores the payment token and cryptographic keys in the TEE in the mobile device (third model described above).[15]

b. Cloud Based

Cloud-based mobile payments technology differs from physical element-based payment technology (such as NFC described above) and leverages mobile connection to the Internet to obtain payment credentials (including tokens) that are stored in the cloud and controlled by a trusted third party rather than being stored on the mobile device itself. For example, with mobile apps, payments will occur on a consumer's device in order to purchase goods from a specific retailer, such as the Starbucks mobile app that generates a "static" bar code scanned at the point of sale for each payment transaction. The static (i.e., unchanging) bar code is stored within the Starbucks mobile app on the user's mobile device.[16] Some mobile payments technologies that are cloud-based use "dynamic" bar codes that are unique with every transaction, but are still tied back to the user's payment account information. QR Pay is a company that provides an application program interface (API) functionality to generate dynamic bar codes.

c. Proximity Based

Proximity-based payments utilize geolocation used to initiate payments. Merchants are able to identify users within range and verify identity, and the credentials (both customer identity verification and payment credentials) are stored in the cloud. Bluetooth low energy (BLE) "triggering" takes place on either the consumer's or merchant's device where data is stored in a mobile payment account. Examples of BLE-enabled mobile payments include PayPal Beacon and Apple's iBeacon.[17]

d. Mobile P2P

A mobile P2P payment initiated on a mobile device can use a recipient's e-mail address, mobile phone number, or other identifier in order to initiate payment. Transfer of funds occurs via ACH, card networks, or intra-FI account transfer (i.e., "book" transfer). Venmo, a mobile P2P transfer service acquired by PayPal, reported transferring more than $1 billion P2P transactions in January 2016 alone.[18] Meanwhile, major banking institutions, such as JPMorgan Chase & Co., Bank of America Corp., Wells Fargo & Co., and U.S. Bancorp, have created a joint venture called Zelle

---

15. *Id.*
16. Rampton, *supra* note 1.
17. *Id.*
18. *Id.*

(now owned by Early Warning) that allows customers to transfer funds instantly to another bank account through their mobile devices.[19] While the technology for the mobile P2P transactions is not particularly complex, technology and security infrastructure must be in place for the P2P transfer system to work and to prevent fraudsters from gaining access to the "directory" that ties personal identifiers to bank account information.

III. RISKS INVOLVED WITH MOBILE WALLETS/MOBILE PAYMENTS

A. Cost of Payments

Whether mobile wallet/mobile payments and P2P transactions will ultimately be more or less costly than traditional methods of payments (credit card, debit card, prepaid card, and ACH) is a matter for speculation. For example, even though in theory the costs of mobile payments should be lower due to issuing banks not having to issue plastic cards (which are even more costly if they are outfitted with an EMV chip), card networks such as MasterCard and Visa were reportedly charging significant "tokenization" fees for issuing device primary account number tokens (D-PANS) for NFC mobile wallets such as Apple Pay. While systems that utilize ACH transaction rails versus credit or debit card transaction rails should theoretically have less expensive transaction costs, the overall cost for processing payments via mobile wallets/mobile payments can remain high due to technology development and security costs for the mobile wallet/mobile payments provider.

In addition, card network association rules leave room for uncertainty regarding whether what constitutes a mobile payments transaction qualifies as a "card present" versus a "card not present" transaction. "Card not present" transactions are generally more expensive to process in terms of interchange fees as they are viewed as carrying heightened risk, but in reality, it appears that the convergence of technology will mean that the distinction between "card present" and "card not present" transactions with regard to risk profiles will diminish, if not disappear, within a short amount of time. As of the writing of this chapter, card networks will only recognize a mobile payments transaction as "card present" if the payment credentials are stored in some form of SE on the mobile device.

B. Fraud and Data Security

Fraud and data security with regard to mobile wallets/mobile payments continues to be a subject for speculation and debate. As with all new and emerging technologies, consumers, issuing FIs, and merchants are all wary of the new technology and unknown security risks. However, as mentioned above, there is a compelling argument that mobile wallets/mobile payments will ultimately prove more secure

---

19. *Id.*

than traditional plastic cards. On one level, a mobile device such as an iPhone that is equipped with Touch ID or other form of biometric recognition allows for mobile wallets/mobile payments to achieve true three-part multifactor authentication.

"Multifactor authentication" is what is currently required by the Federal Financial Institutions Examination Council (FFIEC) for both Internet and mobile transactions and services. In October 2005, the FFIEC issued "Authentication in an Internet Banking Environment,"[20] and in June 2011, it released "Supplement to Authentication in an Internet Banking Environment."[21] This guidance established "multifactor" authentication (as opposed to "single-factor" authentication) where FIs were required to have at least two of three forms of user authentication for online banking transactions: (1) what you have (e.g., ATM card, smart card, physical token); (2) what you know (e.g., password, personal identification number (PIN)); and (3) who you are (e.g., biometric characteristic, such as a fingerprint). Multifactor authentication requirements have been extending to banking services in the mobile channel as well.

Mobile payments that contain a biometric feature can achieve true three-part multifactor authentication if they combine all three form factors. When you add geo-location information as an additional "fourth" factor in a multifactor authentication environment, then that bolsters difficulty in a fraudster simultaneously faking all four authentication factors at once. When one also considers the fact that mobile payments replace the "live" and actionable payment account credentials with "low value" tokens that can only be "re-associated" with actual payment account data by trusted third parties, it becomes clear that two elements that fraudsters must have—authentication credentials and actual payment account information— become extremely difficult to obtain.

But extremely difficult to obtain does not mean impossible. Fraudsters can still "phish" or otherwise steal, and fake, all four form factors discussed above. In addition, if the "token vaults" of a trusted third party that "re-associates" low-value tokens with actual underlying payment account information are ever hacked, then fraudsters would obtain the "keys to the kingdom" and could obtain the underlying payment account credentials. While mobile wallets/mobile payments certainly hold the promise of a more secure, less hacker-prone payments process, whether that promise can ultimately be fulfilled is still unfolding in this new environment.

C. Control over Customer Data

In addition to the potential to achieve greater security at lower cost, merchants are particularly excited about linking the mobile wallet/mobile payment to ads, offers,

---

20. FFIEC, Authentication in an Internet Banking Environment (Oct. 12, 2005), *available at* https://www.ffiec.gov/pdf/authentication_guidance.pdf.

21. FFIEC, Supplement to Authentication in an Internet Banking Environment (June 29, 2011) (Financial Institution Letter FIL-50-2011), *available at* http://ithandbook.ffiec.gov/media/153051/04-27-12_fdic_combined_fil-6-28-11-auth.pdf.

or loyalty/rewards programs. Retailers like Wal-Mart Stores Inc. are rolling out their own products to fuel mobile payments, including use of geolocation technology to deliver localized coupons and deals to customer phones while they are shopping.[22] Many merchants also use loyalty cards and programs to gather information regarding customer behavior and customer spend, often tying product-level information for each purchase to a particular transaction identified with a loyalty/rewards program customer's account.

One of the controversies with merchants when Apple Pay launched was that, due to the device-tokenization and the lack of actual primary account number information being passed to the merchant via the Apple Pay transaction (even in truncated form), merchants were no longer able to identify particular transactions with particular loyalty/rewards customers due to lack of that data being passed from Apple Pay transactions.[23] Similarly, many mobile payments transaction flows and technologies may disintermediate merchants from transaction data and their ability to associate it with item-level purchase information.

This could be one of the significant reasons why many merchants are choosing to implement in-app payments through the merchant's branded mobile app, which allows continued access to customer data and facilitates specific targeted ads, offers, and loyalty/rewards incentives. Issues surrounding ownership of both transaction information and customer personal information are continuing to evolve at a remarkable pace, with many players in the payments ecosystem (card networks, issuing banks, technology service providers and merchants) trying to exercise sole and exclusive "ownership" of transaction data and customer personal information— even if another party in the transaction separately obtained, for example, a customer's e-mail address through a loyalty/rewards program. Ownership and use of transaction and personal information data presents distinct issues that must be resolved with customers' underlying privacy rights. However, while these issues remain unresolved, many companies are engaging in "data grab" to make sure they are not cut out of valuable data streams around mobile payments transactions.

D. Intellectual Property Issues

Due to the fact that mobile wallets/mobile payments involve not only payments technology but also mobile phone technology and mobile app/user interface development—not to mention a whole host of hosted services and cloud computing in the background—there are a lot of intellectual property (IP) issues and potential claims that can arise for developers and users of mobile payments technologies. This chapter does not have room for a detailed discussion of all the IP issues that can arise, but mobile wallet/mobile payments providers that may wish to disclaim all warranties of noninfringement or disclaim any liability or indemnification for

---

22. Rampton, *supra* note 1.
23. Joseph Keller, *Lack of Customer Data Keeping Some Merchants from Supporting Apple Pay*, iMore, June 5, 2015, http://www.imore.com/merchants-want-more-customer-data-theyll-support-apple-pay.

third-party claims of infringement will find significant pushback from merchants on these IP issues, with many demanding either a warranty of noninfringement or indemnification for third-party IP infringement claims at the very least.

IV. REGULATORY FRAMEWORK

Mobile wallet/mobile payments products and services can trigger a surprising number of potentially applicable laws, rules, and regulations because the services touch upon financial services laws, mobile phone/device laws, and privacy/data security laws. In addition, there are card network (e.g., American Express, Discover, Master-Card, Visa) and private network (e.g., National Automated Clearing House Association (NACHA)) rules and requirements governing these transactions as well. This section reviews potentially applicable laws and the regulatory framework in four areas: (1) transactions; (2) privacy/data security; (3) consumer protection; and (4) other miscellaneous regulatory requirements. The discussion below includes applicable federal and state laws, rules, and regulations as well as relevant federal agency guidance.

A. Regulatory Frameworks Governing Transactions

1. Electronic Funds Transaction Act/Regulation E

a. In General

The federal Electronic Funds Transaction Act (EFTA) and Regulation E establish rules for electronic funds transfers (EFTs) involving consumers.[24] The EFTA and its implementing rule, Regulation E, provide a basic framework for establishing the rights, liabilities, and responsibilities of consumers who engage in EFTs and the FIs and other entities who provide EFT services. An "EFT" generally includes any "transaction initiated through an electronic terminal, telephone, computer, or magnetic tape that instructs a financial institution either to credit or debit a consumer's account."[25] This includes debit card transactions, direct deposits and withdrawals, and ATM transactions.[26] The regulation generally applies to FIs, but certain provisions apply to "any person." EFTA/Regulation E applies to any EFT that authorizes an FI to debit or credit a consumer's account. "Financial institution" is defined under the EFTA as "a state or national bank, a state or federal savings and loan association, a mutual savings bank, a state or federal credit union, or any other person who, directly or indirectly, holds an account belonging to a consumer."[27] The term

---

24. Provisions of the EFTA can be found at 15 U.S.C. § 1693 *et seq.* and provisions of Regulation E can be found at 12 C.F.R. pt. 1005.
25. 15 U.S.C. § 1693a(7) (definition of "electronic funds transfer").
26. *Id.* § 1693a(8) (definition of "electronic terminal").
27. *Id.* § 1693a(9) (definition of "financial institution").

"account" generally means a consumer access account held by an FI and established primarily for personal, family, or household purposes.[28]

An entity subject to EFTA/Regulation E must comply with the provisions of the law and regulation, which includes required disclosures to consumers[29] and procedures for consumer notifications and investigation/resolution of alleged fraudulent or unauthorized EFTs within specific timeframes.[30] EFTA/Regulation E also limits consumer liability for fraudulent or unauthorized transactions, with varying limits based upon timing of notification to the FI.[31] Entities that are subject to EFTA/Regulation E must establish a substantial compliance program to oversee and implement compliance.

Many mobile wallet/mobile payments providers have researched applicable definitions of EFTA/Regulation E and concluded that they are not covered by the provisions (although they may be subject to the provisions of Reg E "Lite," as discussed below). However, the Consumer Financial Protection Bureau (CFPB) released its final Prepaid Card Rule (clocking in at 1,689 pages) on October 5, 2016, with most provisions of the new rule effective as of October 1, 2017.[32] The final CFPB Prepaid Card Rule expands Regulation E compliance obligations to a variety of prepaid card accounts, including coverage of certain digital wallets and P2P accounts.

"The new rule applies to traditional prepaid cards as well as mobile wallets, person-to-person payment products and other electronic accounts that can store funds," CFPB Director Richard Cordray said during a press conference October 4, 2016. Kristine Andreassen, senior counsel in the CFPB's Office of Regulations, clarified this by explaining that mobile wallets that can store funds are covered under the final rule, while those that act simply as a "pass-through" are not covered.[33]

The result is that many mobile wallets, such as Google Wallet and PayPal's Venmo, must meet the final rule's requirements, while wallets like Apple Pay are not covered by the revised Regulation E provisions because they only store payment credentials for underlying debit or prepaid accounts issued where funds are held by other entities, rather than storing funds in the mobile wallet provider's account. After the proposed rule had been released, PayPal and Google objected to the CFPB potentially including their mobile wallets because they are capable of P2P transfers and storing funds. Google in 2015 submitted a comment to the CFPB stressing that "overregulation would unnecessarily stifle this emerging market" for mobile wallets, requesting that the CFPB "tread lightly" in regulating them.

---

28. *Id.* § 1693a(2) (definition of "account").

29. *See* 12 C.F.R. § 1005.9(a) (proscribing requirements for receipts at electronic terminals and periodic statements).

30. *See id.* § 1005.11 (setting forth procedures for resolving errors).

31. *See id.* § 1005.6 (setting forth liability of consumers for unauthorized transfers).

32. *See* Press Release, CFBP, CFPB Finalizes Strong Federal Protections for Prepaid Account Consumers (Oct. 5, 2016), *available at* http://www.consumerfinance.gov/about-us/newsroom/cfpb-finalizes-strong-federal-protections-prepaid-account-consumers/.

33. *CFPB Includes Mobile Wallets in Final Prepaid Rule*, PayBefore, Oct. 5, 2016, http://paybefore.com/pay-gov/cfpb-includes-mobile-wallets-in-final-prepaid-rule/.

Despite industry objections, the CFPB did not change its final rule on this issue:

> The Bureau continues to believe that digital wallets that can hold funds operate in large part in a similar manner to physical or online prepaid accounts—a consumer can load funds into the account, spend the funds at multiple, unaffiliated merchants or conduct P2P transfers, and reload the account once the funds are depleted. Accordingly, the bureau believes that consumers who transact using digital wallets deserve the same protections as consumers who use other prepaid accounts. Indeed, as with other prepaid accounts, a consumer's digital wallet could fall victim to erroneous or fraudulent transactions.[34]

The final CFPB Prepaid Card Rule arguably applies to providers as varied as online payments leader PayPal Holdings Inc., owner of the popular Venmo P2P payments service, and banks that use third-party P2P services, such as Popmoney from processor Fiserv Inc. or others. "Everybody involved in bank P2P . . . may have new regs . . . [i]t's hard to tell. There are 1,600 pages here. The rule is so sprawling it's hard to tell where it ends."[35] As of the writing of this publication, many mobile wallet/mobile payments providers are still reviewing the rule to determine its applicability to their products and services.

b. Reg E "Lite"

Even if a mobile wallet/mobile payments provider is not an entity subject to the EFTA/Regulation E under the CFPB Final Prepaid Card Rule, the entity may nevertheless have some EFTA/Regulation E compliance obligations. Regulation E includes provisions that apply specifically to a provider of an "electronic funds transfer service" under 12 C.F.R. § 1005.14.[36] These provisions are colloquially referred to as Reg E "Lite" provisions, and they are particularly applicable to mobile wallet/mobile payments providers whose services are deemed to fall within the definition of "access device," thereby triggering application of Reg E "Lite" requirements.

Reg E "Lite" applies to any person that "provides an electronic fund transfer service to a consumer but that does not hold the consumer's account."[37] An entity is subject to the Reg E "Lite" provisions if the person: (1) issues a debit card (or other access device) that the consumer can use to access the consumer's account held by an FI; and (2) has no agreement with the account-holding institution regarding such access.[38]

An "access device" is defined as "a card, code or other means of access to a consumer's account, or any combination thereof, that may be used by the consumer

---

34. *Id.*

35. Jim Daly, *The CFPB's Final Prepaid Card Rule Raises Concerns about Digital Wallets*, Digital Transactions, Oct. 5, 2016, http://www.digitaltransactions.net/news/story/The-CFPB_s-Final-Prepaid-Card-Rule-Raises-Concerns-About-Digital-Wallets.

36. *See* 12 C.F.R. § 1005.14 (Provider of an Electronic Fund Transfer Service).

37. *Id.*

38. *Id.* § 1005.14(a)(1), (a)(2).

to initiate electronic fund transfers."[39] For mobile wallet providers, provisions that apply to providers of an "access device" used to access accounts are particularly important.

Under the broad definition of "access device," mobile wallet/mobile payments services that store payment credentials for debit or prepaid card accounts and that are used to initiate transactions will be subject to Reg E "Lite" requirements. The Reg E "Lite" provisions contain specific compliance requirements including:

- Required disclosures and documentation[40]
- Error resolution (including primary responsibility for investigations of alleged unauthorized or fraudulent transactions, and requirements to work with the account-holding institution or entity for both investigation and the granting of provisional credit to the consumer during the investigation)[41]
- Final resolution of investigation and transfer funds to or from the consumer's account, in the appropriate amount and within the applicable time period if the investigation concludes that an error occurred for which the consumer is not liable (or has limited liability) under Regulation E[42]

In summary, the rules of the road regarding EFTA/Regulation E compliance for mobile wallet/mobile payments providers are undergoing significant changes over the coming year due to the requirements of the CFPB's final Prepaid Card Rule (provided that rule survives the Congressional Review Act).[43] Mobile wallet/mobile payments providers are well-advised to review the new rule and to remember that even if they are not subject to full-blown EFTA/Regulation E compliance, they may well be subject to Reg E "Lite" requirements as the provider of an "access device" for originating EFTs.

c. EFTA/Regulation E and the Durbin Amendment/Regulation II

The Durbin Amendment, enacted as part of the Dodd-Frank Wall Street Reform and Consumer Protection Act, places limits on the interchange fees and related compensation that may be charged by debit card issuers if the issuer has assets of more than $10 billion.[44] Under Regulation II promulgated under the Durbin Amendment by the Federal Reserve Board, debit cards are broadly defined to include any code or device (other than paper checks or drafts or facsimiles thereof) issued or approved for use through a payment card network to debit an account.[45] This definition also includes many general-use (i.e., open-loop) prepaid cards.[46] Regulation

---

39. *Id.* § 1005.2(a)(1).
40. *Id.* § 1005.14(b)(1).
41. *Id.* § 1005.14(b)(2).
42. *Id.*
43. *See* 5 U.S.C. ch. 8 (Congressional Review of Agency Rulemaking).
44. 12 C.F.R. §§ 235.3–.6.
45. *Id.* § 235.2(f).
46. *Id.* § 235.5(c).

II also requires that an issuer of a covered debit or prepaid account must enable at least two unaffiliated payment card networks on each debit card.[47] The regulation also prohibits an issuer or payment card network from directly or indirectly inhibiting the ability of merchants to direct the routing of electronic debit transactions for processing over any payment card network of the merchant's choosing that may process such transactions.[48]

With regard to mobile wallets/mobile payments, the landscape is still evolving as to whether technology and tokenization efforts are enabling or preventing issuers from offering merchants the unaffiliated network routing options as required under Regulation II. Merchants have claimed that, for example, Apple Pay transactions that are tokenized go straight to Visa and MasterCard networks, and the merchants do not have a choice in routing. However, some PIN networks, including STAR and Fiserv's Accel, have already touted their capability to facilitate Apple Pay transactions and they constitute debit networks that are "unaffiliated" from Visa and MasterCard. As the use of mobile wallets/mobile payments increases, and as both NFC and tokenization technologies continue to evolve, this is an area that may undergo more scrutiny from the regulatory level if merchants are able to show that they are systematically deprived of routing choices with these new technology offerings that are required under the Durbin Amendment/Regulation II.[49]

d. EFTA/Regulation E and the Remittance Transfer Rule

If a mobile wallet/mobile payments provider is involved in facilitating or processing international money transfers, that entity will need to make sure it is in compliance with the CFPB's Remittance Transfer Rule promulgated by the CFPB under the EFTA as an amendment to Regulation E. The Remittance Transfer Rule amended Regulation E regarding international remittances to require that companies that make those services available provide additional protections to consumers.[50] Those provisions include disclosure requirements (including foreign currency conversion fees) and provisions for error resolution and cancellation.

The Remittance Transfer Rule also requires the remittance transfer provider to train their staff on policies and procedures and to adopt new forms and disclosures, including mobile and text message disclosures.[51] Any provider or a mobile wallet/mobile payments service that provides for international remittance will be subject to the Remittance Transfer Rule, and must develop disclosures, policies, and procedures, as well as an internal compliance program, to ensure compliance with the rule.

---

47. *Id.*
48. *Id.* § 235.7(b).
49. *See* Joe Adler, *Apple Pay May Reignite War over Durbin Amendment*, AM. BANKER, Apr. 6, 2015, https://www.americanbanker.com/news/apple-pay-may-reignite-war-over-durbin-amendment.
50. *See* 12 C.F.R. pt. 1005, subpt. B.
51. *Id.* § 1005.31(a)(5) (prescribing disclosures for mobile application or text message transactions).

2. Truth in Lending Act/Regulation Z

The federal Truth in Lending Act (TILA) and Regulation Z[52] promulgated pursuant to TILA establish rules intended to help consumers understand the cost of credit and be able to compare credit options. TILA/Regulation Z generally applies to "creditors" that offer or extend credit to consumers and includes both open-end and closed-end credit products, including credit cards. The purpose of TILA is to assure a meaningful disclosure of credit terms so that the consumer will be able to compare more readily the various credit terms available to him or her and avoid the uniformed use of credit while protecting the consumer against inaccurate and unfair credit billing and credit card practices.

For mobile wallet/mobile payments providers, it is important to note that Regulation Z does not focus on the payment aspect (i.e., the function that provides substantially immediate payment to sellers), but rather the credit aspect (i.e., the commitment by the consumer/purchaser to repay the issuer at some time in the future) of a transaction.

If a mobile wallet/mobile payments service offers an "extension of credit" as defined under TILA/Regulation Z, then these requirements apply (including required disclosures, dispute resolution, investigation, and limitations on consumer liability for fraudulent or unauthorized transactions).

However, most mobile wallet/mobile payments providers currently do not offer extensions of credit, but rather merely store the payment credentials of a credit card account that is issued by an FI. In these instances, the mobile wallet/mobile payments provider will be expected to work with the issuing FI to investigate and resolve claims of unauthorized and fraudulent transactions. Since many mobile wallet/mobile payments providers that store payment credentials often allow use and storage of credit, debit and prepaid cards, many of these providers subject to Reg E "Lite" as discussed above also include credit card investigation and dispute resolution in their compliance programs as they are already doing the same for debit and prepaid cards.

3. Truth in Billing Laws

Mobile wallet/mobile payments providers that charge payments directly to a consumer's mobile wireless or mobile carrier account, instead of a debit, credit, or prepaid card or bank account (so-called "bill to mobile" payment services), must also be aware of the "Truth in Billing" requirements of the Federal Communications Commission (FCC).[53] Under "Truth in Billing" requirements, wireless carriers must provide clear, correct, and detailed billing information to customers, including a description of services provided and charges made. The "Truth in Billing" requirements apply to wireless carriers, but mobile wallet/mobile payments providers must be aware of the requirements to understand how wireless carriers must

---

52. *Id.* pt. 226.
53. 47 C.F.R. § 64.2401.

handle disclosure and dispute resolution requirements and how the "bill to mobile" provider must cooperate and assist with wireless carriers in compliance with their "Truth in Billing" requirements.

4. Bank Secrecy Act/Anti-Money Laundering Regulations

a. In General

The Bank Secrecy Act (BSA) (which includes provisions of the USA PATRIOT Act) and its implementing regulations (collectively referred to as BSA Rules) support government efforts to combat drug trafficking, money laundering, and other crimes such as terrorist financing.[54] The BSA Rules were enacted to prevent banks and other financial services providers from being used as intermediaries for, or to otherwise hide the transfer or deposit of money derived from, criminal activity.[55] The BSA Rules identify transactions and circumstances that must be reported to federal authorities and set forth compliance systems that must be employed, such as screening customers against the U.S. Department of the Treasury's Office of Foreign Asset Control's Sanctions List and Specially Designated Nationals List, which contain countries and individuals barred from doing business with U.S. FIs and other companies.

While some of the functions that processors or mobile wallet/mobile payments providers perform may not fall directly under the BSA Rules, an entity that processes a credit card or certain types of prepaid accounts (such as gift cards, rewards cards, and other stored-value devices) must comply with the BSA Rules and is subject to enforcement actions by the U.S. Department of the Treasury and the U.S. Department of Justice. Payment processors and mobile wallet/mobile payments providers must maintain extensive compliance programs to ensure they conform to BSA Rules, as well as related requirements imposed by contract with any partnering FIs or networks, including card association or card network rules.

A processor or mobile wallet/mobile payments provider that is partnering with an FI may be deemed to be a "service provider" to that FI, and therefore may be subject to "pass through" requirements imposed via contract by the FI. These requirements are designed to ensure that the service provider is conducting appropriate customer due diligence and transmitting appropriate information to allow the FI to meet its obligations under the BSA Rules. FIs will also often require what is colloquially referred to as "fourth-party due diligence" whereby a service provider contractually requires its own vendors and subcontractors to follow all the requirements that the company itself must meet as a service provider.

---

54. 31 U.S.C. §§ 5311–5330; 12 U.S.C. §§ 1829b, 1951–1959; USA PATRIOT Act, 31 U.S.C. § 5312(a)(2) (additions to the anti-money laundering program); 31 C.F.R. tit. X.

55. *See, e.g.*, 31 U.S.C. §§ 5313(a) and 5318(g).

b. Customer Identification Program Requirements

The USA PATRIOT Act in section 326 directs the secretary of the U.S. Treasury to prescribe minimum standards requiring FIs to verify the identity of an entity or any person who wants to open an account with the FI. These standards are known as the "Customer Identification Requirements" (or CIP Rules), which require FIs to implement reasonable procedures to: (1) verify the identity of any individual applying for an account; (2) document the information used to verify that person's identity; and (3) screen potential customers against the U.S. Department of the Treasury's Office of Foreign Asset Control's Sanctions List and Specially Designated Nationals List.

The CIP Rules consider various types of accounts and various methods of opening them, as well as different types of identifying information that can be employed. There are several regulations that govern the different types of FIs, including 31 C.F.R. § 1020.220 applicable to banks. These CIP Rule requirements are, in turn, pushed down by FIs to third-party service providers (including payment processors and mobile wallet/mobile payments providers) as required under various guidance documents issued by the federal functional financial regulators.

Although not defined as a "financial institution," a payment processor or mobile wallet/mobile payments provider that is either "provider" or "seller" related to a "prepaid access program" is subject to the U.S. Department of the Treasury's Financial Crimes Enforcement Network's (FinCEN's) Prepaid Access Rule.[56] The Prepaid Access Rule amends the federal money services business (MSB) registration laws (discussed further in Part IV.A.5 below) as was mandated under the Credit Card Accountability Responsibility and Disclosure (CARD) Act of 2009. "Prepaid access" under the rule covers prepaid devices such as plastic cards, mobile phones, electronic serial numbers, key fobs, and/or other mechanisms that provide a portal to funds that have been paid in advance and are retrievable and transferable.

The Prepaid Access Rule puts in place suspicious activity reporting, and customer and transactional information collection requirements on providers and sellers of certain types of prepaid access similar to other categories of MSBs. The Prepaid Access Rule:

- Renamed "stored value" as "prepaid access," without narrowing or broadening the meaning of the term, but to more aptly describe the underlying activity
- Adopted a targeted approach to regulating sellers of prepaid access products, focusing on the sale of prepaid access products whose inherent features or high dollar amounts pose heightened money laundering risks
- Exempts from the rule prepaid access products of $1,000 or less and payroll products if they cannot be used internationally, do not permit transfers among users, and cannot be reloaded from a non-depository source

---

56. *See* 31 C.F.R. pts. 1010 and 1022.

- Exempts closed-loop prepaid access products sold in amounts of $2,000 or less
- Excludes government-funded and pre-tax flexible spending for health and dependent care-funded prepaid access programs[57]

A "provider" of prepaid access for a prepaid access program can be designated by agreement among the participants in the program or will be determined by their degree of oversight and control over the program—including organizing, offering, and administering the program. Providers of prepaid access are required to register with FinCEN. "Sellers" of prepaid access are retailers of prepaid access devices, which can be physical plastic cards or the virtual equivalent. While sellers of prepaid access are not required to register with FinCEN (just as no MSB that operates solely as an agent for another MSB is required to register), sellers of prepaid access must maintain an anti-money laundering (AML) program if the prepaid access product offered is covered by the Prepaid Access Rule and can be used *without* a later activation process that includes customer identification, or if a retailer sells prepaid access products (regardless of whether offered under a prepaid program) providing a portal to funds that exceed $10,000 to any person during any one day.[58]

The definition of "prepaid access" under the Prepaid Access Rule is broad, definitely covering prepaid access in the mobile wallet/mobile payments arena. Therefore, to the extent that a mobile wallet/mobile payments provider is a provider of prepaid access, the entity will need to register with FinCEN as a federal MSB and maintain a BSA/AML program. If a mobile wallet/mobile payments provider is a seller of prepaid access, the entity will still need to maintain a BSA/AML program for compliance with the Prepaid Access Rule.

c. Know Your Customer's Customer Issues

Over the past several years, various federal agencies have been using their review and examination authority to recommend that FIs take a very close look at categories of customers or lines of business/industry that are deemed risky or undesirable from a safety and soundness perspective. This type of regulatory risk is similar to the regulatory risk faced by processors under the BSA/AML laws where regulators require FIs to evaluate a processor's merchant customer on-boarding and monitoring programs to detect money laundering and terrorist financing, and is referred to as "Know Your Customer's Customer" (KYCC) risk. For a processor or a mobile wallet/mobile payments provider that is processing payments for other third parties, such "nested third-party processing" arrangements may be examined by regulators in evaluating the processor or mobile wallet/mobile payments provider as a third-party service provider to an FI, or merely as an FI customer. The areas of focus by the regulators regarding risk is constantly evolving but monitoring news

---

57. *Id.*
58. *Id.*

developments and interactions with the entity's FI may help the processor or mobile wallet/mobile payments provider stay on top of emerging "risky processing" areas.

5. FinCEN MSB Registration

Chapter 3 reviews the definition of "money transmission" for purposes of regulating businesses (MSB) under federal law and FinCEN regulations. Depending upon the services provided and the "flow of funds" in a mobile wallet/mobile payments transaction, a mobile wallet/mobile payments provider's activities may fall within the definition of "money transmission" at the federal level. While a "payment processor" may be eligible for an exclusion from the requirements to register with FinCEN as an MSB, the parameters of this exclusion require careful evaluation in each case.

In addition, the definition of money transmission and exclusions from MSB registration at the federal level is completely separate and apart from state money transmission licensing regimes. Mobile wallet/mobile payments providers sometimes will mistakenly look only to the federal MSB regulations and not understand that there are still state money transmission laws that apply (as discussed below).

In some instances, a mobile wallet/mobile payments provider may mistakenly believe that registering as a federal MSB takes care of registration as a licensed money transmitter with individual states—this is absolutely not the case, and an entity must comply with both the federal MSB registration and reporting regime as well as the state-level money transmission licensing requirements. Finally, just because an entity determines that it falls within the "processor exemption" of the federal MSB registration requirements, mobile wallet/mobile payments providers should be aware that the presence of a state money transmission law equivalent of a processor exemption must be analyzed on a state-by-state basis, and not every state provides such an exemption from licensing.

6. Unlawful Internet Gambling Enforcement Act

The Unlawful Internet Gambling Enforcement Act (UIGEA) prohibits gambling businesses from knowingly accepting payment (whether by credit card, debit card, electronic funds transfer, check or draft, or proceeds from any form of a financial transaction) in connection with the participation of another person in a bet or wager that involves the use of the Internet and that is unlawful under any federal or state law.[59] The "Internet" under this regulation is not limited to desktop computer access, but also includes transactions conducted online via mobile devices and mobile phones. Regulations promulgated pursuant to UIGEA further require that certain "participants" in payment systems that could be used for unlawful internet gambling must have policies and procedures in place reasonably designed to identify and block or otherwise prevent or prohibit the processing of restricted transactions.[60]

---

59. 31 U.S.C. § 5163.
60. *Id.*

A "participant" is defined as "an operator of a designated payment system, a financial transaction provider that is a member of, or has contracted for financial transaction services with, or is otherwise participating in, a designated payment system, or a third-party processor."[61] "Participants" can include processors or mobile wallet/mobile payments providers. Unless their systems fall within certain narrow exceptions, participants must "establish and implement written policies and procedures reasonably designed to identify and block or otherwise prevent or prohibit restricted transactions."[62] Complying with UIGEA may be problematic for some types of mobile wallet/mobile payments services, and P2P payments may present particular compliance challenges. Nonetheless, given the broad definition of a "participant" under UIGEA, mobile wallet/mobile payments providers should review applicability of this law to their activities and establish a compliance program if needed.

7. State Money Transmitter Laws

Chapter 3 reviews the details regarding the definition of "money transmission" and corresponding state licensure requirements under various state money transmitter laws. Echoing what is discussed in that chapter, state regulators are currently taking a variety of positions with regard to whether their particular state money transmission law applies to payment processors or mobile wallet/mobile payments providers.

As mentioned in Section 5 of this part, the definition of money transmission and exclusions from MSB registration at the federal level are completely separate and apart from state money transmission licensing regimes. Mobile wallet/mobile payments providers should understand that compliance with state money transmission laws may also be required.

As with other areas where state laws are not uniform, or where state laws are layered on top of federal laws, it is a challenge for mobile wallet/mobile payments providers' compliance personnel to comply with often inconsistent, and sometimes conflicting, requirements. Companies such as mobile wallet/mobile payments providers can run into challenges with regard to state money transmission licensing depending on the "flow of funds" in the payment transaction and whether the mobile wallet/mobile payments provider takes legal possession and control of the funds (even for an instant).

Mobile wallet/mobile payments providers that choose to launch their products and services to the U.S. public writ large via the Internet or mobile devices are essentially offering services to consumers in all 50 states (plus the District of Columbia and U.S. territories). Therefore, launching nationwide requires review of the potential application of money transmission laws in all 50 states (plus the District of Columbia and U.S. territories). Because transmitting money without a license

---

61. 12 C.F.R. § 233.2(w) (Regulation GG).
62. 31 C.F.R. § 132.5(a).

carries potential criminal penalties, this is a very important area for mobile wallet/ mobile payments providers to review and ensure compliance.

8. State Unclaimed Property Laws and Escheatment Requirements

Another area of legal compliance that mobile wallet/mobile payments providers can sometimes overlook involves state unclaimed property laws and escheatment requirements. Unclaimed property laws vary state-by-state, but generally require the holder of any tangible or intangible property that is legally owned by another individual to "escheat" or "turn over" that property to the state comptroller, treasurer, or other designated agency in the event that the owner of the property cannot be contacted or located after the statutory abandonment period has expired.

Mobile wallet/mobile payments providers that may also be issuers of closed-loop prepaid access accounts are required under the CARD Act[63] to provide certain gift certificate, store gift cards, and general-use prepaid card account holders with the right to access funds for a period of five years from the date the gift certificate, store gift card, or general-use prepaid card account was loaded with funds.

The CARD Act generally applies to gift certificates, store gift cards, and general-use prepaid cards include cards, codes, or other devices issued in a specified amount, regardless of whether they are issued in card form. Regulations issued under the CARD Act apply to an account number or bar code that can access underlying funds, a device with a chip or other embedded mechanism that links the device to stored funds (such as a mobile phone or sticker containing a contactless chip), and even to an "electronic promise."[64] An "electronic promise" means a person's commitment or obligation communicated or stored in electronic form made to a consumer to provide payment for goods or services; for example, a code given as a gift that can be redeemed in an online transaction would be an electronic promise.[65]

At the state law level, escheatment is the process of identifying a person's funds that are considered abandoned and remitting those funds to the proper state. State unclaimed property laws vary widely in terms of the time period before funds are considered abandoned, what process must be undertaken to contact an account holder or successor-in-interest, and under what circumstances an account is considered abandoned.

An additional challenge with regard to escheatment requirements is that even though funds underlying a prepaid card must remain accessible for a period of five years after the funds were loaded under the federal CARD Act, state laws can still impose a shorter "abandonment" period. Therefore, for states with an unclaimed property abandonment period of less than five years, the holder of the funds on the prepaid account must remit the property to the state according to the shorter

---

63. The CARD Act amended the EFTA, and the rules promulgated by the CFPB with regard to the CARD Act were included within Regulation E at 12 C.F.R. § 1005.20.

64. *See* 12 C.F.R. § 1005.20, officially agency commentary at cmt. 20(a)-1.

65. *Id.*, officially agency commentary at cmt. 20(a)-2.

abandonment period. The holder of the funds must then either (1) make the prepaid account holder whole on transactions that occur before the five-year federal "good funds" expiration period and apply for a refund from the particular state for those amounts, or (2) tell the prepaid account holder that the entity has already remitted funds to a particular state under the state's unclaimed property law, and, therefore, the prepaid account holder will need to obtain the unclaimed property from the state agency to which the company remitted the unclaimed property.

9. Card Association and Network Rules

The credit card networks (Visa, MasterCard, American Express, and Discover), as well as debit card/ATM networks (e.g., New York Currency Exchange (NYCE), STAR) and NACHA, which operates the ACH network, all operate via a nexus of contract relationships that include lengthy operating rules and requirements for network participants. These contracts require compliance with the network operating rules by payment processors, and to the extent that a mobile wallet/mobile payments provider is acting as a processor, they have such "processing" compliance obligations as well. These networks also enforce certain security standards and requirements, such as the Payment Card Industry Data Security Standards (PCI DSS) discussed below.

Over recent years, these various networks have started defining the different roles that third parties play with regard to origination and settlement of transactions into three categories—payment service provider, payment facilitator, and payment aggregator. A "payment service provider" (PSP) is generally a company that supplies merchants with individual merchant accounts and performs functions such as merchant underwriting and payment processing. PSPs help merchants get their merchant accounts and facilitate merchant underwriting and transaction processing. Examples of PSPs include independent sales organizations.[66] But a PSP does not participate in merchant funding and merchants are funded directly by the acquiring FI in credit/debit card transactions.

There are differences between a PSP and a "payment facilitator" and a "payment aggregator." A "payment facilitator" funds merchants directly. Medium and large-size businesses typically obtain their own merchant identification (MID) and they are treated as sub-merchants of the "payment facilitator." If the intermediary entity, which funds the sub-merchants, uses a different MID for each merchant, then it is a "payment facilitator."[67]

Small business and individuals, on the other hand, typically do not obtain their own MIDs and most often work with a "payment aggregator" who uses a single MID to process payments for all sub-merchants in its portfolio. PayPal merchant services

---

66. *See Differences between PSPs, Payment Facilitators, and Aggregators*, UNIPAY GATEWAY, Sept. 4, 2015, https://medium.com/@UniPayGateway/differences-between-psps-payment-facilitators-and-aggregators-c183065e312d#.z93rxjq9w.

67. *Id.*

is a prime example of a "payment aggregator" model. Merchant funding will be performed by the "payment aggregator" that has a lot of small sub-merchants in its portfolio and uses a single merchant ID for all of them. One of the key differences between payment aggregators and payment facilitators is the size of sub-merchants they are servicing. As a merchant's processing amounts grow, it might face the legally imposed need to have its own MID, or even become an independent merchant.[68]

With regard to ACH transactions, NACHA makes a distinction between "third-party senders" (TPS) and "third-party service providers" (TPSPs) and has different rules and requirements for each type of entity. When a third party moves funds on behalf of another through the ACH network, that entity, at a minimum, acts as a TPSP under NACHA rules. To determine whether or not that entity *also* acts as a TPS (a particular type of TPSP), it must be determined whether or not the "originator" (a consumer or business initiating the ACH transaction) or the intermediary entity has an "ACH Origination Agreement" directly with the "originating depository financial institution" (ODFI) for the origination of ACH transactions.[69] If the originator has the ACH Origination Agreement with the ODFI, there is no TPS involved in the transaction, and the intermediary entity is only a TPSP. However, if the intermediary entity has the ACH Origination Agreement with the ODFI, and has a separate agreement with the end-user of the services, the intermediary entity acts as a TPS.[70] This distinction is important because of different NACHA rules applying to each type of entity, and also because the intermediary's FI will need to know they are a TPS as many FIs deem that ACH activity as riskier than merely being a TPSP.

Mobile wallet/mobile payments providers need to understand what role their products and services will fall into within the network rules and the ACH rules. For example, the distinctions between a "payment service provider," "payment facilitator," and "payment aggregator" are important under the network rules because each category of entity may have varying requirements, and pricing for processing services may also vary. In addition, the networks will want some type of representation that a "payment aggregator" has appropriate licensing, such as federal MSB and state money transmission licensing. Because in a payment aggregator model the service provider uses a single MID, takes legal possession and control of the transaction funds, and takes responsibility for getting the transaction funds to the merchants, "payment aggregators" often trigger federal MSB registration requirements and state money transmission licensing requirements. For ACH transactions, NACHA rules impose different requirements on TPS as opposed to TPSP.[71] In addition, the specific role under the ACH rules that the mobile wallet/mobile payments provider is playing will need to be disclosed to that entity's own FI.

---

68. *Id.*
69. NACHA, ACH Operations Bulletin #2-2014: ACH Transactions Involving Third-Party Senders and Other Payment Intermediaries (Dec. 30, 2014), *available at* https://www.nacha.org/news/ach-operations-bulletin-2-2014-ach-transactions-involving-third-party-senders-and-other-payment.
70. *Id.*
71. *See id.*

B. Regulatory Framework Governing Privacy/Data Security

1. Gramm-Leach-Bliley Act

a. In General

The federal Gramm-Leach-Bliley Act (GLBA)[72] requires FIs to provide data security, breach notification, and privacy and data sharing protections to consumers. The Federal Trade Commission (FTC), the CFPB, and each federal functional FI regulatory agency (e.g., Federal Reserve Board, Federal Deposit Insurance Corporation (FDIC), the National Credit Union Administration, and the Office of the Comptroller of the Currency (OCC)) have all issued slightly different regulations promulgated pursuant to GLBA governing the treatment of "nonpublic personal information" (NPI) about consumers by FIs (collectively, the Privacy Rules).[73]

The Privacy Rules generally require FIs to provide notice to customers (and to other consumers in some circumstances) about the FI's privacy policies and practices. The Privacy Rules also require FIs to describe the conditions under which FIs may disclose NPI to nonaffiliated third parties, and to provide a method for consumers to prevent FIs from disclosing NPI to most nonaffiliated third parties through notice that the consumer is "opting out" of that disclosure, subject to certain exceptions.[74]

Under the Privacy Rules, payment processors are considered FIs and, to the extent that a mobile wallet/mobile payments provider is carrying out payment processing functions, the provider is also subject to the Privacy Rules. However, payment processors and mobile wallet/mobile payments providers may not be subject to all of the Privacy Rules. For example, payment processors are not required to comply with the customer notice disclosure requirements promulgated by the FTC and CFPB Privacy Rules because consumers whose ATMs, point-of-service, Internet, or telephone transactions are processed by processors do not become customers simply by carrying out such transactions. A customer relationship is established when the consumer enters into a continuing relationship with the FI.[75]

Processors and mobile wallet/mobile payments providers are also exempt from the customer notice disclosure requirements because any NPI transmitted in connection with a payment transaction is "necessary to effect, administer or enforce a transaction" requested by a consumer, or in connection with servicing or processing of a financial product or service requested or authorized by a consumer.[76]

---

72. 15 U.S.C. § 6804.

73. *See* 16 C.F.R. pt. 313 (FTC Privacy Rule); 12 C.F.R. pt. 1016; *id.* pt. 332 (FDIC Privacy Rule); *id.* pt. 216 (Federal Reserve Board Privacy Rule); *id.* pt. 40 (OCC Privacy Rule); *id.* pt. 573 (National Credit Union Administration Privacy Rule).

74. 16 C.F.R. § 313.1(a); 12 C.F.R. § 1016.1(a); *id.* §§ 332.7 and 332.10; *id.* §§ 216.7 and 216.10; *id.* §§ 40.7 and 40.10; *id.* §§ 573.7 and 573.10.

75. 16 C.F.R. § 313.4(c); 12 C.F.R. § 1016.4(c).

76. 13 C.F.R. § 313.14(a)(1). See also *id.* § 313.14(b)(2)(iv)(A), which states, "In connection with the authorization, settlement, billing, processing, clearing, transferring, reconciling or collection of amounts charged, debited, or otherwise paid using a debit, credit or other payment card, check, or account number, or by other payment means."

Although processing above does not create a customer relationship under the Privacy Rules and does not give rise to customer notice requirements, companies should be aware that *if* a processor or mobile wallet/mobile payments provider also undertakes other activities such as extending credit, deposit of funds, or other services to the consumer, the company must determine whether those additional services give rise to requirements to comply with the Privacy Rules. In addition, a processor or mobile wallet/mobile payments provider that is partnering with an FI to, for example, place credit or debit card accounts into a particular mobile wallet, may find that it must comply as a matter of contract or agreement with "flow through" privacy requirements from the issuing FI's Privacy Rules obligations, which affect its third-party vendors or subcontractors (a category into which a mobile wallet/mobile payments partner will most likely fall).

b. GLBA Customer Information Security Guidelines

Payment processors and mobile wallet/mobile payments providers may be defined as "financial institutions" or "service providers" (or both) depending on the specific services they provide. If the entity falls into either category, the entity is subject to guidelines for safeguarding NPI about customers that the FTC and the federal functional banking regulators have adopted to implement sections 501 and 505(b)(2) of GLBA (the Customer Information Security Guidelines, also known as the Security Rules).[77]

If subject to the Security Rules, then the processor or mobile wallet/mobile payments provider must develop, implement, and maintain a comprehensive written information security program designed to ensure the security and confidentiality of NPI; protect against any anticipated threats or hazards to the security or integrity of such information; and protect against the unauthorized access to or use of NPI that could result in substantial harm or inconvenience to any consumer whose NPI was obtained by an unauthorized individual.[78]

The Security Rules also generally require appropriate due diligence in selecting service providers and contractual obligations to implement appropriate measures designed to meet security objectives. Financial institutions are required to monitor the service provider's compliance with these obligations, such as by conducting or reviewing security audits and requiring summaries of test results and other evaluations of the service provider.[79]

Finally, as part of the written information security program, an entity that is an FI or a service provider must establish a data breach response protocol that includes an incident response team to notify affected customers and to involve law

---

77. 15 U.S.C. §§ 6801(b) and 6805(b)(2).
78. 12 U.S.C. § 3404(1); 16 C.F.R. § 314.3; 12 C.F.R. pt. 364, app. B, § II; *id.* pt. 208, app. D-2, § II; *id.* pt. 30, app. B, § II; *id.* pt. 570, app. B, § II.
79. *See*, *e.g.*, 12 C.F.R. pts. 364 (app. B), 208 (app. D-2), 30 (app. B, § III.D), and 570 (app. B).

enforcement in a timely manner. An FI must also ensure that its TPSPs providers are taking appropriate measures to secure data and respond to a data security incident.[80]

A processor or mobile wallet/mobile payments provider that is partnering with an FI to, for example, place the credit or debit card accounts that the FI issues into a particular mobile wallet will often find that even though it may not be deemed a "financial institution" itself, it will be deemed to be a "service provider" to its partnering FI. As a result, it must comply as a matter of contract or agreement with the service provider data security program summarized above. In addition, FIs will often require what is colloquially referred to as "fourth-party due diligence" whereby service providers subject to GLBA information security requirements must, in turn, make sure all of the service provider's vendors and subcontractors are also following all the requirements that the service provider itself must meet.

c. FTC Safeguards Rule under GLBA

Payment processors and mobile wallet/mobile payments providers fall within the broad definition of an entity that is "significantly engaged" in providing financial products or services and are, therefore, also FIs subject to the FTC's Standards for Safeguarding Customer Information (the Safeguards Rule).[81] The Safeguards Rule requires all FIs over which the FTC has jurisdiction to develop and maintain a comprehensive information security program to safeguard "customer information" which is defined as any record containing NPI. Subject to the Safeguards Rule, entities are required to designate an employee to coordinate the information security program, identify foreseeable security risks, design and implement safeguards to control for such risk, and test and evaluate the program.

Entities subject to the Safeguards Rule are also required to ensure that service providers with access to customer information implement and maintain sufficient security measures. A processor or mobile wallet/mobile payments provider partnering with an FI to place the credit or debit card accounts that the FI issues into a particular mobile wallet will often find that even though it may not be deemed a "financial institution" itself, it will be deemed to be a "service provider" to its partnering FI that must comply as a matter of contract or agreement with the Safeguards Rule. In addition, FIs will often require what is colloquially referred to as "fourth-party due diligence" whereby service providers subject to the Safeguards Rule, in turn, ensure compliance by their vendors and subcontractors.

2. PCI DSS

The PCI DSS are card transaction security requirements published by the Payment Card Industry Security Standards Council (PCI SSC).[82] These security requirements

---

80. *Id.*
81. 16 C.F.R. pt. 314.
82. *See* PCI SSC website, https://www.pcisecuritystandards.org/.

are designed to ensure that all merchants and processors that process, store, or transmit card information maintain such information in a secure environment. The PCI SSC is comprised of the five major global credit card brands and other "strategic members" from the payments industry. The PCI DSS standards are recognized internationally as the governing standards for the payments industry. They are very detailed and are frequently updated by the PCI SSC to address new developments and threats within the card industry.[83] PCI DSS requirements apply to any organization or merchant (regardless of size or transaction volume) that accepts, transmits, or stores any cardholder or card data. All payment processors must comply with these standards, and both merchants and payment processors alike must complete either self-assessments (if small) or be audited by a "qualified security assessor" (QSA) if they have larger transaction volumes.

PCI DSS requires the installation and maintenance of firewalls, system passwords, encryption of cardholder data across open or public networks, use of anti-virus software, employee access restrictions, physical access restrictions, and development of a card information-specific security policy. They also restrict retention of cardholder data. Failure to comply with PCI DSS can result in significant network penalties in the event of a data security breach that compromises cardholder data.[84]

A mobile wallet/mobile payments provider that "accepts, transmits, or stores" cardholder or card data must abide by PCI DSS. In addition, many merchants as well as FI partners with mobile wallet/mobile payments providers that "accept, transmit, or store" cardholder or card data must contractually represent and warrant that they are PCI DSS compliant, which is often confirmed by attestation from a QSA. In addition, FIs will often require what is "fourth-party due diligence" concerning PCI DSS compliance, by vendors and subcontractors.

3. State Data Privacy and Data Security Laws

Almost every state, and even most U.S. territories, has enacted some form of data breach notification law. All of those laws classify financial account or card account information as "personal information." A data security breach incident will thus trigger compliance obligations with both federal law and also state data breach notification laws, which may apply based upon the state of residence of the individual whose personal information (including card or financial account data) was compromised.

In addition, in 2007, Minnesota became the first (and so far only) state to specifically require compliance with PCI DSS for card transactions. The Minnesota Plastic Card Security Act[85] prohibits anyone conducting business in Minnesota from storing sensitive information from credit, debit, or stored-value cards after the transaction has been authorized. The act also makes noncompliant entities responsible for FIs'

---

83. *See, e.g.*, PCI SSC, PCI Mobile Payment Acceptance Security Guidelines (July 2014), *available at* https://www.pcisecuritystandards.org/documents/Mobile_Payment_Acceptance_Security_Guidelines _for_Merchants_v1-1.pdf .

84. *Id.*

85. Minn. Stat. Ann. § 325E.64 *et seq.*

costs related to cancelling and replacing cards compromised in a security breach. As a result, a data security breach of an entity storing "prohibited" cardholder data (e.g., magnetic stripe, card verification value (CVV) codes, etc.) may be required to reimburse banks and other entities for costs associated with blocking and reissuing cards, with enforcement by private lawsuits. Even though the act is entitled the Plastic Card Security Act, the provisions of the act apply to virtually stored payment card data as well.

Mobile wallet/mobile payments providers should understand their obligations under applicable data breach and data security notification laws and develop a data incident response plan. Such a plan should include not only what the entity must do when it suffers a data security breach resulting in the unauthorized access or acquisition of end-user "personal information" (including card or financial account information), but also should cover how the entity must cooperate with business partners, including the merchants it processes for and the FIs issuing the credit, debit, or stored-value cards that are compromised in any data breach incident.

C. Regulatory Framework Governing General Consumer Protection

I. Unfair, Deceptive, or Abusive Acts and Practices and Unfair or Deceptive Acts and Practices

a. Unfair, Deceptive, or Abusive Acts and Practices (Dodd Frank Act)

Title X of the Dodd-Frank Act, like the FTC Act, prohibits covered persons and service providers from engaging in unfair, deceptive, or abusive acts or practices (UDAAP).[86] It further prohibits any person from knowingly or recklessly providing substantial assistance to covered persons and service providers that engage in such practices.[87] The CFPB has not clearly established rules and standards as to what constitutes a UDAAP violation, but has instead chosen to define the parameters of this law by publicizing its enforcement actions.[88] UDAAP actions may be brought for a variety of deceptive, abusive, or unfair violations of the law. Recently, the CFPB brought its first UDAAP action against a mobile wallet/mobile payments provider for failing to provide adequate data security practices.[89] Under the Dodd Frank Act, payment processors, like FIs, are subject to enforcement for alleged UDAAP violations. The CFPB has not yet issued regulations defining UDAAP for payment processors, although it

---

86. 12 U.S.C. § 5531.
87. *Id.* § 5536(a)(3).
88. CFPB Director Richard Cordray announced the precedential value of seeking to glean guidance from previous consent orders, saying that "it would be 'compliance malpractice' for executives not to take careful bearings from the contents of these orders about how to comply with the law and treat consumers fairly." CFPB Director Richard Cordray, Remarks at the Consumer Bankers Association (Mar. 9, 2016), http://www.consumerfinance.gov/newsroom/prepared-remarks-of-cfpb-director-richardcordray-at-the-consumer-bankers-association/.
89. *In the Matter of* Dwolla, Inc., Administrative Proceeding File No. 2016-CFPB-0007, Consent Order (Feb. 27, 2016), http://files.consumerfinance.gov/f/201603_cfpb_consent-order-dwolla-inc.pdf.

has published consumer protection principles for the industry, discussed below. A recent decision from the Northern District of Georgia has held that payment processors are "service providers" within the meaning of the act.[90]

b. Unfair or Deceptive Acts and Practices (FTC Act)

The FTC Act grants the FTC significant investigative and enforcement powers. Relevant for mobile wallet/mobile payments providers and payment processors, section 5 of the FTC Act (15 U.S.C. § 45) empowers the FTC to prohibit unfair or deceptive trade practices. As discussed in the Safeguards Rule section above, mobile wallet/mobile payments providers and payment processors are FIs subject to the FTC's jurisdiction and may be subject to enforcement actions by the FTC. The FTC does not have authority to issue regulations defining unfair or deceptive acts and practices (UDAP), but guidance may be derived from public enforcement actions. Mobile wallet/mobile payments providers' compliance programs must monitor their business practices and all the FTC's enforcement actions to help ensure that the entities do not engage in activities or programs that could be considered UDAP.

2. Telephone Consumer Protection Act

The Telephone Consumer Protection Act (TCPA) restricts telephone solicitations and limits the use of robocalls (made by way of an automatic dialing system), artificial or prerecorded voice messages, SMS text messages, and junk faxes.[91] It also specifies several technical requirements for fax machines, auto dialers, and voice messaging systems, including identifying the entity using the device. The TCPA applies to all entities that engage in telemarketing or the use of auto dialers or prerecorded or artificial voice messages to reach consumers. The law is implemented and generally enforced by the FCC, although a subdivision of the law, the Do Not Call Rule (see below), is enforced by the FTC.[92] The law also imposes time-of-day restrictions for placing telemarketing calls (between 8:00 a.m. and 9:00 p.m. local time), outlines procedures for the FTC's Do Not Call Registry, and grants consumers a private right of action.[93]

With respect to voice calls, the TCPA prohibits a caller from initiating any call to a cell phone or wireless number that was autodialed, or initiating a call that includes a prerecorded or artificial voice without an emergency, or the prior express consent of the recipient (current subscriber or customary user). Any such calls placed to a cell phone that constitutes telemarketing, including telemarketing under an existing business relationship, requires "prior express written consent" from the recipient.[94] Calls made to residential lines that include a prerecorded or artificial voice

---

90. Consumer Fin. Prot. Bureau v. Universal Debt & Payment Solutions, LLC, No. 1:15-CV-00859-RWS (N.D. Ga. Sept. 1, 2015).
91. 47 U.S.C. § 227.
92. 16 C.F.R. pt. 310; 47 C.F.R. § 64.1200.
93. 47 C.F.R. § 64.1200(a)(1)–(4); *id.* § 64.1200(c); *id.* § 64.1200(d).
94. *Id.* § 64.1200(a)(1)(a)(2)(iii)–(iv); *id.* § 64.1200(a)(2).

are prohibited without the "prior express written consent" of the recipient unless the call is made for emergency purposes or not made for commercial purposes; calls made for commercial purposes but that do not include an advertisement or telemarketing are also exempted from the prior consent requirement.[95] Businesses that outsource their telemarketing or informational calls to TPSPs providers can still be held vicariously liable for TCPA violations on the basis of federal common law agency principles.[96]

With regard to mobile wallet/mobile payments providers, the most relevant aspect of TCPA compliance involves SMS text messaging that the provider may use as part of their service. In general, if the SMS text message is used in conjunction with providing the mobile wallet/mobile payments good or service, such as payment transaction confirmation or alerts, then prior express written consent is not required. However, it the SMS text message includes marketing messages, including marketing for the company's own products and services, then prior written express consent is needed. Prior FTC enforcement actions[97] have also clarified that "prior express written consent" does not occur when such consent is buried in the general terms of use, and that such consent must be obtained in a separate clear and conspicuous manner (such as a separate pop-up box in a mobile app) and cannot be structured as an "opt-out" consent.

3. Telemarketer Sales (Do Not Call) Rule

The FTC's Telemarketer Sales Rule (TSR) established the National Do Not Call Registry, where consumers can enter their numbers to reduce the telephone solicitations they receive. The law requires telemarketers to search the registry every 31 days and avoid calling any phone numbers that are on the registry.[98] A telemarketer who disregards the National Do Not Call Registry could be fined up to $16,000 for each call.[99] Further, the TSR prohibits "credit card laundering," which it defines as presenting or depositing into the credit card system for payment a credit card sales draft generated by a telemarketing transaction that is not the result of a telemarketing credit card transaction between the cardholder and the merchant.[100]

The TSR has direct application to consumer-facing businesses. Recently, the FTC has used the TSR as a means of imposing liability on payment processors who provided processing services to telemarketers that violated the TSR, alleging they

---

95. *Id.* § 64.1200(a)(3).

96. *In re* Joint Petition Filed by DISH Network, 28 F.C.C.R. 6574 (2013).

97. *See* Press Release, FCC, FCC Cites First National Bank and Lyft for Telemarketing Violations (Sept. 11, 2015), *available at* https://apps.fcc.gov/edocs_public/attachmatch/DOC-335223A1.pdf.

98. 16 C.F.R. § 310.4(b)(iii)(B).

99. Federal Civil Penalties Inflation Adjustment Act, 74 Fed. Reg. 857 (Jan. 9, 2009) (to be codified at 16 C.F.R. § 1.98(d)) (increasing the maximum civil penalty from $11,000 to $16,000 per violation, effective Feb. 9, 2009).

100. 16 C.F.R. § 310.3(c).

provided "substantial assistance" to the telemarketers.[101] For this reason, mobile wallet/mobile payments providers who are processing transactions for third parties must establish and maintain payment customer "due diligence" programs to help them avoid processing payments for any party that might be accused of violating this TSR.

4. Fair Credit Reporting Act

The Fair Credit Reporting Act (FCRA),[102] as amended by the Fair and Accurate Credit Transactions Act (FACTA),[103] regulates consumer reporting agencies, users of consumer reports, and furnishers of consumer information to consumer reporting agencies.

Of particular note to mobile payments providers, the FCRA also contains a receipt "truncation" requirement that requires that a person who accepts credit or debit cards may not print more than the last five digits of the card number, or print the expiration date, on any electronically printed receipt given to a cardholder at the point of the sale or transaction.[104] Mobile wallet/mobile payments providers must ensure that the receipt truncation requirements are built into their payment transaction functionality whether there will be printed receipts at the point of sale, e-mail receipts, or "in-app" receipts stored within the mobile wallet/mobile payments app.

5. CFPB's "Nine Consumer Protection Requirements for Payment Processors"

On July 9, 2015, CFPB published a list of nine principles that describe the agency's vision for protecting consumers with regard to the Federal Reserve Board's Faster Payments Task Force initiative.[105] While focused on faster payments, this list also provides insight into agency beliefs about consumer protection principles in other payments systems or products. These principles may also provide guidance for likely approaches to UDAAP enforcement actions by the CFPB involving a mobile wallet/mobile payments provider. However, the CFPB has not yet provided any further guidance on how, specifically, these principles are to be implemented.

The nine principles (paraphrased) are:

1. **Consumer control over payments**. A payment system or service should be clear regarding when, how, and under what terms consumers have authorized payments; the authorization should be limited in time and

---

101. *See, e.g.*, Stipulated Order for Permanent Injunction and Monetary Judgment at 2, Fed. Trade Comm'n v. Capital Payments, LLC, No. 16-CV-00526-ADS-AYS (E.D.N.Y. Feb. 3, 2016), https://www.ftc.gov /system/files/documents/cases/160211bluefinorder.pdf.

102. 15 U.S.C. § 1681 *et seq.*

103. Pub. L. No. 108-159, 111 Stat. 1952.

104. 15 U.S.C. § 1681c(g).

105. CFPB, Consumer Protection Principles: CFPB's Vision of Consumer Protection in New Faster Payments Systems (July 9, 2015), *available at* http://files.consumerfinance.gov/f/201507_cfpb_consumer -protection-principles.pdf.

should be clear as to the amount and the payee. There should also be provisions regarding consumer revocation of authorization.

2. **Data and privacy**. Consumers should be informed of how their data is being transferred through a payment system, including what data is being transferred, who has access to it, how that data can be used, and potential risks. As appropriate, the payment system should allow consumers to specify what data can be transferred and whether third parties can access that data. The payment system should also protect against the misuse of the data associated with payment transactions.

3. **Fraud error and resolution protections**. The payment system must include robust protections with respect to mistaken, fraudulent, unauthorized, or otherwise erroneous transactions. Payment system architecture should ensure that information is created and recorded to facilitate post-transaction evaluation. The payment system should provide mechanisms for reversing erroneous and unauthorized transactions quickly once identified. The payment system must also provide consumers with regulatory protections, such as Regulation E and Regulation Z, along with other appropriate safeguards.

4. **Transparency**. A payments system should include real-time or close to real-time information about the status of transactions, including confirmations or payment and receipt of funds. Consumers should receive timely disclosures of the costs, risks, funds availability, and security of payments.

5. **Cost**. Payment systems should be affordable to consumers. Fees charged to consumers should be disclosed in a manner that allows consumers to compare the costs of using different available payment options, and fee structures should not obscure the full cost of making or receiving a payment.

6. **Access**. A payment system should be broadly accessible to consumers. A payment system should permit consumer access through qualified intermediaries and other non-depositories, such as mobile wallet providers and payment processors, except to the extent necessary to protect functionality, security, or other key user values.

7. **Funds availability**. A payment system should make funds availability timelines clear to the consumers using them.

8. **Security and payment credential value**. A payment systems should have strong built-in protections to detect and limit errors, unauthorized transactions, and fraud, as well as detecting and responding to data breaches. Payment systems should also strongly consider limiting the value of consumer payment credentials so that security breaches are of limited worth to fraudsters. Payment systems should also have automated monitoring capabilities, incentives for participants to report misuse, and transparent enforcement procedures.

9. **Strong accountability mechanisms that effectively curtail system misuse**. Payment systems should be organized with goals and incentives that ensure the payment system operators, participants, and end users are aligned against misuse. Participants should be accountable for the risks, harm, and costs they introduce into payment systems and should be incentivized to prevent and correct fraudulent, unauthorized, or otherwise erroneous transactions for consumers.[106]

Compliance departments of mobile wallet/mobile payments providers must analyze this CFPB guidance and monitor litigation and enforcement actions constantly to mitigate risks that they will be accused of UDAAP or other violations that have not been fully articulated by the agencies or the courts.

6. Electronic Signatures in Global and National Commerce Act/State Uniform Electronic Transactions Act

The Electronic Signatures in Global and National Commerce (E-SIGN) Act[107] allows electronic documents and signatures to have the same legal effect as paper documents and "wet" signatures, and was designed to facilitate electronic agreements and disclosures.[108] After obtaining proper agreement and consent under the E-SIGN Act, FIs and financial services providers can provide most written disclosures in electronic form and customers can execute agreements electronically as well. E-SIGN requires a clear and conspicuous statement informing the consumer of his or her rights to a paper copy of records, the right to withdraw E-SIGN consent, and any conditions or limitations to the consumer's consent, such as fees for paper copies the consumer requests. E-SIGN also mandates that companies comply with the law's record retention requirements. In addition to the federal E-SIGN Act, many states have also adopted the model Uniform Electronic Transactions Act (UETA), which in many cases only varies slightly from the federal E-SIGN Act.

For mobile wallet/mobile payments providers, failure to comply with E-SIGN may affect issues such as enforceability of terms of use for the mobile wallet/mobile payments service and the effectiveness of certain required legal disclosures. An agreement such as an "E-SIGN Disclosure and Agreement" should come first in the new customer on-boarding process, before the new customer is presented with any terms of use or disclosures that the entity seeks to conduct electronically. For example, the Square E-SIGN consent that was implemented within the past two years states in part:

> Square, Inc. and its affiliates and third party service providers ("Square") may need to provide you with certain communications, notices, agreements, billing statements, or disclosures in writing ("Communications") regarding our products or

---

106. *Id.*
107. 15 U.S.C. § 7011 *et seq.*
108. E-SIGN does contain exceptions for documents that cannot be executed electronically, and those exceptions are listed at 15 U.S.C. § 7003.

services ("Services"). Your agreement to this E-sign Consent confirms your ability and consent to receive Communications electronically from Square, its affiliates, and its third party service providers, rather than in paper form, and to the use of electronic signatures in our relationship with you ("Consent"). If you choose not to agree to this Consent or you withdraw your consent, you may be restricted from using the Services. [109]

D. Miscellaneous Regulatory Requirements

1. FDIC Supervisory Guidance

A non-FI mobile wallet/mobile payments provider is not directly subject to guidance documents from the FDIC or any federal functional regulator. However, the mobile wallet/mobile payments provider is at the very least subject to certain "pass-through" regulatory requirements by virtue of being the customer of an FI. In addition, if a mobile wallet/mobile payments provider is officially partnered with an FI, then the provider may be subject to additional "pass-through" regulatory requirements due to the provider's status as a "third-party service provider" to an FI. Specifically, mobile wallet/mobile payments providers should be aware of the FDIC's *Financial Institution Letters* (FILs) and *Supervisory Insights* publications regarding payment processor relationships with FIs.[110] These publications provide an overview of the primary risk areas with regard to third-party relationships that FI regulatory examiners and internal audit teams focus on when reviewing any new mobile wallet/mobile payments customer for banking services, or for partnering as a TPSP. A mobile wallet/mobile payments service provider's compliance team should remain up-to-date on the FDIC and other federal functional regulatory guidance (such as the Federal Reserve System, OCC, National Credit Union Administration, and CFPB) and make sure that the provider's internal policies and procedures are in place to provide satisfactory assurance to the provider's FIs that regulatory guidance is followed by the provider.

2. FFIEC Guidance and Examination

The examination authorities of federal banking regulatory agencies,[111] which comprise the FFIEC,[112] include regulating and examination services provided to insured

---

109. Square, *Square E-Sign Consent*, https://squareup.com/legal/sign (last updated Feb. 6, 2017).

110. *See* FDIC, FDIC CLARIFYING SUPERVISORY APPROACH TO INSTITUTIONS ESTABLISHING ACCOUNT RELATIONSHIPS WITH THIRD-PARTY PAYMENT PROCESSORS (July 28, 2014) (Financial Institution Letter FIL-41-2014), *available at* https://www.fdic.gov/news/news/financial/2014/fil14041.pdf; FDIC, FDIC SUPERVISORY APPROACH TO PAYMENT PROCESSING RELATIONSHIPS WITH MERCHANT CUSTOMERS THAT ENGAGE IN HIGHER-RISK ACTIVITIES (Rev. July 2014) (Sept. 27, 2013) (Financial Institution Letter FIL-43-2013), *available at* https:www.fdic.gov/news/news/financial/2013/fil13043.pdf.; FDIC, GUIDANCE ON PAYMENT PROCESSOR RELATIONSHIPS (Rev. July 2014) (Nov. 7, 2008) (Financial Institution Letter FIL-127-2008), *available at* https://www.fdic.gov/news/news/financial/2008/fil08127.pdf; *see also* FDIC, *Supervisory Insights—Summer 2011: Managing Risks in Third-Party Payment Processor Relationships*, https://www.fdic.gov/regulations/examinations/supervisory/insights/sisum11/managing.html (last updated July 14, 2014).

111. 12 U.S.C. §§ 1248(a), 1463(a)(1), 1756, and 1819(a).

112. Financial Institutions Regulatory and Interest Rate Control Act (FIRA) tit. X, Pub. L. No. 95-630, 92 Stat. 3641 (1978) (codified in various provisions of 12 U.S.C.).

FIs by third parties, such as mobile wallet/mobile payments providers. Because mobile wallet/mobile payments providers must typically contract with an FI to have access to the settlement rails to process payments, providers are considered information technology (IT) service providers subject to examination by the FFIEC member regulatory agencies.[113]

The FFIEC provides guidance to FIs regarding considerations that the institution must take into account in third-party relationships, such as data security, availability and integrity of systems, and compliance. As service providers to FIs, mobile wallet/mobile payments providers must comply with the FFIEC's guidance, are subject to examination by all the functional bank regulators (federal and state) and the CFPB, and are also subject to audit by all of the FIs the provider uses and has relationships with.

To help ensure compliance and handle any examination or audit requests, mobile wallet/mobile payments providers must maintain detailed compliance manuals, policies, and procedures, as well as compliance programs and controls. A chief compliance officer is required at a minimum, and other staff depending on the types of payments services and the states in which the company operates.

V. POLICY QUESTIONS AND CONSIDERATIONS REGARDING MOBILE WALLETS/MOBILE PAYMENTS

As illustrated in Part IV, numerous and often overlapping laws govern portions of the mobile wallet/mobile payments process, but many of these laws still operate and respond the same as if the technology behind the business activity has not changed. There are three main areas for legal development as mobile wallets/mobile payments gain traction and use in the marketplace.

A. Resolving Transaction Disputes

One issue that may hold back some consumers from the use of mobile wallets/ mobile payments is the matter of dispute resolution in the case of fraudulent payments or unauthorized charges. Mobile payments services typically function by linking to one or more payment sources. Many mobile payments platforms allow consumers to choose among several different funding sources for payment, such as a credit card, debit card, bank account, or mobile phone account. For instance, a particular payment application on a smartphone may be linked to a credit card so that the credit card is charged when the consumer pays using that application.

---

113. The FFIEC's *Retail Payment Systems Examination Handbook* (2010) provides comprehensive guidance to examiners on risks to FIs that provide payment processing services, as well as step-by-step guidance to preparing for an examination or audit of compliance with customer due diligence regulations and with other expectations of federal regulators.

Depending on the payment source used to fund the mobile payment (e.g., credit card versus prepaid card versus mobile carrier billing), consumers may or may not have statutory protections regarding unauthorized charges.[114]

The FTC convened a mobile payments workshop to look at these issues and found the following:

> Mobile payment users may not recognize that their protections against fraudulent or unauthorized transactions can vary greatly depending on the underlying funding source. Generally, credit cards provide the strongest level of statutory protection, capping liability for unauthorized use at $50. If a mobile payment is linked to a bank debit card, a consumer's liability for unauthorized transfers is limited to $50 if reported within two business days, and up to $500 for charges reported after two business days. However, if consumers do not report unauthorized debit transactions on their bank account within 60 days after their periodic statement is mailed to them, they can face unlimited liability, whether or not the charges result from a lost or stolen card or another electronic transfer. [115]

At the FTC workshop, one consumer group advocated for the extension of the additional federal protections afforded to credit and debit cards to these financial products, specifically pointing out the inequitable situation caused when prepaid or stored-value cards are used as payment vehicles for mobile payments. This issue may have found some resolution in the CFPB's Prepaid Card Rule, but at the time of the writing of this chapter, Congress may nullify the CFPB's Prepaid Card Rule. The inconsistency in protections complicates the landscape for consumers who may not understand the differences between these funding sources.[116]

With multiple parties involved in consumer transactions regarding mobile wallets/mobile payments, additional transaction-related policy questions remain, such as:

- Who is responsible for providing consumer disclosures for products and services requiring such disclosures, and what protocols will apply to proving that these disclosures were given via mobile device?
- To what extent should consumers be responsible for unauthorized or fraudulent mobile payments if they handle their mobile devices carelessly or share their identification information with others? Is that the same as giving someone your debit card and PIN?
- Should consumer disclosures be focused on the liabilities and risks associated with different funding options for mobile wallets/mobile payments (e.g., credit card versus debit card versus ACH)?
- To what extent must mobile wallet/mobile payments services be accessible to the disabled, and how might this be achieved?

114. FTC, PAPER, PLASTIC . . . OR MOBILE? AN FTC WORKSHOP ON MOBILE PAYMENTS (Mar. 2013), *available at* https://www.ftc.gov/reports/paper-plastic-or-mobile-ftc-workshop-mobile-payments.

115. *Id.*

116. *Id.*

- Who will keep records of mobile wallet/mobile payments transactions, and how? How may consumers obtain these records?
- How will theft of mobile devices or hacking of customer authentication data affect responsibility for unauthorized payments?
- What protocols are essential to ensure accuracy of payment data in transmission?
- What obligations and liabilities result when mobile wallet/mobile payments systems "go down"? Is unavailability of a mobile payment system the equivalent of denying consumers the right to their funds?
- Given that all new mobile wallet/mobile payments options thus far operate using existing payments infrastructure, are new transaction-related laws or rules needed at all?

B. Data Security, Privacy, and Data Ownership

With regard to data security, the FTC workshop discussed above also examined data security and mobile payments. It found that a key concern for consumers when making mobile payments is whether or not their sensitive financial information can be stolen or intercepted.[117]

The FTC noted that a 2013 Federal Reserve study reported that 42 percent of consumers were concerned about data security, and this concern was the most cited reason why consumers have not used mobile wallets/mobile payments to a greater extent. Specifically, consumers were concerned about hackers gaining access to their phone remotely, or someone intercepting payment information or other data.[118] Given that a major impediment to consumers' adoption of mobile payments technologies is the perceived lack of security, the incentives for industry to get security right should be strong.

Although technology to provide enhanced security in the mobile wallets/mobile payments market is available, it is not clear that all companies in this market are employing it. Technological advances in the mobile payments marketplace offer the potential for increased data security for financial information. A number of FTC workshop panelists described how, under the traditional payments system, financial data is often transmitted or stored in an unencrypted form at some point during the payment process. By contrast, mobile payments technology allows for encryption throughout the entire payment chain, which is often referred to as "end-to-end encryption." Additionally, under the traditional payments system (and prior to EMV implementation), financial information on a card's magnetic stripe that is transmitted from a merchant to a bank consists of the same information sent each time a consumer makes a payment. Thus, if this information is intercepted, it can be used repeatedly for subsequent, unauthorized transactions. Mobile payments, however, can utilize dynamic data authentication and tokenization (as previously discussed),

---

117. *Id.*
118. *Id.*

whereby a unique set of payment information is generated for each transaction. Accordingly, even if the data is intercepted, it cannot be used for a subsequent transaction. In the mobile context, payment information also can be stored on a secure element that is separate from the rest of a phone's memory, preventing hackers who access a phone OS from compromising sensitive financial information.[119]

Mobile wallet/mobile payments providers should increase data security as sensitive financial information moves through the payment channel and encourage adoption of strong security measures by all companies in the mobile payments chain. Consumers may be harmed when less responsible companies use insecure methods to collect and store payment information. Further, the reputation of the industry as a whole may suffer if consumers believe lax security practices are the norm. Many federal and state laws also impose data security requirements on businesses that collect and use financial information and other sensitive data, as discussed in Part IV above.[120]

With regard to privacy and data ownership, in the traditional payments space, banks, merchants, and payment card networks have access, or potential access, to information about the consumer. In the mobile wallet/mobile payments space, in addition to the traditional actors, payment transactions now include OS and software manufacturers, hardware manufacturers, mobile phone carriers, application developers, and loyalty program administrators.

For example, when a consumer pays using a credit or debit card during a traditional point-of-sale purchase, the merchant typically has detailed data about the products the consumer purchased, but does not have the consumer's contact information. Conversely, the FI that issued the card has a consumer's contact information and the name of the merchant where the consumer shopped, but generally does not have information about specific purchases. Mobile payments can allow multiple players within the mobile payments ecosystem to gather and consolidate personal and purchase data in a way that was not possible under the traditional payments regime. Such consolidation may provide benefits to consumers, such as helping merchants offer products or services that a consumer is more likely to want. This collection of data may also help reduce the incidence of fraud. However, these data practices also raise significant privacy issues. In a current transaction via the use of a credit card, a merchant would get very little information about the consumer due to restricting on data collection imposed by state law, credit card acceptance agreements, and customer loyalty considerations.[121]

Mobile payments systems could provide avenues for merchants to discover shopping habits of the consumer that could be used for marketing or analytical purposes. California is very clear on prohibiting the collection of personal information by merchants from consumers when using credit cards at the physical point of

---

119. *Id.*
120. *Id.*
121. *Id.*

sale,[122] but this is potentially clouded when a mobile wallet/mobile payments system is used. Given that traditional payments are still a near universal option, consumers still have the ability to avoid mobile payments completely without hindering their ability to purchase goods and services.[123]

With regard to data security, privacy, and data ownership relating to mobile wallet/mobile payments transactions, several outstanding policy questions remain, including:

- What privacy rules apply to, and who is responsible for, security of customer data? Should consumers be allowed to select higher or lower levels of identity protection as a matter of their own convenience?
- What consequences should follow if the personal information is compromised in transmission?
- Should those accepting or facilitating mobile payments be allowed to use customer data for marketing or other purposes? Should consumers have a right to opt-in or opt-out of such data sharing?
- Who "owns" the personal information and transaction data? Provisions of Dodd-Frank state that consumers own their financial data, but many agreement provisions from card networks, issuing banks, and mobile wallet/mobile payments providers state that those entities ultimately own transaction data and personal information associated with their products and services.

C. State v. Federal Regulations and Calls for Uniformity

As financial services innovators and fintech have expanded over the past several years, a point of industry consensus is that the U.S. regulatory landscape in particular is challenging to, and in some cases poses a barrier to, innovation and new competition within the fintech arena. Critics of the U.S. regulatory regime point to a confusing web of multiple federal functional regulators and state money transmission regulators. The sheer number of potential laws, rules, regulations, and regulatory entities that can be involved in regulating a particular fintech start-up based upon the product and services provided are subject to increased scrutiny and criticism from the fintech industry.

The perception (and arguably also the reality) that companies are extremely daunted by U.S. regulatory requirements and that some companies choose to launch their payments or fintech products and services outside the United States under more "fintech-friendly" regulatory regimes has gotten the attention of U.S. federal regulators, particularly the OCC, during 2016.

---

122. CAL. CIV. CODE § 1747.08(a)(2) (the Song-Beverly Act) (prohibiting businesses from requesting that customers provide personal identification information, such as e-mail addresses, during credit card transactions).
123. FTC, *supra* note 114.

Many U.S. companies point to the more "fintech-friendly" regimes in other countries. Fintech companies contrast the UK regime under the Financial Conduct Authority, for example, with the much more confusing, inconsistent, and less user-friendly laws, rules, and regulations in the United States. Recently, a U.S. alliance of technology leaders, including Amazon, Apple, Google, Intuit, and PayPal (among others), called "Financial Innovation Now," issued a report entitled "Examining the Extensive Regulation of Financial Technologies," which states in part: "These [U.S.] compliance requirements constitute a significant market barrier, particularly for new entrants, and can sometimes serve to protect incumbent providers from new competition."[124]

The Trump Administration is committed to reducing regulation across the board, which could portend extensive fintech regulatory changes in 2017, at least at the federal level. There are three key areas to monitor during 2017 with regard to fintech regulation and business environment.

1. Potential U.S. Executive and Congressional Action Impacting Mobile Wallet/Mobile Payments Regulation

One of the first big opportunities for full-contact politics under the Trump Administration in 2017 is whether Trump takes action to replace current CFPB Director Richard Cordray. A case currently on appeal addresses whether the president has the authority to do that under the Dodd-Frank Act,[125] but Trump may take steps to remove Cordray regardless of final resolution of the pending constitutional questions. Another looming battle is the repeal of Dodd-Frank either in its entirety or in a manner that will severely change how the CFPB operates, including its overall scope of authority and structure. Any changes to the CFPB will have a direct impact on fintech regulation and climate in the United States as the CFPB currently has broad authority to regulate and enforce against nonbank entities that offer financial services to consumers.

Lobbying of both the executive and legislative branches may also portend changes in the regulatory environment. On November 30, 2016, Financial Innovation Now sent a letter to the Trump-Pence Transition Team that asked President-Elect Trump to make good on his campaign promises of job creation by enacting policies that will enable more rapid development and growth of fintech.[126] Among the "wish list" items in the November 30 letter are:

---

124. Brian Peters, *New Report Examines Regulatory Landscape of Financial Technologies*, FIN. INNO-VATION NOW, July 11, 2016, https://financialinnovationnow.org/2016/07/11/new-report-examines-regulatory-landscape-financial-technologies/.

125. PHH Corp. et al. v. Consumer Fin. Prot. Bureau, No. 15-1177 (D.C. Cir. Oct. 11, 2016), *vacated for reh'g en banc*, Feb. 16, 2017.

126. Brian Peters, *FIN Calls on President-Elect Trump to Promote Innovation in Financial Services, Appoint Senior Financial Technology Leader*, FIN. INNOVATION NOW, Nov. 30, 2016, https://financialinnovationnow.org/2016/11/30/fin-trump-transition-letter/.

- Appoint a U.S. Department of the Treasury undersecretary for technology who will be responsible for developing a national vision and coordinated strategy to ensure that America is the best country to create companies and grow jobs in developing financial technologies
- Promote open, interoperable standards for card payment security that get rid of closed and proprietary networks that lock out innovation
- Streamline money transmission licensing by working on a streamlined federal money transmission licensing system that protects consumers while facilitating access to new payments services across the United States
- Ensure consumer access to financial accounts and data and prevent FIs from blocking consumer-granted access to such information
- Help consumers and businesses manage money with real-time payments, and ensure the availability of a real-time payments network for all Americans by 2020
- Leverage mobile technology to increase financial inclusion[127]

The regulatory reform "wish list" from Financial Innovation Now echoes the sentiments and desires of many other payments and fintech companies in the United States to pursue regulatory reform to ease the regulatory burden on fintech and foster innovation. There will undoubtedly be lobbying on these and similar issues at the executive and congressional levels, and perhaps at the state level in at least some key states (like California, Florida, Illinois, New York, and Texas—the "Big 5" for state money transmission licensing based on those being the top five states in terms of population ranking).

2. OCC Explores a Limited Purpose National Bank Charter for Fintech Companies (and State Regulator Reaction)

On March 31, 2016, the OCC released a much-anticipated white paper entitled "Supporting Responsible Innovation in the Federal Banking System: An OCC Perspective."[128] During the last half of 2016, the OCC undertook several activities to implement the goals of the OCC white paper. On September 13, 2016, the OCC announced a notice of proposed rulemaking to implement the basic legal framework for receiverships for any national bank that is not insured by the FDIC (uninsured banks) and for which the FDIC is not required to be appointed as receiver, such as an uninsured trust bank. Many industry observers viewed this as the first step toward the OCC establishing a special purpose national bank charter for fintech companies anxious to be supervised by a single federal regulator rather than a patchwork of states. By establishing a program under which the OCC would be the receiver of

127. *Id.*
128. OCC, Supporting Responsible Innovation in the Federal Banking System: An OCC Perspective (Mar. 2016), *available at* http://www.occ.treas.gov/publications/publications-by-type/other-publications-reports/pub-responsible-innovation-banking-system-occ-perspective.pdf.

failing non-FDIC insured OCC chartered institutions, with the understanding that an eventual special purpose national bank charter for fintech companies would fall into the "uninsured" category, the OCC may provide a pathway out of the current system's diffused regulatory labyrinth.[129]

In October 2016, the OCC announced the creation of the Office of Innovation. According to the OCC's website, "Responsible Innovation is the use of new or improved financial products, services and processes to meet the evolving needs of consumers, businesses, and communities in a manner that is consistent with sound risk management and is aligned with the bank's overall business strategy."[130]

U.S. Comptroller of the Currency Thomas J. Curry announced on December 2, 2016, at an event at Georgetown Law Center in Washington, D.C., that the OCC will issue new special purpose national bank charters for fintech companies beginning January 2017 after the closing of a comment period ending January 15, 2017. The new special purpose charter will allow fintech companies that collect deposits, issue checks, or make loans (among other traditional banking activities) to have a single national standard for their operations, which would allow them to act throughout the entire United States in exchange for rigorous oversight by the OCC.[131]

In early March 2017, the OCC released "OCC Summary of Comments and Explanatory Statement: Special Purpose National Bank Charters for Financial Technology Companies."[132] This publication summarizes the most common or salient comments that the OCC received in response to its white paper by the January 15, 2017 comment deadline, and the OCC's response or explanation to the comments. At the same time, the OCC released "Evaluating Charter Applications from Financial Technology Companies."[133] This "draft supplement" by the OCC discusses the proposed procedure and standards for fintech companies seeking to obtain a special purpose charter, and the OCC accepted public comments and feedback on the draft supplement until April 15, 2017.

State regulators who oversee, among other things, state money transmission licensing and enforcement and state small dollar lending laws, are vehemently opposed to the OCC's special purpose fintech charter. A press release issued on

---

129. Lalita Clozel, *Cheat Sheet: What the OCC's New Plan Means for a Fintech Charter*, AM. BANKER, Sept. 16, 2016, http://www.americanbanker.com/news/law-regulation/cheat-sheet-what-the-occs-new-plan-means-for-a-fintech-charter-1091365-1.html.

130. *See* OCC, *Responsible Innovation*, https://www.occ.gov/topics/bank-operations/innovation/index-innovation.html (last visited May 20, 2017).

131. Evan Weinberger, *Federal Charters Could Ease Burdens for Fintech Upstarts*, LAW360, Dec. 15, 2016, http://www.law360.com/banking/articles.

132. OCC, OCC SUMMARY OF COMMENTS AND EXPLANATORY STATEMENT: SPECIAL PURPOSE NATIONAL BANK CHARTERS FOR FINANCIAL TECHNOLOGY COMPANIES (Mar. 2017), *available at* https://www.occ.gov/topics/responsible-innovation/summary-explanatory-statement-fintech-charters.pdf

133. OCC, EVALUATING CHARTER APPLICATIONS FROM FINANCIAL TECHNOLOGY COMPANIES (Mar. 2017), *available at* https://www.occ.gov/publications/publications-by-type/licensing-manuals/file-pub-lm-fintech-licensing-manual-supplement.pdf

December 2, 2016, from the Conference of State Bank Supervisors (CSBS)[134] detailed the opposition from state regulators to a new OCC fintech charter, stating:

- A federal fintech charter will distort the marketplace and institute command-and-control innovation. State regulators are concerned that the OCC's subjective criteria for awarding charters, and its intent to not include the normal regulatory safeguards placed on national banks—such as deposit insurance—would result in the OCC choosing winners and losers within the fintech industry as well as the broader banking industry, a sharp departure from the role of a financial regulator.
- The OCC is expanding its mandate absent statutory authority. The National Bank Act does not give the OCC authority to issue full-service bank charters to institutions that do not engage in deposit taking. To get around this, the OCC is relying on its own regulations—not the National Bank Act—to create a non-depository special purpose charter for fintech firms. However, there is no historical precedent for such a charter in the national banking system.
- Despite assurances to the contrary, state regulators believe consumers will be at risk. The state regulators claim that the OCC has a history of preempting state consumer protection laws in ways that damaged consumers. During the early 2000s, many states adopted laws and brought enforcement actions to stop predatory lending. The OCC's response was to preempt the application of state antipredatory lending laws to national banks and their operating subsidiaries, thereby permitting unsafe and abusive lending practices to flourish in the lead up to the U.S. financial crisis.

In addition, after the OCC released the draft supplement outlining the proposed procedure and standards for fintech companies seeking to obtain a special purpose charter, several state banking regulators and the CSBS filed complaints and objections to the draft supplement. In addition, on April 26, 2017, the CSBS sued the OCC in federal court in *Conference of State Bank Supervisors v. OCC*,[135] alleging that the OCC's plan to charter fintech companies as special purpose national banks is unlawful because the process the OCC used to develop the plan was procedurally defective and because issuing such charters would exceed the OCC's authority.

On May 12, 2017, the New York State Department of Financial Services, which is one of the state bank regulators that makes up the CSBS, separately sued the OCC in federal court in *Vullo v. OCC*,[136] alleging, similarly, that the OCC exceeded its

---

134. Press Release, Conference of State Bank Supervisors, Statement by the Conference of State Bank Supervisors on Comptroller's Announcement of New Federal Charters (Dec. 2, 2016), *available at* https://www.csbs.org/news/press-releases/pr2016/Pages/120216.aspx.

135. Conference of State Bank Supervisors v. Office of Comptroller of the Currency, No. 1:17-CV-00763 (D.D.C. Apr. 26, 2017).

136. Vullo v. Office of Comptroller of the Currency, No. 1:17-CV-03574 (S.D.N.Y. May 12, 2017).

authority in planning to issue the charters, and emphasizing that the planned federal charter could threaten New York consumers.

The issues regarding the OCC's limited purpose charter will continue to be debated during 2017 by both policymakers, regulators and now the courts, but inherent in the debate and now court cases around these issues is the tension between a patchwork of state regulations, particularly money transmission laws, which are perceived by the fintech providers, including mobile wallet/mobile payments providers, as stifling innovation and creating barriers for new market entrants.

Chapter 5

Cryptocurrency

Bitcoin and Blockchain Technology

Jillian Friedman

I. INTRODUCTION

Bitcoin is the world's first completely decentralized cryptocurrency.[1] It has been called a "technological tour de force"[2] and a "remarkable conceptual and technical achievement."[3] It consists of an open-source software, a network, and a unit of account that is also called bitcoin. Together, these elements enable the first successful experiment of decentralized digital private money.[4] What began in 2008 as a niche interest relegated to technologists and libertarians has grown to be larger than the economies of some of the world's smaller countries.[5]

Beginning in 2012, substantial investments have been made in Bitcoin and other related ventures based on its underlying distributed ledger or "blockchain" technology. Venture capitalists and financial institutions have expanded the scope of these investments into other applications, reaching an estimated $497 billion in 2016 alone.[6]

---

1. JERRY BRITO & ANDREA CASTILLO, BITCOIN: A PRIMER FOR POLICYMAKERS (Mercatus Center at George Mason University 2013).

2. Kim Lachance Shandrow, *Bill Gates: Bitcoin Is "Better Than Currency,"* ENTREPRENEUR, Oct. 3, 2014, https://www.entrepreneur.com/article/238103.

3. François R. Velde, *Bitcoin: A Primer*, 317 CHI. FED LETTER (Dec. 2013), https://www.chicagofed.org /publications/chicago-fed-letter/2013/december-317.

4. Satoshi Nakamoto, *Bitcoin: A Peer-to-Peer Electronic Cash System* (2008), https://bitcoin.org /bitcoin.pdf.

5. BRITO & CASTILLO, *supra* note 1, at 1.

6. CoinDesk, *Blockchain Venture Capital*, http://www.coindesk.com/bitcoin-venture-capital/ (last visited May 20, 2017); Marc Andreessen, *Why Bitcoin Matters*, N.Y. TIMES, Jan. 21, 2014, http://dealbook .nytimes.com/2014/01/21/why-bitcoin-matters/; Kyle Torpey, *Bitcoin Venture Capital Funding on Pace for $1 Billion in 2015*, INSIDE BITCOINS, Mar. 10, 2015, http://insidebitcoins.com/news/bitcoin-venture -capital-funding-pace-1-billion-2015/30665; BRITO & CASTILLO, *supra* note 1, at 1; Sarah E. Needleman & Spencer E. Ante, *Bitcoin Startups Begin to Attract Real Cash*, WALL ST. J., May 8, 2013, https://www.wsj.com /articles/SB10001424127887323687604578469012375269952.

Blockchain technology has especially captured the interest of the financial services industry with more than $1.3 billion in investments from 2013–2016 as banks throughout the world are becoming involved with blockchain-related projects.[7]

Referred to as the third wave of the Internet,[8] much is anticipated from virtual currency[9] and blockchain technology. This disruptive technology creates new paradigms and legal challenges for lawmakers and financial institutions.[10] Evaluation of the legal rules and challenges applicable to a new technology must be premised on a basic understanding of its functionality and the industry that has formed around it. As such, the first part of this chapter will describe virtual currency and blockchain technology, why it matters, and the emerging industry using this technology. Though there are many different applications that blockchain technology enables, to date bitcoin's use as a payments and money transfer tool is most ubiquitous.[11] The second part of the chapter will describe legal and operational risks and challenges that emerge from blockchain technology and will conclude with an overview of regulatory responses to applications of this technology.

II. WHAT IS VIRTUAL CURRENCY AND BLOCKCHAIN TECHNOLOGY?

A. Functional and Technological Description of Bitcoin

Since it is the most pervasive virtual currency, Bitcoin provides an appropriate focal point as a proxy for a broader discussion of virtual currency. Bitcoin is an open-source, peer-to-peer digital currency whose origins, though mysterious, are clearly set out in a white paper published online in 2008 by a person or group calling itself Satoshi Nakamoto.[12] In elegant simplicity, the paper describes a system for electronic transactions without relying on trust, using a recorded public history of transactions with a built-in consensus mechanism to validate transactions.

Why is Bitcoin significant? Prior to Bitcoin, there was no practically effective way to use a digital representation of cash online without relying on a trusted intermediary. "Digital money" presented challenges similar to other digital data, as it could be easily copied and spent over and over again. A payments system whereby the sender could

---

7. WORLD ECONOMIC FORUM, THE FUTURE OF FINANCIAL INFRASTRUCTURE 14 (2016) [hereinafter THE FUTURE OF FINANCIAL INFRASTRUCTURE], *available at* http://www3.weforum.org/docs/WEF_The_future_of_financial_infrastructure.pdf.

8. P.H. Madore, *CNN Show Inside Man: Morgan Spurlock Lived on Bitcoin for a Week*, CRYPTOCOINS NEWS, Feb. 20 2015, https://www.cryptocoinsnews.com/cnn-show-inside-man-morgan-spurlock-lived-bitcoin-week/.

9. This chapter uses the term "virtual currency" to describe digital assets such as bitcoin that are also often referred to as digital currency and cryptocurrency.

10. Study on the Use of Digital Currency before the Standing Senate Committee on Banking, Trade, and Commerce, Issue 6, 41st Parl., 2nd Sess. (2014) (statement of David Murchison, Director, Financial Sector Division, Department of Finance Canada), https://sencanada.ca/en/Content/Sen/committee/412/banc/06ev-51275-e.

11. NEIL GANDAL & HANNA HAŁABURDA, BANK OF CANADA, COMPETITION IN THE CRYPTOCURRENCY MARKET (2014) (Working Paper No. 2014-33), *available at* http://www.bankofcanada.ca/2014/08/working-paper-2014-33/.

12. NakamotoAKAMOTO, *supra* note 4.

send a digital dollar to an unlimited number of people and save a copy for himself on his desktop would be fatally flawed.[13] In the computer science world, this was dubbed the "double-spend problem." Parties transacting online typically solve this problem by utilizing a trusted third-party intermediary such as a financial institution or a payment processor to keep a ledger of each account holders' balances, to verify the funds exist, and to make sure they are debited from the account of the payor and credited to the account of the payee.[14] Even before the Internet age, non-cash payments between untrusted parties always required an intermediary to verify that the money existed, that it was not already spent, and to effect the transfer on a balance sheet.

Bitcoin was the first to solve the double-spend problem and eliminate the need to trust third parties to transfer value over an untrusted network such as the Internet.[15] The Bitcoin system is based on a ledger that chronologically records every single transaction that occurs within the Bitcoin network, called the Bitcoin blockchain. Each transaction is validated by the network of nodes running the blockchain against the whole transaction history of the public and unchangeable blockchain ledger to make sure that the bitcoin being transferred has not already been spent. Once validated, the transaction is inscribed and broadcast on the blockchain. Each transaction is validated by a global peer-to-peer decentralized network comprised of thousands of users, also called nodes (instead of a single intermediary checking the transaction).[16] There is no central entity operating the Bitcoin protocol and it is a completely open-source initiative.

Transactions are denominated in a token native to the Bitcoin network also called bitcoin and often referred to as virtual currency or cryptocurrency. There is no central authority determining monetary policy for bitcoins. New bitcoins are generated by the computing power of nodes that validate transactions. However, there is a limited supply of bitcoin. The rate of generation of new bitcoin is predetermined by the Bitcoin protocol and designed to decrease over time, set to stop once 21 million bitcoins have been generated. A single bitcoin unit (BTC) is divisible and because the value of one BTC is so high, people deal in milli-bitcoin (0.001) or micro-bitcoin (0.000001), with the smallest unit known as a satoshi (0.00000001). Bitcoin is not government fiat currency and is not designated as legal tender. Legal tender means that, by law or state sanction ("fiat") the currency can be used and accepted as a medium of exchange and as a means to discharge debts.[17] Virtual currency does not currently have legal tender status in any jurisdiction, which is a status that only the state can bestow.[18]

---

13. Brito & Castillo, *supra* note 1, at 5.
14. *Id.*
15. Nakamoto, *supra* note 4.
16. Brito & Castillo, *supra* note 1, at 6.
17. Financial Action Task Force, Virtual Currencies Key Definitions and Potential AML/CFT Risks 4 (June 2014), *available at* http://www.fatf-gafi.org/media/fatf/documents/reports/Virtual-currency-key -definitions-and-potential-aml-cft-risks.pdf.
18. Mann on the Legal Aspect of Money 19–20 (Charles Proctor ed., 7th ed. Oxford U. Press 2012) (citing Hepburn v. Griswold, 75 U.S. 603, 615 (1869), and Juilliard v. Greenman, 110 U.S. 421, 447 (1883)). The Law of Bitcoin 181 (Stuart Hoegner ed., 2015).

Its value is based on market demand. Put otherwise, bitcoin "has value because it is useful and scarce."[19]

There are several components to Bitcoin's functionality. Bitcoin's security derives from public key cryptography, a tool used to secure many different types of digital information and communication. In order to send and receive bitcoin, a user must create a key pair consisting of a private key and a public key. The public key serves as an account identifier and the private key is used to sign transactions.[20] The private key must be kept private and secret, as it is like a password or a personal identification number. Loss or disclosure of one's private key jeopardizes all bitcoins at that public address. The public key is like an address, which is shared publicly (like an e-mail address) and serves as a type of identifier. A person who wishes to receive bitcoin will share a public address that looks something like this: 1DSrfJdB2AnWaFNgSbv3MZC2m74996JafV. The private key is the digital signature that "unlocks" the bitcoin that was sent to its corresponding public address, thus enabling it to be transferred to other addresses. Like a public address, it is also a string of letters and numbers. There is no limit to the number of key pairs that can be generated. For convenience, these key pairs are often held through a "wallet," which is a layer of software that facilitates the management of key pairs.

The Bitcoin protocol, much like the simple mail transfer protocol (SMTP) that enables the sending and receipt of e-mail communications, is a set of rules. These rules are parameters that regulate how value is sent and received, how bitcoins are created, and what makes a transaction valid or invalid. When users send bitcoins, they are creating a message with the pieces of information necessary for the transaction: the public key (or Bitcoin address) of the recipient, the amount of bitcoin being sent, and the "signature" of the private key of the sender. Because Bitcoin uses public key cryptography, anyone can verify that the transaction was signed by the private key simply by examining the public key.

Bitcoin transactions are not anonymous, they are pseudonymous. All transactions are stored publicly on the blockchain, including the public address of the sender and recipient, the amount sent, and the time. Payment network participants are thus linked to the pseudonyms of their public addresses. Anonymity therefore depends on their pseudonym not being linked to their true identity. Bitcoin enthusiasts admit that the current implementation of bitcoin is not very anonymous.[21] Since every transaction is stored publicly in the blockchain, every transaction is publicly known. Knowing who is associated with a Bitcoin address means being able to see all of the associated transactions and the amount of bitcoin that address controls by

19. Erik Voorhees, *The Role of Bitcoin as Money*, Money & State, May 23, 2013, http://moneyandstate.com/role-bitcoin-money/.
20. Malte Möser, *Anonymity of Bitcoin Transactions: An Analysis of Mixing Services* 1 (2013), https://www.wi.uni-muenster.de/sites/wi/files/public/department/itsecurity/mbc13/mbc13-moeser-paper.pdf.
21. *Id.* at 1.

consulting the public blockchain.[22] However, there are numerous techniques available for using bitcoin with increased anonymity.[23]

Hundreds of thousands of computers that run nodes on the Bitcoin network validate each transaction by having it recorded, time stamped, batched with other transactions occurring within a certain timeframe, and publicly broadcast as a "block" of the blockchain. The blocks are chronological and linked to the blocks immediately before and after them. Since the nodes running the blockchain have an updated and verified copy of the ledger with the chronological history of all the transactions within the Bitcoin network, they can verify that there is no double spending or attempt to spend bitcoins not associated with that key pair before authorizing the transaction.[24] The history of transactions on the blockchain is immutable because it is cryptographically secure and cannot be modified. With an updated copy of the ledger on every computer running the system, any change to the blockchain must be validated by a consensus of the majority of the nodes. While it is possible to corrupt some nodes on any system, it is practically impossible to corrupt all the unrelated decentralized nodes on the Bitcoin network.

The role of the network, made up of users or *miners* who provide computing power (by running nodes) to validate transactions, reconcile the ledger, and prevent double spending, is crucial. Remember that there is no central authority verifying transactions, issuing bitcoin, or making sure the network is running properly. Instead, thousands of miners run the Bitcoin network and solve complex mathematical problems in order to verify transactions on the blockchain. As a reward for giving computer power by running nodes (and footing the electric bill) the miners are rewarded with newly generated bitcoin.[25] This incentive structure of rewarding miners with new bitcoin is part of the mathematically predetermined "monetary policy" for bitcoin. After the last bitcoin is generated (which is currently predicted to occur at or near the year 2140), miners will be rewarded via transaction fees.

B. Blockchain and Distributed Ledger Technology

The Bitcoin blockchain is "a distributed database that maintains a continuously-growing list of ordered records called blocks" secured from tampering and revision.[26] Each block contains a timestamp and a link to a previous block[27] and this core technology enables the transfer of value peer-to-peer over an open (and untrusted) network without requiring a trusted intermediary. This technology has applications

---

22. Blockchain.info is an example of a free service that facilitates searching the Bitcoin blockchain. Different types of searches can be made, including searches by public address.

23. *How to Use Bitcoin Anonymously*, CRYPTORIALS, May 22, 2015, http://cryptorials.io/how-to-use-bitcoin-anonymously/.

24. BRITO & CASTILLO, *supra* note 1, at 7.

25. *Id.* at 8; Nakamoto, *supra* note 4.

26. Wikipedia, *Blockchain*, HTTPS://EN.WIKIPEDIA.ORG/WIKI/BLOCKCHAIN (LAST EDITED MAY 19, 2017).

27. Investopedia, *Blockchain*, *http://www.investopedia.com/terms/b/blockchain.asp (last visited* May 20, 2017). Based on the Bitcoin protocol, the blockchain database is shared by all nodes participating in a system.

well beyond bitcoin, digital currency, and payments in general. Realizing the potential of distributed ledger technology (DLT), which is a more general term referencing a type of technology that includes blockchains and the Bitcoin blockchain, the technology and financial services industries have begun to build other types of blockchains or blockchain-inspired distributed ledgers that might replace or complement traditional infrastructure.[28] For consistency, the term "blockchain" will also reference DLT, which is "blockchain-inspired." Though there are different modalities, the following are general characteristics present in all or most blockchain projects:[29]

1. **Ledger**. The data is displayed in the form of an audit trail of transactions or ledger. This ledger is the shared repository of information and is used by multiple parties.

2. **Distributed**. The ledger of transactions is maintained and validated by separate participants, or nodes (in Bitcoin, they are the miners). Copies of the ledger are distributed and replicated on servers on multiple locations. Each node has the same copy of the ledger that is updated in real time.

3. **Multiple participants (or writers)**. Multiple entities generate transactions that require modifications to the shared repository. Only people with certain credentials or "keys" can make ledger entries. Some blockchain platforms also makes use of multiple-signature (multisig) features, which means that a system will require two or more parties to "sign" their private keys in order for a transaction to be signed. Unlike the Bitcoin blockchain, other blockchains may require that the identities of participants be known.

4. **Permissioned/permissionless**. Blockchains can be permissioned or permissionless. The Bitcoin blockchain is permissionless because it is open to anyone who wants to use it. Other distributed ledgers might have restrictions as to who can generate transactions on the shared repository, the type of transaction, who can see the details of the transaction, and who will validate them. For example, a payments system blockchain built for banks that processes millions of transactions on behalf of end users would likely be more closed.[30] These different considerations are in part a response to the legal and regulatory requirements in the financial services industry where the would-be end users already know each other.

5. **Consensus**. In order to change the status or history of the ledger, computers running the different copies of the ledger act as validators. The majority must "agree" that changes to the audit trail are valid and not

---

28. *Blockchains: The Great Chain of Being Sure about Things*, Economist, *Oct. 31, 2015, available at* http://www.economist.com/news/briefing/21677228-technology-behind-bitcoin-lets-people-who-do-not-know-or-trust-each-other-build-dependable.

29. The Future of Financial Infrastructure, *supra* note 7.

30. *Id.* at 36.

being made fraudulently. Unless validators agree by consensus on the state-of-the-network, the change will not be effected on the ledger. This consensus is recorded on the cryptographic audit trial. In public blockchains such as Bitcoin, these validators are the miners and they are unknown. Some private blockchains may require the validators be known.

6. **Immutable**. The ledger is a single historical version of the truth. There is no need for reconciliation. By having data or transactions organized chronologically, distributed, and modifiable only by consensus of participants, it is impossible to change transactions that occurred in the past. The result is information that is tamper-proof and trustworthy, thus reducing the need for central intermediaries that provide reconciliation services.

7. **Transparency**. The ledger is capable of being seen by all participants, allowing for reliable information sharing. Because the ledger is the single version of the truth, it can be a reliable source for past and current transactions and increase visibility of participants and their relative positions.[31]

8. **Minimal trust/autonomy**. Entities generating transactions do not need to fully trust each other. Traditionally, counterparties have needed a central authority to intermediate a transaction, but with a blockchain, counterparties can be "disintermediated" and operate securely without a trusted third party.[32]

9. **Smart contracts**. Though there are many working definitions, a smart contract is a legally binding contract that is both enforceable and automated, whereby the actual transaction associated with the contract is expressed in computer code and independently executed by the code once certain predetermined conditions are met. Blockchain solutions that include smart contracts can ensure that agreements are executed to the agreed upon business outcomes and disintermediate many of the supporting entities set up to resolve disputes. A smart contract facilitates a common agreement as to the nature of the shared facts between the parties.

10. **Security**. Blockchain technology relies on public key cryptography, which is used in many other applications. While this creates an additional control, it does not eliminate security risks.

11. **Speed**. The single version of the ledger is being updated by participant nodes/validators in real time. Reliance on a singular and up-to-date version of the truth allows parties to act in real time with confidence.

---

31. *Id.* at 26.
32. *Id.* at 24.

C. The Industry and Challenges

The industry can be divided into two types of businesses: virtual currency businesses and blockchain businesses. Virtual currency businesses use virtual currency tokens and public networks such as Bitcoin or Ethereum to provide a range of services including payments services to consumers and businesses. Though blockchain businesses may use tokens, they are oriented towards building platforms or providing infrastructure services using blockchain or blockchain-inspired technology.

1. The Virtual Currency Economy

Though virtual currency's genesis apparently stems from a crypto-anarchist, the virtual currency economy is no longer being driven primarily by a libertarian subculture reacting to perceived abuses and excesses of the financial system. Trading volume of bitcoin from 2015 to 2016 increased by 424 percent. Venture capital investment in virtual currency as of the end of the first quarter of 2016 totaled USD 1.1 billion in more than 130 start-ups.[33] Despite being peer-to-peer and thus in principle not requiring an intermediary to use, a niche industry had sprung up around virtual currency focused on payments, exchange trading, and remittance. The size of the Bitcoin network continues to grow exponentially, though the rate of investment has decreased since the 2014 peak with far more money currently being oriented towards DLT projects and start-ups. For the vast majority of the industry, the benefits of digital currency do not derive from its potential to replace traditional currencies, but in the innovation it delivers as a payments service.[34] These are the main components that make digital currency attractive:

Lower transaction costs. Because there is no third-party intermediary, virtual currency transaction costs are substantially lower and transactions occur more quickly than with traditional payment networks. This makes certain activities that were previously cost prohibitive suddenly feasible. Micropayments are one example: you can spend 25 cents worth of bitcoin to tip a blogger or to pay for access to a news article. Lower transaction costs also have important implications for remittances, where traditional remittance fees can be as high as 20 percent.[35]

Peer-to-peer. Virtual currency can protect individuals against government capital controls and facilitate financial privacy where government oppression on financial freedom is a serious concern.[36] Between 1995 and 2010, a total of 37 countries restricted the flow of money out of their economies.[37] But, as long as people retain

---

33. Garrick Hileman, *State of Blockchain Q1 2016: Blockchain Funding Overtakes Bitcoin*, CoinDesk, May 11, 2016, http://www.coindesk.com/state-of-blockchain-q1-2016/.

34. Brito & Castillo, *supra* note 1, at 10.

35. For example, see The World Bank, *Remittance Prices—Sending Money from Canada to Philippines* (select First Quarter 2015 in "Collection period for" dropdown menu), http://remittanceprices.worldbank .org/en/corridor/Canada/Philippines (last updated Feb. 3, 2017).

36. *See id.*

37. Ye Xie, *Capital Controls*, Bloomberg Quick Take, Aug. 18 2015, https://www.bloomberg.com /quicktake/capital-controls.

their private keys, they can send their funds anywhere and no government can stop them. Market activity suggests this is an important driver for the growth of virtual currency. When China introduced stricter capital controls, the bitcoin price soared to a 2016 high in response to rising Chinese demand.[38] For the 2.5 billion of the world's adults who do not use banks or microfinance institutions to borrow, save, or send money, virtual currency has the potential to combat poverty and oppression by providing access to financial services to anyone with a computer or a smartphone and access to the Internet.[39]

Pseudonymity. In its purest form, virtual currency does not require the use of any personal information. In contrast, making an online purchase with a credit card requires credit card information, name, and billing address. When customer credit card data is compromised, customers risk having their identity stolen and need to act to prevent fraudsters from using their accounts. A bitcoin transaction is only the authorization of the transfer of a specific value to a specified recipient. It cannot be used to authorize additional payments, and, in theory, no personal information is associated with the public address.[40] The public address is the only information that is revealed.

Main sectors of the virtual currency economy include:

Payment processing. Through different business models, virtual currency payment providers allow users to make and accept payments in virtual currency. For example, an application program interface (API) connects to the virtual currency payment platform, allowing a payor to choose to pay with bitcoin (or possibly another virtual currency) at online checkout. An invoice can be denominated in bitcoin or fiat currency, with the locked in exchange rate indicated. The payment processor would instantly deposit the equivalent in fiat currency as calculated at the time of purchase into the bank account of the merchant. These services are used for different types of payments including retail, e-commerce, billing, and donations. The processor creates value by removing the price volatility and other risks associated with virtual currency, often allowing users to enjoy the benefits of using virtual currency without ever having to actually possess it. Payments made with virtual currency do not have charge-back mechanisms, reducing the payments fraud risk for the merchant. However, this also presents a challenge for the consumer, who may lack protections found in other payments methods.

Exchange trading. Though not exactly a payments aspect of virtual currency, the most robust sector of the virtual currency economy is exchange and margin trading

38. Tyler Durden, *Bitcoin Surges to 2016 Highs on Rising Chinese Demand; Decouples from Gold*, ZERO-HEDGE, May 27, 2016, http://www.zerohedge.com/news/2016-05-27/bitcoin-surges-2016-highs-rising-chinese-demand-decouples-gold.

39. Alberto Chaia, Tony Goland & Robert Schiff, *Counting the World's Unbanked*, MCKINSEY & CO., Mar. 2010, http://www.mckinsey.com/industries/financial-services/our-insights/counting-the-worlds-unbanked.

40. ANDREAS M. ANTONOPOULOS, MASTERING BITCOIN 236 (O'Reilly Media 2015).

platforms. Exchange platforms allow users to exchange dollars for virtual currencies or to trade virtual currencies for virtual currencies. Settlement may happen in different ways. In one example, virtual currencies purchased by a buyer would be held for the buyer's benefit in the platform provider's settlement wallet and the platform provider holds all the private keys of that wallet. Other methods rely on use of a multisig wallet associated with each user with control retained by the platform provider, or divided between the platform provider and a third party.[41] These exchanges are used as on-off ramps to buy and sell virtual currency. They are also popular with speculators betting on the price fluctuations of different virtual currencies. Margin trading is also a popular feature of exchange trading platforms but beyond the scope of a payments-themed book. There are many bitcoin and altcoin trading platforms with the Chinese bitcoin exchange market share recently at almost 90 percent and more than 95 percent of bitcoin being bought with Chinese yen.[42]

Remittance. Money transfer businesses facilitating the transfer of funds with bitcoin are proliferating in developing countries where remittance fees are extremely high and where the number of people with bank accounts to receive traditional wire transfers is low. These are physical locations where recipients can either "cash out" or the funds are deposited directly into their bank accounts. These services will often guarantee liquidity and will buy the bitcoin from the recipient with a local currency at a locked-in rate. Some offer a suite of financial services beyond remittance.

Wallets. Mobile wallets or plastic debit cards enable the storage and transfer of virtual currency between mobile devices. These include free services such as blockchain.info, which provides a bitcoin wallet for users to manage their key pairs.[43] Some wallet providers only provide the software or hardware for managing a key pair and do not hold any private keys, while others will have a degree of control over the user's funds using different mechanisms such as having a copy of their private key or using multisig wallets.

Trading "desks." Automated teller machines (ATMs) or physical or virtual trading desks allow people to buy and sell virtual currency. These services provide the on-off boarding part of a remittance or payment service of the value chain, enabling users to obtain local or virtual currency. This was one of the highest-growth sectors in 2016.[44]

2. Blockchain Technology

Global payments present a promising opportunity for the application of blockchain technology, specifically for remittances and low-value-high-volume payments

41. Andrew P. Cross, *Making Sense of the CFTC's Enforcement Order and Settlement with Bitfinex*, Derivatives & Repo Rep., June 6, 2016, https://www.derivativesandreporeport.com/2016/06/making-sense-of-the-cftcs-enforcement-order-and-settlement-with-bitfinex/.

42. Hileman, *supra* note 33, at slide 56.

43. Other examples of wallet providers include Xapo (https://www.Xapo.com,) Blockchain (https://www.Blockchain.info), Armory (https://www.bitcoinarmory.com/), and MultiBit (https://multibit.org/).

44. Hileman, *supra* note 33, at slide 36.

currently made by a person or business to another via banks or mone nesses. According to a World Economic Forum (WEF) report, interna transfers using DLT could accomplish "real-time settlement and re enable new business models previously non-feasible, and institute new regulatory oversight."[45] One description of a future state process of international remittance using a blockchain looks like this:[46]

Initiate Relationship →	Transfer Money →	Deliver Funds →	Act Post-Payment
1. KYC [i.e., Know Your Customer authentication] of the sender is established by the bank either traditionally or using a digital identity profile. 2. The obligation between sender and beneficiary to transfer funds would be reflected in a smart contract* and uploaded onto the ledger. 3. Participants on the ledger convert the currency.	4. A regulator monitors transactions in real time and receives AML [i.e., anti-money laundering] alerts. 5. Real-time transfer of funds with minimal fees and guaranteed delivery without the need for a correspondent bank, enabled by smart contract.	6. After KYC is verified, funds are deposited automatically to the beneficiary account via smart contract or otherwise made available.	7. Transaction history is available on the ledger for review by the regulators.

*The smart contract contains the transaction details such as the sender identification (ID), beneficiary ID, foreign exchange (FX) rate, transfer amount, date and time, and payout conditions.

Source: WORLD ECONOMIC FORUM, THE FUTURE OF FINANCIAL INFRASTRUCTURE: AN AMBITIOUS LOOK AT HOW BLOCKCHAIN CAN RESHAPE FINANCIAL SERVICES 51 (2016), *available at* http://www3.weforum.org/docs/WEF_The_future_of _financial_infrastructure.pdf.

The WEF report[47] also consolidates what the core value drivers of blockchain-inspired technology in the payments space could be:

- **Settlement time reduction**. Blockchain tech can enable near real-time point-to-point transfer of funds between financial institutions so that banks could settle global money transfers in near real time. It removes much of the friction of global payments and accelerates settlement by disintermediating third parties that support transaction verification.

---

45. THE FUTURE OF FINANCIAL INFRASTRUCTURE, *supra* note 7, at 39.
46. *Id.* at 5.
47. *Id.* at 19.

- **Frictionless KYC**. The client's digital identity profile could be stored on the ledger and shared between institutions, thus establishing trust between parties and simplifying the KYC authentication process.
- **Operational simplification**. Blockchain reduces manual efforts necessary to perform account reconciliation.
- **Regulatory efficiency improvement**. The transparency and immutability of the ledger can provide the level of detail and the accuracy that regulators need to ensure compliance. By providing direct access to the system, regulated institutions could "permission" a regulator to view transaction data instead of preparing and sending documents. Regulators could access data faster and easier.
- **Liquidity and capital improvement**. Liquidity costs are reduced by opening up the market to foreign exchange traders who can participate via smart contracts on the ledger.
- **Fraud minimization**. It is easier to determine the provenance of funds or assets and establishment of transaction history within a "single source of truth."
- **Cost savings**. A global payments system leveraged on DLT would reduce the number of participants required for it to function and increase operational efficiency, thus reducing costs. While this model may seem a mere conjecture, and indeed there are several critical conditions to be overcome before it is ever commercialized, momentum in the 'blockchain solutions' industry has been growing steadily since about 2013.

3. The Emerging Blockchain-Tech Industry

"Blockchain technology" (also referred to as DLT, but collectively referred to herein as blockchain technology) is outpacing virtual currency in terms of both investment and hype. One report has predicted that by 2017, 80 percent of banks worldwide would be experimenting with blockchain technology in one way or another.[48] From 2013–2016, more than USD 1.4 billion has been invested in blockchain projects and more than 2,500 blockchain-related patents have been filed.[49]

Technology providers. In addition to legacy technology companies such as IBM and Intel, which have their own blockchain projects, an estimated 60 new companies are dedicated exclusively to blockchain.[50] These companies may be providing general infrastructure services using blockchains to register and store information, transfer value, and create and enforce smart contracts. Others provide specific services over a blockchain network. For example, Ripple uses a technology with some blockchain features as a payments settlement rail to enable businesses to send and receive

---

48. *Id.* at 14.
49. *Id.*
50. Hileman, *supra* note 33, at slide 13.

payments in local currency.[51] Their technology uses a netting process of IOUs not unlike that currently used in banking operations. The types of products, technological maturity, and targeted use cases vary.

Blockchain consortia. Some of the biggest investors in blockchain technology are financial institutions and other large corporations. Technology companies such as R3 CEV, have led the creation of consortia made up of banks and other enterprises that collaborate on blockchain research and projects that address common pain points in the financial services ecosystem. Financial institutions, independently or collaboratively, are trialing blockchain technology and smart contracts for a range of use cases: payments, settlement, trade finance, system interoperability, corporate bonds, and more.

Public versus private. There are also public blockchains such as Ethereum, which, with its open software platform, supports the construction of prototypes and self-executing smart contracts making it a testing ground for blockchain solutions. Though bank consortia and technology companies may use these public blockchains for testing purposes, owing to regulatory obligations and other risks, any final blockchain infrastructure used by the financial services industry will likely be on a closed network viewable and accessible only to permissioned users.

III. LEGAL AND OPERATIONAL RISKS AND CHALLENGES

A virtual currency business providing payments-related services to end-users faces legal and operational risks distinct from a blockchain technology business that is primarily focused on building a platform or infrastructure-as-a-service application. The following highlights the key risks of both industries—legal, operational, and otherwise.

A. Risks for Virtual Currency Businesses

Price volatility. The price of bitcoin and other virtual currencies is volatile and can shift several percentage points during any given day. For example, over about six weeks in early 2017, the price of bitcoin fluctuated by as much as 32 percent.[52] A bitcoin trading exchange can see the value of its "inventory" change significantly from one day to the next. This poses challenges for businesses whose assets are held in virtual currency. Most virtual currency businesses hedge this risk by trading on exchanges and selling virtual currency for local currency.

Security. Virtual currency exchange platforms, even reputable ones, have been subject to serious security breaches, frauds, thefts, and losses. One notorious exchange

---

51. Marcel T. Rosner & Andrew Kang, *Understanding and Regulating Twenty-First Century Payment Systems: The Ripple Case Study*, 114 Mich. L. Rev. 649 (2015–2016).

52. Olga Kharif, *Bitcoin Price Sets Record on Trump Policy Uncertainties*, Bloomberg, Feb. 23, 2017, https://www.bloomberg.com/news/articles/2017-02-23/bitcoin-price-sets-intraday-record-on-trump -policy-uncertainties.

platform hack resulted in the theft of $72 million (or 119,756 BTC) worth of users' bitcoin from their wallets.[53] A virtual currency wallet can be hacked by obtaining a copy of the private key, which allows the thief to transfer all the bitcoin to another public address. This risk is both serious and high for businesses that have custody of user funds by possessing a private key associated with a user's virtual currency wallet.

Regulatory and legal uncertainty. Uncertainty remains as to whether and how certain business models engaged in virtual currency activity are subject to regulatory oversight. Some businesses are stuck in limbo because of ambiguity as to how the law applies to them or because new legal frameworks are still in a "pilot" phase. In the state of New York, the process of applying for a BitLicense, the special license for certain types of virtual currency-related business, is long and demanding.[54] In jurisdictions where new regulation of virtual currency businesses is pending but not yet published or in force, establishing a business model that will not fit with future regulatory obligations remains risky. Sections below will review regulatory responses to virtual currency in greater detail.

Negotiability. Virtual currency is not money according to the commercial legal tradition.[55] This is important because the possessor of money enjoys an exception to the *nemo dat quod non habet* principle (literally "no one gives what he doesn't have"). Money therefore passes free and clear of any prior claims or encumbrances.[56] Though the common law concept of money is broader than *legal tender* (which virtual currency certainly is not), virtual currency still falls short of being money. Where money is defined by statute, virtual currency is sometimes clearly out of scope. For example, the definition of money in the Uniform Commercial Code (U.C.C.) requires that money be issued by the state.[57] Since virtual currency is not issued by a government it cannot be money under the U.C.C. Since virtual currency is not money, the holder of virtual currency does not benefit from the holder in due course rights that the holder of cash money or a bill of exchange would possess. Although the innocent purchaser of virtual currency for value in the course of business may be protected from prior claims against him or her, the issue of negotiability is a major barrier to mainstream commercialization of virtual currency assets.[58]

---

53. Clare Baldwin, *Bitcoin Worth $72 Million Stolen from Bitfinex Exchange in Hong Kong*, REUTERS, Aug. 3, 2016, http://www.reuters.com/article/us-bitfinex-hacked-hongkong-idUSKCN10E0KP.
54. Suzanne Barlyn, *New York's Bitcoin Hub Dreams Fade with Licensing Backlog*, REUTERS, Oct. 31, 2016, http://www.reuters.com/article/us-bitcoin-regulations-dfs-idUSKBN12V0CM.
55. THE LAW OF BITCOIN, *supra* note 18.
56. Classic legal definition of money; *see* Moss v. Hancock [1899] 2 Q.B. 111, 116.
57. U.C.C. § 1-201(b)(24) (2013) ("medium of exchange currently authorized or adopted by a domestic or foreign government"). Virtual currency would likely be considered intangible personal property under the U.C.C. *See also* Jeanne L. Schroeder, *Bitcoin and the Uniform Commercial Code*, 24 U. MIAMI BUS. L. REV. 1 (2016).
58. THE LAW OF BITCOIN, *supra* note 18, at 189. Though the U.C.C. codifies various exceptions to nemo dat, it is not likely that virtual currency would meet any of them except for the protection of good faith purchasers. Exceptions include: negotiable instruments (section 3-203(b), protecting holders in due course); document of title (section 7-504(a), where delivered but not duly negotiated); securities (section 8-302(a), and goods (section 2-403(1)); and protecting good faith purchasers (section 9-320 (a)–(b), respecting security interests); Schroeder, *supra*, note 57.

A bankruptcy court judge has found that for the purpose of interpreting section 550(a) of the U.S. Bankruptcy Code relating to actions for fraudulent transfers, bitcoin should be classified as "intangible personal property."[59] While this interpretation is limited to fraudulent transfer actions, this result tends to confirm the nonmonetary status of bitcoin.[60] An analysis of Canadian law arrives at the same conclusions, albeit through slightly different means.[61] The lack of negotiability for an asset that is designed to be used as money is a serious impediment to the adoption of virtual currency as a means of transferring value in commerce.

Privacy. While bitcoin can be used to maintain payor/payee privacy through public key pseudonyms, the public history of all transactions creates unique privacy concerns. Once an identity is associated with a public address, it is possible to view all the bitcoin associated with that address as well as the transaction history. New cryptocurrencies, such as such as Zcash, may be able to preserve privacy by masking both transaction amounts and wallet IDs.

AML/KYC. Transactions between private users require no intermediaries, making AML monitoring extremely difficult (unless a public key is associated with an individual, creating a clear audit trail of the transaction). Many businesses engaged in virtual currency activities such as trading platforms that facilitate the transfer or exchange of virtual currency between users impose KYC on users for AML and anti-fraud purposes and monitor and report suspicious transactions whether or not those practices are imposed by regulators.

Irrevocable transactions. Virtual currency transactions are irrevocable and it is impossible to retrieve virtual currency sent to the wrong address without the cooperation of the recipient. Like cash, once virtual currency is transferred from one public address to another, it cannot be retrieved by appealing to an intermediary such as a payment processor or credit card arbitrator. But regardless of the means of payment, general legal principles are still in play, including the law of contract. A consumer wishing to exercise a contractual right to be refunded should be able to rely on legal recourse, though practical barriers, including jurisdictional constraints, remain.

Loss of key pair. The loss or destruction of a private key means losing any virtual currency associated with that key pair. Like dropping a chest of gold into the sea, you know it is there but can never access it again. Some businesses offer key backups or keep copies of a user's private keys to help users in such an event but doing so substantially heightens security and liability risks.

---

59. 11 U.S.C. § 550 (2006) (Liability of transferee of avoided transfer).

60. Classifying bitcoin as intangible personal property and not as currency allowed the trustee to recover the present value of bitcoin ($1.3 million). The Bankruptcy Code defines "intangible personal property" as something of value that cannot be touched or held, similar to a copyright or trademark. Hashfast Techs. LLC & Hashfast LLC v. Marc A. Lowe, No. 14-30725DM (Bankr. N.D. Cal. Feb. 19, 2016), http://www.esquireglobalcrossings.com/files/2016/09/Hashfast_order.pdf.

61. THE LAW OF BITCOIN, *supra* note 18, at 17–83.

Consumer adoption. For any virtual currency to be viable, the community of users trusting it must be big enough. Trust, whether or not built into a computer program, is something that is earned. Many people have no problem dealing with a bank to handle their funds and are not willing to assume the risks associated with virtual currency. This lack of trust may also be fuelled by virtual currency's association with criminal activity and the so-called dark web.

B. Risks and Challenges for Blockchain Technology[62]

Technological. Blockchain technology is so new that its success relies on many technological assumptions that have not yet been proven. For example, successful blockchain applications will need to be able to integrate other technological capabilities, to interoperate with other systems, and scale to meet volume requirements of an entire payments system while keeping up the speed and efficiency it promises. Perhaps most importantly, security must be sufficiently robust to induce the trust that will be needed for widespread adoption. None of these factors is beyond dispute.

Governance of distributed ledgers. Industrywide legal agreements on how the ledger would work are also needed to ensure a foundation for trust. This is easier said than done. The consensus structures for validating transactions and determining the true state of the ledger currently differs according to the type of blockchain. For public blockchains such as Bitcoin or Ethereum, anyone can participate in the consensus process. Other blockchains, sometimes called consortium or federated blockchains, are those where the consensus process is controlled by a preselected set of nodes, such as the financial institutions on a payments network. A private blockchain that centralizes permissions with one authority would not really be distributed.[63]

The hybrid style consortium model requires careful consideration as to governance, especially if the participants are highly regulated financial institutions. In addition to the role of validating transactions, careful consideration must be given to maintenance (such as decision making for technology investments or fixing any errors to the code) and standardization issues such as authentication services, and legal and regulatory compliance. Participants in a private blockchain will need to determine how decisions regarding a shared infrastructure will be made.

Where prudential regulation applies, how the system is operated and owned will require careful consideration and the involvement of regulators. A shared infrastructure with only some major institutions as participants or owners may bring antitrust issues into play. Since the maintenance or operation of a private blockchain will

62. The Future of Financial Infrastructure, supra note 7, at 53; Gavin Smith et al., Allens & Linklater, Blockchain Reaction (2016), available at http://www.allens.com.au/general/forms/pdf/blockchainreport .pdf?sku=fsdah5e556eqweqwg.

63. Vitalik Buterin, *On Public and Private Blockchains*, Ethereum Blog, Aug. 7, 2015, https://blog .ethereum.org/2015/08/07/on-public-and-private-blockchains/.

likely involve outsourcing either to an information technology (IT) service provider or a consortia-owned blockchain, rules regarding outsourcing for prudentially regulated entities will also need to be considered and may face challenges if a blockchain has no specific owner.[64]

Furthermore, the design will need to consider how errors are corrected and transactions reversed. Some jurisdictions such as Canada have a national payments association that establishes rules for participants and maintains the shared payments system. One wonders whether a regulatory need for a centralized authority would obviate some of the key benefits of blockchain technology.

Risk of error, mistake, or fraud. Blockchain and smart contracts must be error free and built to withstand malicious behavior with appropriate IT controls in place. One high-profile example of what can happen when vulnerabilities are discovered in smart contracts on public systems is the DAO. The DAO was a crowd-funded and crowd-run investment vehicle on the Ethereum blockchain that raised more than $100 million in ethers, the Ethereum virtual currency. Within a few weeks, hackers found "vulnerabilities" in the smart contract that allowed them to siphon off $50 million dollars.[65] With no centralized authority and, in this case, no way to identify the actual users of the DAO, there was little that the other funders could do. This incident resulted in the so-called Ethereum hard fork, a "software update" that was a rewriting of the transaction history to reverse the theft, which required the consensus of network participants to happen.[66]

Where the blockchain relies on smart contracts that execute automatically, mechanisms to correct errors will need to be contemplated. A blockchain is only as valid as the quality of the data on it, which may derive from multiple middle- and back-office systems. The possibility of data errors must be anticipated. If a contract were to execute automatically based on erroneous facts, it could be left to the courts to order the execution of the contract according to the intention of the parties.[67] Participants on a private consortium blockchain will want to determine in their rules how liability is apportioned for any transactions resulting from error or fraud.

The self-executing nature of smart contracts does not eliminate the requirement of the parties to abide by principles of common law and any other regulatory frameworks that may be applicable to the transaction, such as consumer protection law.

Role of regulators. Some central banks and national payments regulators have already been exploring blockchain for the national settlement system. However, any cross-border distributed ledger will need harmonization and collaboration between

---

64. Smith et al., *supra* note 62.

65. Klint Finley, *A $50 Million Hack Just Showed That the DAO Was All Too Human*, Wired, June 18, 2016, https://www.wired.com/2016/06/50-million-hack-just-showed-dao-human/.

66. Pete Rizzo, *Ethereum Hard Fork Creates Competing Currencies as Support for Ethereum Classic Rises*, CoinDesk, July 24, 2016, http://www.coindesk.com/ethereum-hard-fork-creates-competing-currencies -support-ethereum-classic-rises/.

67. Smith et al., *supra* note 62.

regulators, and this could be a challenge. Support and participation of regulators in blockchain innovation, which is already showing optimistic signs, will be crucial.

Standards and interoperability. Participating financial institutions and regulators will need to agree on which blockchain platform they will use and significant standardization for certain processes are needed to achieve efficiency gains. Aligning stakeholders will be a challenge where priorities and resources differ and significant time and investment is required to replace existing financial infrastructure.

Compliance and AML. In order to benefit from real-time compliance, participants on a blockchain such as money transfer businesses and banks will need to use a standard KYC dataset. Each institution's policies and processes for on-boarding customers differ and are subject to different requirements according to the jurisdiction in which they operate. Furthermore, the benefits of real time AML monitoring rely on technological assumptions that sophisticated AML platforms can be built and deployed.

Current financial services and payments legislation. The implementation of new financial infrastructure, including national and international payments systems and networks will likely require changes to regulations and perhaps even new legal and liability frameworks. If legacy payments systems migrate to a blockchain infrastructure, then any regulation that is not technology neutral will need to be revised. There is also the question of the nature of the asset on the blockchain and whether it is a token of true value or simply a form of IOU. This is particularly relevant with respect to implementing smart contracts, where issues of liability and governance must be addressed.[68]

Privacy and confidentiality. When the users of a network are financial institutions, it is not desirable for all parties on the network to receive all of the information about all of the transactions. Legal, regulatory, and business reasons that financial institutions have to keep transaction information private must be balanced with the benefits of transparency and accountability that come from an open system. The success of blockchain applications may thus depend on new technological means to protect financial privacy. It is possible to configure smart contracts and data on the blockchain so that sensitive data is hidden and only select data is exposed to specific participants at specific times. Participating institutions will need to establish privacy and security policies for the collection, use, transfer, and disclosure of customer data on a ledger, taking into account the immutability and permanency of the data record on the ledger.[69]

Liquidity. Most blockchain systems, including the original Bitcoin blockchain, rely on tokens, such as bitcoins or ethers that are native to that system. The expanded use of blockchain as financial infrastructure will likely require high levels of liquidity between the tokenized assets and fiat currency.[70] One possible solution for this

---

68. The Future of Financial Infrastructure, *supra* note 7, at 23.
69. Smith et al., *supra* note 62.
70. The Future of Financial Infrastructure, *supra* note 7, at 22.

would be digital currencies representing fiat currency issued by central banks. This would require policy changes and legal review of currency laws. Whether digital assets or tokens representing off-ledger assets are used, the associated legal implications need to be assessed.

IV. REGULATORY RESPONSES TO VIRTUAL CURRENCY AND BLOCKCHAIN TECHNOLOGY

Virtual currencies such as bitcoin are distinct from blockchain technology (whether permissioned or permissionless). The first refers to a unit of value or unit representing value while the latter refers to a type of infrastructure technology and record of truth that can serve many purposes, including recording the chain of possession and providing payment rails for the transfer of virtual currency. Though they are related, the legal and regulatory approaches for virtual currency and blockchain technology are distinct.

A. Virtual Currency

Regulators in most national jurisdictions have expressed concern about the risk of fraud, money laundering, and tax evasion associated with virtual currency along with the acknowledgment that regulations should avoid stifling innovation. Practically, the Bitcoin blockchain (and any other open, decentralized ledger) and network itself does not fit comfortably within any regulatory jurisdiction because instead of a central entity or financial intermediary running it, the network is maintained by validators (miners) who are unknown individuals or entities running the Bitcoin protocol on their computers. Because all you need is the Internet and people willing to use it, Bitcoin cannot be shut down.

However, bitcoin and other virtual currencies do not exist in a legal vacuum. Even where legislators have not taken steps to adopt or amend legislation specifically targeting virtual currency, those engaged in activities involving virtual currency are still subject to legal obligations. In some cases, the law is not clear or does not extend to new technologies where regulators or law enforcement believe it should. For example, tax laws, money transmission laws, and AML legislation can apply to holders, users, or businesses dealing in virtual currencies. These topics are addressed below in greater detail.

1. Defining Virtual Currency

Among the most frequent questions about the law and virtual currency is: *is it money?* We have already reviewed why virtual currency likely is not money under commercial law, but confusion remains owing to the reality that that virtual currency is characterized differently depending on the agency, its purpose, and jurisdiction. Court decisions equating virtual currency with money have done so narrowly within the confines of the facts and law in question. While virtual currency may be considered money for the purpose of certain legal interpretations and the application of specific laws, this is not indicative of its treatment across all legal domains (such as commercial law).

One of the most widely referenced definitions of virtual currency comes from the Financial Action Task Force (FATF), which has been frequently followed by other legislators or agencies. The FATF defines virtual currency as:

> a digital representation of value that can be digitally traded and functions as (1) a medium of exchange; and/or (2) a unit of account; and/or (3) a store of value, but does not have legal tender status (i.e., when tendered to a creditor, is a valid and legal offer of payment) in any jurisdiction. It is not issued nor guaranteed by any jurisdiction, and fulfills the above functions only by agreement within the community of users of the virtual currency.[71]

The FATF has identified virtual currency as being subject to higher money laundering and terrorist financing risks because it allows greater anonymity than traditional payment systems, it is easy to access, and it allows for the transfer of funds across any border.[72]

The U.S. Commodity Futures Trading Commission (CFTC) and the U.S. Internal Revenue Service (IRS) have also characterized bitcoin as either property or commodities for the purposes of enforcement of the laws under their jurisdiction. The IRS ruled in April 2014 that virtual currencies are property. Hence, the profit from an investment in virtual currencies is eligible for capital gains tax rates if held longer than one year.[73] By asserting that it is a commodity, the CFTC extended its regulatory jurisdiction over any leveraged, margined, or financed transaction of virtual currency. Subsequently, enforcement actions have been taken against platforms offering margin and options trading of virtual currency that were not properly registered.[74]

The Canada Revenue Agency also characterizes virtual currency as a commodity and when it is used to buy goods and services, these transactions are considered barter transactions.[75] Thus, the value of the goods and services provided should be included in the taxpayer's income and value added tax (VAT) should be applied to the value received.[76] The buying and selling of virtual currency for speculative

---

71. FINANCIAL ACTION TASK FORCE, *supra* note 17.

72. *Id.* at 11.

73. I.R.S. Notice 2014-21, 2014-16, IRB, *available at* https://www.irs.gov/pub/irs-drop/n-14-21.pdf.

74. Press Release, CFTC, CFTC Orders Bitcoin Exchange Bitfinex to Pay $75,000 for Offering Illegal Off-Exchange Financed Retail Commodity Transactions and Failing to Register as a Futures Commission Merchant (June 2, 2016), *available at* http://www.cftc.gov/PressRoom/PressReleases/pr7380-16; bitcoin falls within the definition of a "commodity" under section 1a(9) of the Commodity Exchange Act (CEA), Press Release, CFTC, CFTC Orders Bitcoin Options Trading Platform Operator and Its CEO to Cease Illegally Offering Bitcoin Options and to Cease Operating a Facility for Trading or Processing of Swaps without Registering (Sept. 17, 2015), *available at* http://www.cftc.gov/PressRoom/PressReleases/pr7231-15.

75. Study on the Use of Digital Currency before the Standing Senate Committee on Banking, Trade, and Commerce, Issue 6, 41st Parl., 2nd Sess. (2014).

76. For tax purposes, the fair market value of the goods or services provided in exchange for virtual currency will be used to calculate taxes payable.

purposes or as a store of value is taxable "like a commodity" and "resulting gains or losses could be taxable income or capital."[77] One of the outstanding questions for tax authorities in several jurisdictions is how VAT applies to the purchase and sale of virtual currency. In 2015, the European Court of Justice ruled that the exchange of traditional currency for units of virtual currency is exempt from VAT.[78]

The European Parliament and European Council's second Electronic Money Directive governs the issuance of e-money and sets the standards by which e-money products are issued and operated. A closer look at the definition of e-money under the directive clearly excludes virtual currencies such as bitcoin from its scope because e-money is classified as monetary value represented as a claim on the issuer.[79] This characteristic is absent with decentralized, open, permissionless virtual currency such as bitcoin where there is no "issuer."

2. AML

One of the first U.S. agencies to take a position on virtual currency was the U.S. Treasury Department's Financial Crimes Enforcement Network (FinCEN) when it issued an interpretive guidance in March 2013 clarifying the applicability of the Bank Secrecy Act to certain parties dealing in convertible virtual currencies.[80] "Exchangers" and "administrators," defined as a person engaged as a business "in the exchange of virtual currency for real currency, funds, or other virtual currency" and "in issuing (putting into circulation) a virtual currency and who has the authority to redeem (withdraw from circulation) such virtual currency," respectively, are considered money transmitters under FinCEN's regulations and are thus subject to the BSA.[81] FinCEN has issued a number of rulings relating to the types of activities that qualify a person as an exchanger or administrator and have confirmed that a virtual currency trading platform is considered a money transmitter while excluding miners, those trading virtual currency for personal use or investment, and users who obtain virtual currency and use it to buy or sell goods.[82]

The position taken by regulators in other jurisdictions has been similar in focusing on certain types of businesses as being subject to AML laws, rather than users

---

77. Canada Revenue Agency, *What You Should Know about Digital Currency*, http://www.cra-arc .gc.ca/nwsrm/fctshts/2013/m11/fs131105-eng.html (last modified Dec. 3, 2014). If a taxpayer is in the business of buying and selling virtual currency, the gain is fully taxable as an income transaction. If it is an investment, only half of the gains are taxable as a capital transaction.

78. Press Release, Court of Justice of the European Union, The Exchange of Traditional Currencies for Units of the "Bitcoin" Virtual Currency Is Exempt from VAT (Oct. 22, 2015), *available at* http://curia .europa.eu/jcms/upload/docs/application/pdf/2015-10/cp150128en.pdf.

79. Directive 2009/110/EC of the European Parliament and of the Council of 16 September 2009 on the Taking Up, Pursuit, and Prudential Supervision of the Business of Electronic Money Institutions Amending Directives 2005/60/EC and 2006/48/EC, 2009 O.J. (L 267) 7 (E.U.).

80. FinCEN, Application of FinCEN's Regulations to Persons Administering, Exchanging, or Using Virtual Currencies (Mar. 18, 2013), *available at* https://www.fincen.gov/sites/default/files/shared/FIN-2013-G001.pdf.

81. Note that FinCEN divides virtual currency into two categories: centralized and decentralized virtual currencies. Both types apply to their interpretation. "Administrators" only applies to centralized virtual currency systems.

82. FinCEN, *supra* note 80; The Law of Bitcoin, *supra* note 18, at 199.

of virtual currency. The European Commission has proposed bringing "virtual currency exchange platforms and custodian wallet providers under the scope of the Anti-Money Laundering Directive" to prevent the misuse of virtual currencies for money laundering and terrorist financing purposes.[83] Canada's Proceeds of Crime (Money Laundering) Terrorist Financing Act (PCMLTFA) requires certain persons and entities such as money services businesses to comply with obligations under the act, including recordingkeeping, KYC, reporting suspicious transactions, and registration with the Financial Transactions and Reports Centre (FINTRAC), Canada's financial crime reporting agency. In 2014, the PCMLTFA was amended to expand the scope of application of this law to "persons and entities that have a place of business in Canada and that are engaged in the business of dealing in virtual currencies, as defined in the regulations." The act also applies to persons and entities that do not have a place of business in Canada, which means that banks may not provide banking services for persons or entities dealing in virtual currency that do not have a place of business in Canada unless that person or entity is registered with FINTRAC.[84] The corresponding regulations are not yet in place and as a result these changes are not yet in force as of March 2017. The government has indicated that virtual currency businesses subject to the law will be exchanges and trading platforms but not individuals.

3. Case Law

Not many cases have been rendered yet on the legal status of virtual currency (at the time of writing). One of the first was the prosecution of a Ponzi scheme using bitcoin brought by the U.S. Securities and Exchange Commission (SEC), in *SEC v. Shavers*.[85] The defendants had run an investment scheme promising a 7 percent weekly return on bitcoin purchased by the clients through bitcoin arbitrage. The SEC argued that the offering of bitcoin as investments gave the illusion that they were securities.[86] The court ruled that bitcoin acted as a form of money, was used towards a common enterprise (the market expertise of Shavers), and there was an expectation of profits. Thus, bitcoin can be used as the basis of an investment contract.[87] In another case, the SEC has also fined individuals accepting virtual currency for the sale of securities without proper registration filings.[88]

In criminal cases, courts have rejected the defense that because bitcoin is not "money" it cannot be used to commit financial crimes, and in some cases it has been

83. Press Release, European Commission, Commission Strengthens Transparency Rules to Tackle Terrorism Financing, Tax Avoidance, and Money Laundering (July 5, 2016), *available at* http://europa.eu/rapid/press-release_IP-16-2380_en.htm.

84. *Economic Action Plan 2014 Act, No. 1, S.C. 2014, ch. 20, §§ 256, 256(2), 258, amends Proceeds of Crime (Money Laundering) and Terrorist Financing Act, S.C. 2001, ch. 17, §§ 5, 5(h)(h.1), 9.31(1).*

85. SEC v. Shavers, No. 4:13-CV-416 (E.D. Tex. Sept. 18, 2014).

86. *Id.*

87. *Id.*

88. *In the Matter of* Erik T. Voorhees, Administrative Proceeding File No. 3-15902, *available at* https://www.sec.gov/litigation/admin/2014/33-9592.pdf.

qualified as money under the common meaning of the word or certain criminal law provisions.[89] In *United States v. Ulbricht*,[90] Mr. Ulbricht was accused of having created, owned, and operated the Silk Road website, which functioned as a marketplace for illegal goods and services and included a bitcoin-based payment system that allowed buyers and sellers to conceal their identities. One of Mr. Ulbricht's arguments was that since bitcoins are not "money" or "funds" he could not be guilty of money laundering. The court rejected this and found that bitcoin can be considered "funds" under 18 U.S.C. § 1956 because it can be used to pay for things. The court found that the money laundering statute was "broad enough to encompass use of bitcoins in financial transactions."[91] The treatment of virtual currency by courts is by no means uniform and is highly dependent on the facts of the case.[92]

4. Money Transfer Businesses

State money transmission laws, in general, do not impose different obligations on virtual currency businesses than other money transmitters. Some states have amended legislation to expand and/or clarify the definition of the business of money transmission to regulate activities undertaken with virtual currency. For example, North Carolina amended their Money Transmitters Act (MTA)[93] to encompass certain virtual currency activities. The business of money transmission requires a license and one is engaged in the business of money transmission when they solicit or advertise money transmission services from a website that someone in North Carolina can access. According to the new amendments, money transmission involves "receiving money or monetary value for transmission or holding funds incidental to transmission within the United States or to locations abroad by any means . . . primarily for personal, family or household purposes. This includes maintaining control of virtual currency on behalf of others."[94]

By expanding money transmission to include maintaining control of virtual currency on behalf of others, North Carolina's MTA captures virtual currency wallet providers and trading platforms that have custodial services exercising some degree of control over the users' virtual currency, for example, through multisig wallets or private key backups. Exchange services that hold customer funds, even

---

89. *See* United States v. Faiella, No. 14-cr-243, at 47 (S.D.N.Y. Aug. 18, 2014) (mem. order); United States v. Ulbricht, No. 14-CR-68 (S.D.N.Y. July 9, 2014); *Shavers*, No. 4:13-CV-416; United States v. Liberty Reserve et al., No. 13-CR-368 (S.D.N.Y Sept. 23, 2015).

90. *Ulbricht*, No. 14-CR-68, at 5.

91. *Id.* at 49–50.

92. *See for example* Order Granting Defendant's Motion to Dismiss the Information, Florida v. Espinoza, No. F14-2923 (11th Cir. July 22, 2016).

93. Chris Finney, *North Carolina Introduces #Bitlicence for Virtual Currency Exchanges and Wallet Providers*, Lexology, July 7, 2016, http://www.lexology.com/library/detail.aspx?g=324ce96e-dc91-4a55-9e 0e-5d2d56002418&utm_source=Lexology+Daily+Newsfeed&utm_medium=HTML+email+-+Body+-+General +section&utm_campaign=Lexology+subscriber+daily+feed&utm_content=Lexology+Daily+Newsfeed+2016 -07-11&utm_term=.

94. North Carolina Money Transmitters Act, N.C. Gen. Stat. § 53-208.42(13)(b) (2015), *available at* http://www.ncleg.net/Applications/BillLookUp/LoadBillDocument.aspx?SessionCode=2015&DocNum =1327&SeqNum=0.

for a short period in order to arrange a buy/sell order and facilitate the exchange of virtual/fiat currency between parties, may also be considered money transmitters under the law.

Note that some of the bigger virtual currency businesses have taken steps to obtain money transmitter licenses even before laws were amended requiring such licenses.[95] Legislative activity in this domain is fast paced, and much may have occurred since this chapter was written. New Hampshire has amended its money transmission laws to include virtual currency businesses, and proposals have been forwarded in Florida, California, Georgia, New York, Pennsylvania, Tennessee, and Wyoming.[96] Wallet software providers of multisig solutions, wallet services that have no custody or control of the wallets, users of virtual currency, and miners are often beyond the scope of money transmission legislation.

The state of New York stands out internationally with its "BitLicense" regulatory framework.[97] The regime is separate from money transmission laws and is aimed to "put in place guardrails that protect consumers and root out illicit activity—without stifling beneficial innovation."[98] The law applies to financial intermediaries holding customers' funds in virtual currency and requires such entities to have a special license in order to conduct business in the state of New York.[99] The license approval process requires a background investigation by the superintendent of the New York State Department of Financial Services and a $5,000 fee. After becoming a license holder, a business must comply with a rigorous regulatory framework, including the requirements to hold capital in an amount deemed sufficient by the superintendent, obtain a surety bond in U.S. dollars, ensure cybersecurity, provide consumer data protection, follow AML policies, and disclose any material risks to the business and its customers.[100] The superintendent's prior written approval is needed to introduce any new product, service, or activity, or to make a material change to an existing product or service.[101] In addition to submitting quarterly financial statements,

95. Charles M. Horn, Melissa R.H. Hall, Michael M. Philipp & Sarah V. Riddell, *North Carolina Captures Bitcoin Custodians in New Money Transmitter Law*, Lexology, July 15, 2016, http://www.lexology.com/library/detail.aspx?g=48870bcd-4bde-4f56-9b49-2692c65de167&utm_source=Lexology+Daily+Newsfeed&utm_medium=HTML+email+-+Body+-+General+section&utm_campaign=Lexology+subscriber+daily+feed&utm_content=Lexology+Daily+Newsfeed+2016-07-18&utm_term.

96. N.H. Rev. Stat. Ann. § 399-G:1 (2015); Luke Parker, *New Hampshire Money Transmitter Rule Change Will Include Bitcoin Businesses*, BraveNewCoin, Dec. 8, 2015, http://bravenewcoin.com/news/new-hampshire-money-transmitter-rule-change-will-include-bitcoin-businesses/; Vic Lance, *State Regulation Changes the Game for Bitcoin Sellers in New Hampshire*, CoinDesk, Mar. 19, 2016, http://www.coindesk.com/state-regulation-changes-the-game-for-bitcoin-in-new-hampshire/; Stan Higgins, *Florida Senator Drafting Bill That Could Recognize Bitcoin as Money*, CoinDesk, Sept. 6, 2016, http://www.coindesk.com/florida-senator-drafting-bill-recognize-bitcoin-money/.

97. N.Y. Comp. Codes R. & Regs. tit. 23.

98. Michael J. de la Merced, *Bitcoin Rules Completed by New York Regulator*, N.Y. Times, June 3, 2015, https://www.nytimes.com/2015/06/04/business/dealbook/new-york-regulator-announces-final-rules-on-bitcoin.html?_r=0.

99. Virtual currency under the regulations includes any type of digital unit that is utilized as a medium of exchange or as a form of digitally stored value.

100. N.Y. Comp. Codes R. & Regs. tit. 23., §§ 200.7, 200.8, 200.9, *available at* http://www.dfs.ny.gov/legal/regulations/adoptions/dfsp200t.pdf.

101. *Id.* § 200.10.

license holders are also subject to examination of their business and their financial condition at least once every two years.[102]

The BitLicense licensing, disclosure, and reporting obligations may legitimize license holders and facilitate consumer confidence and their ability to do business with traditional financial institutions. Conversely, many have criticized the rules as being too strict, limiting the potential of this developing industry. The developers of the BitLicense were early advocates of virtual currency who apparently desired to attract businesses to their jurisdiction. However, following its coming into force in June 2015, only two BitLicenses had been issued, and another 15 applications were still pending as of October 2016.[103] The regulations have a "safe harbor" provision that deems any business that filed an application within 45 days of the law coming into force to be in compliance with the licensing requirements unless advised otherwise by the superintendent.[104]

The New York approach is one of two policy approaches towards regulating virtual currency businesses: light versus tough. Some regulators and policy makers have taken a light touch approach or have decided to "wait and see" how the industry develops. While jurisdictions such as New York opted for tougher regulations, presumably to eliminate the regulatory uncertainty that many virtual currency businesses encounter as an obstacle to doing business, other government bodies such as the Canadian Senate have suggested the technology requires a light-touch approach.[105] The downside of a BitLicense approach is that the regulations themselves can be a barrier to entry, especially if the licensing process takes many months. Several virtual currency businesses have decided that the New York BitLicense is "not worth the effort."[106]

The only Canadian province with specific money transmitter legislation is Quebec. Quebec's regulatory authority responsible for enforcing the Money-Services Businesses Act issued guidance in February 2015 stating that virtual currency ATMs and virtual currency trading platforms must obtain a license to operate in Quebec.[107]

B. Blockchain Technology

Public, open, permissionless ledgers such as Bitcoin or Ethereum have received different regulatory responses from the permissioned private ledgers being built by

---

102. *Id.* §§ 200.14, 200.13.

103. Barlyn, *supra* note 54.

104. N.Y. Comp. Codes R. & Regs. tit. 23., § 200.21, *available at* http://www.dfs.ny.gov/legal/regulations /adoptions/dfsp200t.pdf.

105. Barlyn, *supra* note 54; Report to the Standing Senate Committee on Banking, Trade, and Commerce, Digital Currency: You Can't Flip this Coin! 13 (June 18, 2015), *available at* https://sencanada.ca/Content/SEN /Committee/412/banc/rep/rep12jun15-e.pdf.

106. Barlyn, *supra* note 54.

107. Press Release, Autorité des Marchés Financiers, Virtual Currency ATMs and Trading Platforms Must Be Authorized (Feb. 12, 2015), *available at* https://www.lautorite.qc.ca/en/press-releases-2015 -corpo.html_2015_virtual-currency-atms-and-trading-platforms-must-be-authorized12-02-2015-09-4.html.

financial institutions and technology companies. With permissioned or private blockchains (see Section I.A.2 above), the technology can be used for many purposes and can crosscut many sectors and regulatory jurisdictions. The actors using the technology are likely to be subject to the same regulatory framework as the infrastructure the blockchain technology replaces. For example, a payments network replaced or augmented by blockchain technology may need new legal agreements between the participants and the operator. While it is too soon to tell what will become of this technology, regulators generally are intrigued or excited about the potential of blockchain as a tool to provide greater transparency and reduced costs. For example, the CFTC commissioner has emphasized that regulators across the board should take a no-harm strategy inspired by the way the Internet was left to develop in the 1990s.[108] A June 2016 resolution adopted by the European Parliament also supported a "hands-off" approach to the regulation of blockchain.[109] The CFTC commissioner also called for a coordinated regulatory response to blockchain technology, echoing other regulators that it should be addressed multilaterally and not be fragmented by jurisdiction.[110] One early stand out is the state of Vermont, which adopted legislation to recognize blockchain data as admissible in court as "authentic" under certain conditions.[111]

Some regulators and governments are even participating in blockchain consortia efforts, such as the Bank of Canada.[112] This can be seen as part of a broader trend of regulatory authorities cautiously supporting new technology in the financial services industry through special programs such as regulatory sandboxes or new types of banking licenses.[113] The United Kingdom's Financial Conduct Authority is another regulator that has opted to give innovators space to develop and is engaging in discussion with industry before regulating.[114]

---

108. CFTC Commissioner J. Christopher Giancarlo, Special Address before the Depository Trust & Clearing Corp. 2016 Blockchain Symposium (Mar. 29, 2016), http://www.cftc.gov/PressRoom /SpeechesTestimony/opagiancarlo-13.

109. *Report on Virtual Currencies*, Eur. Parl., Comm. on Economic and Monetary Affairs, Doc. No. A8-0168/2016 (2016), *available at* http://www.europarl.europa.eu/sides/getDoc.do?pubRef=-//EP //TEXT+REPORT+A8-2016-0168+0+DOC+XML+V0//EN.

110. Giancarlo, *supra* note 108; Greg Medcraft, *Blockchain: How We Can Harness the Benefits of this New Technology While Mitigating the Risks*, MARKETVOICE, Jan. 2016, at 23.

111. Thomas Moore, *Vermont Breaks New Ground in Cryptocurrency Technology*, DCEBRIEF, May 23, 2016, https://dcebrief.com/vermont-breaks-new-ground-in-cryptocurrency-technology/; Cory Dawson, *Vt. Eager for Blockchain, but Agencies Slow to Change*, BURLINGTON FREE PRESS, July 26, 2016, http://www .burlingtonfreepress.com/story/news/local/vermont/2016/07/26/vt-eager-blockchain-but-agencies-slow -change/87524558/; http://legislature.vermont.gov/bill/status/2016/H.868.

112. Ethan Lou & Leah Schnurr, *Bank of Canada Studies Payments System Using Tech Behind Bitcoin*, REUTERS, June 16, 2016, http://www.reuters.com/article/us-canada-cenbank-payments-idUSKCN0Z22F9.

113. Rachel Witkowski, Telis Demos & Peter Rudegeair, *Regulator Will Start Issuing Bank Charters for Fintech Firms*, WALL ST. J., Dec. 2, 2016, https://www.wsj.com/articles/regulator-will-start -issuing-bank-charters-for-fintech-firms-1480691712; Michael del Castillo, *The Swiss Government Is Paving the Way for Crypto Banks*, COINDESK, Nov. 18, 2016, http://www.coindesk.com/swiss-government -paving-way-bitcoin-blockchain-banks/.

114. *See* Financial Conduct Authority, *Fintech and Innovative Businesses*, https://www.fca.org.uk /firms/fintech-and-innovative-businesses (last visited May 20, 2017); Financial Conduct Authority, *Regulatory Sandbox*, https://www.fca.org.uk/firms/innovate-innovation-hub/regulatory-sandbox (last updated Apr. 21, 2017).

V. CONCLUSION

Virtual currency and its most ubiquitous use-case, bitcoin, as well as the distributed ledger technology platforms and services that have burst onto the financial services industry in recent years, have the potential to seriously impact the payments land-scape. These disruptions will not happen overnight. As this chapter has demon-strated, there are many unknowns and obstacles to be overcome. Development is fast-paced and catching the attention of technology companies, financial technology companies (fintechs), financial institutions, and all of the governmental and regu-latory apparatus that oversee these players. This chapter reviewed some, not all, of the highlights with respect to this domain, but lawyers must be vigilant about changes to the legal framework, of which we can certainly expect more to come.

Chapter 6

Emerging Technologies

In Pursuit of Consumers—
Merchant Payments via Contextual Commerce

Sean Ruff and Crystal Kaldjob

Emerging payment technologies are changing the way in which merchants and the financial services industry operate. The introduction of new business models, new players entering the financial services space, and new and innovative methods of customer service have all significantly impacted one of the most important interactions between merchants and customers—payments.

Against this backdrop, this chapter addresses the concept of "contextual commerce" as a private-label vehicle for merchants to target both existing and potential customers outside of traditional merchant e-commerce channels, including social media platforms and other web-based consumer gathering points. In doing so, this chapter discusses some of the key legal and regulatory considerations that govern the application of these types of payment transactions, including the use of digital wallets and stored value. While it is beyond the scope of this chapter to cover all legal and regulatory issues that may impact payments facilitated via contextual commerce, those legal and regulatory issues identified represent a collection of the most interesting and, in some cases, difficult applications of current law.

Sean Ruff is of counsel in the Financial Services Practice Group of Morrison & Foerster LLP and co-chair of the firm's Fintech Practice Group. Crystal Kaldjob is an associate in the Financial Services Practice Group of Morrison & Foerster LLP.

I. INTRODUCTION

The technological capability of smartphones and other portable electronic devices that can access the Internet has increased dramatically.[1] These capabilities have taken advantage of improvements in communication enabled by mobile phones and mobile "apps" and combined them with existing payment platforms, thus facilitating more efficient payment communications between the payment parties (e.g., merchants and holders of debit cards and credit cards). This enhanced functionality has led to the development of new ways for consumers to engage in traditional financial services transactions, which have transformed the payments industry by establishing new channels through which merchants can seamlessly interact with consumers.[2]

The notion that merchants can enable consumers to execute purchase transactions via channels not typically associated with a merchant's physical or virtual location is not new.[3] But as much as the smartphone and other electronic portable devices have changed the face of payments, so too have these devices changed the way consumers lead their lives.[4] For example, the proportion of online time Americans spend on their mobile devices increased from 12.7 percent in 2008 to 54.6 percent in 2015.[5] As smartphones become more prevalent, users tend to access their social networks more on their mobile devices. At the end of 2013, 98 percent of time spent on Instagram was via mobile device, 92 percent for Pinterest, 86 percent for Twitter, and 68 percent for Facebook.[6] As more of a consumer's time is spread among an ever-growing number of social media platforms, merchants find it necessary to interact with consumers in these consumer-dictated contexts, as opposed to merchant-defined contexts.

This concept of dealing with a consumer on the consumer's own terms is sometimes referred to as "contextual commerce," which embodies the idea that consumers can make purchases seamlessly inside the environments that they use regularly

---

1. Hemant Bhargava, David Evans & Deepa Mani, *The Move to Smart Mobile Platforms: Implications for Antitrust Analysis of Online Markets in Developed and Developing Countries*, 16 U.C. Davis Bus. L.J. 157, 162 (2016) ("This new generation of phones employs a full-blown operating system and has essentially unlimited capabilities, primarily because they enable end-users to install third-party application programs (or 'apps'). Leveraging Internet standards and cloud computing, these small portable devices imported the full power of modern computing, through easy-to-use apps connected with powerful computers, software, and data over the Internet."). Additionally, smartphone ownership has risen from 44 percent of U.S. adults in 2011 to 77 percent in 2016. Board of Governors of the Federal Reserve System, Consumers and Mobile Financial Services 2016, at 4 (2016) [hereinafter Consumers and Mobile Financial Services 2016], *available at* https://www.federalreserve.gov/econresdata/consumers-and-mobile-financial-services-report-201603.pdf.
2. Consumers and Mobile Financial Services 2016, *supra* note 1, at 1, 16–17; *see* Bhargava, Evans & Mani, *supra* note 1, at 161.
3. *See* Douglas Arner, Janos Barberis & Ross Buckley, *The Evolution of FinTech: A New Post-Crisis Paradigm?*, 47 Geo. J. Int'l L. 1271 (2016).
4. Carolyn Lowry, *What's in Your Mobile Wallet: An Analysis of Trends in Mobile Payments and Regulation*, 68 Fed. Comm. L.J. 353, 357 (2016).
5. Bhargava, Evans & Mani, *supra* note 1, at 168.
6. Pengtao Li, *Current and Future Years of E-Commerce*, *in* 1 Encyclopedia of E-Commerce Development, Implementation, and Management 1031, 1031 (In Lee ed., 2016).

for other reasons.[7] The idea that, with the touch of a button, consumers could buy anything, anywhere, at any time was the impetus behind the effort of several high-profile social media platforms to operationalize contextual commerce.[8]

For example, in September 2014, Twitter began the rollout of its "buy button" technology, which allowed a consumer to purchase a product directly from a tweet.[9] With the initial rollout of the buy button, a small percentage of U.S. users would see a buy button on tweets from Twitter's test partners.[10] After hitting the Twitter buy button, customers received additional product details and then could enter shipping and payment information.[11] By September 2015, Twitter joined with several e-commerce platforms to make it easier for merchants to sell products with buy-button tweets.[12]

Pinterest followed Twitter with the launch of its buy-button technology in mid-2015. Prior to launching the Pinterest buy button, users interested in buying an item would be directed to the retailer's website, where the user would have to search for the item again.[13] The Pinterest buy button launched with several large retailer partners, including Macy's, Nordstrom, and Neiman Marcus.[14] When purchasing with the Pinterest buy button, users were able to scroll through different views of a product and select product colors.[15] The Pinterest buy button allowed checkout using a credit card.[16]

Instagram launched its buy-button technology in November 2016,[17] with just 20 retail partners.[18] With Instagram's buy button, when one of the partner brands posts a picture on Instagram, users can tap a button to make prices appear for up to five pictured items.[19] A user can then tap one of the items to shop for it on the brand's website though Instagram's in-app browser.[20] Facebook first started testing

---

7. Karen Webster, *Why Contextual Commerce Is the Next Big Thing*, PYMNTS.COM, Apr. 4, 2016, http://www.pymnts.com/news/merchant-innovation/2016/why-contextual-commerce-is-the-next-big-thing/.

8. *See* MONICA GONCALVES & PETTERI RAATIKAINEN, HOW SOCIAL MEDIA PLATFORMS WILL REVOLUTIONIZE RETAIL SHOPPING: A SHOWROOMING AND WEBROOMING ANALYSIS (2012), *available at* https://www.contextuallearning.nl/wp-content/uploads/2016/02/Group_Assignment_356509_354079.pdf.

9. Erin McCarthy, *Twitter Tests Mobile Commerce with "Buy" Button*, WALL ST. J., Sept. 8, 2014, https://www.wsj.com/articles/twitter-tests-mobile-commerce-with-buy-button-1410183730.

10. *Id.*

11. *Id.*

12. Yoree Koh, *Twitter Makes Click-Through Purchases Easier*, WALL ST. J., Sept. 30, 2015, https://www.wsj.com/articles/twitter-makes-click-through-purchases-easier-1443618000.

13. Yoree Koh, *Pinterest to Soon Add a "Buy" Button*, WALL ST. J., June 2, 2015, https://www.wsj.com/articles/pinterest-to-soon-add-a-buy-button-news-digest-1433289211.

14. *Id.*

15. *Id.*

16. *Id.*; Yoree Koh, *Pinterest Hits 100 Million Monthly Users in Bid for Ad-Search Dollars*, WALL ST. J., Sept. 17, 2015, https://blogs.wsj.com/digits/2015/09/17/pinterest-hits-100-million-monthly-users-in-bid-for-ad-search-dollars/.

17. Nathan Olivarez-Giles, *Instagram Adds "Shop Now" Button for In-App Impulse Buying*, WALL ST. J., Nov. 1, 2016, https://www.wsj.com/articles/instagram-adds-shop-now-button-for-in-app-impulse-buying-1478041969.

18. *Id.*

19. *Id.*

20. *Id.*

buy buttons on users' news feed pages, posts, and ads in 2014.[21] More recently, Facebook launched technology that facilitates a merchant's ability to add a buy button to artificial intelligence (AI) bot interactions with a consumer through the Messenger app.[22]

Each of these implementations was an effort to reach consumers more effectively to turn "social engagements" into sales.[23] With nearly 80 percent of the U.S. population using social media, and with this percentage expected to increase each year, buy-button technology can link customers within social media apps to merchants, and thereby enable merchants to reach these customers.[24]

Despite the advantages of contextual commerce in targeting interested consumers, the friction caused by the underlying payment function may continue to present barriers to consumer acceptance.[25] While transaction friction is an issue that has beleaguered online payments generally,[26] it appears that it may play a significant role in the consumer failure to embrace buy-button and other related technology meant to facilitate contextual commerce.[27] For example, contextual commerce solutions that effectively target consumers, but then redirect the consumer back to the merchant's own website to complete a purchase transaction, have seen reduced conversion rates.[28] Add to the process an inefficient payments flow, such as a consumer having to key in various pieces of information such as user name, password, or billing information, and the rate of transaction abandonment increases significantly.[29]

Given such challenges, potential solutions are beginning to appear. For example, ride-sharing platforms such as Uber have attempted to address the issue of

---

21. Josh Constine, *Facebook Tests Buy Button to Let You Purchase Stuff without Leaving Facebook*, TechCrunch, July 17, 2014, https://techcrunch.com/2014/07/17/facebook-buy-button/.

22. Stephanie Condon, *Facebook Messenger Adds Buy Button, Native Payments*, ZDNet, Sept. 12, 2016, http://www.zdnet.com/article/facebook-messenger-adds-buy-button-native-payments/.

23. *See* Goncalves & Raatikainen, *supra* note 8.

24. Statista, *Number of Social Network Users in the United States from 2015 to 2021 (in Millions)*, https://www.statista.com/statistics/278409/number-of-social-network-users-in-the-united-states/ (last visited May 20, 2017).

25. *Contextual Commerce: From Single-Purpose Apps to All-in-One Platforms*, Let's Talk Payments, Aug. 29, 2016, https://letstalkpayments.com/contextual-commerce-from-single-purpose-apps-to-all-in-one -platforms/.

26. *Why Paying and Buying Should Break Up at Checkout*, PYMNTS.com, Feb. 26, 2016 (noting that checkout friction and shopping cart abandonment is "plaguing online merchants"), http://www.pymnts .com/news/ecommerce/2016/why-paying-and-buying-should-break-up-at-checkout/.

27. Karen Webster, *What's More Valuable—A Buy Button or a Digital Wallet?*, July 13, 2015 (noting the "obvious" limitation of buy buttons—"they can only be used on the site that is enabling it"), http://www .pymnts.com/news/2015/whats-more-valuable-a-buy-button-or-a-digital-wallet/.

28. Ashwin Shirvaikar, *Contextual Commerce*, *in* Disruptive Innovations IV: Ten More Things to Stop and Think About 22 (Citi 2016), *available at* https://ir.citi.com/TRk1lgLXY1sehGYbkjzU8ZK8ajrDvDGgoUxZKCl2 Cv2nKapNyHQQ4cYJkWzeg5c0JjxlYbk337o%3D.

29. Michael Cheng, *Braintree: Frictionless, Invisible Mobile Payments Are Crucial for Businesses*, Payment Wk., July 31, 2015, http://paymentweek.com/2015-7-31-braintree-frictionless-invisible-mobile -payments-are-crucial-for-businesses-7884/.

payments friction by making payment for a transaction all but invisible.[30] The luxury of being able to exit a car at one's destination without having to worry about the physical payment transaction cannot be overstated.[31] And the card-on-file payment process that runs in the background serves as the cloaking device for the physical payment process, without which a quick exit from the car free from fumbling for (or worrying about) a payment method would be impossible.[32]

While centrally stored payment credentials within a digital wallet (or similar device) may alleviate at least some of the friction that can arise in contextual payments transactions, other solutions such as centralized stored-balance accounts have the potential of addressing the issue as well.[33] Nevertheless, facilitating a true "one button" contextual payments solution in which consumers can seamlessly pay for goods and services across many different digital platforms without having to visit other websites or provide substantial additional information to complete the transaction will require collaboration and partnership across many entities, including merchants, payment processors, and digital platforms.[34]

As with most issues concerning financial services, the legal framework upon which contextual commerce payments are built is complex, including a mix of federal and state laws and regulations. While other chapters in this book address these laws and regulations in greater detail, the remainder of this chapter will provide an overview of *some* of the most important legal and regulatory issues that face participants in this area, with an emphasis on laws that may provide the greatest functional hurdle for participants in contextual commerce payments. These include state money transmission laws and the prospect of state money transmitter licensing; federal Bank Secrecy Act (BSA) compliance; federal laws aimed at services that provide stored value; as well as nonlegal frameworks, such as the Payment Card Industry Data Security Standards (PCI DSS), and the implications of that framework for contextual commerce stakeholders.

---

30. Aaron Strout, *Frictionless Mobile Commerce: 5 Examples of Companies That Are Leading*, Marketing Land, May 1, 2014, http://marketingland.com/frictionless-commerce-5-examples-companies-leading-81351.

31. *See id.* (noting that "Uber is a godsend" because it is so "frictionless"; "when you are done with your ride, you just get out of the car").

32. *See* Karen Webster, *Is "The Uber Experience" Really the Future of Payments?*, PYMNTS.com, Aug. 11, 2014, http://www.pymnts.com/news/2014/is-the-uber-experience-really-the-future-of-payments/.

33. This includes centralized stored-balance accounts with Venmo and PayPal. *See* Jon Russell, *Venmo Opens Its Payment Service to Third-Party Apps*, TechCrunch, Jan. 27, 2016, https://techcrunch.com/2016/01/27/venmo-becomes-a-payment-platform/; *see also* Fitz Tepper, *You Can Now Use Venmo to Pay for Things Inside Other Apps*, TechCrunch, July 26, 2016, https://techcrunch.com/2016/07/26/you-can-now-use-venmo-to-pay-for-things-inside-other-apps/.

34. Andrew B. Morris, *Why Context Matters in Commerce*, N>genuity J., Oct. 18, 2016 (noting that "there is greater need for collaboration and partnership, often between payments industry competitors, as the commerce ecosystem becomes increasingly integrated and complex"), http://tsys.com/ngenuity-journal/why-context-matters-in-commerce.html.

II. KEY LEGAL AND REGULATORY ISSUES

A. State Money Transmission Laws/Federal BSA

1. State Money Transmission Laws

Almost all U.S. states require nonbank entities engaging in the business of money transmission to be licensed.[35] There are a variety of actions that can trigger state money transmission licensing and compliance obligations, including receiving and transmitting money, selling or issuing payment instruments or money orders, providing bill payment services, issuing or selling stored value, etc.[36] With respect to facilitating contextual commerce payments, however, there are two primary licensing triggers: the receipt and transmittal of funds, and the issuance of open-loop stored value.

a. Receipt and Transmittal of Funds

State money transmitter laws generally define money transmission to include "receiving" money for transmission.[37] While this definition is broad, the "classic" money transmission model is a service in which an entity *receives* funds from a sender and makes a promise *to that sender* to deliver the funds to another party, on the sender's behalf.[38] In this scenario, the transmitting entity is acting as an "agent" of the sender who holds funds in trust for the sender in the course of transmitting those funds consistent with the sender's instructions. State money transmission licensing laws, with their emphasis on safety and soundness, are often interpreted as seeking to protect the sender of funds by ensuring that when an intermediary (i.e., a money transmitter) receives those funds, it will deliver the funds as promised (and have funds available to do so). Nevertheless, in some cases, regulators have suggested that even if an entity does *not* physically control funds (i.e., actually *receive* the funds), the entity may still be subject to regulation as a money transmitter if it has "constructive control" of the funds.[39]

---

35. *See, e.g.*, Fla. Stat. § 560.125(1) (requiring a license to engage in the business of a money services business); 205 Ill. Comp. Stat. 657/10 (requiring a license to engage in the business of transmitting money); Md. Code Ann., Fin. Inst. § 12-405(a) (requiring a license to engage in the business of money transmission).

36. *See, e.g.*, Md. Code Ann., Fin. Inst. § 12-401(m) (defining money transmission to include "selling or issuing payment instruments or stored value devices, or receiving money or monetary value . . ." and including bill payment services).

37. *See, e.g.*, Cal. Fin. Code § 2003(q); Va. Code § 6.2-1900; Tex. Fin. Code Ann. § 151.301(b)(4).

38. Only a few states explicitly exempt business-to-business funds transfers. *See, e.g.*, N.C. Gen. Stat. § 53-208.42(12) (defining money transmission to involve activity "primarily for personal, family, or household purposes"). Most states interpret their money transmission laws to apply to the transmission of funds on behalf of businesses as well.

39. California Department of Business Oversight, Data Processor That Does Not Have Possession or Control of Money Not Subject to California Money Transmission Act (May 20, 2014), http://www.dbo .ca.gov/Laws_&_Regs/dfi_orders_files/2014_MTA_opinion.5.20.14.pdf. Similarly, the Washington Department of Financial Institutions, in its Interpretive Statement 2015-1, as revised May 2, 2016, suggested that a money transmitter could include a company that "constructively control[s] the flow of money without actual receipt of the money," http://dfi.wa.gov/sites/default/files/opinions/is-2015-01.pdf.

Ultimately, however, nonbank entities not otherwise exempt from state money transmitter licensing that facilitate contextual commerce payments by receiving funds for transmission to the merchant may be subject to state money transmitter laws. As the entity processing payments on behalf of merchants, and typically (but not always) receiving settlement funds prior to settling such funds to the merchant in the context of contextual commerce payments transactions, nonbank payment processors, including payment facilitators (and any other nonbank entity performing similar activities) should be aware of these laws and licensing requirements and assess potential applicability.

However, in the context of "payment processing," based on the specific activity of the nonbank payment processor (or an entity acting in a substantially similar manner to a payment processor), state-by-state exemptions to money transmitter licensing and compliance requirements may be available on a fact-specific, case-by-case basis. Because nonbank payment processors typically (but not always) act on behalf of the ultimate *recipient* of the funds (i.e., the merchant), as opposed to providing a service to a *sender* of funds, a nonbank payment processor may not be subject to certain state money transmission laws by its actions as an agent of the recipient of transaction funds, or, in other words, its role as an "agent of the payee." Under this theory, when the payment processor receives the funds, it is as if the funds have been received, as a matter of agency law, by the ultimate recipient. Based on this interpretation, it follows that there is no "transmission" to another party, nor is there a promise made to any sender to make funds available at another location or to another party.[40]

Nevertheless, state money transmission regulators have struggled with how to treat "payment processor" and "agent of the payee" transactions. While many state regulators have not taken a formal position on whether their state law governs "agent of the payee" transactions, some states have determined in recent years that "payment processors" acting as "agents of the payee" are not money transmitters[41]

---

40. *See, e.g.*, Texas Department of Banking, Op. No. 14-01 (May 9, 2014) (observing that when the "agent" receives the funds, "it is the Biller receiving the funds. . . . In essence, the agency relationship renders the exchange a two-party transaction between the Biller and the customer. Without receipt of money in exchange for a promise to make it available at a later time or different location, there is no money transmission."); Illinois Department of Financial and Professional Regulation, Statement Regarding Third-Party Payment Processors and the Transmitter of Money Act (observing that "due to the contractual relationship with the third-party payment processor, the merchant will always have a method to address any issues with the third-party payment processor" and reasoning that because the third-party processor is acting as agent for the merchant in accepting and processing funds, "there is no transaction that would fall under the definition of transmitting money" under the Illinois money transmitters law), http://www.idfpr.com/DFI/CCD/pdfs/07292015StatementThirdPartyProcTOMA.pdf.

41. In recent years, states that have established or otherwise indicated by regulation, statutory change, guidance, or other formal communication that an agent of the payee and/or a payment processor is not subject to licensing as a money transmitter include: California, Idaho, Illinois, Kansas, Kentucky, North Carolina, Pennsylvania, Texas, and Virginia. States including Nebraska, Nevada, New York, and Ohio have historically had payee agent exemptions in their money transmitter statutes.

and are exempt from regulation under such states' money transmitter licensing laws, provided that certain criteria are met.[42]

The most notable example is California, which exempts from its money transmission law a "transaction in which the recipient of the money or other monetary value is an agent of the payee pursuant to a preexisting written contract and delivery of the money or other monetary value to the agent satisfies the payor's obligation to the payee."[43]

b. Issuance or Sale of Open-Loop Stored Value/Prepaid Access

At the state level, "open-loop" stored value (i.e., may be used with multiple unaffiliated sellers of goods or services) is generally subject to state money transmission licensing and compliance obligations. Specific definitions (as well as the terminology) of stored value (e.g., "closed loop" versus "open loop," "prepaid access," etc.) vary under state laws, but the general concept of a covered stored-value product (i.e., an open-loop stored-value product) is money or monetary value evidenced by an electronic record that is prefunded and for which value is reduced on each use—and that is not otherwise exempt as closed-loop stored value.[44] Closed-loop products are generally those issued by a merchant that can be redeemed only by that merchant or at a defined set of related merchants.[45] Typically, closed-loop stored value would not include a product that had functionality enabling users to make cash withdrawals or funds transfers, or to obtain a cash redemption of the balance. A product that is otherwise closed loop but permits any required de minimis cash out under state gift card laws should not be deemed open loop by that feature alone.[46]

Accordingly, an entity that issues or sells open-loop stored value may be subject to state money transmitter laws. With respect to contextual commerce payments transactions, this could include, for example, nonbank entities that issue a stored-value service that can be used in connection with a consumer's ability to fund (or prefund) payment transactions across a wide variety of digital platforms. An entity

---

42. For example, the state of Washington, in an Interpretive Statement produced by the Department of Financial Institutions, provides that payment processors/payee agents may be exempt from regulation as money transmitters *if* they meet certain requirements. *See* Washington Department of Financial Institutions, Interpretive Statement 2015-1, *supra* note 39.

43. CAL. FIN. CODE § 2010(l). "Agent" is defined as "one who represents another, called the principal, in dealings with third persons." A "payee" is the provider of goods or services, who is owed payment of money or other monetary value from the payor for the goods or services, while the "payor" is the recipient of goods or services, who owes payment of money or monetary value to the payee for the goods or services. *See id.*

44. *See, e.g.,* TEX. FIN. CODE ANN. § 151.301(b)(8); CAL. FIN. CODE § 2003(x); KAN. STAT. ANN. § 9-508(d) (definition of "electronic instrument").

45. *See, e.g.,* TEX. FIN. CODE § 151.301(b)(8)(C) (exempting from the definition of "stored value" an electronic record that is "redeemable only for goods or services from a specified merchant or set of affiliated merchants").

46. *See, e.g.,* CAL. CIV. CODE § 1749.5(b)(2) (making any gift card with a cash value of less than $10 redeemable for cash); VT. STAT. ANN. tit. 8, § 2704 (making any gift card with cash value of less than $1 redeemable for cash).

that offers such functionality should be aware of these laws and licensing requirements and appropriately assess applicability.

2. Federal BSA—Money Services Business Requirements

The BSA[47] requires that a "money services business" (MSB), which includes an entity that provides money transmission services, comply with certain registration requirements, customer identification procedures, and transaction monitoring, recordkeeping, and reporting requirements.[48] The regulations implementing the BSA define "money transmission services" in a similar fashion to state licensing laws (i.e., as the acceptance of funds from one person and the transmission of those funds to another location or person by any means).[49] Under the BSA, however, whether an entity is a money transmitter "is a matter of facts and circumstances."[50]

3. Exemptions from the Definition of Money Transmitter
a. Payment Processor Exemption

The BSA regulations exempt from the definition of "money transmitter" a person that only "[a]cts as a payment processor to facilitate the purchase of, or payment of a bill for, a good or service through a clearance and settlement system by agreement with the creditor or seller"[51] ("payment processor exemption"). The Financial Crimes Enforcement Network (FinCEN), which implements the BSA, explained in the section-by-section analysis accompanying its final rule adding the payment processor exemption that "[a]lthough payment processors may provide a money transmission service, the service is ancillary to their primary business of coordinating payments either from a debtor to a creditor or, if operating at the point of sale, from a purchaser to a merchant."[52]

Through administrative rulings, FinCEN has established a four-part test for determining whether the payment processor exemption applies to a payment intermediary:[53]

- The entity providing the service must facilitate the purchase of goods or services, or the payment of bills for goods or services (other than money transmission itself)
- The entity must operate through clearance and settlement systems that admit only BSA-regulated financial institutions

---

47. 31 U.S.C. § 5311 et seq.
48. 31 C.F.R. ch. X, pts. 1010, 1022.
49. *Id.* § 1010.100(ff)(5)(i)(A).
50. *Id.* § 1010.100(ff)(5)(ii).
51. *Id.* § 1010.100(ff)(5)(ii)(B).
52. 76 Fed. Reg. 43,585, 43,593 (July 21, 2011).
53. *See* FinCEN Ruling FIN-2013-R002, Whether a Company That Offers a Payment Mechanism Based on Payable-Through Drafts to Its Commercial Customers Is a Money Transmitter (Nov. 13, 2013); *accord* FinCEN Ruling FIN-2014-R009, Application of Money Services Business Regulations to a Company Acting as an Independent Sales Organization and Payment Processor (Aug. 27, 2014).

- The entity must provide the service pursuant to a formal agreement
- The entity's agreement must be at a minimum with the seller or creditor that provided the goods or services and receives the funds

b. Integral to the Provision of Services Exemption

In addition to the payment processor exemption, the BSA definition of money transmitter excludes a person that "[a]ccepts and transmits funds only integral to the sale of goods or the provision of services, other than money transmission services, by the person who is accepting and transmitting the funds."[54] FinCEN explains that this provision is intended to address instances in which the acceptance and transmission of funds by a particular entity is "an integral part of the execution and settlement of a transaction other than the funds transmission or transfer" provided by that entity.[55] In determining whether the money transmission is integral to the provision of a service, and thus eligible for exemption, FinCEN has set forth three "fundamental conditions" that must be met:

1. The money transmission component must be part of the provision of goods or services distinct from money transmission itself
2. The exemption can only be claimed by the person that is engaged in the provision of goods or services distinct from money transmission
3. The money transmission component must be integral (that is, necessary) for the provision of the goods or services[56]

Accordingly, to the extent that an entity accepts funds from one person/entity and then transmits those funds to another location or person/entity by any means, there is a possibility that such entity, outside of applicable exemptions, may be subject to federal MSB registration and BSA compliance. With respect to contextual commerce payments transactions, this could include, for example, nonbank entities that receive settlement funds prior to settling such funds to a merchant. Nonbank payment entities performing similar activities should be aware of these laws and licensing requirements and assess potential applicability.

B. FinCEN Prepaid Access Rule

In 2011, FinCEN published the final Prepaid Access Rule, implementing its delegated authority to regulate "prepaid access" under the BSA.[57] The Prepaid Access Rule imposes BSA obligations on "providers of prepaid access" and "sellers of prepaid access"—two categories of MSBs. The Prepaid Access Rule exempts from coverage as an MSB certain categories of prepaid access products and services—including

---

54. 31 C.F.R. § 1010.100(ff)(5)(ii)(F).
55. 64 Fed. Reg. 45,438, 45,443 (Aug. 20, 1999).
56. FinCEN Ruling FIN-2014-R011 (Oct. 27, 2014); FinCEN Ruling FIN-2014-R012 (Oct. 27, 2014).
57. 76 Fed. Reg. 45,403 (July 29, 2011) (codified at 31 C.F.R. pt. 1010).

closed-loop products—that, in FinCEN's view, generally pose lower risks of money laundering and terrorist financing.

Under the Prepaid Access Rule, "prepaid access" is defined as "[a]ccess to funds or the value of funds that have been paid in advance and can be retrieved or transferred at some point in the future through an electronic device or vehicle, such as a card, code, electronic serial number, mobile identification number, or personal identification number."[58] Interpretive guidance from FinCEN suggests that an online account that operates "like a fungible payment instrument in traditional commerce, usable at any number of as-yet-unidentified merchants" meets the definition of "prepaid access" even if there is no separate electronic device such as a physical card associated with the account.[59]

Even if an arrangement involves prepaid access, whether an entity is a *provider* of prepaid access, and thereby subject to the Prepaid Access Rule, depends on whether the entity (1) has "principal oversight and control" over (2) a "prepaid program."[60] An arrangement for providing prepaid access is not a "prepaid program" if it

- provides access solely to funds not to exceed $1,000 maximum value and from which no more than $1,000 maximum value can be initially or subsequently loaded, used, or withdrawn on any day; *and*
- does *not permit* (1) transfers of prepaid access funds between or among users; (2) reloads from a non-depository source; or (3) international transfers.[61]

If an arrangement does constitute a prepaid program, a "provider of prepaid access" is the "participant within a prepaid program that agrees to serve as the principal conduit for access to information from its fellow program participants."[62] If no participant in the program is designated the "provider of prepaid access," determining which participant in a prepaid program has principal oversight and control "is a matter of facts and circumstances." Activities that indicate principal oversight and control include: organizing the prepaid program; setting the terms and conditions of the prepaid program and determining that the terms have not been exceeded; determining the other businesses that participate in the prepaid program, which may include the issuing bank, the payment processor, or the distributor; controlling or directing the appropriate party to initiate, freeze, or terminate prepaid access; and engaging in activity that demonstrates oversight and control of the prepaid program.[63] (FinCEN subsequently clarified, however, that for a bank-controlled prepaid

---

58. 31 C.F.R. § 1010.100(ww).
59. FinCEN Ruling FIN-2014-R006, Whether a Company That Provides Online Real-Time Deposit, Settlement, and Payment Services for Banks, Businesses, and Consumers Is a Money Transmitter Rather Than a Provider of Prepaid Access (Apr. 29, 2014).
60. 31 C.F.R. § 1010.100(ff)(4)(ii).
61. *Id.* § 1010.100(ff)(4)(iii)(D)(1)(ii), (D)(2).
62. *Id.* § 1010.100(ff)(4)(i).
63. *Id.* § 1010.100(ff)(4)(ii)(A)–(E).

access program, no entity would be required to register as a provider of prepaid access if the bank has principal oversight and control over the prepaid program.[64])

A participant that is determined to be a "provider of prepaid access" would be regulated as an MSB under FinCEN's BSA regulations. As an MSB, the "provider of prepaid access" would be subject to compliance obligations, including:

- Registering with FinCEN as an MSB and submitting, as part of its registration and registration renewals, a complete list of the prepaid programs for which it serves as provider[65]
- Reporting transactions in currency in amounts greater than $10,000[66]
- Reporting on transactions of $2,000 or more that it determines to be suspicious[67]
- Establishing procedures to verify the identity of a person who obtains prepaid access under a prepaid program[68]
- Obtaining identifying information concerning such a person, including name, date of birth, address, and identification number[69]
- Retaining access to such identifying information for five years after the last use of the prepaid access[70]

A *seller* of prepaid access is a person that "receives funds or the value of funds in exchange for an initial loading or subsequent loading of prepaid access" *if* the prepaid access is sold under a prepaid program and can be used before customer information is verified.[71] In other words, if the "prepaid access" product is part of a prepaid program, and the provider of prepaid access does not verify the customer's identity as described above, then the entity selling the prepaid access would be subject to the BSA as an MSB and required to collect and verify identifying information in its own right.[72]

Accordingly, any entity that issues or sells prepaid access, as defined above, may be subject to regulation as a federal MSB. With respect to contextual commerce payments transactions, this could represent, for example, a nonbank entity operating as a provider or seller of prepaid access (as defined above) that could be used in connection with a consumer's ability to fund payment transactions across a wide

---

64. *See* FinCEN Ruling FIN-2012-R003, Application of the Prepaid Access Rule to Bank-Controlled Programs (June 8, 2012).

65. 31 C.F.R. § 1022.380(a)(1).

66. *Id.* § 1010.311.

67. *Id.* § 1022.320(a)(2).

68. *Id.* § 1022.210(d)(1)(i).

69. *Id.* § 1022.210(d)(1)(iv).

70. *Id.* Certain of the above-listed requirements are incremental to the BSA compliance requirements to which an entity would be subject as a money transmitter.

71. 31 C.F.R. § 1010.100(ff)(7).

72. An entity is also a seller of prepaid access if it sells prepaid access (open or closed loop, and regardless of whether part of a prepaid program or not) to funds "that exceed $10,000 to any person during any one day, and has not implemented policies and procedures reasonably adapted to prevent such a sale." *See id.* § 1010.100(ff)(7)(ii).

variety of digital platforms. Any entity offering such functionality should be aware of these requirements to appropriately assess applicability.

C. Consumer Financial Protection Bureau Prepaid Accounts Rule[73]

The Consumer Financial Protection Bureau's (CFPB's) final rule regulating prepaid accounts (Prepaid Accounts Rule) amends the CFPB's Regulation E, which implements the Electronic Fund Transfer Act (EFTA), and Regulation Z, which implements the Truth in Lending Act (TILA).[74] In general, the Prepaid Accounts Rule extends a modified version of the regulatory compliance regime currently applicable to payroll card accounts (i.e., Reg E "Lite") to "prepaid accounts," including by providing an alternative to requiring written periodic statements, modified error resolution procedures, limited initial disclosures and an annual error resolution notice, and limitations on cardholder liability. The Prepaid Accounts Rule requires certain preacquisition disclosures and extends modified versions of certain requirements of the Credit Card Accountability Responsibility and Disclosure Act[75] to prepaid accounts, including account agreement submission and posting requirements and certain statement disclosures.[76]

1. Scope of the Prepaid Accounts Rule

The Prepaid Accounts Rule amends Regulation E to include "prepaid accounts" as one type of "account" subject to Regulation E. There are two relevant prongs of the "prepaid account" definition.[77]

The first relevant prong of the prepaid account definition (the "marketed or labeled prong") applies to an account (1) that is marketed or labeled as "prepaid"; and (2) that is redeemable upon presentation at multiple, unaffiliated merchants for goods or services, or are usable at automated teller machines (ATMs). The official staff interpretations of the Prepaid Accounts Rule (the Commentary) provide that

---

73. The Prepaid Accounts Rule was scheduled to take effect, with certain exceptions, on Oct. 1, 2017; however, on Mar. 15, 2017, the Consumer Financial Protection Bureau published a proposed rule to delay the effective date of the rule. Prepaid Accounts under the Electronic Fund Transfer Act (Regulation E) and the Truth in Lending Act (Regulation Z); Delay of Effective Date, 82 Fed. Reg. 13,782 (proposed Mar. 15, 2017). On Apr. 20, 2017, the CFPB released a final rule delaying the effective date of the Prepaid Accounts Rule, as proposed, to Apr. 1, 2018. 82 Fed. Reg. 18,975 (Apr. 25, 2017) [hereinafter Release].

74. *See* 15 U.S.C. § 1693 *et seq.* (EFTA) and § 1601 *et seq.* (TILA); 12 C.F.R. pts. 1005 (Regulation E) and 1026 (Regulation Z). The final rule was issued on Oct. 5, 2016. Prepaid Accounts under the Electronic Fund Transfer Act (Regulation E) and the Truth in Lending Act (Regulation Z), 81 Fed. Reg. 83,934 (Nov. 22, 2016).

75. Pub. L. No. 111-24, 123 Stat. 1734 (2009).

76. For the sake of simplicity, in this section on the CFPB's prepaid accounts rule, references are made to issuers, rather than financial institutions. The amendments to Regulation E will, however, be imposed on "financial institutions," which include any "person that directly or indirectly holds an account belonging to a consumer, or that issues an access device and agrees with a consumer to provide electronic fund transfer services." 12 C.F.R. § 1005.2(i).

77. Prepaid accounts also include payroll card accounts and government benefit accounts currently subject to Regulation E.

"marketed or labeled as 'prepaid'" means "promoting or advertising" an account using the term "prepaid."[78] Essentially, if an issuer calls a product "prepaid," it is a prepaid account under the marketed or labeled prong.

The second relevant prong of the prepaid account definition (the "functional prong") applies to an account (1) that is issued on a prepaid basis or capable of being loaded with funds; (2) whose "primary function" is to conduct transactions with multiple, unaffiliated merchants or at ATMs, or to conduct peer-to-peer (P2P) transfers; and (3) that is not a checking account, share draft account, or negotiable order of withdrawal (NOW) account.

For participants facilitating contextual commerce payments, it is worth noting that prepaid accounts are not limited to traditional physical cards. While the Prepaid Accounts Rule will not apply in the context of a mobile or digital wallet that *only* stores a consumer's payments credentials (i.e., card on file) in order to facilitate payments transactions via a wide variety of digital platforms, the Prepaid Accounts Rule will apply to the extent that a mobile or digital wallet is capable of storing funds.[79] Moreover, it appears that the entire wallet would be subject to the Prepaid Accounts Rule if only a portion of the wallet can store funds. Therefore, as of the writing of this chapter, in situations in which an entity issues a mobile or digital wallet for purposes of facilitating contextual commerce payments transactions and the mobile or digital wallet stores both (1) payment credentials of consumers (i.e., card on file) and (2) prepaid funds, but the consumer does not use the stored value functionality of the wallet, the Prepaid Accounts Rule would nonetheless apply.

However, on April 20, 2017, the CFPB released a follow-on final rule concerning a delay in the effective date of the Prepaid Account Rule[80] but also noted that it would revisit "the linking of credit cards into digital wallets that are capable of storing funds."[81] As of the time of this writing it is unclear as to how the CFPB will address the applicability of the Prepaid Accounts Rule to situations described above in which a digital wallet has the capability of storing both payments credentials and funds, but the consumer does not use the stored value functionality of the wallet. Given the regulatory implications for contextual commerce participants that issue digital wallets capable of storing payments credentials *and* funds for the use across a wide variety of digital platforms, this issue will remain a significant concern and should be closely monitored.

---

78. *See* cmt. 1005.2(b)(3)(i)–3 (stating, as an example, that a prepaid account would be marketed or labeled as prepaid if the term "prepaid" appeared on the access device or on the packaging materials of the access device, or on a display, advertisement, or other publication to promote purchase or use of the account).

79. A digital wallet that only stores a consumer's payment credentials is not covered, provided that the digital wallet is incapable of storing funds.

80. Release, *supra* note 73.

81. *Id.* at 18,977.

D. Compliance with PCI DSS

Given the number of participants in a contextual commerce payments transaction that potentially can encounter consumer payments credentials, the application of and compliance with the PCI DSS is of paramount concern. Importantly, payment processors, merchants, and any other entity that stores, processes, or transmits cardholder data as part of a contextual commerce payments transaction must comply with PCI DSS.[82] PCI DSS identifies the requirements applicable to securing cardholder information, including technical security standards, access controls, monitoring functions, and governance policies.[83] The Payment Card Industry Security Standards Council, which was established by the payment card associations, administers PCI DSS and specifies the controls and steps that entities must take to verify or report on their compliance with the standard.[84]

As founding members of the Payment Card Industry Security Standards Council, the payment card networks enforce compliance with PCI DSS, either directly for member banks, or indirectly through member banks for payment processors, merchants, and other entities that store, process, or transmit cardholder data in the card processing value chain.[85] Member banks typically include compliance with PCI DSS as a requirement in contracts with other payment processing participants, or otherwise require compliance with the card association rules, which in turn mandate PCI DSS compliance. Thus, PCI DSS is, most directly, a contractual requirement.

PCI DSS compliance is not mandated by federal law, but three states have mandated compliance with PCI DSS, at least in part. Nevada goes furthest in mandating compliance with the standard for any company doing business in the state that collects payment card information in connection with the sale of goods or services.[86] Washington exempts "processors, businesses, and vendors" from certain data breach liabilities if these entities are certified compliant with the current version of PCI DSS at the time of the breach.[87] Minnesota incorporated into state law one aspect of PCI DSS—a prohibition against storing the card verification value, personal identification number (PIN), or full magnetic stripe data.[88] As a result, noncompliance with PCI DSS can not only result in a contractual breach, but can also violate certain state laws.

Noncompliance with PCI DSS also can be a factor in litigation in determining whether a breached company implemented reasonable security safeguards to protect cardholder data. Merchants and other companies where payment card data was

---

82. *See* PCI Security Standards Council, *Maintaining Payment Security*, https://www.pcisecurity standards.org/pci_security/maintaining_payment_security (last visited May 20, 2017).
83. See *id.* for an overview of PCI DSS.
84. *See* PCI Security Standards Council, *PCI Security*, https://www.pcisecuritystandards.org /pci_security/ (last visited May 20, 2017).
85. *See* PCI Security Standards Council, *About Us*, https://www.pcisecuritystandards.org/about _us/ (last visited May 20, 2017).
86. *See* Nev. Rev. Stat. § 603A.215.
87. *See* Wash. Rev. Code § 19.255.020(2).
88. *See* Minn. Rev. Stat. § 325E.64 subd. 2.

accessed without authorization from the companies' systems have been subjected to lawsuits by companies that allegedly suffered damages from the breach, such as card-issuing banks. In some of these cases, plaintiffs have alleged that the defendant company that suffered the breach was negligent because, among other things, the defendant company was not in compliance with PCI DSS.[89]

III. CONCLUSION

Given the recent history of contextual commerce as viewed through the lens of merchant and digital platform experimentation with buy-button technology and other similar attempts to move commerce to consumers, it might be easy to discount the impact of contextual commerce based on indicators of poor consumer response. After all, while the idea of taking commerce to consumers wherever they may be makes perfect sense on paper, it is also obvious that consumers need to be willing and able to make purchases when presented with the opportunity.

Of course, issues pertaining to whether consumers will be "willing" to make a purchase outside of what the consumer considers to be an appropriate purchase channel are beyond the scope of this chapter. Issues pertaining to whether consumers are "able" to make the purchase, however, are largely within the ability of contextual commerce stakeholders to control and, as pointed out in the introduction to this chapter, may be positively influenced through further reductions in payments friction via solutions that limit the need for consumer interaction with the payment process.

In order to provide that kind of functionality, it is likely that providers will need to implement end-to-end contextual commerce solutions, including (1) the maintenance of relationships with digital platforms that utilize the provider's contextual commerce solution; (2) the maintenance of relationships with merchants looking to transact on a wide variety of digital platforms; and (3) the ability to provide payment services to consumers via digital wallets and/or stored value that will either fund or facilitate the funding of merchant transactions that occur via the participating digital platform. In doing so, the contextual commerce provider will be able to orchestrate, at least in theory, the type of "invisible" payments process that has been so successful in other contexts.

It is, however, this positioning as the conduit through which contextual commerce payments transactions occur that brings to bear many of the legal issues discussed in this chapter. And while each of these legal and regulatory issues might be applicable today depending upon the structure of the contextual commerce solution, the evolving nature of the payments industry as well as the legal landscape will trigger the possibility of further regulatory obligations. As a result, contextual commerce stakeholders—whether merchants, payments processors, digital platforms, or others—may benefit from the advice of legal counsel concerning the impact of these and future developments.

---

89. *See, e.g.*, Complaint, Trustmark Nat'l Bank v. Target Corp., No. 14-CV-2069 (E.D. Ill. Mar. 24, 2014).

PART III

Legal and Policy Insights in the Payments Environment

Chapter 7

Money Laundering and Tax Enforcement

U.S. Foundations

Eileen Lyon

I. INTRODUCTION

The great challenges of the increased availability and cutting-edge technology in electronic payments systems, which have undoubtedly provided access to financial systems to the unbanked and new businesses, are how to keep criminals from using the same systems for laundering criminal proceeds and to prevent terrorists from using the systems to accumulate resources to aid their political goals.

In the United States, financial institutions are subject to a comprehensive set of laws, regulations, and guidance designed to identify, detect, and deter money laundering and terrorist financing activities. Financial institutions are on the front line of anti-money laundering (AML) regulations. Through enactment of various laws since 1970, financial institutions have been required to develop and implement programs that are reasonably designed to detect and deter money laundering and terrorist financing activities. This chapter will focus on how these laws affect and are applied to payment systems.

II. MONEY LAUNDERING

The colloquial meaning of the term "money laundering" is the process of turning profits from illegal activities ("dirty" money) into "clean" money so that the funds appear to be the proceeds of legal activities. In essence, it is a means of hiding the illegal source of funds. Money laundering also serves to:

- Facilitate tax evasion

- Convert large sums of currency into more manageable assets
- Separate illegal proceeds from the crime for purposes of avoiding prosecution and seizure

The Federal Financial Institutions Examination Council (FFIEC)[1] breaks money laundering down into three steps, all of which can occur simultaneously: placement, layering, and integration.

The *placement* phase involves introducing unlawful proceeds into the financial system without attracting the attention of financial institutions or law enforcement. For example, placement includes:

- Dividing a large sum of money into smaller sums for deposit into one or more accounts so as to evade a depository financial institution's currency transaction reporting requirements (also known as "structuring")
- Commingling of currency derived from legal activity with currency derived from illegal activity

Layering involves moving funds around the financial system in an attempt to create confusion and complicate the paper trail. For example, layering might involve:

- Exchanging monetary instruments, such as money orders, for larger or smaller amounts
- Wiring money to and from several accounts in one or more financial institutions

The final phase and the ultimate goal of money laundering is *integration* of the illegal funds to create the appearance of legality. Criminals attempt to obscure their connection to the funds through additional transactions, such as the purchase and resale of real estate, investment securities, foreign trusts, or other assets, which have the effect of creating a plausible explanation for the source of funds as other than the criminal activity.

III. OVERVIEW OF AML REGULATION IN THE UNITED STATES

The AML regulatory scheme in the United States is referred to as the Bank Secrecy Act (BSA or BSA/AML).[2] These regulations are paired with sanctions programs

---

1. The FFIEC consists of the Board of Governors of the Federal Reserve System (FRB), which examines state-chartered banks that are members of the FRB, Federal Deposit Insurance Corporation (FDIC), which examines state-chartered nonmember banks, Office of the Comptroller of the Currency (OCC), which examines national banking associations and federal savings associations, and National Credit Union Administration (NCUA), which examines credit unions, as well as the U.S. Securities and Exchange Commission (SEC), which regulates the securities markets, and the Commodity Futures Trading Commission (CFTC), which regulates commodity futures and options markets.

2. The BSA is sometimes referred to as an "anti-money laundering" (AML) law or jointly as BSA/AML. Several AML acts, including provisions in title III of the USA PATRIOT Act of 2001, have been enacted up to the present to amend the BSA. *See infra* note 4 and accompanying text. The BSA is codified at 12 U.S.C. §§ 1829b, 1951–1959, 31 U.S.C. §§ 5311–5314, 5316–5332, and 31 C.F.R. ch. X (formerly 31 C.F.R. pt. 103).

administered by the U.S. Department of the Treasury's Office of Foreign Assets Control (OFAC). The BSA arose out of a series of federal laws passed since 1970. The Currency and Foreign Transactions Reporting Act[3] first established recordkeeping and reporting requirements for banks and other financial institutions designed to assist law enforcement in identifying and tracking currency and other monetary instruments transported into and out of the United States. While other legislation incrementally enhanced the BSA regime, significant new requirements were imposed by the Uniting and Strengthening America by Providing Appropriate Tools Required to Intercept and Obstruct Terrorism Act of 2001 (USA PATRIOT Act),[4] adopted in the wake of the September 11, 2001, terrorist attacks on the United States.

IV. SIGNIFICANT U.S. MONEY LAUNDERING LEGISLATION

A. BSA

The BSA,[5] adopted in 1970, established recordkeeping and reporting requirements for individuals and financial institutions in order to aid in the identification of the source, volume, and movement of currency and other monetary instruments. The principal reporting and recordkeeping requirements created were the Currency Transaction Report (CTR),[6] the Report of International Transportation of Currency or Monetary Instruments (CMIR),[7] and the Report of Foreign Bank and Financial Accounts (FBAR).[8]

B. Money Laundering Control Act[9]

"Money laundering" (i.e., placement, layering, and integration)[10] was not a federal crime until passage of the Money Laundering Control Act (MLCA) in 1986. The MLCA also added a provision to the BSA prohibiting the "structuring" of transactions, established money laundering as a separate criminal offense, and clarified that each financial transaction constitutes a separate offense giving rise to separate liability.

---

3. 31 U.S.C. § 5311, 12 U.S.C. §§ 1829b and 1951–1959 (1970). The Currency and Foreign Transactions Reporting Act of 1970 (the legislative framework of which is commonly referred to as the "Bank Secrecy Act" or "BSA") requires U.S. financial institutions to assist U.S. government agencies to detect and prevent money laundering. Specifically, the act requires financial institutions to keep records of cash purchases of negotiable instruments, file reports of cash transactions exceeding $10,000 (daily aggregate amount), and to report suspicious activity that might signify money laundering, tax evasion, or other criminal activities. It was passed by the Congress in 1970.

4. Pub. L. No. 107-56, 115 Stat. 272.

5. 31 U.S.C. § 5311 et seq., 12 U.S.C. §§ 1829b, and 1951–1959, and 31 U.S.C. §§ 5311–5332 (1970).

6. FinCEN Form 112, Currency Transaction Report. A financial institution may also designate persons that are exempt from CTR filings by filing a FinCEN Form 110, Designation of Exempt Person (DOEP).

7. FinCEN Form 105, Report of International Transportation of Currency or Monetary Instruments.

8. FinCEN Report 114, Report of Foreign Bank and Financial Accounts.

9. Pub. L. No. 99-570, 100 Stat. 5071.

10. See supra note1 and accompanying text.

Among other things, the MLCA established money laundering as a federal offense that carries with it a fine of up to $500,000 or twice the value of the property involved, whichever is greater, and/or imprisonment for up to twenty years. Under the statute, it is a crime to conduct (or attempt to conduct) a financial transaction with the proceeds of "specified unlawful activity,"

- knowing that the property involved comes from some form of unlawful activity with the intent to promote the carrying on of the unlawful activity;
- with the intent to engage in tax evasion or the filing of false tax documents;
- knowing that the transaction is designed to conceal or disguise the nature, location, source, ownership, or control of the proceeds; or
- knowing that the transaction is designed to avoid a transaction reporting requirement under state or federal law.[11]

Specified unlawful activity is defined to include a number of offenses such as manufacture, importation, sale, or distribution of a controlled substance, as well as bank robbery, murder, mail fraud, and even certain environmental crimes.[12]

The MLCA imposes criminal liability on a person or financial institution that "structures" transactions to avoid their reporting.[13] Structuring a transaction includes, for example, breaking down a single sum of currency exceeding $10,000 into smaller sums at or below $10,000. The transactions need not exceed the $10,000 reporting threshold at any single financial institution on any single day in order to constitute structuring.

The MLCA also clarified that money laundering is not a continuing offense, meaning that each of several deposits by a person in a "structured" transaction is a distinct violation of the BSA. If the depositor then withdrew some of the money and used it to purchase an asset, he or she would have committed two more violations, one for the withdrawal and one for the purchase.[14] In addition, money laundering is a separate and distinct offense from the underlying criminal activity that resulted in the "dirty money" being "laundered."

C. Anti-Drug Abuse Act of 1988[15]

The Anti-Drug Abuse Act of 1988 (ADAA) was part of the Reagan Administration's War on Drugs. Section 6181 of the ADAA, subtitled the Money Laundering Prosecution Improvements Act of 1988, amended the BSA to require recordkeeping and reporting in connection with the purchase and sale of bank checks, cashier's checks, traveler's checks, and money orders for currency in amounts between $3,000 and $10,000, inclusive.[16]

---

11. 18 U.S.C. § 1956.
12. *Id.* § 1956(c).
13. *Id.* § 1956(a)(1)(A)(ii).
14. *Id.* § 1957.
15. Pub. L. No. 100-690, 102 Stat. 4181.
16. 31 U.S.C. § 6185(b).

As a result of the ADAA, financial institutions are required to verify the identity of a person purchasing monetary instruments for currency in amounts between $3,000 and $10,000.[17] This applies to customers and noncustomers alike. Financial institutions may either verify that the purchaser of monetary instruments is a deposit accountholder with identifying information on record with the institution, or it may verify the identity of the purchaser by viewing a form of identification containing the person's name and address that is acceptable as a means of identification for cashing checks for noncustomers.

D. Annunzio-Wylie Anti-Money Laundering Act[18]

The Annunzio-Wylie Anti-Money Laundering Act (AWAMLA)[19] added the requirement that financial institutions report "suspicious activity" and maintain records of certain funds transfers.[20] Today, suspicious activity reports (SARs) and the underlying monitoring of customers' accounts are key components of the BSA/AML regulatory structure and provide law enforcement with information that has led directly to the capture and prosecution of money launderers.[21]

E. USA PATRIOT Act[22]

The USA PATRIOT Act was enacted in the months following 9/11, and massively expanded law enforcement investigatory tools to detect, deter, and punish terrorists in the United States and around the world. The primary revisions to the BSA are contained in title III, subtitled the International Money Laundering Abatement and Financial Anti-Terrorism Act of 2001.[23] The act, among other things, expanded U.S. scrutiny of foreign financial institutions and applied the BSA to all appropriate elements of the financial services industry that had not previously been captured within the BSA's scope.

The USA PATRIOT Act is sweeping. The definition of "financial institutions" was significantly broadened due to the USA PATRIOT Act. Prior to the act, only depository financial institutions and casinos were required to establish an AML program. The USA PATRIOT Act expanded this requirement by applying the BSA to "financial institutions"[24] to require compliance by, among others:

---

17. *Id.* § 5325(a).

18. Title XV of the Housing and Community Development Act of 1992, Pub. L. No. 102-255, 106 Stat. 3672.

19. 12 U.S.C. § 1811.

20. 31 U.S.C. § 5314(g).

21. *See, e.g.*, Financial Crimes Enforcement Network, The SAR Activity Review—Trends, Tips & Issues, Issue 14 (Oct. 2008) (BSA Records "Critical" in Conviction of Money Launderer in Organized Retail Theft Case).

22. Pub. L. No. 107-56, 115 Stat. 272 (2001).

23. *Id.*

24. Pub. L. No. 107–56, tit. III, §§ 321(a), (b), 359(a), 365(c)(1), (2)(A), 115 Stat. 315, 328, 335 (2001), 31 U.S.C. § 5312.

- U.S. Securities and Exchange Commission (SEC)-registered brokers and dealers
- Commodities brokers and dealers
- Investment bankers or investment companies
- Currency exchangers
- Issuers, redeemers, and cashiers of travelers' checks, checks, money orders, or similar instruments
- Operators of a credit card system
- Insurance companies
- Dealers in precious metals, stones, or jewels
- Pawnbrokers
- Loan or finance companies
- Travel agencies
- Money transmitters, including licensed and unlicensed, and formal or informal senders of money, domestic or international
- The U.S. Postal Service

The application of the BSA to "financial institutions" also extended the AML law to businesses as well as federal, state, and local government agencies that engage in activities that the secretary of the U.S. Department of the Treasury determines, by regulation, to be an activity that is similar to, related to, or a substitute for any activity in which enumerated financial institutions are authorized to engage and any other business designated by the secretary whose cash transactions have a high degree of usefulness in criminal, tax, or regulatory matters.[25]

The predicate criminal acts, or specified unlawful activities, for money laundering offenses were increased to target foreign corruption, and the list of predicate offenses now includes any violation of foreign law that would be an extraditable offense under a treaty between the United States and the foreign jurisdiction.[26]

A key principle in the USA PATRIOT Act was to ascertain the identity of the nominal and beneficial owners of, and the source of funds deposited into, bank accounts in order to understand the source of funds, guard against money laundering, and report any suspicious transactions. Accordingly, the USA PATRIOT Act required the secretary of the treasury and the federal financial regulators to promulgate regulations for a financial institution's identification of its customers prior to opening accounts, or a customer identification program (CIP).[27] The CIPs required by the USA PATRIOT Act require financial institutions to adopt reasonable procedures for (1) verifying the identity of any person seeking to open an account to the extent reasonable and practicable; (2) maintaining records of the information used to verify a person's identity, including name, address, and other identifying information; and (3) consulting lists of known or suspected terrorists or terrorist organizations

---

25. 31 U.S.C. § 5312(a)(2)(Y), (Z).
26. 18 U.S.C. § 1956(c).
27. 31 U.S.C. § 5318(l)(1).

provided to the financial institution by any government agency to determine whether a person seeking to open an account appears on any such list. A financial institution's CIP must be "risk based," meaning that it must be tailored to address the risks presented by the institution's size, location, customer base, product offerings, and account opening procedures, for example. However, the applicable regulations require that financial institutions obtain certain minimum identification information, including a customer's name, address, date of birth of natural persons, and, subject to certain exceptions, a taxpayer identification number or government-issued document if the customer is not a "U.S. person."[28] In addition, financial institutions must have procedures in place for the documentary or nondocumentary verification of the identifying information provided by customers and also must maintain records of the information obtained in connection with the verification procedures.

The USA PATRIOT Act mandated all financial institutions must implement and maintain an AML program that must include, at a minimum, the following elements, known as the "Four Pillars":[29]

- The development of internal policies, procedures, and controls
- The designation of a BSA compliance officer
- An ongoing employee training program
- An independent audit function to test the effectiveness of the AML programs

The BSA/AML programs that financial institutions are required to develop should be risk based; that is, the financial institutions are required to evaluate the risk within their institution's products, services, customers, and geographic locations. Some factors will be weighted more heavily than others. In general, however, a large international financial institution with a multitude of products, particularly those that facilitate the movement of money across borders, will be expected to have a significantly more robust BSA/AML program than a small community savings and loan with traditional mortgage and deposit products.

V. REGULATORY ADMINISTRATION

The secretary of the treasury is authorized to issue regulations requiring financial institutions administer the BSA.[30] The treasury secretary's administrative authority has been delegated to the director of the Financial Crimes Enforcement Network

---

28. 31 C.F.R. § 1020.220(a).

29. The issuance of a final rule outlining regulatory expectations regarding beneficial ownership has been referred to as a "Fifth Pillar." *See* Customer Due Diligence Requirements for Financial Institutions, 81 Fed. Reg. 29,398, 29,420 (May 5, 2016). *See also* Memo, Covington & Burling, LLP, FinCEN Releases Final Rule on Beneficial Ownership and Risk-Based Customer Due Diligence (May 10, 2016), *available at* https://www.cov.com/-/media/files/corporate/publications/2016/05/fincen_releases_final_rule_on _beneficial_ownership_and_risk_based_customer_due_diligence.pdf. *See also infra* note 43 and accompanying text.

30. 31 U.S.C. § 5318(a)(2).

(FinCEN).[31] FinCEN was established in 1990 as a division of the Treasury Department to support law enforcement agencies by collecting, analyzing, and coordinating financial intelligence information to combat money laundering. FinCEN is the administrative agency over BSA[32] with "[o]verall authority for enforcement and compliance, including coordination and direction of procedures and activities of all other agencies exercising delegated authority under [Chapter 31]."[33]

FinCEN became the primary financial intelligence unit of the United States by the Treasury Department after adoption of the USA PATRIOT Act.[34] FinCEN has implemented the BSA through rules and regulations contained in 31 C.F.R. chapter X.[35] The basic concept underlying FinCEN's core activities is to "follow the money"[36] in partnership with law enforcement at all levels of government that supports the nation's foreign policy and national security objectives by tracking the financial trails left by criminals and terrorists. The depository institution financial regulators that constitute the FFIEC[37] oversee financial institutions' AML efforts.

VI. IMPACTS OF BSA/AML REGULATION ON PAYMENTS SYSTEMS

Payments systems in the United States consist of financial intermediaries, financial services firms, and nonbank businesses that create, process, and distribute payments. Some participants and distribution channels in these sectors may be at greater risk for misuse by terrorists, money launderers, and other criminals.[38]

Most payment transactions are conducted through legacy systems[39] by large banking institutions. Nonbank businesses engaged in payments typically need access to banking services in order to operate. However, some types of payments, such as stored-value cards, remittances, mobile payments, and cryptocurrency, can be created and processed by nonbank businesses.[40] As a result of the USA PATRIOT Act, most of those entities now come within the coverage of the BSA.[41] Those activities and nonbank businesses become subject to the BSA/AML regime when an entity

---

31. Treasury Order 180-01 (July 1, 2014).
32. 31 C.F.R. § 1010.810.
33. *Id.*
34. *See* 31 U.S.C. § 310.
35. FinCEN's regulations were transferred from 31 C.F.R. pt. 103 to 31 C.F.R. ch. X on Mar. 1, 2011.
36. "'Follow the money'—a phrase that's now part of our national lexicon—was supposedly whispered to reporter Bob Woodward by Deep Throat as a way to cut through the lies and deceptions and find the truth about the Watergate scandal." Kee Malesky, quoted from *Follow the Money: On the Trail of Watergate Lore*, NPR, June 16, 2012.
37. *See supra* note 1 and accompanying text.
38. Interagency Interpretive Guidance on Providing Banking Services to Money Services Businesses Operating in the United States (Apr. 26, 2005).
39. These include FedWire, Automated Clearing House (ACH), and the Society for Worldwide Interbank Financial Telecommunication (SWIFT).
40. FIN-2013-G001, Application of FinCEN's Regulations to Persons Administering, Exchanging, or Using Virtual Currencies (Mar. 18, 2013).
41. *See supra* note 25 and accompanying text.

is engaged in a "money services business" (MSB).[42] MSB is a term created by FinCEN for nonbank financial institutions that offer specific services and do not have a functional federal regulator. As such, FinCEN has the authority to deem such businesses to be "financial institutions" within the meaning of the BSA.[43] The BSA obligations of MSBs are different depending on the activities engaged in, and also depending on whether the MSB is acting as a principal or agent.

In 1999, FinCEN issued a rule requiring registration of MSBs.[44] FinCEN regulations define the term "money services business" to include each agent, agency, branch, or office within the United States of any person doing business, whether or not on a regular basis or as an organized business concern, in one or more of the following capacities:

- Currency dealers or exchangers
- Check cashers
- Issuers of traveler's checks, money orders, or stored value[45]
- Sellers or redeemers of traveler's checks, money orders, or stored value
- Money transmitters
- The U.S. Postal Service (except with respect to the sale of postage or philatelic products)

Banks, by definition, are not MSBs. MSBs also do not include securities dealers, persons who transmit less than $1,000 in payments per day, and natural persons who engage in money transmission on an infrequent basis and not in a for-profit capacity.[46]

A. Depository Institutions

As discussed above, financial institutions have a legislative and regulatory mandate to monitor their customers' accounts for suspicious activities in order to detect and deter money laundering and terrorist financing. BSA responsibilities for depository financial institutions are based on the Four Pillars,[47] and they can be wide-ranging and demanding. Financial institutions are not expected to ascertain whether an underlying crime has actually been committed, but instead are required to monitor and report suspicious activities.[48] While banks are expected to manage risk associated with all accounts, they are generally not held responsible for their customers'

---

42. 31 C.F.R. § 1010.100(uu).

43. 31 U.S.C. § 5312(a)(2)(Y).

44. Definitions Relating to, and Registration of, Money Services Businesses, 64 Fed. Reg. 45,439 (Aug. 20, 1999).

45. Although considered a form of MSB, sellers, issuers, and redeemers of stored-value cards were not initially required to register with FinCEN, but were required to file CTRs and establish AML programs. In 2011, FinCEN issued a final rule which, among other things, renamed "stored value" as "prepaid access." *See infra* note 78 and accompanying text.

46. 31 C.F.R. § 1010.100(ff).

47. *See supra* note 29 and accompanying text.

48. FFIEC, BSA/AML Examination Manual 67 [hereinafter BSA Manual], *available at* https://www.ffiec .gov/bsa_aml_infobase/pages_manual/manual_online.htm.

compliance with the BSA and other applicable federal and state laws and regulations.[49] The largest internationally active depository financial institutions have spent billions on AML systems and have financial investigation teams consisting of thousands of employees.[50] Since FFIEC's issuance of the first edition of a BSA/AML examination manual in 2005,[51] the functional bank regulatory agencies have become progressively clearer and more consistent about their compliance expectations and depository financial institutions who failed to meet those expectations have seen enforcement actions and fines in the millions of dollars.[52]

Since most of the dollar value of all payments is concentrated in the electronic funds transfer systems used for large-dollar payments between banks (i.e., FedWire and the Clearing House Interbank Payments System (CHIPS)), depository financial institutions are subject to stringent regulatory expectations to monitor payments systems and identify unusual activity.[53] Detection of money laundering can be difficult, particularly because funds transfer systems enable the instantaneous transfer of funds, including both domestic and cross-border transfers, using numerous financial institutions. The funds transfer rules adopted as part of the AWAMLA in 1992[54] are designed to help law enforcement agencies detect, investigate, and prosecute money laundering and other financial crimes by preserving an information trail about persons sending and receiving funds through funds transfer systems.

Under a regulation known as the Travel Rule[55] information identifying the originator and ultimate beneficiary of transmittals of funds equal to or greater than $3,000 (or its foreign equivalent) is subject to this rule—regardless of whether or not currency is involved—and must be preserved and passed along to successive intermediary financial institutions involved in the funds transfer. An intermediary financial institution must pass on all of the information it receives from a transmitter's financial institution or the preceding intermediary financial institution; however, it has no general duty to retrieve information not provided by the transmitter's financial institution or the preceding intermediary financial institution. BNP Paribas's systematic practice of omitting (and not replacing) sanctioned parties' names from payment messages pursuant to specific instructions from OFAC sanctioned parties led to an $8.9 billion fine against the bank in 2014.[56]

---

49. *See id.* at 299.

50. Daniel P. Stipano, *Time to Bring BSA into This Century*, AM. BANKER, Feb. 21, 2017, https://www.americanbanker.com/opinion/time-to-bring-bsa-into-this-century.

51. The FFIEC issued updated editions in 2006, 2007, 2009, and 2014. The BSA Manual purportedly did not set new standards but was described as a compilation of existing regulatory requirements, supervisory expectations, and sound practices for BSA/AML compliance.

52. *See* Sullivan & Cromwell LLP, *2015 Year-End Review of BSA/AML and Sanctions Developments and Their Importance to Financial Institutions* (Mar. 3, 2016), *available at* https://sullcrom.com/siteFiles/Publications/SC_Publication_2015_Year_End_Review_of_BSA_AML_3_3_16.pdf.

53. *See* BSA MANUAL, *supra* note 48, at 207.

54. *See supra* note 18 and accompanying text.

55. 31 C.F.R. § 1010.410(f).

56. *See* U.S. Treasury Department, Complaint COMPL-2013-193659.

Financial transparency is paramount in the fight to safeguard the financial system against illicit use. Requiring financial institutions to perform effective customer due diligence (CDD) so that they understand who their customers are and what type of transactions they conduct is a critical element of an effective BSA program. The minimum expectation for CDD includes:

- Identifying and verifying the identity of customers
- Identifying and verifying the identity of beneficial owners of legal entity customers (i.e., the natural persons who own or control legal entities)
- Understanding the nature and purpose of customer relationships
- Conducting ongoing monitoring[57]

Although BSA monitoring depends on financial institutions knowing their customers, there were widely divergent beneficial ownership practices among financial institutions. Some institutions had robust compliance procedures but feared that they risked losing customers to other institutions with less rigorous procedures. Similarly, institutions felt that there were inconsistencies among regulatory examiners in enforcing compliance standards.[58]

In 2012, FinCEN issued an advance notice of proposed rulemaking[59] with respect to strengthening existing customer due diligence requirements and to establish a categorical requirement for financial institutions to identify beneficial ownership of their accountholders. Treasury acknowledged the need to mitigate these concerns by creating an environment where clearer rules and guidance may foster more consistent practices by financial institutions and examiners.[60] After several years of reviewing comments and hosting roundtable meetings with stakeholders to continue gathering information on the proposal, in July 2016, FinCEN issued final rules to clarify and strengthen customer due diligence requirements for banks, brokers or dealers in securities, mutual funds, and futures commission merchants and introducing brokers in commodities (the CDD Rules). The CDD Rules contain explicit customer due diligence requirements and include a new requirement to identify and verify the identity of beneficial owners of legal entity customers, subject to certain exclusions and exemptions.[61]

Effective as of July 11, 2018, the final CDD Rules will require that "covered financial institutions" include CDD procedures in their AML programs that facilitate the

---

57. *See* BSA Manual, *supra* note 48, at 56.

58. *See, e.g.*, News Release, FinCEN, Summary of Roundtable Meeting: Advance Notice of Proposed Rulemaking on Customer Due Diligence (Oct. 5, 2012) ("Participants expressed varied views as to whether, how and in what circumstances, financial institutions obtain beneficial ownership information."), *available at* http://www.fincen.gov/whatsnew/html/20121130NYC.html.

59. Customer Due Diligence Requirements for Financial Institutions, 77 Fed. Reg. 13,046 (Mar. 5, 2012).

60. FinCEN, Summary of Roundtable Meeting: Advance Notice of Proposed Rulemaking on Customer Due Diligence (Dec. 3, 2012), *available at* https://www.fincen.gov/whatsnew/pdf/SummaryofHearing-MiamiDec3.pdf.

61. Customer Due Diligence Requirements for Financial Institutions, 81 Fed. Reg. 29,398 (May 5, 2016).

understanding of the nature and purpose of customer relationships for the purpose of developing a customer risk profile, and maintain ongoing monitoring of these relationships to identify and report suspicious activities. In addition, covered financial institutions must maintain and update customer information. The level of detail required is based on the perceived BSA/AML risk that the customer brings in terms of the customer's business type, nature of transactions, and activities. "Covered financial institutions" include:

- Depository institutions, including insured banks, commercial banks, savings associations, federally insured credit unions, federally regulated trust companies, U.S. agencies and branches of a foreign bank, and Edge Act corporations
- Securities broker-dealers
- Mutual funds
- Futures commission merchants and introducing brokers in commodities

Under the CDD Rules,[62] covered financial institutions[63] are required to establish and maintain written procedures designed to identify and verify beneficial owners of legal entity customers, such as corporations and limited liability companies. The term "beneficial owner" includes each individual who, directly or indirectly, owns 25 percent or more of the equity interests of the legal entity customer, or a single individual with significant responsibility to control, manage, or direct the legal entity customer. At least one beneficial owner is required to be identified for each legal entity customer. A covered financial institution may rely on another financial institution (including an affiliate) to perform the requirements of the CDD Rule with respect to any legal entity customer of the covered financial institution that is opening, or has opened, an account or has established a similar business relationship with the other financial institution.[64]

The level of a depository financial institution's scrutiny of an MSB should reflect the level of risk that it presents. Not all MSBs will pose the same level of risk for money laundering and other illegal activities, but bank customers that are MSBs can expect scrutiny of their accounts. At a minimum, with the new CDD Rule, depository institutions will be required to identify at least one beneficial owner. In addition, under guidance issued by the FFIEC in 2005[65] (2005 Guidance), depository financial institutions are expected to conduct minimum customer due diligence when opening or maintaining accounts for MSBs, including the following:

- Apply CIP
- Confirm the customer's FinCEN registration, if required
- Confirm the customer's state licensing status, if applicable

---

62. 31 C.F.R. § 1010.230.
63. *Id.* § 1010.605(e)(1).
64. *Id.* § 1010.230(j).
65. Interagency Interpretive Guidance on Providing Banking Services to Money Services Businesses Operating in the United States (Apr. 26, 2005).

- Confirm the customer's agent status, if applicable
- Conduct a risk assessment to determine the level of risk associated with each account of the customer and whether further due diligence is required

When performing this basic risk assessment, depository financial institutions will consider, at a minimum:

- The types of products and services offered by an MSB
- The locations and markets served by the MSB
- The types of banking account services needed by the MSB
- The purpose of each depository financial institution account

This means that a depository financial institution may need to obtain additional information from an MSB that falls into a higher risk category. Most depository financial institutions will make certain inquiries at account opening and conduct ongoing account monitoring to uncover activities such as check cashing that may require registration and licensure. Once a depository financial institution has identified an MSB as a high-risk customer, the 2005 Guidance suggests other due diligence steps that a depository financial institution may need to take. These include:

- Making an on-site visit to the MSB
- Reviewing the MSB's own AML program
- Reviewing the MSB's employee screening practices
- Reviewing lists of the MSB's agents and locations in and outside of the United States that receive services through the MSB's depository financial institution account
- Reviewing the MSB's procedures for its operations
- Reviewing results of the MSB's independent testing of its AML program
- Reviewing written agent management and termination practices for the MSB[66]

Because of the significant additional monitoring that is required and, to some extent, because of the lack of BSA governance adopted by the MSBs themselves, depository financial institutions have been reluctant to continue doing business with MSBs.[67]

B. MSBs

In addition to providing information to their depository institutions and being subject to transaction monitoring, many MSBs are themselves subject to the full range of BSA regulatory requirements, including adopting a BSA/AML program, monitoring for suspicious activity, filing currency transaction reports, and

---

66. *See* BSA Manual, *supra* note 48, at 299–308.

67. *See* David Landsman, National Money Transmitters Association, How to Bank Money Services Businesses and Payments Companies (Dec. 2015).

various other identification and recordkeeping rules. MSBs' BSA responsibilities are activity-based. In the payments category, MSBs could include:

- Money transmitters and their agents
- Providers of prepaid access
- Sellers of prepaid access
- Exchangers and administrators of virtual currency

Regardless of the industry that comprises the main activity of the enterprise, such as a grocery store, convenience store, or check cashing operation, a business can be an MSB for BSA purposes if it engages in those activities.

1. Money Transmitters

FinCEN's regulations, as amended, define the term "money transmitter" to include a person that provides money transmission services and other persons engaged in the transfer of funds.[68] The term "money transmission services" means the acceptance of currency, funds, or other value that substitutes for currency from one person and the transmission of currency, funds, or other value that substitutes for currency to another location or person by any means. "Any means" includes, but is not limited to, through a financial agency or institution; a Federal Reserve Bank or other facility of one or more Federal Reserve Banks, the Board of Governors of the Federal Reserve System, or both; an electronic funds transfer network; or an informal value transfer system.[69]

Whether a person is a money transmitter is a matter of facts and circumstances. However, the definition of "money transmitter" in FinCEN's regulations defines six sets of circumstances—variously referred to as limitations or exemptions—under which a person is not a money transmitter despite accepting and transmitting currency, funds, or value that substitutes for currency. A "money transmitter" does not include a person that

- only provides the delivery, communication, or network access services used by a money transmitter to support money transmission services;
- acts as a payment processor to facilitate the purchase of, or payment of a bill for, a good or service through a clearance and settlement system by agreement with the creditor or seller;
- operates a clearance and settlement system or otherwise acts as an intermediary solely between BSA-regulated institutions, such as the FedWire system, and electronic funds transfer networks;
- certain registered clearing agencies regulated by the SEC, and derivatives clearing organizations, or other clearing house arrangements established by a financial agency or institution;

---

68. 31 C.F.R. § 1010.100(uu)(5(A), (B).

69. *See* FinCEN, Bank Secrecy Act/Anti-Money Laundering Examination Manual for Money Services Businesses 9 (2008) [hereinafter MSB Manual], *available at* https://www.fincen.gov/sites/default/files/shared/MSB_Exam_Manual.pdf.

- physically transports currency, other monetary instruments, other commercial paper, or other value that substitutes for currency as a person primarily engaged in such business, such as an armored car, from one person to the same person at another location or to an account belonging to the same person at a financial institution, provided that the person engaged in physical transportation has no more than a custodial interest in the currency, other monetary instruments, other commercial paper, or other value at any point during the transportation; or
- provides prepaid access, or accepts and transmits funds only integral to the sale of goods or the provision of services, other than money transmission services, by the person who is accepting and transmitting the funds.[70]

Agents[71] of money transmitters may include grocery stores, truck stops, check cashers, pharmacy stores, travel agents, and supermarkets. Entities that are paid commission on the fees paid to transfer money are agents. Western Union is a money transmitter "principal"; the convenience stores that facilitate Western Union money transfers might be "agents."

2. Prepaid Access

The prepaid card industry originated when companies began replacing paper gift certificates with magnetic stripe-bearing gift cards based on existing credit and automated teller machine (ATM) or debit card models. Over time, prepaid cards gained broad acceptance as their accessibility and capabilities have expanded. These capabilities include the ability to deposit additional funds by reloading the card, withdraw cash from an ATM, transfer funds between users, and pay bills. The ease of obtaining prepaid cards and their potential anonymous use make prepaid access products vulnerable to illicit activity. Internationally capable prepaid cards with large-dollar cash withdrawal functionality have raised the most consistent concern for U.S. law enforcement.[72]

Prepaid access can be issued in an electronic or physical form and linked to funds held in a pooled account. Consumers use both electronic and physical prepaid products to access funds held by banks in pooled accounts that are linked to subaccounts. As with other payment instruments, money laundering, terrorist financing, and other criminal activity may occur through prepaid access and prepaid card programs if effective controls are not in place. For example, law enforcement investigations have found that some prepaid holders have used false identification and funded their initial loads with stolen credit cards, or have purchased multiple prepaid cards under aliases.

---

70. *Id.*
71. *Id.* at 8.
72. *See, e.g.*, Amendment to the Bank Secrecy Act Regulations—Definitions and Other Regulations Relating to Prepaid Access, 75 Fed. Reg. 36,589, 36,595 n.44 (June 28, 2010).

The essential elements of prepaid access are "an arrangement of one or more persons acting together to provide access to funds or the value of funds that have been paid in advance and can be retrieved or transferred at some point in the future through an electronic device or vehicle such as a card, [or] code . . ."[73]

Until 2011, FinCEN had regulated "stored value" to a lesser degree than other forms of MSB activity, in part to allow the fledgling industry to develop. Since that time, "prepaid access" (as it is now more commonly called) has become increasingly prevalent in American commerce. In an effort to establish a more comprehensive regulatory regime for an industry whose technological advances have outpaced existing rules, FinCEN promulgated new requirements for prepaid access on July 26, 2011.[74] The final prepaid access rule recognizes the increasing potential for money laundering that prepaid access presented.[75] The final prepaid access rule was intended to balance the risks presented by certain types of prepaid access cards and bring the riskier products and their providers under the AML regime.

The final prepaid access rule primarily focused on the determination of who was a "provider" of prepaid access, but also identified a smaller subset of "sellers" that represented risk for money laundering. A provider must register with FinCEN as an MSB and identify each prepaid program for which it is the provider of prepaid access. In the final rule, prepaid access is defined as access to funds or the value of funds that have been paid in advance and can be retrieved or transferred at some point in the future through an electronic device or vehicle, such as a card, code, electronic serial number, mobile identification number, or personal identification number.[76]

As an MSB, providers of prepaid access are subject to certain BSA/AML responsibilities. The final rule also put in place SAR reporting and information collection requirements for providers and sellers of certain types of prepaid access. Those types of risks are present when a product is reloadable, available to transfer funds to other consumers, or available to transfer funds internationally.[77]

This final rule also amended and updated some of the existing provisions of FinCEN's rules applicable to MSBs that related to certain products that were previously defined as "stored value." It renamed "stored value" as "prepaid access," and clarified that a "provider" of "prepaid access" for a prepaid access program can be designated by agreement among the various participants in the program.[78] Prepaid access programs often rely on multiple third parties to accomplish the design, implementation, and maintenance of their programs, including program managers,

---

73. 31 C.F.R. § 1010.100(ww). *See* FIN-2014-R006, Whether a Company that Provides Online Real-Time Deposit, Settlement, and Payment Services for Banks, Businesses, and Consumers Is a Money Transmitter Rather Than a Provider of Prepaid Access (Apr. 29, 2014).

74. Bank Secrecy Act Regulations—Definitions and Other Regulations Relating to Prepaid Access, 76 Fed. Reg. 45,403 (July 29, 2011).

75. *Id.* at 45,404–04.

76. 31 C.F.R. § 1010.100(ww).

77. *See* 75 Fed. Reg. 36,589, 36,599–600 (June 28, 2010).

78. *Id.*

networks, distributors, providers of prepaid access, payment processors, issuing banks, and sellers or retailers. As a general rule, businesses offering check cashing, money orders, traveler's checks, money transfers, foreign currency exchange, and prepaid access products are "agents." Under the final prepaid access rule, the participants determine among themselves who should register; the final prepaid access rule presumes that the participant registering as the provider of prepaid access has agreed to perform all of the duties required for providers of prepaid access under the rule.[79] If none of the participants in a prepaid program registers with FinCEN as the provider of prepaid access for that program, the provider of prepaid access is the participant in the program with principal oversight and control over the program, which could be the program manager.[80]

The final rule excludes certain providers and sellers of prepaid access from the definition of MSB, such as arrangements that:

- Provide closed-loop prepaid access to funds (e.g., such as store gift cards) in amounts not to exceed $2,000 maximum value per device on any day
- Provide prepaid access solely to funds provided by a government agency
- Provide prepaid access to funds for pretax flexible spending for health and dependent care, or from health reimbursement arrangements for health care expenses[81]

Additionally, under the final rule, open-loop prepaid access limited to $1,000 per day and arrangements for access to employment benefits, incentives, wages, or salaries have a *qualified exclusion* and are not considered prepaid access programs subject to BSA regulatory requirements *unless* they can be used internationally, allow transfers of value from person to person within the arrangement, or be reloaded from a nondepository source. If any one of these features is part of the arrangement, however, it would be a covered prepaid program under the final rules.

The final rule also addressed the obligations of certain sellers of prepaid access, defined to include any person that receives funds or the value of funds in exchange for an initial loading or subsequent loading of prepaid access if that person

- sells prepaid access offered under a prepaid program that can be used before verification of the customer's identification under 31 C.F.R. § 1022.210(d)(1)(iv); or
- sells prepaid access (including closed-loop prepaid access) to funds that exceed $10,000 to any person during any one day, *and has not* implemented policies and procedures reasonably adapted to prevent such a sale.[82]

FinCEN acknowledged that sellers meeting this definition, while small in number, posed heightened money laundering risk. Accordingly, those sellers would be

---

79. 31 C.F.R. § 1010.380.
80. *Id.* § 1010.100(ff)(4)(ii).
81. *Id.* § 1010.100(ff).
82. *Id.* § 1010.100(ff)(7).

obligated to comply with the requirements to maintain an AML program, report suspicious activity, and collect customer identifying information.[83]

3. Virtual Currency

A subset of money transmitters are certain participants in virtual currency businesses.[84] FinCEN's regulations define currency (sometimes referred to as "fiat currency") as "the coin and paper money of the United States or of any other country that is designated as legal tender; and that circulates; and is customarily used and accepted as a medium of exchange in the country of issuance."[85]

In contrast, "virtual" currency is a medium of exchange that operates like a currency in some environments, but does not have legal tender status in any jurisdiction. Virtual currency must be converted into fiat currency through the services of an administrator or exchanger prior to deposit into the banking system. An administrator or exchanger of virtual currency is an MSB under FinCEN's regulations (specifically, a money transmitter) unless a limitation to or exemption from the definition applies to the person.

Specifically, "exchangers" and "administrators" of virtual currencies are money transmitters under FinCEN's regulations and therefore required to register with FinCEN as MSBs. The 2013 Guidance defines an "exchanger" as a person or entity "engaged as a business in the exchange of virtual currency for real currency, funds, or other virtual currency." The 2013 Guidance also defines an administrator of virtual currency as a person or entity "engaged as a business in issuing (putting into circulation) a virtual currency, and who has the authority to redeem (to withdraw from circulation) such virtual currency."[86]

The BSA requirements and supervisory expectations for providing banking services to administrators or exchangers of virtual currencies are the same as for money transmitters.

VII. MSB OBLIGATIONS TO COMPLY WITH BSA

This section summarizes the obligations of MSBs under FinCEN's BSA rules.[87] With certain exceptions, MSBs are required to establish written AML programs, file CTR and SARs, and maintain certain records. In addition to their BSA obligations, MSBs are required to be licensed by FinCEN. These are independent obligations.

---

83. 76 Fed. Reg. at 45,412.
84. FIN-2013-G0001, Application of FinCEN's Regulations to Persons Administering, Exchanging, or Using Virtual Currencies (Mar. 18, 2013).
85. *Id.*
86. *Id.* at 2.
87. 31 C.F.R. ch. X.

A. Registration

The owner or controlling person of the MSB must register with FinCEN by electronically filing FinCEN Form 107 within 180 days after the date the MSB was established. Foreign-located MSBs must designate a person who resides in the United States to function as an agent to accept service of legal process, including with respect to BSA compliance.[88] A copy of the filed registration form and other supporting documentation must be retained at a location in the United States for a period of five years.

B. Maintenance of Agent List

A person that is an MSB solely because it is an "agent" of another MSB is not required to separately register. As part of the registration rule, each MSB that is required to register must prepare and maintain a list of its agents that are authorized to sell or distribute its MSB services.[89] An "agent" is a separate business entity from the issuer (also sometimes referred to as the "principal") that the issuer authorizes, through a written agreement or otherwise, to sell its instruments or, in the case of funds transmission, to sell its send-and-receive transfer services. A person who is solely an employee of the MSB is not an agent of that MSB.[90]

An "agent" is distinguished from a "branch" of the MSB, which is a place of operation that is owned by the issuer of the MSB product or service.[91] An issuer may own numerous branches through which the issuer sells its own instruments or transmits funds.

The agent list is not filed with the registration form but must be maintained at a location in the United States that is identified on the form. The list must be revised each January 1 for the immediately preceding 12-month period. A copy of the MSB's initial agent list and of each revised list must be retained for a period of five years. Upon request, the MSB must make its list of agents available to FinCEN, or its designee, the Internal Revenue Service (IRS), in the performance of its examination function.[92] In addition to identifying information, the agent list provides information regarding the specific type of service or services the agent provides, and the gross amount of transactions conducted in the preceding 12 months that exceeded $100,000 (excluding fees and commissions) received from transactions with MSBs and identification of depository institutions at which the agent maintains accounts for all or part of the funds received in or for the financial products or services issued by the MSB, whether the account is maintained in the agent's or the business principal's name.[93]

---

88. *Id.* § 1022.380(a)(2).
89. 31 U.S.C. § 5330; 31 C.F.R. § 1022.380(a).
90. 31 C.F.R. § 1022.380(a)(3).
91. *Id.* § 1022.380(b)(1)(ii).
92. *Id.*
93. *Id.* § 1022.380(d).

C. AML Program

Each MSB is required by law to have an effective AML program.[94] An effective AML program is one that is reasonably designed to prevent the money services business from being used to facilitate money laundering and the financing of terrorist activities. MSBs, both principals and their agents, are required to establish and maintain an effective written AML program.[95] An MSB's AML program must, at a minimum, cover the Four Pillars:[96]

- Incorporate policies, procedures, and internal controls reasonably designed to assure compliance with the BSA and its implementing regulations
- Designate a person to assure day-to-day compliance with the program and the BSA and its implementing regulations
- Provide education and training of appropriate personnel concerning their responsibilities under the program, including training in the detection of suspicious transactions to the extent that the MSB is required to report such transactions under the BSA
- Provide for independent review to monitor and maintain an adequate program

1. Risk Assessment

Each MSB AML program is expected to be risk-based.[97] That is, the program should be commensurate with the risks posed by the location and size of the MSB, and by the nature and volume of the products and services it offers. A written risk assessment is generally encouraged, which identifies the products, services and customer types, the volumes of activity, and the risk mitigation measurements employed.[98]

In addition, an effective AML program must include agent monitoring policies and procedures sufficient to allow the principal to understand and account for associated risks. Both principals and agents are liable for compliance with the AML program. An MSB principal is exposed to risk when an agent engages in transactions that create a risk for money laundering, terrorist financing, or other financial crime. Risk factors that principals should consider when conducting agent monitoring include, but are not limited to:

- Whether the owners are known or suspected to be associated with criminal conduct or terrorism
- Whether the agent has an established and adhered-to AML program

---

94. *Id.* § 1022.210.
95. *Id. See also* Interpretive Release 2004-1, Anti-Money Laundering Program Requirements for Money Services Businesses with Respect to Foreign Agents or Foreign Counterparties, 69 Fed. Reg. 74,439 (Dec. 14, 2004).
96. *See supra* note 29 and accompanying text.
97. 31 C.F.R. § 1022.210(b).
98. *See* MSB Manual, *supra* note 69, at 14.

- The nature of the markets the agent serves and the extent to which the market presents an increased risk for money laundering or terrorist financing (Note that this does not mean that principals with agents providing services involving regions affected by conflict or terrorism cannot manage such risks, but rather that principals must take steps to account for and mitigate such risks.)
- The services an agent is expected to provide and the agent's anticipated level of activity
- The nature and duration of the relationship

2. Internal Controls

Internal controls are the policies, procedures, and processes designed to limit and control risks and to achieve compliance with the BSA. The level of sophistication of the internal controls should be commensurate with the size, structure, risks, and complexity of the entity. In order to reduce exposure to risks posed by agents, the MSB principal must have procedures in place to identify those agents conducting activities that appear to lack commercial purpose, lack justification, or otherwise are not supported by verifiable documentation.[99] The principal must implement risk-based procedures to monitor the agents' transactions to ensure that they are legitimate. The procedures must also ensure that, if the agents' transactions trigger reporting or recordkeeping requirements, the principal handles the information in accordance with regulatory reporting and recordkeeping obligations. In addition, the MSB principal should implement procedures for handling noncompliant agents including, where appropriate, terminating the agent relationship.[100]

Principals must periodically reassess risks associated with their agents and update the principals' programs to address any changing or additional related risks. Principals must also take corrective action after becoming aware of any weaknesses or deficiencies in their AML programs. MSB principals and agents are required to conduct reviews with a scope and frequency commensurate with the risks of money laundering or other illicit activity such principal or agent faces. A principal must conduct internal and/or external independent testing to ensure there are no material weaknesses (e.g., inadequate training) or internal control deficiencies (e.g., monitoring agents). In addition, the testing must factor in products and services provided to determine if the procedures are sufficient to detect and report suspicious activity.

3. CIP

As part of their risk assessment and risk mitigation plans, MSBs are required to implement know-your-customer/know-your-counterparty procedures.[101] Such

---

99. 31 C.F.R. § 1022.210(d)(1).
100. *See* MSB Manual, *supra* note 69, at 50.
101. 31 C.F.R. § 1022.210(d)(1)(i)(A).

procedures allow the MSB to assess the risk involved in providing account-based or transactional services to customers based on their identity and profile, and to comply with their AML program requirements regarding foreign agents or foreign counterparties.[102] MSBs are also subject to the Travel Rule.[103] MSBs are not covered financial institutions for purposes of the new CDD Rules, however.[104]

4. Transaction Monitoring and Suspicious Activity Reporting

Money transmitters, issuers, sellers and redeemers of money orders and traveler's checks, as well as the U.S. Postal Service are required to monitor their customers' transactions and report suspicious activity that involves $2,000 or more. The monitoring and reporting must include, at a minimum: (1) risk rating of accounts based on the particular gateway used; (2) dynamic risk tools to facilitate investigation of suspicious activity, including counterparty reporting, flow of funds reporting, account flagging of suspicious accounts, and degrees of separation reporting; and (3) other reports of protocol-wide activity regarding any unlawful activity.

If the MSB knows, suspects, or has reason to suspect that the transaction or pattern of transactions (or a pattern of transactions of which the transaction is a part) either involves funds derived from illegal activity; is intended or conducted in order to hide or disguise funds or assets derived from illegal activity; is designed to evade the requirements of the BSA, whether through structuring or other means; serves no business or apparent lawful purpose; or that the reporting business knows of no reasonable explanation for the transaction after examining all available facts, the MSB must file a SAR if the transaction involves $2,000 or more.[105] SAR filings are detailed reports describing the activity observed and categorizing the report into one of eight types of suspicious activities: structuring, fraud, identification, insurance, securities futures and options, terrorist financing, money laundering, and a catchall of other suspicious activities.[106] Even if an MSB concludes after investigation that the activity is not suspicious, it must maintain documentary evidence to support that conclusion.[107]

5. CTR Filings

MSBs must also file CTRs if the transaction involves currency of more than $10,000.[108] When an MSB receives more than $10,000 in one transaction or a series of related transactions, while conducting their trade or business, a CTR must be filed electronically by the covered MSB.

---

102. *See supra* note 96 and accompanying text.
103. *See supra* note 56 and accompanying text.
104. *See* 31 C.F.R. §§ 1010.230(f), 1010.605(e)(1).
105. SAR FinCEN Form 111.
106. *See* 75 Fed. Reg. 63,545 (Oct. 10, 2010).
107. *See* MSB MANUAL, *supra* note 69, at 94.
108. However, money transfers in excess of $10,000 solely for the purpose of purchasing postage or philatelic products from the U.S. Postal Service do not require the filing of a CTR. 31 C.F.R. § 1010.311.

6. Recordkeeping Requirements

MSBs are required to make and keep certain records, which are to be made available to FinCEN or law enforcement during examinations or upon subpoena.[109] Required records include:

- Purchases of bank checks or drafts, cashier's checks, money orders, or traveler's checks for $3,000 or more in currency[110]
- Certain transactional records relating to prepaid access[111]
- Additional records to be maintained by prepaid access providers and sellers to collect and retain customer information relating to prepaid access[112]

Records are generally required to be kept for five years and failure to maintain records is considered a recordkeeping violation.[113]

D. Examination and Enforcement

FinCEN has delegated authority to investigate MSBs for compliance with the BSA to the IRS.[114] The IRS has issued its own *Bank Secrecy Act/Anti-Money Laundering Examination Manual for Money Services Businesses* (the MSB Manual).[115] Similar to the FFIEC BSA Examination Manual, the MSB Manual provides guidance to examiners for performing BSA examinations, but it also provides guidance to MSBs on developing and maintaining effective AML programs. The MSB Manual contains an overview of the program requirements, BSA/AML risks and risk management expectations, and industry practices, in addition to examination procedures.

In the exercise of its enforcement authority, FinCEN may bring an enforcement action for violations of the reporting, recordkeeping, or other requirements of the BSA. FinCEN's Office of Enforcement evaluates enforcement matters that may result in a variety of remedies, including the assessment of civil money penalties. Civil money penalties may be assessed for recordkeeping violations,[116] failing to file a CTR,[117] failing to file an SAR,[118] or failing to file an FBAR.[119] FinCEN also takes enforcement actions against MSBs for failure to register with FinCEN.[120]

---

109. *Id.* § 1010.410(e).
110. *Id.* § 1010.415.
111. *Id.* § 1022.420.
112. *Id.* § 1022.210(d)(1)(iv).
113. *Id.* § 1010.430.
114. *Id.* §§ 56(b)(8), 103.125(c).
115. MSB Manual, *supra* note 69.
116. 31 C.F.R. § 1010.415.
117. *Id.* § 1010.311.
118. *Id.* § 1021.320.
119. *Id.* § 1010.350.
120. *Id.* § 1022.380.

VIII. OFAC[121]

The OFAC is a division of the U.S. Department of the Treasury that administers and enforces economic and trade sanctions based on U.S. foreign policy and national security goals against targeted foreign countries and regimes, terrorists, international narcotics traffickers, those engaged in activities related to the proliferation of weapons of mass destruction, and other threats to the national security, foreign policy, or economy of the United States. OFAC acts under presidential national emergency powers,[122] as well as specific legislation, to prohibit transactions and block (or "freeze") assets subject to U.S. jurisdiction.[123] OFAC's regulations apply to all U.S. persons, certain foreign persons living in the United States, and, for certain sanctions programs, foreign subsidiaries of U.S. persons.[124]

OFAC administers two general types of programs. The first is economic sanctions against particular countries. This is commonly referred to as sanctions programs and includes countries such as Cuba, Russia-Ukraine, Syria, North Korea, and Sudan, as well as programs targeted at terrorists and weapons of mass destruction. Each sanctions program is different since they are designed to achieve a specific foreign policy objective that varies from program to program.

The second type of program is the Specially Designated Nationals (SDN) List.[125] While the country sanctions may apply to all transactions associated with the government of Cuba, the SDN List specifically identifies an entity that U.S. persons may not "do business with." SDNs typically include terrorist groups, Latin American drug lords, and charities that provide funding to terrorists.

The OFAC SDN List is updated regularly as a result of law enforcement investigations or presidential actions. For example, shortly after the attacks of 9/11, the president, utilizing his statutory authority, issued an Executive Order seizing the property of the suspected terrorists. Upon issuance of this Executive Order, all U.S. persons were expected to comply with the requirements of the Executive Order.[126]

---

121. According to the U.S. Department of the Treasury website, https://www.treasury.gov, OFAC is the successor to the Office of Foreign Funds Control, established during World War II to prevent the Nazis from using occupied countries' holdings of foreign currency and securities. OFAC was formally created in December 1950, during the Korean War, when President Harry S. Truman ordered the blocking of all Chinese and North Korean assets in the United States. *See* U.S. Department of the Treasury, *About—Terrorism and Financial Intelligence—Office of Foreign Assets Control (OFAC)*, https://www.treasury .gov/about/organizational-structure/offices/Pages/Office-of-Foreign-Assets-Control.aspx (last updated Apr. 20, 2017).

122. 50 U.S.C. ch. 35.

123. *See* OFAC Economic Sanctions Enforcement Guidelines, 74 Fed. Reg. 57,593, 57,594 (Nov. 9, 2009) [hereinafter OFAC Guidelines].

124. *See* U.S. Department of the Treasury, *OFAC FAQs: General Questions*, FAQ No. 11, https://www .treasury.gov/resource-center/faqs/Sanctions/Pages/faq_general.aspx#basic (last updated Mar. 14, 2017).

125. *Id.* FAQ No. 18.

126. Exec. Order No. 13,224, Blocking Property and Prohibiting Transactions with Persons Who Commit, Threaten to Commit, or Support Terrorism Notice of Sept. 24, 2001—Continuation of Emergency with Respect to UNITA, 66 Fed. Reg. 49,079 (Sept. 25, 2001).

OFAC and BSA impose separate and distinct legal obligations, which are authorized by different statutes and serve different public policy purposes. Most importantly, these laws apply to different constituencies—OFAC applies to almost every U.S. person, while BSA only applies to certain financial institutions. However, there is overlap between the two requirements and they are often considered together. One reason for this treatment is that the OFAC SDN List contains names of terrorists and drug dealers, which also signal potential BSA violations.

Each of the more than twenty-some sanctions programs[127] and several thousand SDNs[128] varies in the extent and scope of the prohibited transactions. Generally, businesses must determine how they comply with the OFAC regulations. Although the OFAC regulations do not specifically require the checking of the OFAC SDN List or country sanctions list, if a prohibited transaction occurs with entities on either list, then an OFAC violation has occurred.[129] These are "strict liability" statutes and a violator will probably incur both a fine and potential reputational harm as well.[130] OFAC fines are published on the OFAC website.[131]

Compliant businesses typically compare transactions against the SDN List and the list of embargoed or blocked countries by using technology solutions that will not permit a payment to be completed to a blocked person or country. If a prohibited transaction is identified, OFAC requires the reporting of this information within ten days and annually each September 30. Failure to make reports constitutes a violation subject to civil money penalties.[132]

IX. CONCLUSION

International crime syndicates and terrorist organizations continue to evolve and invent new methods to launder proceeds of crime and financing of worldwide terrorist activities. The federal financial regulators will likely continue to respond by adopting increasingly robust BSA/AML regulations applicable to payments systems to combat these changing threats to the global financial system.

---

127. 31 C.F.R. ch. V. A list of active sanctions programs can be found at U.S. Department of the Treasury, *Resource Center—Sanctions Programs and Country Information*, https://www.treasury.gov/resource-center /sanctions/Programs/Pages/Programs.aspx (last updated May 19, 2017).

128. 31 C.F.R. ch. V, app. A. The SDN list is updated regularly and can be searched at U.S. Department of the Treasury, *Resource Center—Specially Designated Nationals and Blocked Persons List (SDN) Human Readable List*, https://www.treasury.gov/resource-center/sanctions/SDN-List/Pages/default.aspx (last updated May 19, 2017).

129. *See* OFAC Guidelines, *supra* note 123, at 57,594.

130. 31 C.F.R. pt. 501, app. A.

131. *See, e.g.*, Enforcement Actions against MasterCard for Violations of the Reporting, Procedures, and Penalties Regulations (RPPR), 31 C.F.R. pt. 501, Enforcement Information for Mar. 16, 2016, *available at* https://www.treasury.gov/resource-center/sanctions/CivPen/Documents/20160316_MasterCard.pdf.

132. 31 C.F.R. § 501.603.

Chapter 8

Money Laundering and Sanctions Regimes

Cross-Border Payments

Paul Lanois[1]

I. INTRODUCTION

The world of global payments is evolving rapidly, driven by an increasingly global economy, expanding consumer buying power in Asia and South America, and rising adoption of digital payment methods. According to Bloomberg News, PayPal alone processed $354 billion in transactions in 2016, with about half of the business taking place overseas.[2] Cross-border payments are on the rise, and this has not gone unnoticed by regulators. For example, the U.S. Department of Justice recently sought transaction information from PayPal as part of a money laundering investigation.[3]

Since money laundering is by nature clandestine and hidden, it is extremely difficult to estimate the total volume of money involved. According to the United Nations Office on Drugs and Crime, the amount laundered globally in one year is estimated to be 2–5 percent of global gross domestic product (GDP), or USD 800 billion to USD 2 trillion.[4] Back in 1998, the International Monetary Fund also stated that the aggregate size of money laundering in the world could be somewhere between 2 and 5 percent of the world's GDP—the value of the total output of an economy the size of Spain.[5]

---

1. Paul Lanois is Vice President and Senior Legal Counsel at Credit Suisse.
2. Spencer Soper, *PayPal Says Anti-Money Laundering Program Subpoenaed by DOJ*, Bloomberg, Feb. 8, 2017, https://www.bloomberg.com/news/articles/2017-02-08/paypal-says-anti-money-laundering-program-subpoenaed-by-doj.
3. *Id.*
4. United Nations Office on Drugs and Crime, *Money-Laundering and Globalization*, http://www.unodc.org/unodc/en/money-laundering/globalization.html (last visited May 22, 2017).
5. Financial Action Task Force (FATF), *FAQ—Money Laundering*, http://www.fatf-gafi.org/faq/moneylaundering/ (last visited May 22, 2017).

Sanctions and regulations are very closely intertwined with global markets, since these are often the tools used by governments around the world to prevent actors from undertaking certain activities within their territory and enjoying the benefits of globalization at the expense of local entities. According to a 2016 survey on global economic crime conducted by PwC, nearly a dozen global financial institutions have been assessed fines in the hundreds of millions to billions of dollars for money laundering and/or sanctions violations over the past few years in the United States alone.[6] For example, in December 2012, HSBC agreed to settle money laundering charges for a record $1.9 billion.[7] In addition, U.S. authorities also required HSBC to improve its in-house controls after investigators found that it allowed billions of dollars to be transferred in violation of U.S. sanctions laws and anti-money laundering (AML) statutes. As other countries are expected to ramp up their regulation and enforcement efforts, the increased regulatory expectations on financial services organizations will continue to grow and represent a greater challenge. The same 2016 PwC survey found that many financial services organizations are generally struggling to cope with the ever-shifting regulatory environment, with one in five financial services respondents having experienced enforcement actions by a regulator.[8]

Nevertheless, the regulatory challenges faced by financial services organizations are no longer limited to simply complying with local money laundering rules or banking regulations, as demonstrated by the record fine imposed in 2014 by the U.S. Department of Justice on BNP Paribas, the largest retail bank in France and also one of the world's top ten largest banks. The French bank was sentenced for conspiring to violate two U.S. laws, the International Emergency Economic Powers Act (IEEPA) and the Trading with the Enemy Act (TWEA), by processing billions of dollars of transactions through the U.S. financial system on behalf of Sudanese, Iranian, and Cuban entities subject to U.S. economic sanctions.[9] BNP was sentenced to a five-year term of probation, ordered to forfeit more than $8.8 billion to the United States, and required to pay a $140 million fine. According to the U.S. Department of Justice, this is "the first time a financial institution has been convicted and sentenced for violations of U.S. economic sanctions, and the total financial penalty—including the forfeiture and criminal fine—is the largest financial penalty ever imposed in a criminal case." The severity of the sentence indicates the intention to send a clear message to financial institutions around the world that simply complying with local money laundering rules or banking regulations is not enough. More recent enforcement actions

---

6. PwC, GLOBAL ECONOMIC CRIME SURVEY 2016 (2016), *available at* http://www.pwc.com/gx/en /economic-crime-survey/pdf/GlobalEconomicCrimeSurvey2016.pdf.

7. Halah Touryalai, *Massive Money Laundering Hits Keep Coming, HSBC Said to Pay $1.9B Settlement*, FORBES, Dec. 10, 2012, http://www.forbes.com/sites/halahtouryalai/2012/12/10/massive-money -laundering-hits-keep-coming-hsbc-said-to-pay-1-9b-in-u-s-settlement/.

8. PwC, *supra* note 5.

9. Press Release, U.S. Department of Justice, BNP Paribas Sentenced for Conspiring to Violate the International Emergency Economic Powers Act and the Trading with the Enemy Act (May 1, 2015), *available at* https://www.justice.gov/opa/pr/bnp-paribas-sentenced-conspiring-violate-international -emergency-economic-powers-act-and.

from the U.S. authorities, such as the sanctions imposed on Deutsche Bank,[10] have led some observers to worry that the importance of U.S. sanctions may threaten the financial stability of the European banking sector.[11]

This chapter provides an overview of recent money laundering developments throughout the Europe, Middle East, and Africa (EMEA) region.

II. THE CURRENT EUROPEAN FRAMEWORK: THE FOURTH EU DIRECTIVE ON AML

The European Union has adopted important directives on the matter of money laundering, with the latest one—the European Union's Fourth AML Directive[12]—being adopted on May 20, 2015. This directive incorporates rules to combat money laundering and terrorist financing within the EU financial system.

Previous directives addressed the threat of money laundering, but this directive goes a step further. European Directive 91/308/EEC[13] defined money laundering in terms of drug offenses and imposed obligations solely on the financial sector. Directive 2001/97/EC[14] then extended its scope, both in terms of the crimes covered and the range of professions and activities included. In June 2003, the Financial Action Task Force (FATF) revised its recommendations to cover terrorist financing and provided more detailed requirements in relation to customer identification and verification. FATF *identified* situations where a higher risk of money laundering or terrorist financing may justify enhanced measures, as well as those situations where a reduced risk may justify less rigorous controls. Those changes were reflected in Directive 2005/60/EC[15] and in Directive 2006/70/EC[16] laying down further implementing measures.

---

10. Ely Razin, *Deutsche Bank Was Fined $14 Billion. What Does That Mean for U.S. Commercial Real Estate?*, FORBES, Sept. 19, 2016, http://www.forbes.com/sites/elyrazin/2016/09/19/deutsche-bank-was-fined-14-billion-what-does-that-mean-for-u-s-commercial-real-estate/#107739d15225.

11. Matt Clinch & Geoff Cutmore, *EU Boss Wants an End to Large US Fines on Europe Banks: "It's Becoming a Risk,"* CNBC, Oct. 7, 2016, http://www.cnbc.com/2016/10/07/eu-boss-wants-an-end-to-large-us-fines-on-europe-banks-its-becoming-a-risk.html.

12. Directive (EU) 2015/849 of the European Parliament and of the Council of 20 May 2015 on the Prevention of the Use of the Financial System for the Purposes of Money Laundering or Terrorist Financing, Amending Regulation (EU) No 648/2012 of the European Parliament and of the Council, and Repealing Directive 2005/60/EC of the European Parliament and of the Council and Commission Directive 2006/70/EC, *available at* http://eur-lex.europa.eu/legal-content/EN/TXT/?uri=CELEX:32015L0849.

13. Directive 91/308/EEC of 10 June 1991 on Prevention of the Use of the Financial System for the Purpose of Money Laundering, *available at* http://eur-lex.europa.eu/legal-content/EN/TXT/?uri=CELEX%3A31991L0308.

14. Directive 2001/97/EC of the European Parliament and of the Council of 4 December 2001 Amending Council Directive 91/308/EEC on Prevention of the Use of the Financial System for the Purpose of Money Laundering, *available at* http://eur-lex.europa.eu/legal-content/EN/ALL/?uri=CELEX%3A32001L0097.

15. Directive 2005/60/EC of the European Parliament and of the Council of 26 October 2005 on the Prevention of the Use of the Financial System for the Purpose of Money Laundering and Terrorist Financing, *available at* http://eur-lex.europa.eu/legal-content/en/ALL/?uri=CELEX:32005L0060.

16. Commission Directive 2006/70/EC of 1 August 2006 Laying Down Implementing Measures for Directive 2005/60/EC of the European Parliament and of the Council as Regards the Definition of Politically Exposed Person and the Technical Criteria for Simplified Customer Due Diligence Procedures and for Exemption on Grounds of a Financial Activity Conducted on an Occasional or Very Limited Basis, *available at* http://eur-lex.europa.eu/legal-content/EN/TXT/?uri=CELEX%3A32006L0070.

The Fourth AML Directive takes into account the recommendations issued by the FATF in its International Standards on Combating Money Laundering and the Financing of Terrorism and Proliferation adopted in February 2012.[17] It sets high standards to ensure that credit and financial institutions are equipped to detect and take action against such risks. For instance, it introduced a requirement for European Member States to put in place national registers of beneficial owners to ensure transparency around certain ownership structures.

The Fourth AML Directive applies to the financial sector and certain other actors such as lawyers, estate agents, auditors, trusts, or company service providers. The scope of "obliged entities" falling under the Fourth AML Directive has been extended to include persons trading in goods (e.g., precious metals and stones) where payments of €10,000 or more are made in cash. In addition, all providers of gambling services[18] now fall within the scope of the Fourth AML Directive, whereas the previous directives only applied to casinos. Also, the Fourth AML Directive expressly mentions in recital 8 that estate agents should be understood to include letting agents, where applicable. The Fourth AML Directive requires covered participants to identify and verify the identity of their customers, including the beneficial owners of their entity customers, thereby disclosing the identity of the person who ultimately owns or controls a company. It imposes obligations to report suspicions of money laundering or terrorist financing to the public authorities, usually the financial intelligence unit, and to adopt supporting measures, such as proper training of personnel, appropriate internal preventive policies and procedures, and enhanced customer due diligence practices for higher-risk situations such as trading with banks situated outside the European Union. The Fourth AML Directive requires the industry to adopt a more risk-based approach and new processes for determining eligibility for simplified due diligence, and more public officials to be included in the politically exposed person (PEP) definition.

European Member States are required to update their respective money laundering laws and "transpose" the new requirements into their local law by June 26, 2017.

III. PROPOSED AMENDMENTS TO THE FOURTH AML DIRECTIVE

Even though the Fourth AML Directive was only recently adopted (i.e., May 2015), the European Commission continued its initiatives to address money laundering

---

17. FATF, INTERNATIONAL STANDARDS ON COMBATING MONEY LAUNDERING AND THE FINANCING OF TERRORISM AND PROLIFERATION (Feb. 2012), *available at* http://www.fatf-gafi.org/media/fatf/documents/recommendations/pdfs/FATF_Recommendations.pdf.

18. As per article 3(14) of the Fourth AML Directive, "gambling services" means a service that involves wagering a stake with monetary value in games of chance, including those with an element of skill, such as lotteries, casino games, poker games, and betting transactions that are provided at a physical location, or by any means at a distance, by electronic means, or any other technology for facilitating communication, and at the individual request of a recipient of services.

concerns. The Commission's action plan issued in February 2016 indicates that amendments to the Fourth AML Directive are very considerable, and include: enhancing checks ("due diligence measures/counter-measures") aimed towards high-risk third countries; bringing virtual currency exchange platforms under the scope of the customer due diligence controls within the Fourth AML Directive, thereby ending the anonymity associated with such exchanges; strengthening transparency measures applicable to prepaid instruments (such as prepaid cards) by lowering thresholds for required identification from €250 to €150 and widening customer verification requirements; and enhancing the powers of financial intelligence units (FIUs) and facilitating their cooperation by further aligning the rules for such FIUs with the latest international standards and giving FIUs swift access to information on the holders of bank and payment accounts through centralized registers or electronic data retrieval systems.[19]

Proposed amendments to the Fourth AML Directive were issued by the European Commission on July 5, 2016, to virtual currency exchange platforms as well as custodian wallet providers.[20] According to the proposed amendment, virtual currency transfers are currently not monitored in any way by public authorities within the European Union, as neither the Union nor its Member States have adopted specific binding rules to set out conditions for such monitoring.[21]

Under the proposed article 1, virtual currency exchanges "*engaged primarily and professionally in exchange services between virtual currencies and fiat currencies*"[22] and "*wallet providers offering custodial services of credentials necessary to access virtual currencies*"[23] will be entities subject to the requirements of the Fourth AML Directive. The new changes mean that virtual currency exchange platforms and custodian wallet providers will soon be required to apply customer due diligence controls to manage and mitigate risks, and anonymous virtual currency holding and transfers will no longer be possible via EU exchanges and wallet companies. It is unclear based on the current wording of the proposed article 1 whether currency exchanges that only deal with virtual currencies (i.e., only exchange virtual currency for different virtual currencies) would be subject to the new AML requirements or not.

Additionally, the proposed directive would amend article 65 of the Fourth AML Directive to grant FIUs across European Member States "with respect to virtual currencies, empowerments to set-up and maintain a central database registering users' identities and wallet addresses accessible to FIUs, as well as self-declaration forms

---

19. Fact Sheet, European Commission, Questions and Answers: Anti-Money Laundering Directive (July 5, 2016), *available at* http://europa.eu/rapid/press-release_MEMO-16-2381_en.htm.

20. Commission Proposal for a Directive of the European Parliament and of the Council Amending Directive (EU) 2015/849 on the Prevention of the Use of the Financial System for the Purposes of Money Laundering or Terrorist Financing and Amending Directive 2009/101/EC (July 5, 2016), *available at* http://ec.europa.eu/justice/criminal/document/files/aml-directive_en.pdf.

21. *Id.* at 12.

22. Id. at art. 1.

23. Id. at art. 1.

for the use of virtual currency users."[24] Last but not least, the proposed directive would include the first legal definition under EU law for "virtual currencies," which European Member States would be required to implement in their legislation once the proposed directive is formally adopted. As set out in the proposed article 1, the term "virtual currencies" would be defined as "a digital representation of value that is neither issued by a central bank or a public authority, nor necessarily attached to a fiat currency, but is accepted by natural or legal persons as a means of payment and can be transferred, stored or traded electronically."[25]

This would not be the first legislation to include virtual currency businesses within the scope of AML requirements. The U.S. Financial Crimes Enforcement Network (FinCEN), the regulator empowered to administer the Bank Secrecy Act (BSA), issued guidance on March 18, 2013, clarifying that an administrator or exchanger of virtual currencies falls within the definition of "money services businesses" (MSB).[26] More specifically, an administrator or exchanger that (1) accepts and transmits a convertible virtual currency or (2) buys or sells convertible virtual currency for any reason is a money transmitter under FinCEN's regulations, unless a limitation to or exemption from the definition applies to the person.[27] In contrast to the proposed amendments to the Fourth AML Directive, the FinCEN guidance clearly states that there is no difference between real currencies and convertible virtual currencies for the purposes of the BSA and that "accepting and transmitting anything of value that substitutes for currency makes a person a money transmitter under the regulations implementing the BSA."[28]

IV. FURTHER PROPOSED AMENDMENTS TO THE CURRENT EUROPEAN FRAMEWORK

In December 2016, the European Commission adopted a package of additional measures that are intended to strengthen the fight against the financing of terrorism and organized crime.[29] These proposals were meant to complete and reinforce the European legal framework in the areas of money laundering, illicit cash flows, and government powers for freezing and confiscation of assets.

One of the proposed amendments is a legislative proposal for a "directive on countering money laundering by criminal law,"[30] which sets minimum rules con-

---

24. *Id.* at 38–39.

25. *Id.* at 30.

26. FinCEN Guidance on the Application of FinCEN's Regulations to Persons Administering, Exchanging, or Using Virtual Currencies (Mar. 18, 2013) (FIN-2013-G001), *available at* https://www.fincen.gov/sites/default/files/shared/FIN-2013-G001.pdf.

27. *Id.* at 3.

28. *Id.* at 3.

29. Press Release, European Commission, Security Union: Commission Adopts Stronger Rules to Fight Terrorism Financing (Dec. 21, 2016), *available at* http://europa.eu/rapid/press-release_IP-16-4401_en.htm.

30. Commission Proposal for a Directive of the European Parliament and of the Council on Countering Money Laundering by Criminal Law, *available at* http://eur-lex.europa.eu/legal-content/EN/TXT/PDF/?uri=COM:2016:826:FIN&qid=1378484867646&from=EN.

cerning the definition of criminal offenses and sanctions related to money launder-ing. Although European Member States already criminalize money laundering, the proposal attempts to harmonize across the European Union the significant differ-ences in the respective definitions of what constitutes money laundering as well as the level of sanctions.[31] The Commission was concerned that differences in legal frameworks in European Member States could be exploited by criminals and ter-rorists, who choose to carry out their financial transactions where they perceive AML measures to be weakest. The proposed change is meant to improve existing cross-border cooperation, facilitate the exchange of information between compe-tent authorities, and help prevent criminals from exploiting differences between national legislations.

Under article 3 of the legislative proposal, the three criminal offences are

(i) the conversion or transfer of property, knowing that such property is derived from criminal activity or from an act of participation in such activity, for the pur-pose of concealing or disguising the illicit origin of the property or of assisting any person who is involved in the commission of such an activity to evade the legal consequences of that person's action; (ii) the concealment or disguise of the true nature, source, location, disposition, movement, rights with respect to, or owner-ship of, property, knowing that such property is derived from criminal activity or from an act of participation in such an activity; (iii) the acquisition, possession or use of property, knowing at the time of receipt, that such property was derived from criminal activity or from an act of participation in such an activity.[32]

Criminal activity is defined widely since the legislative proposal would make it com-pulsory for European Member States to criminalize the acquisition, possession, or use of property derived from criminal activity. This is a departure from the existing framework, where the mere possession of criminal proceeds is not considered money laundering in most European Member States.[33] According to article 4, aiding and abet-ting, inciting, and attempting an offence would also be punishable. Last but not least, article 5 provides that an offence committed by an individual would be punishable by a maximum term of imprisonment of at least four years in serious cases.

In addition to the above proposal, the European Commission is planning to introduce a regulation on the recognition of freezing and confiscation orders across borders.[34] The proposed regulation comes in the wake of the 2015[35] and 2016[36] terror

---

31. *Id.* at 2.

32. *Id.* at 22.

33. Brigitte Unger et al., Project "ECOLEF"—The Economic and Legal Effectiveness of Anti-Money Launder-ing and Combating Terrorist Financing Policy 16 (Feb. 2013).

34. Fact Sheet, European Commission, Security Union: Regulation on the Mutual Recogni-tion of Freezing and Confiscation Orders (Dec. 21, 2016), *available at* http://europa.eu/rapid/press-release_IP-16-4401_en.htm.

35. *2015 Paris Terror Attacks Fast Facts*, CNN, Nov. 30, 2016, http://edition.cnn.com/2015/12/08/europe/2015-paris-terror-attacks-fast-facts/index.html.

36. Tim Hume, Tiffany Ap & Ray Sanchez, *Here's What We Know About the Brussels Terror Attacks*, CNN, Mar. 25, 2016, http://edition.cnn.com/2016/03/23/europe/brussels-belgium-attacks-what-we-know/index.html.

attacks and is meant to fix one of the perceived gaps in the current framework by facilitating cross-border recovery of criminal assets and more efficient freezing and confiscation of illicit funds. New rules on cash controls will also be introduced, whereby travelers entering or leaving the European Union would legally be obliged to declare amounts of cash valued at €10,000 or more, or its equivalent in other currencies or bearer negotiable instruments, to customs authorities.[37]

V. RECENT DEVELOPMENTS

It is often said that the leak of the Panama Papers in 2016 has thrust money laundering into the spotlight. In fact, European parliamentarians have credited the Panama Papers with helping to "*focus minds and speed up this work.*"[38] At the 2017 World Economic Forum in Davos, Swiss anti-corruption expert Mark Pieth said that "*the Panama Papers showed the world how the crooks of this world stash away their money.*"[39] However, even if the Panama Papers leak had not occurred, terrorism threats provide ample incentives for regulators to increase their enforcement actions against the means of financing those attacks.[40]

In the United Kingdom, the Financial Conduct Authority (FCA) has indicated in its Business Plan 2016/17[41] that its key priorities include supervision and investigation, using its "*enforcement powers to send a deterrent message to industry and/or impose business restrictions to limit the level of risk,*" as well as to foster collaboration with law enforcement partners and other agencies. For example, the FCA recently imposed penalties on the UK operations of Bangladesh's biggest bank, Sonali Bank, as well as its former money laundering reporting officer, for serious failings in its AML systems.[42] In January 2017, the FCA fined Deutsche Bank £163 million for failing to maintain an adequate AML control framework during the period between January 1, 2012, and December 31, 2015.[43] The FCA stated that:

---

37. Fact Sheet, European Commission, Q&A on the Update of EU Rules on Cash Controls (Dec. 21, 2016), *available at* http://europa.eu/rapid/press-release_MEMO-16-4458_en.htm.

38. Press Release, European Commission, Fair Taxation: The Commission Sets Out Next Steps to Increase Tax Transparency and Tackle Tax Abuse (July 5, 2016), *available at* http://europa.eu/rapid/press-release_IP-16-2354_en.htm.

39. Julian Bonnici, *Panama Papers Show How "The Crooks of This World Stash Away Their Money"— Mark Pieth*, MALTA INDEP., Jan. 17, 2017, http://www.independent.com.mt/articles/2017-01-17/local-news/Former-Panama-Papers-probe-member-giving-talk-on-ending-corruption-6736169166.

40. SamuelRubenfeld,*ParisAttackstoBoostMoneyLaunderingEnforcement*,WALLST.J.,Nov.20,2015,http://blogs.wsj.com/riskandcompliance/2015/11/20/paris-attacks-to-boost-money-laundering-enforcement/.

41. FCA, BUSINESS PLAN 2016/17 (2016), *available at* https://www.fca.org.uk/publication/corporate/business-plan-2016-17.pdf.

42. Press Release, FCA, FCA Imposes Penalties on Sonali Bank (UK) Limited and Its Former Money Laundering Reporting Officer for Serious Anti-Money Laundering Systems Failings (Oct. 12, 2016), *available at* https://www.fca.org.uk/news/press-releases/fca-imposes-penalties-sonali-bank-uk-limited-money-laundering.

43. Press Release, FCA, FCA Fines Deutsche Bank £163 Million for Serious Anti-Money Laundering Controls Failings (Jan. 31, 2017), *available at* https://www.fca.org.uk/news/press-releases/fca-fines-deutsche-bank-163-million-anti-money-laundering-controls-failure.

Deutsche Bank exposed the UK financial system to the risks of financial crime by failing to properly oversee the formation of new customer relationships and the booking of global business in the UK. As a consequence of its inadequate AML control framework, Deutsche Bank was used by unidentified customers to transfer approximately $10 billion, of unknown origin, from Russia to offshore bank accounts in a manner that is highly suggestive of financial crime.[44]

According to the FCA, this is the largest financial penalty for AML controls failings ever imposed by the FCA or its predecessor, the Financial Services Authority.[45]

Countries outside the European Union are also taking note of the growing risk of money laundering as they become more closely integrated into global markets. For example, the People's Bank of China, which is the central bank of the People's Republic of China with the power to carry out monetary policy and regulate financial institutions in mainland China, stated that the "risks of money laundering and terrorist financing are further increasing in line with cross-border uses of the yuan, the rise of internet financing and the opening of capital accounts."[46] In December 2016, the People's Bank of China issued new requirements applicable to financial institutions (including banks, securities firms, fund management firms, insurers, and trust companies).[47] In particular, as of July 1, 2017, financial institutions are required to report any cross-border transfer between an individual's bank account and another bank account in excess of 200,000 yuan ($28,800).[48] In February 2017, the People's Bank of China announced that it would step up its AML supervision activities and further improve mechanisms to prevent money laundering.[49] According to media reports, China is developing its own digital currency, which could give the government real-time readings on the pulse of consumers.[50] Other reports suggest that the People's Bank of China digital currency initiative is likely motivated by the authorities' efforts to combat money laundering.[51]Other countries, such as Australia and Switzerland, have instead provided position papers laying out the principles that the regulator will follow to ensure cross-border financial regulation. For example, the Australian Securities and Investments Commission (ASIC) published a guide setting

---

44. *Id.*

45. *Id.*

46. Wendy Wu, *China Faces Higher Risk of Money Laundering and Financing of Terrorist Groups, Central Bank Official Warns*, S. CHINA MORNING POST, Apr. 26, 2016, http://www.scmp.com/news/china /policies-politics/article/1938519/china-faces-higher-risk-money-laundering-and-financing.

47. Yinan Zhao, *China Tightens Anti-Money Laundering Regulations for Banks*, BLOOMBERG, Dec. 30, 2016, https://www.bloomberg.com/news/articles/2016-12-30/china-tightens-anti-money-laundering -regulations-for-banks; Dong Tongjian, *PBOC Tightens Bank-Reporting Requirements in Bid to Curb Money Laundering*, CAIXIN, Dec. 30, 2016, http://www.caixinglobal.com/2016-12-30/101032182.html.

48. *Id.*

49. Richard Borsuk, *China Will Step Up Anti-Money Laundering Supervision—Central Bank*, REUTERS, Feb. 17, 2017, http://uk.reuters.com/article/uk-china-economy-cenbank-idUKKBN15W15T?il=0.

50. Yinan Zhao, *China Is Developing Its Own Digital Currency*, BLOOMBERG, Feb. 23, 2017, https:// www.bloomberg.com/news/articles/2017-02-23/pboc-is-going-digital-as-mobile-payments-boom-transforms -economy.

51. Brian Yap, *PBOC Uses Blockchain Technology to Combat Money Laundering*, INT'L FIN. L. REV., Feb. 14, 2017, http://www.iflr.com/Article/3661468/PBOC-uses-blockchain-technology-to-combat-money -laundering.html.

out its approach to recognizing overseas regulatory regimes for the purpose of facilitating cross-border financial regulation.[52] In the guide, the ASIC states that it provides "conditional relief from certain Australian regulatory requirements to foreign providers" and seeks "similar relief from foreign requirements for Australian providers where possible."[53] In Switzerland, the Financial Market Supervisory Authority (FINMA) issued a position paper on risks in cross-border financial services, calling on all supervised institutions to comply with foreign supervisory law and define an appropriate service model for each target market.[54]

The case of Switzerland is particularly interesting, since Swiss law entrenched banking secrecy back in 1934, making it a criminal offense for a bank to reveal its client's identity. Yet in May 2015, Switzerland signed an agreement with the European Union regarding the introduction of the automatic exchange of information, ending the tradition of banking secrecy that existed until then.[55] Switzerland has since stepped up its enforcement efforts in relation to money laundering. In June 2015, HSBC was ordered to pay a record-breaking 40 million Swiss francs[56] as "compensation." It was also given a final warning by the Geneva authorities for "organizational deficiencies" that allowed money laundering to take place in the bank's Swiss subsidiary. According to media reports, the Swiss authorities will not prosecute HSBC following the entry into the settlement or publish the findings of their investigation into alleged aggravated money laundering.[57]

More recently, the FINMA ordered the bank Coutts & Co. Ltd. to disgorge "unlawfully generated profits" of 6.5 million Swiss francs, stating that Coutts had "seriously breached money-laundering regulations by failing to carry out adequate background checks into business relationships and transactions" associated with the alleged corruption scandal involving the Malaysian sovereign wealth fund 1MDB.[58] The FINMA also pointed out that it is considering initiating enforcement proceedings against the relevant bank employees responsible. According to the FINMA, the Coutts bank opened a business relationship in Zurich with a young Malaysian businessman in the summer of 2009 with the expectation that USD 10 million would be transferred

---

52. ASIC, RG 54 Principles for Cross-Border Financial Regulation (June 29, 2012), *available at* http://asic.gov.au/regulatory-resources/find-a-document/regulatory-guides/rg-54-principles-for-cross-border-financial-regulation/.

53. *Id*. RG 54.2, at 4.

54. Press Release, FINMA, FINMA Position Paper on Risks in Cross-Border Financial Services (Oct. 22, 2010), *available at* https://www.finma.ch/en/news/2010/10/mm-finma-positionspapier-rechtsrisiken-20101022/.

55. Swiss Confederation—Federal Department of Finance, *Automatic Exchange of Information (AEOI)*, https://www.efd.admin.ch/efd/en/home/themen/wirtschaft–waehrung–finanzplatz/finanzmarktpolitik/automatic-exchange-of-information–aeoi-/fb-AIA.html (last visited May 22, 2017).

56. Juliette Garside, *HSBC Pays Out £28m over Money-Laundering Claims*, Guardian, June 4, 2015, https://www.theguardian.com/business/2015/jun/04/hsbc-fined-278m-over-money-laundering-claims; *see also* Joshua Franklin & Stephanie Nebehay, *HSBC to Pay $43 Million Geneva Money Laundering Settlement*, Reuters, June 4, 2015, http://www.reuters.com/article/us-hsbc-tax-swiss-iduskbn0ok1g220150604.

57. *Id.*

58. Press Release, FINMA, FINMA Sanctions Coutts for 1MDB Breaches (Feb. 2, 2017), *available at* https://www.finma.ch/en/news/2017/02/20170202-mm-coutts/.

to it from the account holder's family assets. Instead, in the autumn of 2009, approximately USD 700 million was transferred to the account from the Malaysian sovereign wealth fund 1MDB. The reasons given for this transaction were inconsistent, documents presented in support of the transaction contained obvious mistakes, and some information was changed retrospectively. The case is also a good example of the increased cross-border cooperation between authorities: the FINMA indicates that it coordinated its actions with a number of other authorities, including the Monetary Authority of Singapore (MAS) and the United Kingdom's FCA, since the Coutts bank belonged to the United Kingdom-based Royal Bank of Scotland Group during the relevant period.

Chapter 9

Regulatory Developments in the European Union

Structures and Frameworks

Jane K. Winn

"Retail payments are the backbone of the real economy."

—Benoît Cœuré, executive board member, European Central Bank[1]

I. REENGINEERING EUROPEAN PAYMENT LAW

Within the field of financial services, retail payment services once received little attention from bank managers, regulators, academic commentators, or even the consumers of such services. In recent years, however, payment services have been catapulted from obscurity to prominence by a wave of innovation in business models and technologies for payment services. The focus of this chapter will be on the strategies that the Commission of the European Union is using in its efforts to usher in fundamental reforms in markets for payment services in Europe. Because this chapter was written with U.S. lawyers in mind, some comparisons between U.S. and EU legislative strategies will be offered wherever they might help to clarify similarities and differences in the two approaches.

In recent decades, innovations in the field of information technology have lowered some of the traditional barriers to entry into markets for payment services, and

---

1. Press Release, European Central Bank, New Euro Retail Payments Board Will Reinforce Market Governance (Dec. 19, 2013) [hereinafter ECB Press Release], *available at* https://www.ecb.europa.eu/press/pr/date/2013/html/pr131219.en.html.

thus have spawned a swarm of new nonbank payment services. The idea that payment services may be provided by enterprises other than banks has gradually gained acceptance from both the public in the form of increased willingness to use nonbank payment services and from regulators in the form of alternative licensing regimes. Because these new payment service providers are not banks, they can choose to compete with banks in only those markets where the newcomers enjoy a competitive advantage. Commercial banks are then left to figure out how to maintain their profitability as more nimble competitors selectively pick off the most valuable parts of the portfolio of financial services they are required by regulators to offer. This chapter describes more than a decade of efforts in the European Union to establish a new regulatory framework designed to achieve a politically acceptable balance among innovation, competition, safety and soundness, and convenience for consumers.

The starting point for the reform of EU payment law as with many other EU law reforms was the construction of the "Single Market." The goal was to create an "internal market" in Europe that operates as seamlessly as the domestic market of a national economy. Diversity in national payment laws and in the technology of national payment systems fragmented the European market for payment services and threatened to diminish the value of the euro as a single currency.[2] Following the creation of the euro, the EU and European banks have struggled to create a seamless "Single Euro Payments Area" (SEPA) that could serve the Single Market well. As a result of those efforts, the scope of EU payments policy has gradually expanded from merely harmonizing existing laws to include promoting innovation and competition in markets that often did not seem very receptive to either.

At the apex of European payment systems is the European Central Bank (ECB), which works with central banks of eurozone countries to lead what is known as the Eurosystem. In the wake of the Global Financial Crisis, payment law reforms in Europe are now taking place in the context of a much broader overhaul of European banking regulation. In 2011, the European Banking Authority (EBA) was established to provide a more effective pan-European bank regulator, taking over from the Committee of European Banking Supervisors.[3] In 2013, legislation authorizing ECB to create a European-level "single supervisory mechanism" for bank examination was enacted.[4]

---

2. Press Release, European Commission, New Rules on Payment Services for the Benefit of Consumers and Retailers (July 24, 2013) [hereinafter EC Press Release] ("[T]he payment market in the EU is fragmented and expensive with a cost of more than 1% of EU GDP or €130 billion a year."), *available at* http://europa.eu/rapid/press-release_IP-13-730_en.htm.

3. Regulation (EU) No 1093/2010 of the European Parliament and of the Council of 24 November 2010 Establishing a European Supervisory Authority (European Banking Authority), Amending Decision No 716/2009/EC and Repealing Commission Decision 2009/78/EC, 2010 O.J. (L 331) 12 [hereinafter Regulation (EU) No 1093/2010].

4. Council Regulation (EU) No 1024/2013 of 15 October 2013, Conferring Specific Tasks on the European Central Bank Concerning Policies Relating to the Prudential Supervision of Credit Institutions, 2013 O.J. (L 287) 63; on the emerging European "banking union," see generally Jeffrey N. Gordon & Wolf-Georg Ringe, *Bank Resolution in the European Banking Union: A Transatlantic Perspective on What It Would Take*, 115 COLUM. L. REV. 1297 (2015). "Eurosystem" is the term used to describe the increasingly integrated financial system regulated by the ECB working together with the national central banks of the countries whose currency is the euro. ECB, *Eurosystem Mission*, https://www.ecb.europa.eu/ecb/orga/escb/html/mission_eurosys.en.html (last visited May 29, 2017).

Thus, the trend in recent years has been for EU-level prudential regulation over markets for financial services—including payment services—to be strengthened.

The desire of EU-level payment system regulators to "reengineer" the architecture of retail payments in Europe has also strengthened in recent years. The notion of reengineering institutions was popularized in the 1990s by the embrace of "business process reengineering" by corporate leaders around the world.[5] Reengineering consists of fundamentally rethinking how business processes are organized to make them more efficient and responsive to market conditions. Starting in 2001, the European Union has enacted the following laws in order to reengineer European payment markets by spurring innovation, lowering costs, and improving customer service:

- **EC Regulation 2560/2001**: capped the price of cross-border euro credit transfers at the same (much lower) level as domestic euro transfers, triggering the creation of the European Payments Council (EPC) and SEPA in an effort to bring bank processing costs down to the same level as prices[6]
- **Payment Services Directive 2007/64/EC (PSD1)**: harmonized the rights and obligations of parties to payments transactions throughout the Single Market, and authorized a new category of nonbank "payment service providers" to compete with banks in markets for payment services[7]
- **E-Money Directive II 2009/110/EC (EMD2)**: liberalized the regulatory regime for "e-money" institutions (i.e., nonbanks issuing monetary value stored outside of a bank account to make payments to third parties); it repealed and replaced the more restrictive first E-Money Directive 2000/46/EC[8]
- **EC Regulation 924/2009**: expanded the scope of pricing parity between domestic and cross-border euro transfers to cover more types of payments and pushed for greater use of the new International Bank Account Number (IBAN) and Business Identifier Code (BIC) in cross-border euro payments[9]
- **EU Regulation 260/2012/EU and Regulation 248/2014**: in the face of widespread resistance to migrating domestic as well as cross-border euro transfers from diverse national schemes to the new harmonized SEPA

---

5. MICHAEL HAMMER & JAMES CHAMPY, REENGINEERING THE CORPORATION: A MANIFESTO FOR BUSINESS REVOLUTION 35 (1993).

6. Regulation (EC) No 2560/2001 of the European Parliament and of the Council of 19 December 2001 on Cross-Border Payments in Euro, 2001 O.J. (L 344) 13.

7. Directive 2007/64/EC of the European Parliament and of the Council of 13 November 2007 on Payment Services in the Internal Market Amending Directives 97/7/EC, 2002/65/EC, 2005/60/EC, and 2006/48/EC and Repealing Directive 97/5/EC, 2007 O.J. (L 319) 1 [hereinafter Internal Market Payment Services Directive].

8. Directive 2009/110/EC of the European Parliament and of the Council of 16 September 2009 on the Taking Up, Pursuit, and Prudential Supervision of the Business of Electronic Money Institutions Amending Directives 2005/60/EC and 2006/48/EC and Repealing Directive 2000/46/EC, 2009 O.J. (L 267) 7 [hereinafter E-Money Directive II 2009/110/EC].

9. Regulation (EC) No 924/2009 of the European Parliament and of the Council of 16 September 2009 on Cross-Border Payments in the Community and Repealing Regulation (EC) No 2560/2001, 2009 O.J. (L 266) 11.

schemes, the Commission set (then postponed) a mandatory deadline for shutting down the old national electronic fund transfer schemes and ensuring that both domestic and cross-border transfers conformed to the new SEPA schemes[10]

- **Payment Accounts Directive 2014/92/EU (PAD)**: required banks to offer basic bank accounts, standardize fee disclosures to make comparison shopping easier, and simplify procedures for cross-border account opening in addition to requiring banks to make it quick and easy to transfer payment accounts—including all standing electronic payment instructions—from one institution to another[11]

- **Payment Services Directive II 2015/2366/EU (PSD2)**: strengthened consumer protection and security requirements for payment services; recognized two new categories of nonbank payment service providers; and required banks and credit card issuers to accommodate "open application programming interface" (open API) payment processing by third parties (i.e., to prohibit banks from interfering with their customers' ability to make transfers into and out of their bank accounts, or access their account information, with the assistance of third parties)[12]

- **Interchange Fee Regulation (EU) 2015/751 (IFR)**: following more than a decade of competition, law enforcement actions, and negotiations with card networks, imposed tough mandatory price caps on multilateral card network interchange fees[13]

- **Instant Payments**: the Euro Retail Payments Board (ERPB) with the assistance of the EPC is now promoting the development of a pan-European system for immediate small-value electronic payments accessible from mobile phones and through other online channels[14]

- **Regulatory Technical Standards**: when harmonized technical standards are required to establish or maintain the interoperability of European electronic payment systems as a result of law reform, the Commission may

---

10. Regulation (EU) No 260/2012 of the European Parliament and of the Council of 14 March 2012 Establishing Technical and Business Requirements for Credit Transfers and Direct Debits in Euro and Amending Regulation (EC) No 924/2009, 2012 O.J. (L 94) 22 [hereinafter Regulation on Credit Transfers and Direct Debits]; Regulation (EU) No 248/2014 of the European Parliament and of the Council of 26 February 2014 Amending Regulation (EU) No 260/2012 as Regards the Migration to Union-Wide Credit Transfers and Direct Debits, 2014 O.J. (L 84) 1 [hereinafter EU Regulation 248/2014].

11. Directive 2014/92/EU of the European Parliament and of the Council of 23 July 2014 on the Comparability of Fees Related to Payment Accounts, Payment Account Switching, and Access to Payment Accounts with Basic Features, 2014 O.J. (L 257) 214 [hereinafter Payment Accounts Directive].

12. Directive (EU) 2015/2366 of the European Parliament and of the Council of 25 November 2015 on Payment Services in the Internal Market, Amending Directives 2002/65/EC, 2009/110/EC, and 2013/36/EU and Regulation (EU) No 1093/2010, and Repealing Directive 2007/64/EC, 2015 O.J. (L 337) 35 [hereinafter EU Directive 2015/2366].

13. Regulation (EU) 2015/751 of the European Parliament and of the Council of 29 April 2015 on Interchange Fees for Card-based Payment Transactions, 2015 O.J. (L 123) 1 [hereinafter Interchange Fee Regulation].

14. ECB, Eurosystem Expectations for Clearing Infrastructures to Support pan-European Instant Payments in Euro (2016).

issue a mandate to the EBA to develop those standards by following a statutory public consultation process[15]

This chapter will first provide an overview of the framework of EU law reform before turning to brief descriptions of some important provisions of each law and some of the political factors that contributed to their enactment.

II. EU-LEVEL COORDINATION

The formulation of policy in Europe for specific economic sectors such as payment services takes place within an overarching framework of formal European economic policies. An explicitly hierarchical, integrated approach to national or regional economic strategy is rare in countries such as the United States that incline toward more "bottom-up," market-driven approaches to economic challenges. Such an approach is, however, very common in countries that have what political scientists have labeled a "coordinated market economy," which includes most continental European countries. Because EU policy with regard to innovation and competition in payment systems is developed within a coordinated market economy policy framework, rather than the "liberal market economy" policy framework characteristic of Anglo-Saxon countries, there is more emphasis on the role of government in guiding economic development in EU policy than most Americans would be accustomed to seeing in equivalent U.S. policies.[16]

By contrast, in both the United States and Europe, there was a general consensus for much of the 20th century that banks were not subject to antitrust or competition law in the same way that commercial or industrial enterprises might be.[17] Banks enjoyed this de facto exemption from antitrust or competition law in part because of concerns that harm to the rest of the economy caused by excessive competition in banking markets would outweigh any benefits of competition. In addition, banks were generally subject to a highly restrictive, comprehensive, prudential regulatory regime designed to protect the public from financial crises. By the end of the 20th century, however, the consensus had moved in the other direction, forcing banks to confront active antitrust and competition law enforcement on both sides of the Atlantic.[18] The Commission published the results of its sector inquiry investigating

---

15. EBA, ANNUAL REPORT 23 (2015).

16. Peter A. Hall & David Soskice, *An Introduction to Varieties of Capitalism, in* VARIETIES OF CAPITALISM: THE INSTITUTIONAL FOUNDATIONS OF COMPARATIVE ADVANTAGE (Peter A. Hall & David Soskice eds., 2001).

17. ELENA CARLETTI & XAVIER VIVES, IESE BUSINESS SCHOOL–UNIVERSITY OF NAVARRA, REGULATION AND COMPETITION POLICY IN THE BANKING SECTOR 7 (Occasional Paper OP-159, Oct. 2008).

18. United States v. Phila. Nat'l Bank, 374 U.S. 321 (1963). *See also* Case 172/80, Züchner v. Bayerische Vereinsbank, 1981 E.C.R. 2021; Edward Pekarek & Michela Huth, *Bank Merger Reform Takes an Extended Philadelphia National Bank Holiday*, 13 FORDHAM J. CORP. & FIN. L. 595, 622 (2008); John A. Usher, *Financial Services in EEC Law*, 37 INT'L & COMP. L.Q. 144 (1988). Market discipline was recognized as the third pillar of bank regulation by the Basel Committee in 2001 (Pillars 1 and 2 were capital requirements and supervisory review). BASEL COMMITTEE ON BANKING SUPERVISION, BANK FOR INTERNATIONAL SETTLEMENTS, CONSULTATIVE DOCUMENT PILLAR 3 (MARKET DISCIPLINE) (2001), *available at* http://www.bis.org/publ/bcbsca10.pdf.

the European retail payment sector in 2007, concluding that the lack of competition merited follow-up.[19] There is also evidence, however, that a major factor contributing to the Global Financial Crisis was efforts by financial market regulators generally in the United States and United Kingdom to promote more competition that unfortunately overshot the mark.[20]

As noted above, a cardinal EU economic policy is completion of the Single Market. When diversity in national laws impedes the functioning of the Single Market, the Commission may propose legislation to remove those impediments by harmonizing national laws. As a union of individual countries each of which had established its own national market before accession to the European Union, harmonization of different national technical standards is often treated as an element of EU law reform.[21] The European system of harmonizing technical standards across Member States as part of constructing the internal market resembles the World Trade Organization (WTO) Technical Barriers to Trade Agreement system for harmonizing technical standards.[22] By contrast, a nationwide domestic economy had already emerged in the United States in the 19th century before harmonization of technical standards was a major issue, while the Commerce Clause of the U.S. Constitution gave the federal government the authority to ensure that technical standards never became a barrier to interstate commerce. As a result of early economic integration and a liberal market economic culture, the United States lacks a counterpart to the European system of treating the development of harmonized technical standards as an integrated part of economic regulation.[23] Before turning to the specific provisions of individual EU payment law reforms, each of these general structural characteristics of EU law reform will be considered.

A. Digital Single Market Strategy

The fact that power in the European Union is exercised in such a diffuse and ambiguous manner[24] may help to explain why EU leaders are so fond of announcing grand strategic plans that employees of the Commission must then dutifully reference in all their policy discussions. In the area of payment law reform, the foundational

---

19. Sector Inquiry under Article 17 of Regulation (EC) No 1/2003 on Retail Banking (Final Report), COM(07)33 final.

20. Organization for Economic Cooperation & Development, Competition and Financial Markets: Key Findings 7 (2009).

21. *See* Michelle Egan, Constructing a European Market: Standards, Regulation, and Governance (2001).

22. Agreement on Technical Barriers to Trade, Apr. 15, 1994, Marrakesh Agreement Establishing the World Trade Organization, Annex 1A, 1868 U.N.T.S. 120. *See generally* Alan O. Sykes, Product Standards for Internationally Integrated Goods Markets (1995).

23. *See* American National Standards Institute, United States Standards Strategy (2015), *available at* https://www.ansi.org/standards_activities/nss/usss.aspx; Michelle Egan, Single Markets: Economic Integration in Europe and the United States (2015); U.S. Congress, Office of Technology Assessment, Global Standards: Building Blocks for the Future (1992) (OTA-TCT-512); Jane K. Winn, *Globalization and Standards: The Logic of Two-Level Games*, 5 I/S: J.L. & Pol'y for Info. Soc'y 185 (2009).

24. One famous remark highlighting this issue, "Who do I call if I want to speak to Europe?," is attributed to Henry Kissinger. Gideon Rachman, *Kissinger Never Wanted to Dial Europe*, Fin. Times, July 22, 2009, http://blogs.ft.com/the-world/2009/07/kissinger-never-wanted-to-dial-europe/.

grand strategy can be found in the reference to "efficient and transparent financial markets" in the Lisbon Agenda announced in 2000. The goal of the Lisbon Agenda was to "make Europe, by 2010, the most competitive and the most dynamic knowledge-based economy in the world."[25] For a variety of reasons, this never occurred.[26] In 2015, the president of Deutsche Bundesbank described the successor to the Lisbon Agenda in these terms:

> Some of you may remember the European Council's Lisbon Agenda . . . Given the apparent failure of this strategy and in the face of an unprecedented crisis, the goals set out in its successor, Europe 2020, are somewhat less ambitious: the priorities of Europe 2020 are smart, sustainable and inclusive growth.[27]

One foundation of the new Europe 2020 strategy is the "Digital Agenda," which is intended to leverage the potential of information and communication technologies to foster innovation, economic growth, and progress in Europe.[28] In turn, a major part of the Digital Agenda strategy is the "Digital Single Market" strategy, which the Commission has described in the following terms:

> Too many barriers still block the free flow of online services and entertainment across national borders. The Digital Agenda will update EU Single Market rules for the digital era. The aims are to boost the music download business, establish a single area for online payments, and further protect EU consumers in cyberspace . . . EU payment market suffers from a number of drawbacks. The costs of acceptance of cards, as the most common payment instrument online are high, payments markets are still fragmented, in some cases the industry has not yet agreed on a set of technical standards for the whole of the EU. The markets are not as dynamic and innovative as they should. There are many new technologies, such as using electronic wallets or smartphone at the point of sale. However—except in a few EU countries—it is difficult for these services to enter cross-border market for payments.[29]

The Digital Agenda thus targets payment services in Europe as a policy arena where removing barriers to economic integration and fueling the acceleration of innovation and competitiveness in Europe is of paramount importance.

The notion of the Single Market itself dates back to the 1985 Jacques Delors white paper that articulated the "completion of the internal market" as the next phase for

25. Lisbon European Council, Presidency Conclusions (Mar. 24, 2000), http://www.consilium.europa.eu/en/uedocs/cms_data/docs/pressdata/en/ec/00100-r1.en0.htm.

26. Reinhard Bütikofer, *Is Europe2020 the Right Consequence after the Failure of the Lisbon Strategy?*, New Federalist, Aug. 28, 2010 (Lina Ohltmann trans.), http://www.thenewfederalist.eu/3641; Charles Wyplosz, *The Failure of the Lisbon Strategy*, VOX, Jan. 12, 2010, http://voxeu.org/article/failure-lisbon-strategy.

27. Deutsche Bundesbank President Jens Weidmann, Keynote Speech at the Official Monetary and Financial Institutions Forum (OMFIF) Global Investment Seminar (June 11, 2015), http://www.bis.org/review/r150611b.pdf. *See also* Europe 2020, *Europe 2020 in a Nutshell*, http://ec.europa.eu/europe2020/europe-2020-in-a-nutshell/index_en.htm (last updated Aug. 18, 2016).

28. European Commission, *Europe 2020 Strategy*, https://ec.europa.eu/digital-single-market/en/europe-2020-strategy (last updated May 16, 2017).

29. European Commission, *Digital Single Market*, https://ec.europa.eu/digital-single-market/our-goals/pillar-i-digital-single-market (last updated May 16, 2017).

European integration and the 1986 Single European Act that launched a major push culminating in 1992 toward greater European integration.[30] The goal was to create an internal market "without internal frontiers in which the free movement of goods, persons, services and capital is ensured . . ."[31] Financial institutions regulated under harmonized European financial services law in one Member State of what was then known as the European Economic Community could do business in another Member State without being required to comply with the "host" country's licensing regime.[32] The ability of European financial services firms to establish branches throughout Europe based on their home country regulation merely upon notifying their home country regulator is referred to informally as "financial passporting."[33]

Payment service providers operating under harmonized EU law can take advantage of financial passporting to establish branches throughout the European Union without the burden of compliance with multiple national regulatory systems. Perhaps the closest analog that exists to financial passporting in the United States is federal licensing of banks. Because there is no federal regime for licensing "money services businesses" and the attempt by the Uniform Law Commission to harmonize the state law regimes governing such businesses has enjoyed only modest success,[34] financial technology (fintech) start-ups may face much heavier compliance burdens in the United States than they would in the European Union due to the fragmented structure of U.S. financial services law.[35] As one commentator noted, "The U.S. alone has ten regulating bodies which oversee different parts of the financial sector and additionally each state has its own rules and regulators."[36]

---

30. Single European Act, June 29, 1987, 1987 O.J. (L 169) 1, 2 C.M.L.R. 741 [hereinafter SEA] (amending the Treaty Establishing the European Economic Community, Mar. 25, 1957, 298 U.N.T.S. 11; Completing the Internal Market: White Paper from the Commission to the European Council, COM(85)310 final [hereinafter White Paper on Completion of Internal Market].

31. The Treaty Establishing the European Economic Community, Mar. 25, 1957, 298 U.N.T.S. 3 (also known as the Treaty of Rome), established a "common market." Article 8A of the Treaty of Rome was amended to include the definition of a "Single Market" by the SEA.

32. Second Council Directive 89/646/EEC of 15 December 1989 on the Coordination of Laws, Regulations, and Administrative Provisions Relating to the Taking Up and Pursuit of the Business of Credit Institutions and Amending Directive 77/780/EEC, 1989 O.J. (L 386) 1 [hereinafter Second Banking Directive] (creating a "Single Banking License" recognized throughout the European Economic Community).

33. Brandon Daniels, *Brexit Achieves the Opposite of Intended Effect in Banking*, Law360, Aug. 12, 2016, http://www.law360.com/articles/827870/brexit-achieves-the-opposite-of-intended-effect-in-banking. *See also* White Paper on Completion of Internal Market, *supra* note 30 (calling for a single banking license, home country control, and mutual recognition). These were accomplished with the Second Banking Directive, *supra* note 32.

34. Uniform Law Commission, *Legislative Fact Sheet—Money Services Act*, http://www.uniformlaws.org/LegislativeFactSheet.aspx?title=Money%20Services%20Act (last visited May 20, 2017) (showing that by 2016, only nine jurisdictions including Puerto Rico and the U.S. Virgin Islands had enacted the Uniform Money Services Act of 2000).

35. Lalita Clozel, *State Regulators Balk at OCC Fintech Charter*, Am. Banker, Aug. 19, 2016, https://www.americanbanker.com/news/state-regulators-balk-at-occ-fintech-charter; Benjamin Saul & Matthew Bornfreund, *Translating the Success of UK Fintech Measures to the US*, White & Case, Aug. 9, 2016, https://www.whitecase.com/publications/article/translating-success-uk-fintech-measures-us.

36. Falguni Desai, *The Fintech Boom and Bank Innovation*, Forbes, Dec. 14, 2015, http://www.forbes.com/sites/falgunidesai/2015/12/14/the-fintech-revolution/.

B. New Legal Framework for Payments

In 2003, the Commission issued a "New Legal Framework for Payments in the Internal Market" that reviewed the then-current state of EU-level payment law and proposed changes to address some of the problems it uncovered.[37] This discussion document marks something of a watershed in EU thinking about the role of the law applicable to payment systems in building the internal market: up to this point, the accent was on "negative integration," or the removal of barriers to the operation of markets already in existence, while after this point, the accent shifted to "positive integration," or the creation of new EU-level institutions that shape or counterbalance the operation of existing markets.[38]

The priorities that the Commission established with its 2003 proposal for a New Legal Framework for payments remain visible in later legislation. These include:

- Liberalizing licensing regimes for nonbank payment service providers
- Defining the role of payment service providers in disputes between customers and merchants
- Harmonizing terms and conditions for payment transfers such as information disclosure obligations, liability for failure to execute payment transfers as instructed, liability for unauthorized transactions, mandatory time frames for completing transactions, and the use of strong authentication methods

In its proposal for a New Legal Framework, the Commission clearly signaled its intention to move payment law from the traditional private law domain of commercial law to the modern administrative law fields of consumer protection and antitrust/competition law. It also embraced the principles of technology neutrality and better regulation.

C. EU-Level Standard Setting

As manual transaction processing and paper records are replaced by computer processes and digital records in modern payment systems, the interoperability of the different computer systems that make up payment systems has emerged as a salient issue in payment law. When regulators determine that technical standards are needed to support legislation in Europe, it is conventional to have a public sector standard-setting organization invite private sector representatives to participate in the process of developing the standards.[39] While this process was widely followed for industrial economy standards in Europe,[40] such a public process had

---

37. Communication from the Commission to the Council and the European Parliament Concerning a New Legal Framework for Payments in the Internal Market (Consultative Document), COM(03)718 final.

38. John Pinder, *Positive Integration and Negative Integration: Some Problems of Economic Union in the EEC*, 24 World Today 88 (1968).

39. *See generally* Egan, *supra* note 23; U.S Congress, *supra* note 23; Winn, *supra* note 23.

40. Egan, *supra* note 21.

not yet been established for financial market standards when the euro was launched in 1999.

When European banks made the strategic decision to support the development of pan-European technical standards for payment transactions, they also made the decision to create the EPC, a new private sector standard-setting body to lead the process. The structure of the EPC was similar to that of American private sector standard-setting organizations such as the National Automated Clearing House Association (NACHA), and thus something of an anomaly in Europe. For reasons discussed in Part VI.C below, in 2013, the ECB transferred the power to set the strategic direction for European payment systems from the industry-led EPC to the ERPB, which is firmly under the ECB's direct control.[41] The EPC plays an active role in the maintenance of SEPA standards and, if it receives a mandate to do so by the ERPB, to develop new standards. However, the scope of its role in defining the architecture of European payment markets is narrower today than it was at its inception.

As the standard-setting role of the EPC declined, the standard-setting role of the EBA increased. The EBA's involvement in technical standard-setting activities as part of the law reforms discussed in this chapter is not market-driven but instead is triggered by mandates given to it by the Commission. Under the 2010 European Banking Authority Regulation, the EBA has the authority to develop "regulatory technical standards" as part of the process of implementing EU-level banking law reforms when requested to do so by the Commission.[42] Harmonized "regulatory technical standards" developed by the EBA will play a significant role in the implementation of directives such as EMD2, PAD, PSD2, and IFR. Under the 2010 European Banking Authority Regulation, in theory, the EBA should not become embroiled in political controversies surrounding payment law reforms: "[r]egulatory technical standards shall be technical, shall not imply strategic decisions or policy choices and their content shall be delimited by the legislative acts on which they are based."[43] As will be discussed below, however, the EBA's task will be daunting because it will be required simultaneously to build broad support for technical standards in fields undergoing rapid change and also resolve many controversial aspects of European payment law reform.

III. E-MONEY DIRECTIVE II

During the 1990s, the success of a few stored-value payment systems such as the Octopus card issued by the Hong Kong mass transit authority sparked enormous interest in the idea of a digital substitute for the cash most consumers carry in their

---

41. *EU to Replace SEPA Council and Revise EPC and Governance Programme*, Bobs Guide, June 27, 2013, http://www.bobsguide.com/guide/news/2013/Jun/27/eu-to-replace-sepa-council-and-revise-epc-and-governance-programme/. *See also* ECB Press Release, *supra* note 1.

42. Regulation (EU) No 1093/2010, *supra* note 3, recitals 21–26, arts. 8(2), 10–16.

43. *Id.* art. 10.

pockets.[44] In 2000, the European Union enacted the First E-Money Directive (EMD1) in order to permit any new e-money services to enjoy access to the entire European internal market based on regulation only in the EU Member State where the service was established.[45] While many e-money services firms did take advantage of the new regulatory framework in many countries—including U.S. companies such as Pay-Pal, Google, American Express, and Airbnb, which have obtained e-money services licenses in the United Kingdom—the overall rate of uptake was less than expected.[46]

In 2005, a study was undertaken as required under the EMD1 to evaluate its transposition by the Member States. By then, however, it was apparent that e-money had not caught on as expected, so the Commission expanded the scope of the inquiry to try to uncover the cause of EMD1's lack of success and whether or not it had anything to do with how Member States had transposed the directive into their national laws.[47] The study revealed that outside of Belgium, card-based e-money had not caught on in any Member State, and efforts to launch such e-money schemes had already been abandoned in some. While contactless cards were gaining ground in some public transportation systems, it was unclear whether they would be able to make the leap into general payment services. At the time of the study, there were fewer than ten e-money institutions operating under the EMD1 licensing scheme in all of Europe, although applications to launch new services were in process. The report noted that "server-based" e-money (e.g., PayPal) had enjoyed more success than card-based services, although the application of the EMD1 to such services was unclear. There was uncertainty about how EMD1 should be applied to mobile network operators because the law seemed to indicate that a licensed e-money institution had to limit the scope of its activities to payment services, thus making it impossible to offer co-branded products.[48] The requirement of initial capital of €1 million in addition to 100 percent float coverage was also thought to be excessive.[49]

When the revised EMD2 was enacted in 2009, it lowered the initial capital requirement to €350,000, expanded the scope of activities an e-money institution could undertake, and relaxed the definition of what constitutes e-money.[50] Nevertheless,

---

44. *See, e.g.*, Task Force on Stored-Value Cards, *A Commercial Lawyer's Take on the Electronic Purse: An Analysis of Commercial Law Issues Associated with Stored-Value Cards and Electronic Money*, 52 Bus. Law. 653, 654 (1997).

45. Directive 2000/46/EC of the European Parliament and of the Council of 18 September 2000 on the Taking Up, Pursuit of, and Prudential Supervision of the Business of Electronic Money Institutions, 2000 O.J. (L 275) 39.

46. *See* Leo Van Hove, *Electronic Purses: (Which) Way to Go?*, First Monday Special Issue #3 (Dec. 5, 2005), http://firstmonday.org/ojs/index.php/fm/article/view/1515/1430.

47. Evaluation Partnership Ltd., Evaluation of the E-Money Directive (2000/46/EC), Final Report for DG Internal Market, European Commission (2006), *available at* http://ec.europa.eu/internal_market/bank /docs/e-money/evaluation_en.pdf.

48. Melissa Thornton, *Perfect Har-money? The New E-money Directive*, Lexology, Oct. 1, 2009, http:// www.lexology.com/library/detail.aspx?g=e03f2a34-3e5e-479a-b33b-5dddd709b317.

49. Commission of the European Communities, Commission Staff Working Document on the Review of the E-Money Directive (2000/46/EC) (July 19, 2006) (SEC (2006) 1049), *available at* http://ec.europa.eu/internal_market /bank/docs/e-money/working-document_en.pdf.

50. E-Money Directive II 2009/110/EC, *supra* note 8, arts. 2(2), 4, 6.

how much market demand there is for e-money products remains unclear. When Facebook registered as an e-money institution in Ireland in 2016, it was only the second firm to do so.[51] Google had braved the EMD1 regime by registering as an e-money institution in the United Kingdom in 2007 and maintained that license under the new regime despite the fact that the Google Wallet payment service for the Android phone had still not taken off in 2016.[52] In 2016, bitcoin payment service Circle chose a UK e-money institution license as the framework for its operations in Europe.[53] If virtual currency businesses began to apply for e-money licenses, then EBA would be authorized to develop any standards that might be needed.

IV. PAYMENT ACCOUNTS DIRECTIVE

Although the challenges of achieving financial inclusion may be particularly acute in developing countries,[54] they also confront regulators in advanced economies. Redesigning the delivery of financial services so that both the privileged and disadvantaged have easy access to them is a profoundly difficult problem.[55] A simpler solution that looks good in theory but does not usually work very well in practice is simply to mandate that regulated depository institutions provide access in the form of "basic bank accounts."[56] In a 2009 study of financial services in developing countries, the World Bank found that roughly a quarter of the countries surveyed had mandatory basic banking laws but noted that they were generally not very successful in increasing financial inclusion.[57]

Political controversy surrounding the issue of disparate access to conventional financial services periodically erupts in the United States.[58] Although the United States does not impose a general mandate on licensed depository institutions to

---

51. Peter Oakes, *Facebook Now Authorised in Ireland by the Central Bank as an EU E-Money Directive Firm*, Fintech Ir., Nov. 23, 2016, http://fintechireland.com/1/post/2016/11/facebook-now-authorised-in -ireland-by-the-central-bank-as-an-eu-e-money-directive-firm.html.

52. Google's current registration status can be viewed on the UK Financial Conduct Authority's website at https://register.fca.org.uk (last visited May 24, 2017). *See also* Charles Arthur, *How Many Google Wallet Users Are There? Google Won't Say—But We Can*, Guardian, Sept. 25, 2014, https://www.theguardian. com/technology/2014/sep/25/google-wallet-apple-pay-nfc.

53. Pete Rizzo, *What Circle's UK E-Money License Means for Bitcoin and Blockchain*, CoinDesk, Apr. 12, 2016, http://www.coindesk.com/circles-uk-license-blockchain-impact/.

54. *See, e.g.*, John D. Villasenor, Darrell M. West & Robin J. Lewis, The 2015 Brookings Financial and Digital Inclusion Project Report (2015).

55. *See, e.g.*, Bill & Melinda Gates Foundation, The Level One Project Guide—Designing a New System for Financial Inclusion (2015), *available at* https://leveloneproject.org/wp-content/uploads/2015/04/The-Level -One-Project-Guide-Designing-a-New-System-for-Financial-Inclusion1.pdf.

56. Jane K. Winn, *Mobile Payments and Financial Inclusion: Kenya, Brazil, and India as Case Studies*, *in* Research Handbook on Electronic Commerce Law 62 (John A. Rothchild ed., 2016).

57. World Bank, Banking the Poor 10 (2009).

58. *See generally* Robert W. Emerson, *Franchisees in a Fringe Banking World: Striking the Balance between Entrepreneurial Autonomy and Consumer Protection*, 46 Akron L. Rev. 1 (2013); Margot F. Saunders & Johnson M. Tyler, *Past, Present, and Future Threats to Federal Safety Net Benefits in Bank Accounts*, 16 N.C. Banking Inst. 43 (2012); Penny Crosman, *Reaching the Underbanked? Try Offering Control, Research Says*, Am. Banker, Mar. 6, 2013, https://www.americanbanker.com/news /reaching-the-underbanked-try-offering-control-research-says.

provide basic bank accounts, the Consumer Financial Protection Bureau recently put major U.S. banks on notice that it was monitoring the issue of whether some low-income consumers were being unfairly denied access to bank accounts.[59] Even before the PAD, some European countries had used moral suasion to encourage depository institutions to increase access to financial services. In 2013, the UK banking industry in the absence of any government mandate but under the looming shadow of the threat of regulation established a "current account switch service" that would allow consumers to switch bank accounts—including all standing debit and credit instructions—between banks quickly and easily.[60]

In 2014, the European Union moved in the direction of making financial services more inclusive and promoting greater competition in retail financial services with the PAD.[61] The PAD provides EU consumers with the following rights:

- Access to a payment account that allows them to perform essential operations, such as receiving wages or pensions and paying utility bills
- The right to make payments across borders without residency restrictions within the European Union (e.g., this would permit a German retiree living in Spain to pay utility bills in Spain with euros from a German bank account)
- The ability to compare payment account fees by requiring disclosure of relevant information in a standardized format
- A simple, quick procedure for switching payment accounts between financial institutions, including those in different Member States[62]

Obligations under the PAD apply to both bank and nonbank payment service providers.

The PAD imposes significant disclosure obligations on payment service providers, requiring not only that disclosures be accurate, but that they be easy to understand and compare with disclosures of other payment service providers.[63] The EBA was put in charge of setting standards for the disclosure of fee information as well

---

59. Press Release, Consumer Financial Protection Bureau, CFBP Takes Steps to Improve Checking Account Access (Feb. 3, 2016), *available at* http://www.consumerfinance.gov/about-us/newsroom /cfpb-takes-steps-to-improve-checking-account-access/.

60. *See* PaymentsUK, *Current Account Switch Service*, http://www.paymentsuk.org.uk/projects /current-account-switch-service (last visited May 21, 2017). This service was developed by the UK banking industry in what appears to have been a vain attempt to stave off the replacement of its industry self-regulation body with a government regulator. If so, it turned out to be too little, too late. *See* HM Treasury, *Consultation Outcome: Designation of Payment Systems for Regulation by the Payment Systems Regulator*, https://www.gov.uk/government/consultations/designation-of-payment-systems -for-regulation-by-the-payment-systems-regulator/designation-of-payment-systems-for-regulation-by -the-payment-systems-regulator (last updated Mar. 18, 2015). The UK current account switch service has suffered some growing pains. Elliott Holley, *BACS Admits Disappointment as UK Current Account Switching Stalls*, BANKING TECH., July 23, 2015, http://www.bankingtech.com/346942/bacs-admits-it-is -disappointed-as-uk-current-account-switching-stalls/.

61. Payment Accounts Directive, *supra* note 11.

62. *Id.* arts. 3, 4, and 9.

63. *Id.* art. 20.

as technical interoperability standards for account switching. [64] The EBA's mandate covered:

- Issuing guidelines to the Member States regarding the process of gathering information about the most representative payment account terms in their domestic markets
- Collecting the lists of 10–20 most representative terms from each Member State
- Issuing technical standards setting out the standardized EU terminology to be used by payment service providers to describe common services available in a majority of the Member States
- Issuing technical standards for the presentation of the standardized fee information and symbols[65]

The depth and breadth of the effort to collect and analyze relevant data before issuing disclosure standards designed to support a new consumer protection law is remarkable. The difficulty of ensuring the adequate representation of consumer interests in technical standard-setting problems is one that has dogged the process of harmonizing legislation with technical standards for decades.[66] The difficulty of striking the right balance between expanding participation for political legitimacy and restricting access based on technical competence in setting standards intended to shape regulatory obligations was described eloquently in 1978 by an American who was both a political science and law professor:

> In private standards-making the adequacy of the information base is more critical than in regard to general legislation. Many of the relevant questions are scientific or technical. To be sure, a perfect truth is not being pursued, and the standards are spoken of as consensus standards based on reasonableness, not ultimates. At the same time, there is probably more of an intrinsic rightness or wrongness quality than, for example, in respect to making legislative judgments about the intricacies of the spongy mass known as the federal income tax. Achieving the relevant input for wise standards-making is essentially a question of touching base with a sufficient number of informed and affected people. That process has at best a coincidental relationship to direct representation and committee voting power as derived from disparate constituencies of interest.[67]

The complex process that the EBA and Commission must follow prior to issuing the new disclosure standards required to implement the PAD reflects the European Union's commitment to improving the odds that its law reforms will achieve

---

64. *Id.* art. 3.
65. *EBA Consults on Technical Standards on Fee Terminology and Disclosure Documents under the Payment Accounts Directive*, EBA, Sept. 22, 2016, https://www.eba.europa.eu/-/eba-consults-on-technical-standards-on-fee-terminology-and-disclosure-documents-under-the-payment-accounts-directive.
66. Andrew McGee & Stephen Weatherill, *The Evolution of the Single Market—Harmonisation or Liberalisation*, 53 Mod. L. Rev. 578 (1990).
67. Robert G. Dixon, Jr., Standards Development in the Private Sector: Thoughts on Interest Representation and Procedural Fairness: A Report to the National Fire Protection Association 53 (1978).

their intended objectives by following "Better Regulation" principles in crafting legislation.[68]

V. INTERCHANGE FEE REGULATION

Before the Commission terminated the conflict by imposing mandatory, permanent price caps on the "interchange fees" they charge merchants in 2015, the Commission had been fighting Visa and MasterCard for nearly two decades over how much discretion the card networks should have to set interchange fees.[69] The Commission explained the definition of interchange fees found in the IFR in the following terms:

> Each time a consumer uses a credit, debit or prepaid card to buy something in a shop or online, the retailer's bank (the "acquiring bank") pays a fee called "interchange fee" to the consumer's bank that issued the card (the "issuing bank"). As retailers generally incorporate interchange fees in the prices they charge consumers, these fees increase the retail prices of goods and services.
>
> Interchange fees are normally set by operators of payment card schemes, such as Visa or MasterCard, or the banking community. Retailers have no possibility to influence the level of the fees, as they are not involved in the process.[70]

Even before the 2015 Interchange Fee Regulation was enacted, Visa Europe and MasterCard had suffered some serious setbacks in Europe to their efforts to preserve their discretion to set the level of interchange fees:

- In 2001, the Commission agreed that most of Visa's scheme rules did not violate EU competition law and in 2002, the Commission granted a temporary exemption to Visa allowing it discretion to set interchange fees up to a cap until 2007 after Visa agreed to make significant changes in the system.[71]
- In 2007, the Commission decided that Visa's decision in 1999 refusing to allow Morgan Stanley join the Visa network in Europe because it owned

---

68. *See* Commission Staff Working Document: Better Regulation Guidelines, COM(15)215 final.

69. The intensity and persistence of the conflict between regulator and industry reflected in part the intensity and persistence of the lack of consensus among economists regarding the significance of the fact that card networks could be characterized as "two-sided markets." *See, e.g.*, MARIA CHIARA MALAGUTI & ALESSANDRA GUERRIERI, MULTILATERAL INTERCHANGE FEES (2014); Jean-Charles Rochet & Jean Tirole, *Cooperation among Competitors: Some Economics of Payment Card Associations*, 33 RAND J. ECON. 549 (2002); Jean-Charles Rochet & Jean Tirole, *Platform Competition in Two-Sided Markets*, 1 J. EUR. ECON. ASS'N 990 (2003) (launching the debate about interchange and platform markets); Jean-Charles Rochet & Julian Wright, *Credit Card Interchange Fees*, 34 J. BANKING & FIN.1788 (2010) (discussing the fact that capping interchange fees is a regulatory strategy that may raise consumer surplus); Marc Rysman & Julian Wright, *The Economics of Payment Cards*, 13 REV. NETWORK ECON. 303 (2014) (summarizing the current state of the debate as of 2014).

70. Interchange Fee Regulation, *supra* note 13, art. 2; Fact Sheet, European Commission, Antitrust: Regulation on Interchange Fees (June 9, 2016), http://europa.eu/rapid/press-release_MEMO-16-2162_en.htm.

71. Case COMP/29.373—Visa Int'l, Comm'n Decision (Aug. 9, 2001) (2001 O.J. (L 293) 24); Case COMP/29.373—Visa Int'l—Multilateral Interchange Fee, Comm'n Decision (July 24, 2002) (2002 O.J. (L 318) 17).

Discover Card, which Visa Europe deemed to be a competitor, violated EU competition law;[72] that decision was upheld by the General Court.[73]

- In 2007, the Commission issued a prohibition against MasterCard with regard to its merchant fees on intraregional card transactions (e.g., a French card used in Germany).[74] MasterCard committed to reduce its fees to 0.30 percent of the transaction value for consumer credit cards and 0.20 percent of the transaction value for consumer debit cards while it appealed the decision.[75] MasterCard lost its appeals at both the General Court[76] and the European Court of Justice.[77]

- In 2010, the Commission issued a decision confirming Visa Europe's[78] agreement to lower the fees it charged on debit transactions to 0.2 percent on all debit card transactions in the European Union.[79] In 2014, Visa Europe committed to lower its fees to 0.3 percent on all credit card transactions in the European Union, and Visa Europe also agreed to modify its cross-border acquiring rules to allow merchants in one Member State to acquire card transactions through an acquirer in another Member State at these levels.[80]

Neither the Commission nor the European Court of Justice were ultimately persuaded by arguments that the Visa and MasterCard networks had unique characteristics that placed them outside the scope of the Commission's competition law authority under the EU treaties.[81] The 2015 IFR made permanent the 0.2 percent fee limit for debit cards and 0.3 percent fee limit for credit cards that Visa and Master-Card had consented to as temporary measures.[82]

The Interchange Fee Regulation includes many other provisions designed to provide merchants and consumers with more choices in retail payment services:

---

72. Case COMP/37—Morgan Stanley/Visa Int'l & Visa Europe (Summary: 2009 O.J. (C 183) 5).

73. Case T-461/07, Visa Eur. Ltd v. Eur. Comm'n, Judgment of Gen. Court, ECLI:EU:T:2011:181 (Apr. 14, 2011).

74. Case COMP/34.579—MasterCard (Case No COMP/36.518)—EuroCommerce (Case No COMP/38.580)—Commercial Cards (Summary: 2009 O.J. (C 264) 8).

75. Press Release, European Commission, Antitrust: Commissioner Kroes Takes Note of Master-Card's Decision to Cut Cross-Border Multilateral Interchange Fees (MIFs) and to Repeal Recent Scheme Fee Increases (Apr. 1, 2009), *available at* http://europa.eu/rapid/press-release_IP-09-515_en.htm.

76. Case T-111/08, MasterCard, Inc. v. Eur. Comm'n, Judgment of Gen. Court, ECLI:EU:T:2012:260 (May 24, 2012).

77. Case C-382/12P, MasterCard, Inc. v. Eur. Comm'n, Judgment of Court, ECLI:EU:C:2014:2201, ¶ 229 (Sept. 11, 2014).

78. Visa Europe was originally part of the global Visa network, but was spun off as a separate entity in 2007 when the main Visa network became a publicly listed company; in 2016, Visa Europe was merged back into the global network. Richa Naidu & Steve Slater, *Visa Is Buying Visa Europe in a Deal Worth up to $23.3 Billion*, Bus. Insider, Nov. 2, 2015, http://www.businessinsider.com/visa-buys-visa-europe-2015-11.

79. Case COMP/39.398—Visa Multilateral Interchange Fee, Comm'n Decision (Dec. 8, 2010) (2011 O.J. (C 79) 8).

80. Case COMP/39.398—Visa Multilateral Interchange Fee, Comm'n Decision (Feb. 26, 2014) (2014 O.J. (C 147) 6).

81. *See generally* David S. Evans, Interchange Fees: The Economics and Regulations of What Merchants Pay for Cards (2011).

82. Interchange Fee Regulation, *supra* note 13, arts. 3 and 4.

- Consumers can request that mobile phone wallet providers allow them to choose among compatible alternative payment services, and that cards issued by banks allow consumers to choose among alternative card products (although banks retain the right to refuse to offer premium products to individual consumers).[83]
- Retailers are required to inform consumers of which cards they accept as well as their preferred payment method.[84]
- Card networks are now required to support consumer and retailer choice among payment methods. Retailers may set up their point-of-sale payment terminals to default to their preferred payment method, but consumers retain the right to override the retailer's default setting and make a different selection from among the payment methods that the retailer accepts.[85]
- Merchant acquirers are required to provide merchants with a breakdown of fees paid into merchant service fees, interchange fees, and scheme fees.[86]
- Territorial restrictions by card schemes on card issuing or transaction acquiring are no longer permitted, so any institution authorized to issue cards or acquire card transactions from merchants may operate throughout the Single Market.[87]
- Card networks are being required to separate into entities that process network traffic and entities that develop and enforce payment card scheme policies.[88]

EU-level coordination will be required to maintain the interoperability of different network services following these changes in payment card network functionality. Under a mandate from the Commission, the EBA has begun issuing regulatory technical standards to clarify what is required by separation.[89]

VI. SINGLE EURO PAYMENTS AREA AND PAYMENT SERVICES DIRECTIVES I AND II

The first glimmerings of what would later become SEPA became visible during the 1990s with the creation of the European Monetary Union. With the benefit of

---

83. *Id.* art. 8.
84. *Id.* art. 10.
85. *Id.* arts. 8, 10, and 11.
86. *Id.* arts. 9 and 12. According to the UK Payment System Regulator, "interchange fees may differ even amongst the same brand and category of card, for example depending on the type of transaction (e.g. cardholder present or not-present, secure or non-secure, etc.) and scheme fees may differ depending on factors such as the volume of transactions." FINANCIAL CONDUCT AUTHORITY PAYMENT SYSTEM REGULATOR, CONSULTATION PAPER: THE APPLICATION OF THE INTERCHANGE FEE REGULATION IN THE UK: PHASE 2, at 10 (May 2016) (CP16/3).
87. Interchange Fee Regulation, *supra* note 13, art. 6.
88. *Id.*
89. EBA, EBA Final Draft Regulatory Technical Standards on Separation of Payment Card Schemes and Processing Entities under Article 7 (6) of Regulation (EU) 2015/751, EBA/RTS/2016/05, July 27, 2016.

hindsight, it is also clear that few anticipated what a long, slow, difficult task it would be.[90] The ECB and Commission were not in a position to establish a cross-border payment system for the eurozone, but had to rely on the banks to do it for them.[91] In 2001, the ECB informed the banking industry that it expected the Single Market to have its own electronic fund transfer system providing equivalent service levels and prices to the legacy national systems by 2004.[92] Internal contradictions between political priorities and economic logic bedeviled the project from the start, however.[93] As a result, the ECB's expectations were not met until 2014.

In 1999, the ECB published a report outlining its vision for an internal market where cross-border euro transactions would be as quick and easy for EU citizens as domestic euro transfers.[94] It noted that although the European banks and payment processors had already committed to making fully automated "straight-through processing" (STP) of transactions possible for cross-border transactions, thus lowering the cost of providing them, very little concrete progress had been made in implementing the technological changes required to make that possible. In 1992, European banks had established the European Committee for Banking Standards, which had developed the IBAN and BIC standards, but they had not yet been widely implemented.[95]

Both the ECB and the Commission pushed hard for the banks to overhaul their interbank payment infrastructures and internal bank processes so that cross-border STP euro transactions would be possible. The banks resisted, arguing that there was no business case for such a large investment when cross-border transactions amounted to only about 1 percent of all fund transfers they processed. While the ECB and Commission did not deny that current volumes were low, they believed that once the vicious circle of low transaction volumes and high fees was stopped, then latent demand would surface. In 2000, the Commission announced its strategy for working with the ECB and other stakeholders to achieve a single market in retail payments within the broader framework of the Commission's 1999 "Financial Services Action Plan."[96]

The ECB's research had revealed that the processing times were longer and the fees for cross-border payment were often dramatically higher than for domestic payments. Processing times for domestic payment transactions were 1–3 days, while cross-border transactions averaged 4.8 days, with 15 percent taking more than

---

90. *See generally* THE FUTURE OF FINANCE AFTER SEPA (Chris Skinner ed., 2008); DESPINA MAVROMATI, THE LAW OF PAYMENT SERVICES IN THE EU (2008); RUTH WANDHÖFER, EU PAYMENTS INTEGRATION: THE TALE OF SEPA, PSD, AND OTHER MILESTONES ALONG THE ROAD (2010).

91. Martijn van Empel, *Retail Payments in the EU*, 42 COMMON MKT. L. REV. 1425, 1436 (2005).

92. ECB, TOWARDS AN INTEGRATED INFRASTRUCTURE FOR CREDIT TRANSFERS IN EURO 5 (2001).

93. Martijn van Empel, *Retail Payments and the Arduous Road to SEPA*, 46 COMMON MKT. L. REV. 921, 940 (2009).

94. ECB, IMPROVING CROSS-BORDER RETAIL PAYMENT SERVICES: THE EUROSYSTEM'S VIEW (1999).

95. Agnieszka Janczuk-Gorywoda, *Evolution of EU Retail Payments Law*, 40 EUR. L. REV. 858 (2015).

96. Financial Services: Implementing the Framework for Financial Markets: Action Plan, adopted by the European Commission on May 11, 1999, COM(99)232; Commission of the European Communities, Retail Payments in the Internal Market, COM(00)36, final.

a week. In 1993/1994, the Commission had found that the average cost of a cross-border transfer was the equivalent of €24 for a transfer of €100. In 1999, ECB found that they remained stubbornly high: €3.5 to €26 for small amounts and €31 to €400 for large amounts. Furthermore, banks in some countries added additional fees on top of that for balance of payments reporting, currency conversion, or postage and other communication charges.

The high cost and slow processing time for cross-border transactions were due in large part to the use of correspondent banking relations rather than an integrated, computerized network. Although the ECB had been pressing Member States to create links among their different national automated clearing house systems, little progress had been made by the time the euro was launched. In 1998, the Euro Banking Association[97] established the EURO1 network.[98] In 1999, the ECB established the Trans-European Automated Real-time Gross Settlement Express Transfer (TARGET) system for real-time large value transfers.[99] However, nothing equivalent had yet been created for small value payments or payments that were not time sensitive, in part because the ECB's attention with regard to payments was focused on managing operational risk, which was not as great for smaller or slower electronic payments. Nevertheless, the ECB made clear its expectations that new cross-border STP services providing settlement times and fees equivalent to domestic STP services be available by 2002.[100] In a 2001 report critical of the European banking industry's slow progress, the ECB reminded the banks that its goal was cross-border euro transfers so cheap, easy, and quick that bank customers could not discern any significant difference between domestic and cross-border transfers.[101]

Once it was clear that the ECB's goals were not going to be achieved within the time frame it had set, the Commission responded with a regulation in December 2001 mandating that the price for cross-border euro transfers be reduced to the same level as domestic euro transfers (which in some cases were offered for free).[102] This price cap went into effect immediately in January 2002 for automated electronic fund transfers such as automated teller machine (ATM) withdrawals and from January 2003 for all other cross-border euro transfers.[103] The regulation required all banks to inform their customers of their IBANs and BICs so they could start using them for cross-border transfers, to disclose clearly to the sender the total amount

---

97. There are two major banking law institutions in the European Union that may be referred to with the acronym EBA: the Euro Banking Association is a private trade association while the European Banking Authority is an independent regulatory authority; in this chapter, EBA refers only to the latter and not the former.

98. EBA Clearing, *EURO1: The Pre-eminent Privately-Owned Large Value Payment System*, http://www.abe.org/EURO1-N=EURO1-L=EN.aspx (last visited May 21, 2017).

99. ECB, *About Its Forerunner TARGET1*, https://www.ecb.europa.eu/paym/t2/target/html/index.en.html (last visited May 21, 2017).

100. ECB, *supra* note 94, at 7.

101. ECB, *supra* note 92.

102. Regulation (EC) No 2560/2001 of the European Parliament and of the Council of 19 December 2001 on Cross-Border Payments in Euro, 2001 O.J. (L 344) 13.

103. *Id.* art. 3.

of fees due at the outset of a payment transaction, and to request IBANs and BICs for all beneficiaries of cross-border euro transfers.[104] Suddenly, the high transaction costs, lack of standardization, and lack of infrastructure for cross-border euro payments were no longer problems for the ECB and Commission: they were the banks' problems.

A. Launch of the Single Euro Payments Area

By setting fees for cross-border euro payment equal to fees for domestic euro payments, the European Union forced the banks to internalize the high transaction costs created by the lack of a comprehensive infrastructure, which is a form of "taxation by regulation."[105] In 2001, when the banks realized that the Commission was preparing to mandate lower prices for cross-border euro payments, they proposed a "Multilateral Interchange Fee Convention" permitting an interchange fee of €3 to be charged to help defray the costs of building the SEPA system. Such an interchange fee would have created a financial incentive similar to those provided by the international Visa and MasterCard networks to drive adoption of the new SEPA network. But having first-hand experience with how difficult it was to get card interchange fees lowered after the cost of operating the card networks declined, the Commission was unwilling to agree to such an incentive system at the outset of the SEPA project.[106] After the Commission rejected the interchange fee proposal, the banks were left with no viable mechanism for recovering the costs of "reengineering" their national Automated Clearing House (ACH) systems to conform to SEPA standards.

In May 2002, a large group of European banks and several European bank trade associations met to look for ways to halt the losses they were now incurring on cross-border euro transfers. After the meeting, they issued a white paper entitled "Euroland: Our Single Euro Payments Area"[107] describing the solution they had found: while the term "Euroland" was quickly forgotten, the acronym SEPA stuck. In June 2002, the bankers established the EPC, which was composed of representatives of 65 banks representing all the different categories of European banks (such as commercial banks and savings banks), several banking industry trade associations, and the Euro Banking Association. In addition, stakeholders from Iceland, Liechtenstein, Monaco, Norway, and Switzerland were allowed to participate. The EPC plenary was organized as the primary decision making and coordinating body.[108] The EPC

---

104. *Id.* arts. 4 and 5.

105. Richard A. Posner, *Taxation by Regulation*, 2 Bell J. Econ. & Mgmt. Sci. 22 (1971).

106. Opinion of the Economic and Social Committee on the "Proposal for a Regulation of the European Parliament and of the Council on Cross-border Payments in Euro" (2002/C 48/29), ¶ 2.12, 2002 O.J. (C 048) 141.

107. European Credit Sector Association, Euroland: Our Single Payment Area! (2002).

108. Bank for International Settlements, Committee on Payment and Settlement Systems, 2 Payment, Clearing, and Settlement Systems in the Euro Area 85 (2012).

began work developing standards, rulebooks, and frameworks for different types of transactions that are collectively known as "schemes."[109]

The bankers themselves estimated that they might be able to complete the work of reengineering their fragmented national ACH systems into a pan-European network by 2010. In effect, they committed to muddle through as best they could, hoping that once the standards had been developed, a business case for adoption would emerge, but leaving the question of incentives to participate unresolved. After the EPC began work in earnest, it quickly became apparent how daunting the task of creating SEPA was going to be, given the complexity of the technology challenges and the lack of a business case for the banks to invest in finding a solution. To ensure that bankers stayed focused on the task of constructing SEPA even in the absence of any business case for it, the ECB also pointedly reminded the banks that it could always impose a mandatory solution if self-regulation proved to be inadequate: "[s]hould banks, however, not be able to deliver the promised results within the committed timeframe, the ECB might step up its involvement, using its regulatory tools more actively."[110]

On January 28, 2008, the SEPA Credit Transfer scheme was officially launched. A "scheme" in this sense refers to a combination of business rules and technology standards that define mandatory service levels to be achieved by all participating financial institutions. Banks become participants in schemes by entering into contractual agreements with the EPC agreeing to implement them. The goal of the SEPA Credit Transfer scheme was to permit any bank customer anywhere in the eurozone to reach any other bank customer by providing the other party's IBAN and BIC. The maximum execution time when the program was launched was three business days, although this was later shortened to one business day in 2012. The format for all EPC fund transfer messages is defined by the UNIFI (ISO 20022) XML message standards.[111] Use of the SEPA Credit Transfer scheme is independent from the question of which network to use. By 2008, the Euro Banking Association had launched the pan-European ACH STEP2 but banks remained free to engage in bilateral clearing and settlement systems, or to use a different clearing house such as Equens, which operates in the Netherlands, Germany, and Italy.[112]

On November 1, 2009, the SEPA Direct Debit scheme was officially launched.[113] The first step in using the SEPA Direct Debit scheme is for the payor to deliver a

---

109. EPC, *What Is a Payment Scheme?*, http://www.europeanpaymentscouncil.eu/index.cfm/sepa -credit-transfer/what-is-a-payment-scheme/ (last visited May 21, 2017).

110. ECB, Towards a Single Euro Payments Area—Progress Report 6 (2003).

111. *See generally* EPC, *ISO 20022 Message Standards*, http://www.europeanpaymentscouncil.eu /index.cfm/sepa-credit-transfer/iso-20022-message-standards/ (last visited May 21, 2017).

112. *See* EBA Clearing, *STEP2: The Pan-European ACH*, http://www.abe.org/STEP2-N=STEP2-L=EN .aspx (last visited May 21, 2017); European Automated Clearing House Association, *Members* (list of European automated clearing houses), http://www.eacha.org/members.php (last visited May 21, 2017); Equens Worldline, *Automated Clearing House* (Netherlands, Germany, and Italy coverage), https://www .equensworldline.com/payments/automatedclearinghouse/index.jsp (last visited May 21, 2017).

113. EPC, *SEPA Direct Debit Core Scheme (SDD Core)*, http://www.europeanpaymentscouncil.eu /index.cfm/sepa-direct-debit/sepa-direct-debit-core-scheme-sdd-core/ (last visited May 21, 2017).

signed mandate to the payee who in turn gives it to the payor's payment service provider. The mandate is an instruction from the payor to the payment service provider to process debit transactions from the payee against the payor's account. SEPA Direct Debit can be used for one-time transactions or recurring transactions. The payor and the payee must both maintain accounts with payment service providers in the European Union. The most common users of the SEPA Direct Debit scheme are corporations that bill consumers for recurring payments such as those for mortgages, rent, utilities, or insurance premiums. Anyone who does not wish to permit a SEPA Direct Debit to be charged to their accounts may so instruct their payment service provider. A mandate ceases to be valid 36 months after the last debit transaction is processed. During the eight weeks after a SEPA Direct Debit transaction has been processed, a payor may request a "no-questions-asked" refund. In the event of an unauthorized charge, the payor may request a refund within 13 months.

In addition to the SEPA Credit Transfer scheme, the SEPA Core Direct Debit scheme and the SEPA Business-to-Business Direct Debit scheme, the EPC also developed a SEPA Card Framework to harmonize card processing policies and procedures across Europe. Because considerable progress in achieving pan-European technical interoperability had already been achieved for card networks, there was no need for the EPC to develop and maintain a full scheme for card payments. However, the European card payment network was fragmented into national markets with regard to the terms and conditions imposed for domestic and cross-border transactions. At the request of the ECB, the EPC developed the SEPA Card Framework to ensure that the user experience for domestic and cross-border card transactions was equivalent.[114] The ECB also hoped that the European banks would launch a third, European card network to compete with Visa and MasterCard but never succeeded in persuading the banks that this would be a good idea.[115] In 2009, a "Card Stakeholder Group" made up of five different industry sectors (retailers/wholesale; technology vendors; processors of card transactions; card schemes; and payment service providers) was established to develop and maintain the SEPA Card Standardisation Volume, a comprehensive description of voluntary implementation standards.[116] In 2016, the European Card Stakeholder Group was established and it took over the work of maintaining the SEPA Card Standardisation Volume from the Card Stakeholder Group.

---

114. ECB, Towards a Single Euro Payments Area—Third Progress Report 4–5 (2004) [hereinafter Third Progress Report].

115. ECB, Single Euro Payments Area Seventh Progress Report: Beyond Theory into Practice 22 (2010). By contrast, India and China, where Visa and MasterCard had not yet become well established by the time the government made a national payments network a priority, were able to successfully launch new national card payment networks. Jane K. Winn, *Innovation Governance Competition: Payment Modernization Strategies in India and China*, in The Routledge Handbook on Asian Law (Christoph Antons ed., 2016), *available at* http://ssrn.com/abstract=2548684.

116. EPC, *The EPC Welcomes the Creation of the European Card Stakeholders Group*, https://www.europeanpaymentscouncil.eu/news-insights/news/epc-welcomes-creation-european-cards-stakeholders-group (last visited May 21, 2017).

B. Payment Services Directive I

To establish a solid legal foundation for the SEPA project and to advance the progress in harmonizing EU payment law both inside and outside the eurozone, PSD1 was promulgated in 2007.[117] As one commentator noted, "A robust and secure payments system requires a consistent and reliable legal framework specifying in particular when a payment transaction is completed and can no longer be reversed, as well as distributing risks between parties involved in a payment transaction."[118] The PSD1 established mandatory minimum requirements for the rights and obligations of the parties to retail credit transfers, direct debit transactions, and card payments as well as a new licensing regime governing nonbank payment service providers. While the SEPA project was designed to remove barriers to STP for cross-border euro payments, the focus of the PSD1 was to harmonize the law governing retail payments throughout the internal market without regard to the currency used.

C. Completion of the Single Euro Payments Area

In 2002, the EPC launched the Convention for Cross-border Payments in Euros (also known as the Credeuro Convention) and in 2003, the Euro Banking Association launched a Pan-European ACH that could process those credit transfers. The implementation of these early efforts at harmonization was based largely on the efforts of the banks that had previously operated the legacy correspondent banking system and, in effect, permitted other banks to outsource the processing of cross-border euro transactions to those banks rather than come into compliance themselves. In 2006, the Commission made it clear that any solution that was not based on the participation of all payment service providers would not be acceptable:

> [SEPA] will be deemed a success when the full potential of economies of scale and scope and competition are realised with the euro-zone. This means savings for users and lower costs for providers. This vision does not allow for developments that will only take us half the way. A mini-SEPA that only delivers solutions for cross-border payments in Europe is not acceptable.[119]

The business process reengineering challenges of achieving such a comprehensive solution to the problem of inefficient cross-border euro transfers was probably one order of magnitude greater than anything the European banking industry had in mind in 2002 when it issued its Euroland white paper.

The ECB expected that once the SEPA system was up and running, then the legacy national systems could be shut down:

> [I]n a first phase banks would be able to offer to customers pan-European instruments, services and standards in parallel to national services, standards and instruments. The pan-European services would allow customers to make all their

---

117. Internal Market Payment Services Directive, *supra* note 7.
118. Janczuk-Gorywoda, *supra* note 95.
119. European Commission, Consultative Paper on SEPA Incentives (2006) [hereinafter SEPA Incentives Paper].

euro payments—national and cross-border—in one format from one account. In a second phase, once national instruments, services and standards have been gradually phased out and replaced by pan-European ones, national infrastructures would be either abolished or transformed into pan-European ones.[120]

The second phase did not follow automatically after the first phase as expected. In September 2011, the ECB determined that only 21.1 percent of credit transfers had migrated to SEPA while 0.13 percent of direct debit transactions had migrated, and almost all the national ACH systems were still up and running.

After enduring years of ECB complaints about how ineffectual the SEPA migration process was, as the 2010 target date for completion of SEPA grew nearer, the banking industry found itself in the unlikely position of facing complaints from competition law regulators on the grounds that it might be too effective and thus stifle competition.[121] As a matter of EU competition law, when the Commission determined that the way MasterCard administered interchange fees was unlawful,[122] then the interchange fee that the EPC had proposed as an incentive for adoption of the SEPA Direct Debit was no longer viable. One commentator explained the consternation among banks that greeted the directorate-general for competition's 2007 Master-Card decision in these terms:

> The decision came as a shock to banks and seriously undermined the SEPA process insofar as banks had constructed not only the SEPA Cards Framework but also the SEPA Direct Debit scheme on the basis of [multilateral exchange fee (MIF)] as a financing mechanism. Once the legality of MIF was questioned, banks—never actually enthusiastic for SEPA—complained that any business case for SEPA had ceased to exist. As a result, SEPA migration became seriously jeopardized, and even more so the spontaneous "market-driven" migration. In these circumstances, the EPC called for clarification of the EU law's stance towards MIF in direct debits and for a legal end-date for the existing national payment systems.[123]

At this point, the only obvious way forward was for the EPC to turn to the Commission for help.

The Commission responded with EC Regulation 924/2009, which repealed EC Regulation 2560/2001 and replaced it with an expanded framework to support the SEPA system.[124] While the 2001 regulation applied only to credit transfers and card payments, the 2009 regulation extended to debit transactions the "nondiscrimination" rule for domestic versus cross-border euro transfer fees. The 2009 regulation granted the banks a temporary authorization to collect a €0.088 per transaction

---

120. THIRD PROGRESS REPORT, *supra* note 114, at 3–4.
121. van Empel, *supra* note 93.
122. Case COMP/34.579—MasterCard (Case No COMP/36.518)—EuroCommerce (Case No COMP/38.580)—Commercial Cards (Summary: 2009 O.J. (C 264) 8).
123. Janczuk-Gorywoda, *supra* note 95.
124. Regulation on Cross Border Payments, *supra* note 4.

interchange fee until November 2012, although the Commission also recognized that EU competition law would not generally permit such an interchange fee.[125]

By 2010, however, it had become clear that the migration of legacy national ACH systems to the new SEPA schemes would never be completed in a timely fashion without even more forceful intervention on the part of the Commission and ECB.[126] In 2012, the EU Parliament and Council authorized additional support for the SEPA migration process with the "SEPA End Date Regulation."[127] For the euro area, February 1, 2014, was set as the deadline for shutting down legacy national ACH systems, while the deadline for migrating euro-denominated payments in non-euro area countries was set for October 31, 2016. All banks in the euro area that offer credit transfer or direct debit payment services were required to be "reachable" by any other bank in the euro area. SEPA "reachability" refers to having implemented SEPA compliant standards and procedures internally plus participating in a clearing and settlement system that can process SEPA transactions originating anywhere else in the internal market. In addition, the transaction upper limit of €50,000 for equal fees to apply was eliminated. In 2014, when it became clear that the February 1, 2014, deadline was not going to be met by certain Member States, the Commission extended the deadline for SEPA migration by six months with Regulation 248/2014.[128]

Although the Commission intervened in the SEPA migration process with legislation to support the EPC's work, the Commission and ECB remained concerned that EPC governance processes excluded the interests of certain stakeholders. In 2006, the Commission noted that end users, nonbank payment service providers, and infrastructure providers such as ACHs were not well integrated into the EPC governance process.[129] In 2010, the ECB and Commission established the SEPA Council as a vehicle through which all these nonbank stakeholder groups could participate in the SEPA process.[130] These governance reforms were still not satisfactory to the ECB, which decided in 2013 to replace the SEPA Council with the ERPB, a high-level strategy body under the ECB's control designed to maintain momentum toward an "integrated, innovative and competitive" euro retail payments market. The Commission had launched a competition law investigation of the EPC in 2011, and although it closed the investigation in 2013 without taking action, it did announce its intention

---

125. Press Release, ECB, Joint Statement by the European Commission and the European Central Bank Clarifying Certain Principles Underlying a Future SEPA Direct Debit (SDD) Business Model (Mar. 24, 2009), *available at* https://www.ecb.europa.eu/press/pr/date/2009/html/Jointstatement24032009.pdf?d7b50bb5c6cc2eb5dc3b0968165ae51a.

126. SEPA Council Formal Declaration on SEPA Migration End-Date(s) (June 7, 2010), http://www.europeanpaymentscouncil.eu/index.cfm/knowledge-bank/other-sepa-information/sepa-council-formal-declaration-on-sepa-end-dates/sepa-council-formal-declaration-on-sepa-end-datespdf/.

127. Regulation on Credit Transfers and Direct Debits, *supra* note 10.

128. EU Regulation 248/2014, *supra* note 10.

129. SEPA Incentives Paper, *supra* note 119.

130. EPC, *About SEPA: The Political Drivers*, http://www.europeanpaymentscouncil.eu/index.cfm/about-sepa/the-political-drivers/ (last visited May 21, 2017).

to continue monitoring the EPC.[131] Receiving a clear mandate from a public body such as the ERPB reduced the EPC's exposure to possible competition law liability.

Although the EPC no longer exercised a leadership role in setting the strategic direction of euro retail payments policy, it remains an active participant in the SEPA ecosystem. The EPC maintains the existing SEPA schemes, which are being continuously updated. As will be discussed in the following section, it was also invited in 2015 by the ERPB to contribute technical expertise and then standard-setting services for a new SEPA "instant payments" scheme.

D. Payment Services Directive II

Article 87 of PSD1 required the Commission to report to the European Parliament, European Council, and ECB three years after the effective date for PDS1 on the possible need for additional legislation to expand its scope. In 2012, the Commission outlined its strategy to use SEPA as the springboard for the next phase of reform in European payment law.[132] The Commission noted that the mass adoption of smartphones in EU markets was changing the payments landscape. It highlighted strategic priorities favoring competition, innovation, increased choice and transparency for consumers, and better integration of security into payment processes. In 2013, the Commission published a payment law reform proposal that included a draft of a revised Payment Services Directive together with a draft of the interchange fee regulation discussed above in Part V.[133] After extensive consultation and negotiations among the Commission, European Parliament, and European Council, PSD2 was enacted in 2015 with a 2018 deadline for Member States to transpose its provisions into national law.[134]

The scope of PSD2 was expanded to cover transactions with only "one leg" in the European Union (i.e., one of two payment processors is located outside the European Union) as well as "two leg" transactions (i.e., both payment processors inside the European Union), which were within the scope of PSD1. Under PSD2, many consumer protections first mandated in PSD1 were expanded, including reducing consumer liability for unauthorized transactions from €150 to €50; prohibiting payment service providers from charging customers for giving notice of the loss of a payment device or unauthorized transactions; and prohibiting surcharging consumers for paying with cards. Payment service providers are required to improve the security of their systems and provide their customers with strong authentication technologies. The licensing requirements for nonbank payment institutions were strengthened somewhat by adding a requirement of professional indemnity insurance and clarifying some aspects of the supervision process. The scope of the EBA oversight

---

131. Memo, European Commission, Antitrust: Commission Closes Investigation of EPC but Continues Monitoring Online Payments Market (June 13, 2013), *available at* http://europa.eu/rapid/press-release_MEMO-13-553_en.htm.

132. Green Paper Towards an Integrated European Market for Card, Internet, and Mobile Payments, COM(11)941 final.

133. EC Press Release, *supra* note 2.

134. EU Directive 2015/2366, *supra* note 12.

of retail payment systems was expanded by requiring the EBA to develop a central registry of authorized payment institutions, to assist in resolving disputes among national payment regulators, to promote cooperation and information exchange among national payment regulators, and to develop regulatory technical standards for strong customer authentication and secure communication channels.

On the surface, the PSD2 provisions governing "account information service providers" (AISP) and "payment information service providers" (PISP) may not appear to be the most controversial part of PSD2, but they are. They are generally understood as requiring European banks to publish APIs that disruptive fintech innovators can then use to disintermediate the banks themselves. For obvious reasons, these provisions triggered a firestorm of controversy among financial services firms in Europe.[135] In order to understand how and why the Commission devised this novel policy instrument, it may be helpful first to recall how widespread the practice of "screen scraping" is among fintech innovators and the relevance of APIs to disruptive business models generally.

Screen scraping is a data collection technique that permits one computer system to "scrape" data displayed on the screen or other output device of a second computer system.[136] Screen scraping can be used within a single system of computers, for example, as a method to collect data from a legacy system in order to overcome incompatible file formats. It can also be used by the operator of one independent computer system to collect data without the consent or knowledge of the operator of a second computer system. The practice of screen scraping is widespread among nonbank financial services firms. A customer can provide his or her Internet bank account user identification and password credentials to a financial services software provider such as Intuit or Mint. Using these customer credentials, the third party captures and transmits customer data from the bank to its own computer system. In many instances, the bank may not be aware that a third party has used its customer's credentials to capture and reuse the customer's information.[137]

Financial aggregators such as Mint in the United States or Money Dashboard in the United Kingdom pioneered business models that correspond to AISP. These aggregators can collect and integrate information from a consumer's different financial accounts in order to display it in a way that is meaningful to the consumer. In Europe, Sofort, an independent German fintech start-up, and iDeal, a collaborative effort among Dutch banks, pioneered business models that correspond to PISP.[138]

---

135. Javier Santamaría, *On the Difference between Innovation and the Wild West: How to Ensure the Security of Bank Customers' Funds and Data with Payment Account Access Services*, EPC NEWSL., Apr. 17, 2014, http://www.europeanpaymentscouncil.eu/index.cfm/newsletter/article/?articles_uuid =D7124BB7-5056-B741-DBD57544389D7A1A.

136. *See generally* JANE K. WINN & BENJAMIN WRIGHT, LAW OF ELECTRONIC COMMERCE § 2.04[B] (4th ed. & Supp. 2016) (discussing screen scraping cases under U.S. law).

137. PwC, PSD2 IN A NUTSHELL, TWO (2016), *available at* http://www.pwc.com/it/en/industries/banking /assets/docs/psd2-nutshell-n02.pdf.

138. Memo, European Commission, Payment Services Directive and Interchange Fees Regulation: Frequently Asked Questions (July 24, 2013), http://europa.eu/rapid/press-release_MEMO-13-719_en.htm.

These payment services can transfer payments between consumers and merchants without opening an account with the PISP and without the payment through an ATM or credit card network, thus radically simplifying the transaction flow. While many of these new services collect the information they need by screen scraping or a similar process without the active participation of the financial institution where the account is housed, it would be more efficient if the traditional financial institution and the new service coordinated their efforts.

While neither the definition of AISP nor the definition of PISP use the term "API," it is generally understood that banks will have to publish APIs or do something very similar in order to comply with PSD2.[139] An API is a framework that specifies how different software program components interact with each other. APIs can be used to define how software interacts with hardware or access databases, or it may simplify the process of writing software by reusing elements of other programs.[140] Information economy firms as diverse as Google, Netflix, Uber, Airbnb, Spotify, Twitter, Facebook, Instagram, Amazon, eBay, Alibaba, PayPal, Stripe, FedEx, United Parcel Service, the *New York Times*, and Marvel Comics have all learned to engage in e-commerce based on APIs to link mobile phones, cloud computing, data analytics, artificial intelligence, and social production.[141]

In effect, the AIS and PIS provisions of the PSD2 have recast the banks as involuntary "platform as a service" (PaaS) providers for disruptive fintech start-ups seeking to disintermediate them.[142] Banks are also concerned that the PSD2 may not correctly allocate liability for money laundering or data protection breaches.[143] If disruptive fintech innovators are not held to the same compliance and supervisory standards as the banks and there is a risk that liability for any technical or regulatory failures attributable to the PSD2's open API banking mandate may fall on the banks, then banks can be expected to resist assuming their new role as PaaS for disruptive fintech innovators. Under the PSD2, much of the responsibility for aligning the functions of AISPs and PISPs (collectively, providers of "third-party payment," or TPP services), together with "account servicing payment service providers" (ASPSPs,

---

139. By contrast, regulators in the United Kingdom do use the term API in payment regulations. Mary Wisniewski, *U.K. Push for Open Bank APIs Makes U.S. Look So Last Century*, Am. Banker, Nov. 25, 2015, http://www.americanbanker.com/news/bank-technology/uk-push-for-open-bank-apis-makes-us-look-so-last-century-1078015-1.html.

140. *See generally* Winn & Wright, *supra* note 136, § 13.03 (discussing APIs under U.S. law).

141. José Manuel de la Chica, *PSD2 and Open APIs in Banking: Is This the Start of the Exponential Era in FinTech and Online Payments?*, BBVA Open 4 U Blog, June 3, 2016, https://bbvaopen4u.com/en/actualidad/psd2-and-open-apis-banking-start-exponential-era-fintech-and-online-payments.

142. "Platform as a service (PaaS) is a cloud-based computing environment designed to support the rapid development, running and management of applications. It is integrated and abstracted from the lower-level infrastructure components." Sunil Joshi, *What Is Platform as a Service Pass (PaaS)?*, IBM Cloud Computing News, Feb. 17, 2014, https://www.ibm.com/blogs/cloud-computing/2014/02/what-is-platform-as-a-service-paas/. *See also* Peter Mell & Timothy Grance, U.S. Department of Commerce, National Institute of Standards and Technology, The NIST Definition of Cloud Computing (2011) (NIST SP 800-145).

143. Peggy Valcke, Niels Vandezande & Nathan Van de Velde, Swift Institute, The Evolution of Third Party Payment Providers and Cryptocurrencies under the EU's Upcoming PSD2 and AMLD4 (Working Paper No. 2015-001, Sept. 23, 2015).

i.e., the banks), with AISPs in the new world of "access to account" (XS2A)[144] services, falls on the EBA as the architect of the "regulatory technical standards" with which ASPSPs, AISPs, and PISPs will all have to comply.

VII. INSTANT/FASTER PAYMENTS

The first "instant payments" or "faster payments" scheme in the world was the Zengin system launched in 1973.[145] In 2016, there were at least 19 live faster payment schemes operating in different countries around the world with nine more in various stages of development.[146] In 2014, the financial services firm FIS provided the following definition of an "instant" or "faster" payment scheme:

> Domestic, inter-bank (i.e. not alternative payment schemes), purely electronic payment systems in which irrevocable funds are transferred from one bank account to another and where confirmation back to the originator and receiver of the payment is available in one minute or less.[147]

When Switzerland built its "real time gross settlement" platform in 1987, it decided to run all payments through it, including small value payments.[148] In 2001, Korea successfully launched its Interbank Home/Firm Banking Network (HOFINET) faster payment system[149] and in 2002, Brazil launched its Sistema de Transferência de Fundos (Sitraf) faster payments system.[150]

The first EU member state to build such a system was the United Kingdom, which launched its Faster Payments scheme in 2008. This new system for retail electronic payments with prompt, same-day settlement was launched in response to the recommendations of the Cruickshank Report issued in 2000. When the Faster Payments scheme went live in 2008, all major UK banks participated in the new scheme.[151] The infrastructure was provided by VocaLink, a new infrastructure service provider created by the merger of Voca and Link, two existing payment network service providers. When the scheme was launched, the value limit on electronic fund transfers was £10,000. In 2008, the cap was lifted to £100,000, and in 2015, it was

---

144. Anne Boden, *Explaining PSD2 without TLAs Is Tough!*, STARLING BANK, Oct. 9, 2015, https://www.starlingbank.com/explaining-psd2-without-tlas-tough/.

145. JAPANESE BANKS' PAYMENT CLEARING NETWORK, THE ZENGIN DATA TELECOMMUNICATION SYSTEM (2014), *available at* https://www.zengin-net.jp/en/zengin_net/pdf/pamphlet_e.pdf.

146. FIDELITY NATIONAL INFORMATION SERVICES INC., FLAVOURS OF FAST: A TRIP AROUND THE WORLD IN IMMEDIATE PAYMENTS 5 (2016).

147. *Id.* at 13.

148. DANIEL HELLER, THOMAS NELLEN & ANDY STURM, SWISS NATIONAL BANK, PAYMENT SYSTEM SUBSECTION, THE SWISS INTERBANK CLEARING SYSTEM 4 (June 2000).

149. PRESIDENT'S MESSAGE, KOREA FINANCIAL TELECOMMUNICATIONS & CLEARINGS INSTITUTE 41 (2015).

150. Banco Central do Brasil, *New SPB—The Brazilian Payment System*, http://www.bcb.gov.br/pom/spb/Ing/InterbankFundsTransfer/CIPIngles.asp (last visited May 21, 2017).

151. *Faster Bank Transfers under Way*, BBC NEWS, May 27, 2008, http://news.bbc.co.uk/2/hi/business/7417303.stm; KPMB & ASSOCIATION FOR PAYMENT CLEARANCE SERVICES, BRINGING FASTER PAYMENTS TO THE UK BANKING SYSTEM (2009).

lifted again to £250,000.[152] The customer receives confirmation of the transaction within 15 seconds and transactions post to the customer's account in two hours. The Faster Payments scheme may be faster and cheaper than other electronic payment schemes in the United Kingdom, but it is not an "immediate payment" system based on "real time gross settlement." It provides instead three deferred net settlement cycles a day.

In 2014, when the ERPB considered the question of whether the internal market needed an immediate payment system, it had considerably higher expectations of how such a system would function:

> [an] electronic retail payment solutions available 24/7/365 and resulting in the immediate or close-to-immediate interbank clearing of the transaction and crediting of the payee's account with confirmation to the payer (within seconds of payment initiation). This is irrespective of the underlying payment instrument used (credit transfer, direct debit or payment card) and of the underlying arrangements for clearing (whether bilateral interbank clearing or clearing via infrastructures) and settlement (e.g. with guarantees or in real time) that make this possible.[153]

The ERPB did not want the emergence of separate national immediate payment systems to fragment the European Union and reverse any of the hard-won harmonization gains achieved through the creation of SEPA. As an official at the ECB noted, "Nobody would accept having to subscribe to a Spanish mobile operator just to be able to phone a friend in Spain."[154] In addition, the ERPB thought existing payment infrastructures should be leveraged as much as possible, and wanted to prevent the creation of any new payment systems that were not interoperable with existing systems. The ERPB requested the EPC conduct a study of the feasibility of creating a pan-European instant payment system, which was issued in 2015.[155]

In light of the findings of the June 2015 EPC report on the feasibility of a European instant payment services, the ERPB authorized the EPC to begin work on an instant payment scheme based on existing SEPA Credit Transfer standards. A draft of the SEPA Credit Transfer Inst (instant SEPA credit transfer, or SCT Inst) scheme was released for comments in July 2016, and in November 2016, version 1.0 of the SEPA Credit Transfer Inst scheme was issued with a target date of November 2017 to process the first transaction. Participation in the SCT Inst will be open to all payment service providers and voluntary, unlike participation in the "basic" SEPA

---

152. Faster Payments, *History/Timeline*, http://www.fasterpayments.org.uk/sites/default/files/downloads/page/history_timeline.pdf (last visited May 30, 2017).

153. ERPB, Statement Following the Second Meeting of the Euro Retail Payments Board (Dec. 1, 2014), http://www.ecb.europa.eu/paym/retpaym/shared/pdf/eprb_statement_2.pdf?72f16eb99abfaef ce9292143f0344227.

154. ECB Executive Board Member Yves Mersch, Speech at the Belgian Financial Forum: Challenges of Retail Payments Innovation (Oct. 26, 2015).

155. EPC Ad-hoc Task Force on Instant Payments, EPC Report to the ERPB on Instant Payments (2015) (EPC 160-15).

Credit Transfer and SEPA Core Direct Debit schemes, which became mandatory in 2012 for depository institutions.[156]

VIII. CONCLUSION: PAST AS PROLOGUE?

Long before "fintech" became a buzzword, the European Union began the process of overhauling the legal framework of payment systems in Europe to lay a foundation for the success of the euro as its common currency. In 2003, the Commission announced its intention to construct a "New Legal Framework" for payments in Europe as part of the process of building the internal market. While grappling with challenges such as credit card interchange and SEPA, the Commission gradually shifted the focus of its law reform efforts from merely reducing transaction costs and increasing consumer protection to inciting new forms of competition in sluggish retail financial services markets in an effort to accelerate innovation and increase Europe's global competitiveness. After the rise of fintech in London demonstrated the potential of innovations in payment services to help fuel the growth of a broader knowledge economy, the overhaul of European retail payment systems became a strategic priority in the EU Digital Single Market strategy.

As a result of this distinctly European effort at completing its internal market, the European Union finds itself today at the vanguard of global "fintech" regulation. Over the past 20 years, the scope of EU payment law expanded from modest efforts to harmonize the terms and conditions of payment services governed by private agreements to laying one of the cornerstones of the Digital Single Market program. This expansive new approach to payment law includes startlingly bold strategies and politically controversial strategies to fuel competition in retail payments such as mandating open API banking and account number portability. Because the EU law reforms discussed in this chapter are based on treaty provisions giving EU institutions the authority to build a single market, EU institutions have been able to develop and implement a much more forceful fintech regime than has the United States, where financial regulators such as the Federal Reserve Board currently lack express authority to enact similarly broad legislation.

A fundamental contradiction between the construction of the internal market as a political goal and the pursuit of efficiency, innovation, and competitiveness as economic goals lies at the heart of EU payment law reforms in recent decades. This contradiction is often papered over with "Eurospeak" rhetoric about the importance of "market-led" reforms embedded in coercive mandates imposed on what the Commission appears to regard as a recalcitrant banking industry. This contradiction is clearly visible in the most novel payment law reforms such as open API banking and

---

156. Press Release, EPC, The Launch of the EPC's SEPA Instant Credit Transfer Scheme Marks a Further Step in European Payments Integration (Nov. 30, 2016), *available at* http://www.europeanpayments council.eu/index.cfm/knowledge-bank/epc-documents/press-release-the-launch-of-the-epce28099s-sepa-instant-credit-transfer-scheme-marks-a-further-step-in-european-payments-integration/press-release-the-launch-of-the-epce28099s-sepa-instant-credit-transfer-scheme-marks-a-furt/.

account number portability, which raise many complex technological and political issues that will have to be resolved by the EBA through the complex new process for setting "regulatory technical standards." It remains to be seen whether an updated form of the old "comitology" process will be up to the task of resolving fundamental conflicts between political and economic goals at the same time as setting interoperability standards for emerging financial services. As one commentator noted, "Hard choices will have to be made one day or the other, though, and should not be allowed to be fudged by ambiguous drafting."[157]

The European Union still has significant hurdles to overcome in order to achieve its Digital Single Market strategy in markets for payment services. In 2014, Google chief executive officer Eric Schmidt famously suggested that "heavy-handed regulation" to protect incumbents "risks creating an innovation desert in Europe."[158] In 2016, the *Economist* opined, "The fundamental problem is both that there are too many banks in Europe and that many are not profitable enough because they have clung to flawed business models."[159] Furthermore, the ongoing political woes of the European Union have been compounded by Brexit. While it is still too soon to know how many of the EU payment law reforms described in this chapter will succeed, it is clear that the Commission's goal is to drive innovation with law reform rather than block it.[160]

---

157. van Empel, *supra* note 93, at 1443.

158. Eric Schmidt, *About the Good Things Google Does: A Chance for Growth*, Frankfurter Allgemeine (Ger.), Apr. 9, 2014, http://www.faz.net/aktuell/feuilleton/debatten/eric-schmidt-about-the-good-things -google-does-a-chance-for-growth-12887909.html. Schmidt was responding to articles published in newspapers in France and Germany that were highly critical of Google. *See, e.g.*, Robert M. Maier, *Angst vor Google*, Frankfurter Allgemeine (Ger.), Apr. 3, 2014, http://www.faz.net/aktuell/feuilleton/debatten /weltmacht-google-ist-gefahr-fuer-die-gesellschaft-12877120.html; Pascal de Lima, *Google ou la Route de la Servitude*, Le Monde (Fr.), Apr. 3, 2014, http://www.lemonde.fr/economie/article/2014/04/03/google-ou -la-route-de-la-servitude_4395186_3234.html. *See generally* Francisco J. Jariego, *Googlecracy*, Mind Post Blog, May 11, 2014, https://pacojariego.me/2014/05/11/googlecracy/.

159. *Falling Bank Shares: A Tempest of Fear*, Economist, Feb. 13, 2016, http://www.economist.com /news/business-and-finance/21692863-european-banks-are-eye-new-financial-storm-tempest-fear.

160. Mersch, *supra* note 154.

Chapter 10

E-payments Systems in the United Kingdom

Implementing EU Directives and UK Privacy Laws

Julian Hamblin, Emma Radmore,
and Malcolm Dowden

I. INTRODUCTION

In recent years, the pace of reform in UK payments laws has substantially been determined by the relentless pace of EU payments law reform, discussed in more detail in Chapter 9. The UK popular vote in the referendum of June 23, 2016, to exit the European Union ("Brexit") has now cast a shadow over that process, adding uncertainty to the mix. This chapter describes how retail e-payment systems and associated payments laws are evolving in the United Kingdom, and offers some provisional thoughts on how Brexit is likely to affect the regulatory footprint.

E-payments have the potential to facilitate and promote the growth of online and omnichannel commerce and retailing, not only within and between EU Member States but more broadly around the world. As consumer confidence and convenience are important byproducts of effective regulation, we consider how the regulatory regimes affect consumers' daily experiences by promoting confidence and security or creating barriers or inconvenience. At root, our view is that the most effective incentive for investors and entrepreneurs is a market populated by consumers who are both able and willing to participate in a vibrant, seamless, and reliable market for goods and services; appropriate regulation contributes significantly toward creating that marketplace.

At the time of writing, it is likely that the United Kingdom will remain a full Member State of the European Union when key legislation discussed in this chapter comes into full operation in 2018. However, it is not yet clear how far (or whether) the United Kingdom will remain part of the legislative and policy projects relating to payment services. It is possible that the United Kingdom will become (or remain) a member of the European Economic Area (EEA), in which case the rules discussed in this chapter would apply in full. It is also possible, and at present it seems more likely, that the United Kingdom will simply cease to be a Member State at the expiry of the two-year period following notification under article 50 of the Lisbon Treaty. In that case, payment transactions between the United Kingdom and EU/EEA Member States would be caught by the newly extended geographical reach of EU payment services regulation as "one leg" transactions, involving some information and consumer protection requirements, but by no means amounting to full participation.

II. CASE STUDY: MIKE AND JENNY HILL AND NOTJUSTFOOD CO.

Mike and Jenny Hill are loyal customers of NotjustFood, a leading UK supermarket chain. They like to shop with NotjustFood because of the broad range of goods and services it provides, both in-store and online. When they visit a store, they will typically purchase groceries, but they may also grab a coffee at the in-store CforCoffee franchise, and before heading home, fill up their car at the NotjustFood filling station.

NotjustFood prides itself on being able to meet most of its customers' needs. It has branched out into banking and insurance, as well as providing mobile phone and broadband packages online and through kiosks in their stores. In addition, it offers a range of services through its wholly-owned bank, which is an authorized deposit-taker. Using their NotjustFood mobile phones, Mike and Jenny can purchase certain goods and services that are then charged to their mobile phone bill, and paid through their bank account, all within the NotjustFood corporate umbrella.

NotjustFood has a loyalty card scheme that can be used to earn points in its stores. NotjustFood sells gift cards for various other retailers, including the CforCoffee card, which can be used only in CforCoffee outlets, some of which can be found in NotjustFood stores. The CforCoffee card is a stored-value card that carries a monetary value. It can also be topped up online, in-store, and automatically. It can also be put into an Apple Pay wallet.

Jenny Hill signed up for a NotjustFood loyalty card in 2005 shortly after NotjustFood launched its loyalty program. As with most loyalty card schemes, the Hills earn points on the value of purchases made in-store, but they can also use the card to earn points when they fill up their cars at the supermarket filling station. The points accumulate to provide vouchers with a monetary value or special "money off" discounts on promotional products. The vouchers are only redeemable when shopping at NotjustFood, online or in-store.

Mike and Jenny Hill have a current account (with an overdraft facility) with NotjustFood Bank, including a contactless enabled chip-and-PIN Visa card, which

Mike has set up on his iPhone as his linked Apple Pay payment card. NotjustFood Bank is a wholly-owned subsidiary of NotjustFood plc and is authorized by the United Kingdom's Prudential Regulation Authority and Financial Conduct Authority in its deposit-taking and consumer credit business. The Hills own a house in France and have another bank account with a French bank, and they frequently transfer sterling sums into their French euro account.

Sometimes Mike and Jenny will do their grocery shopping online but, despite their best efforts, NotjustFood cannot provide for the Hills' every need. When they want to buy non-grocery goods they often use an online marketplace like Amazon or eBay to research products and price ranges. If online prices are sufficiently attractive, or if an online order is simply more convenient, Mike and Jenny will readily take their business to competitors who offer advantages in price or convenience.

When checking their NotjustFood Bank statement this morning, Jenny was shocked to find that they had somehow reached their overdraft limit of £1,500. Working through the transactions listed on the statement, Mike and Jenny found several that they did not recognize. During a call to the bank's helpline, the operator commented that they had been inundated with calls and complaints that morning. Later, the evening news bulletin included reports that NotjustFood Bank had been the victim of a cyberattack resulting in a leak of account and other personal information relating to nearly 200,000 customers.

Mike and Jenny Hill represent both an asset and a challenge for retailers like NotjustFood. Their loyalty to the NotjustFood brand means that they are willing to be "multichannel" customers, buying a variety of goods and services from NotjustFood's supermarket and online retail channels, and through its bank and mobile network, operated as a mobile virtual network operator (MVNO). However, Mike and Jenny Hill would also be prized customers for a growing range of NotjustFood's competitors.

"Multichannel" is rapidly giving way to "omnichannel." Multichannel sought to push and apply consistent branding across a retailer's range of outlets, devices, and networks. Omnichannel begins with customer experience, applying sophisticated predictive analytics to data gathered from previous purchases and searches, customer profiling, real-time location monitoring, and data such as shopping lists created in smartphone applications (apps) to track, respond to, and shape customer behavior. A key objective with the omnichannel model is to make the customer's experience as seamless and as streamlined as possible, including stages such as product research and comparison, order fulfillment, and, of course, payment.

Mike and Jenny's current shopping habits and the range of their interactions suggest that NotjustFood is, for the moment at least, doing well. However, providing a seamless customer experience requires NotjustFood to draw on and to integrate a wide range of technologies, regulated activities, and contractual relationships. NotjustFood also faces intense competition; it cannot take customer loyalty for granted. Trust and consumer confidence are essential, and a business can suffer potentially fatal damage to its reputation and customer base if that trust and confidence are lost.

What are the relevant practical, legal, and regulatory challenges faced by NotjustFood in its quest to secure and retain its market-leading position? In Part A below, we first provide an overview of the regulatory environment. Those who are familiar with that environment can skip directly to Part B, in which we address some particulars about the case.

A. Legal and Regulatory Overview

1. What Is E-payment and M-payment?

Minimizing the gap between a customer's interest in a product or service and actual receipt of payment is a perennial business challenge. Electronic payment can be instantaneous and, given the range of contactless payment technologies now readily available, can be accomplished by a gesture. However, true omnichannel retailing relies on a clear understanding of the types of e-payment and m-payment currently available or in development.

In its 2012 green paper, *Towards an integrated European Market for Card, Internet, and Mobile Payments*, the European Commission distinguished between electronic (e-payment) and mobile (m-payment), but observed that "the line between them was blurred, and may become even more so in the future." That prediction has been borne out by experience. Although e-payments are now frequently referred to simply using the label of "m-payments," there is, in fact, a range of quite different ways in which a consumer can make a payment using a mobile phone or other device.

M-payments typically fall into one of the following categories:

- **Physical mobile device payment**. The mobile device is used (in place of a card) at the electronic point of sale, often using near-field communication (NFC) technology, to communicate with the sale terminal equipment (in a similar manner to a contactless card) and to transmit tokenized information regarding a card that the device owner has linked with the handset (e.g., in a "digital wallet" on the device). Examples of this type of payment are Apple Pay (launched in the United Kingdom in 2015) and the recently launched Android Pay.
- **Direct carrier billing**. The relevant charges are added to the consumer's mobile phone bill. This method is typically used to purchase small items such as ringtones.
- **Internet-based payment**. The mobile device's web browser is used to interact with the merchant's online shopping channel (typically now optimized for mobile devices) in the normal way using online banking-based transfers or direct debits.
- **Alternative payment platform**. The mobile device links to (and sometimes becomes part of the authentication process for) a mobile version of an

alternative payment platform (such as PayPal or, in the United Kingdom, Paym). Consumers' individual accounts may be funded through methods such as bank transfers or credit card payments.

- **Closed-loop payments**. A gift- or loyalty-based approach operated by a particular merchant that enables a customer to load funds onto an app, collect loyalty points, and use the app to pay for purchases. The Starbucks app is one of the most well-known examples of this model, which enables customers to pay using the app against an account balance and that provides an auto top-up option.

Given the speed of development in the technology sector, new and alternative payment methods can continue to be expected as both new entrants and established players continue to vie for their share in this market. UK and European regulators are keen to foster greater competition for the traditional banks and payment platforms that have an inevitable head start with consumers, including because they have existing authorizations.

While all of these payment methods involve the use of a mobile device, no single framework legislation or regulation governs them. Payment providers need to analyze the specific way in which their solution operates, and their position in the chain, to identify which regulations they need to be aware of and, accordingly, which authorization or registration requirements (if any) apply to them.

2. The Payment Services Regulations: What Are Payment Services?

The Payment Services Directive[1] (PSD) was introduced by the European Commission at the end of 2007 as a means of: (1) regulating payment services across the European Union and EEA; and (2) increasing competition in the payments industry across Europe. In the United Kingdom, the PSD was implemented by the Payment Services Regulations 2009[2] (PSRs), which came into effect in March 2009.

A second Payment Services Directive[3] (PSD2) has followed. It repeals the PSD and by building on and, where necessary, modifying the principles established by the PSD, PSD2 seeks to address the advances in technology relevant to payments and the ever-growing need for increased security. PSD2 came into force on January 13, 2016, with a two-year implementation period before full compliance is required (by January 13, 2018).

Although it is likely that the United Kingdom will implement PSD2 fully, the detailed political and institutional outcome of Brexit negotiations will determine whether the United Kingdom is in fact able to achieve full implementation. Simply replicating the wording of the law (for example, through the UK government's proposed "Great Repeal Bill") would not necessarily engage the institutional arrangements and consistency mechanisms forming part of the European Union's legislative

---

1. Directive 2007/64/EC.
2. SI 2009/209, as amended by SI 2012/1791 and SI 2015/422.
3. Directive 2015/2366/EC.

scheme. If the United Kingdom remains a member of the EEA, it would retain access to bodies such as the European Banking Authority (EBA), albeit with observer status rather than as a voting member. If the United Kingdom does retain EEA membership, it would be treated as an outside country for payment services purposes.

The PSRs apply to any type of m-payment that amounts to a "payment service."[4] Moreover, the assessment of payment service status also requires analysis of definitions and exclusions in schedule 1 (parts 1 and 2) of the PSRs and section 15.3 of the Financial Conduct Authority (FCA) Perimeter Guidance Manual (PERG), which provides additional relevant details.

In summary, m-payments will be broadly categorized as a "payment service" if they involve:

> the execution of payment transactions where the consent of the payer to execute the payment transaction is given by means of any telecommunication, digital or IT [information technology] device and the payment is made to the telecommunication, IT system or network operator acting only as an intermediary between the payment service user and the supplier of the goods or services.[5]

However, a number of exclusions are particularly relevant here, including:

Supporting technology services. Services that support the provision of a payment service, where the provider never has possession of the funds to be transferred. These services include: (1) processing and storage of data; (2) trust and privacy protection services; (3) data and party authentication; (4) IT; (5) communication network; and (6) the provision and maintenance of terminals and devices used for payment services.[6]

The "limited network" exemption. Services based on instruments that can only be used to buy goods or services (1) in or on the issuer's premises; or (2) under a commercial agreement with the issuer, either within a limited network of service providers or for a limited range of goods or services.[7] There is little meaningful guidance on what a "limited network" or "limited range" means in this context. Recital (12) to PSD2 reflects the European Commission's view that the exemption has been used more broadly than was initially intended. PSD2 therefore aims to narrow this exemption, but the amendments (discussed later in this chapter) still leave room for interpretation. The ability to qualify for this exemption can be expected to become more difficult as its range narrows.

The "value add" exemption. Payment transactions made by means of any telecommunication, digital, or IT device, where the goods/services bought are delivered to and are to be used through a telecommunication, digital, or IT device, provided that the telecommunication, digital, or IT operator does not act only as an intermediary

---

4. As defined in regulation 2 of the PSRs.
5. PSRs sched. 1, pt. 1, reg. 1(g).
6. PSRs sched. 1, para. 2(j).
7. PSRs sched. 1, para. 2(k).

between the payment service user and the supplier of the goods and services.[8] Guidance on the amount of "value add" needed to avoid having only intermediary status suggests that the threshold is not significant. Examples of value added activities include providing access (including a short message service (SMS) center), search, or distribution facilities.[9] However, similar to the "limited network" exemption, PSD2 restricts the potential use of this exemption to 50 euros per transaction and 200 euros per month. Qualification for this exemption will therefore be much harder to achieve in the context of general payment services once PSD2 comes into effect.

3. Obligations of Providers of "Payment Services"

The PSRs brought with them a broad range of obligations, including:

- A requirement that any provider that is not already an authorized credit institution seeks authorization as a payment institution or registration as a small payment institution[10]
- Minimum capital requirements (unless qualifying as a "small payments institution") and rules regarding the safeguarding of funds requirements[11]
- Restricting the use of funds held in a payment account to payment transactions rather than being held as deposits or applied for any other purpose[12]
- Minimum consumer information and consent requirements[13]
- Potential liability for unauthorized transactions[14]

These obligations imposed by the PSRs deserve serious attention, as a failure to obtain the relevant authorization/registration constitutes a criminal offense. Service providers should prioritize understanding how the PSRs apply to their solution and their resulting responsibilities and potential liabilities in this context.

4. Electronic Money Regulations: Overlapping Concerns

Also relevant to m-payments is the Second Directive on Electronic Money[15] (2EMD), which came into effect in October 2009. 2EMD was implemented in the United Kingdom by the Electronic Money Regulations 2011[16] (EMRs), which govern the activity of issuing electronic money.

In 2008, the European Commission concluded that the e-money market was developing more slowly than expected and that the directive was holding it back. The EMRs were therefore designed to encourage new entrants, such as mobile

---

8. PSRs sched. 1, para. 2(l).
9. PERG question 23.
10. PSRs pt. 2.
11. PSRs pt. 3.
12. PSRs pt. 4.
13. PSRs pts. 5 and 6.
14. PSRs pt. 6.
15. Directive 2009/110/EC.
16. SI 2011/99.

operators, to the market by imposing lower capital requirements and a lighter regulatory regime for small "e-money issuers" (EMIs).

"E-money" is defined in EMRs regulation 2 as "electronically (including magnetically) stored monetary value as represented by a claim on the e-money issuer which:

(a) is issued on receipt of funds for the purpose of making payment transactions;

(b) is accepted by a person other than the electronic money issuer; and

(c) is not excluded by Regulation 3."

Regulation 3 then contains two exclusions that are similar to the limited network and value add exemptions under the PSRs. Accordingly, a service that involves the loading of e-money onto a mobile device generally must either be authorized or registered under the EMRs unless they are already authorized as a traditional credit institution, such as a bank or building society.

Where EMIs also wish to provide payment services, they may be able to do so without requiring separate authorization or registration under the PSRs. Issuing e-money is not itself regarded as a payment service, although it may entail the provision of payment services. For example, issuing a payment instrument is a payment service and e-money is likely to be issued on a payment instrument in order to make a payment transaction. To cover those situations, the PSRs contain conduct-of-business rules that are applicable to most EMIs for the payment services part of their business.

EMRs also bring with them similar obligations to the PSRs, such as capital requirements, safeguarding of funds, and accounting/audit and recordkeeping requests. Failure to obtain the relevant permissions also presents a risk of criminal sanctions. Consequently, providers of m-payment services must also consider how the EMRs apply to their business models.

5. Other Regulatory Considerations

a. General

Within the NotjustFood group, it is important that each relevant entity has the correct authorizations. The delineation of activities between the group bank and the supermarket operating company will be essential to ensure regulatory compliance.

b. European Operations

For organizations conducting business on a pan-European basis, both the PSRs and the EMRs contain a right to passport the firm's business within the EEA. The United Kingdom's Brexit-related negotiations with the European Union can be expected to include a significant focus on passporting in the financial institutions sector. The effects of a potential loss of the ability to passport could be significant. The results of those negotiations will only start to become clear after the date of publication of this book.

c. Carrier Billing

Payment service providers also have to consider whether their solution will be regulated by PhonepayPlus (the specialist regulator of "premium rate" phone paid services under the remit of the Office of Communications (Ofcom), the UK communications regulator) under its Code of Practice. Premium rate services include anything that a consumer can buy on his or her phone and charge to his or her mobile phone bill and/or prepay account. The relevant rules, as contained in the Code of Practice, are outcomes-based. PhonepayPlus's *Guidance Note: Application Based Payments* emphasized that the rules are designed to be "flexible and adept enough to incorporate technological innovations as mobile payments continue to evolve."

Details of the PhonepayPlus Code of Practice are beyond the scope of this chapter. However, key principles can be summarized as follows:

- A compulsory registration regime applies to all providers of a premium rate service, including the payment of a yearly fee
- Providers are required to satisfy a number of "outcomes" designed to protect consumers (e.g., clear disclosure regarding pricing details, a clear method of exit, an appropriate complaints process, and technical compatibility with different devices on which the services are promoted)
- Responsibilities depend on the level at which a provider is performing its element of the service (i.e., whether as a network operator or organization responsible for providing the content of the service)
- Failure to comply with the Code of Practice can lead to significant fines being issued by PhonepayPlus

B. Application to NotjustFood

1. Mobile Payment Considerations

Returning to the NotjustFood example, different regulatory permutations could be involved in its m-payment offering. If NotjustFood Bank is making a payment solution available, its existing authorization as a bank means that it will not require separate authorization or registration as a payment institution or e-money issuer. But it will require separate permission to issue e-money under its existing authorization and it will need to comply with several PSR/EMR requirements.

Alternatively, if another nonbank entity within the NotjustFood group is providing the payment solution, separate authorization or registration requirements could apply, although this is not a foregone conclusion. For example, Apple Pay is designed so that Apple only receives a tokenized version of its user's card details and does not come into possession of any of the funds being transferred by the user (i.e., the contactless device authentication simply links to existing card payment schemes). As a result, Apple is not required to be authorized as a payment service provider. Nevertheless, Apple Pay is still being seen as one of the main drivers of consumer adoption in the m-payments market.

If carrier billing is utilized, the PhonepayPlus Code of Practice applies. Additional "outcomes"-based requirements apply, with the detail of how to comply with those requirements dependent on NotjustFood's role in the provision of the service. In this context, NotjustFood (in providing own-brand mobile phone services) will want to ensure its MVNO agreement contains a requirement for the underlying mobile network operator to comply with its obligations under the Code of Practice, while also needing to be aware of its own responsibilities (which it can expect to see reflected in its agreement with its mobile network operator, as well as its responsibility to PhonepayPlus under the Code of Practice).

In practice, a mobile wallet offering may well include a combination of different types of m-payment—whether linking to existing card payment schemes or ending in a charge being added to the consumer's mobile phone bill. As a result, there may be a range of different requirements applicable to one m-payment solution. This, in turn, requires a close analysis of the different types of regulation involved and how the provider and its offering sit within that overall framework.

2. Store Loyalty Cards

Recall that Jenny Hill signed up for a NotjustFood loyalty card, which allows her to earn points on the value of in-store purchases and on purchases at the supermarket filling station. The points accumulate to provide vouchers with a monetary value or special "money off" discounts on promotional products. The vouchers are only redeemable when shopping at NotjustFood, online or in-store.

A store loyalty card is not a payment instrument and the provision of one does not constitute a payment service. The card cannot be used to pay for goods or services, and it is merely a method to measure customer loyalty by providing vouchers for their patronage. The goods that lead to the points will be paid for using cash or a debit or credit card, which is the payment instrument.

3. Gift Cards

NotjustFood sells gift cards for various other retailers, including the CforCoffee card. The cards are preloaded with various values and can be used instead of cash or a debit or credit card to pay for goods in the relevant retailers' outlets, and in the case of the CforCoffee card, any CforCoffee outlet, whether adjoining a NotjustFood store or elsewhere. Gift cards such as the CforCoffee card, and those who issue and sell them, benefit from the "limited network" exemption under both the EMRs and the PSRs. For EMR payments, they provide monetary value stored on instruments that can be used to acquire goods and services only in or on the issuer's premises or under a commercial agreement with the issuer, either within a *limited* network of service providers or for a *limited* range of goods or services. For PSR purposes, their services are based on instruments that can be used to acquire goods and services only in these limited circumstances.

Unfortunately, the PSD exemption did not clarify what constituted a "limited network," which led to concerns within the European Commission that some issuers have adopted a more liberal interpretation of the exemption than intended, with a consequential expansion of risk to consumers. As referenced earlier in this chapter, PSD2 seeks to address this concern by imposing a narrower exemption for services based on specific payment instruments that can be used only in a limited way and that must meet one condition, including the following:

1. Instruments allowing the holder to acquire goods or services only in the premises of the issuer or within a limited network of service providers under direct commercial agreement with a professional issuer
2. Instruments that can be used only to acquire a very limited range of goods or services

Where a service provider like NotjustFood meets these conditions and the value of the total payment transactions in a given year exceeds €1 million (or its sterling equivalent), it will be required to notify the FCA, which will assess whether or not it considers the provider can still use the limited network exemption. The detail of how sterling equivalence is to be calculated by a PSP is yet to be established.

4. Other Financial Services and Extraterritorial Considerations

The Hills have a current account (with an overdraft facility) with NotjustFood Bank, including a contactless enabled chip-and-PIN Visa card that Mike has set up on his iPhone as his linked Apple Pay payment card. They frequently transfer sterling sums from their NotjustFood Bank account into euros deposited in another account at a bank in France, where they maintain a second home.

NotjustFood Bank will need to be authorized under the Financial Services and Markets Act 2000 (FSMA) for several of the "regulated activities" it carries on. This is because any person carrying on or purporting to carry on a regulated activity in the United Kingdom must be authorized to do so unless otherwise exempt.[17]Because it accepts deposits, the bank is subject to authorization and regulation by the Prudential Regulation Authority (PRA) and the FCA. Its consumer credit and insurance mediation business will require additional regulatory permission and oversight from the FCA.

The bank must also comply with the expectations of the regulators set out in the PRA's Fundamental Rules and in the FCA's Principles for Business in respect of its entire business, including any payment services or e-money business it carries out. Detailed discussion on the application of FSMA and PRA and FCA rules is outside the scope of this chapter, but overarching requirements include the duties to conduct business with due skill, care, and diligence and to treat customers fairly.

Once authorized, a regulated firm has to comply with the relevant prudential (financial resources and governance) and conduct rules. For NotjustFood Bank, these will include the applicable conduct of business rules for banking, consumer credit, and insurance. Insofar as it provides a payment service, it also has to comply

---

17. FSMA section 19.

with the customer information and contract provisions in the PSRs. Additionally, it will need to comply with all relevant financial crime prevention legislation, not least the Money Laundering Regulations 2017, which require firms to conduct customer due diligence, and the Proceeds of Crime Act 2002, which requires firms to report any knowledge or suspicion of money laundering. The FCA imposes additional expectations on regulated firms with respect to systems and controls to prevent financial crime, and has often taken significant enforcement action against firms for failing to have in place adequate systems and controls.

Where another NotjustFood entity carries on regulated activities (for example, the promotion by the supermarket group company of the store cards and insurance services), it may require separate FSMA authorization, or it may need to be appointed a representative of NotjustFood Bank. An appointed representative arrangement allows unauthorized firms to legally carry on certain regulated activities (including insurance and credit broking) under the regulatory protection and responsibility of an authorized firm (such as a bank).

Each relevant sectoral EU legislation (for these purposes, the Capital Requirements Directive and Regulation and PSD) includes a "passporting" mechanism, whereby an authorization for relevant services from the authorities in one Member State of the European Union (and invariably also the EEA, where the EEA Agreement has incorporated the EU laws) allows the firm to provide the relevant services in or into any other Member State based on a single notification to its "home state" regulator.

Passporting has emerged as a key issue in the context of Brexit. Once the United Kingdom ceases to be a Member State of the European Union, its continuation would depend upon the United Kingdom either becoming (or remaining) a member of the EEA or securing a separately negotiated deal with the European Union for that purpose.

The Single Euro Payments Area (SEPA) Regulation applies to cross-border e-payments (by credit card, debit card, bank transfer, or direct debit) across the euro area. It enables customers to make cashless payments within the euro area using a single payment account with the same basic conditions, regardless of location within the EEA. This regime was introduced with the aim of integrating financial services within SEPA and improving all payments, whether they are domestic payments or cross-border payments between two euro area countries. SEPA also brings benefits to people like the Hills when transferring sterling in their NotjustFood Bank account to their euro-denominated French bank account. They will still benefit from the same improved services and rules information that apply to pure euro payments, although currency conversion may mean that payments cannot be made quite as fast as a pure euro payment.

5. "Always-on" Consumers/Online Marketplaces

The Hills are "always-on" consumers. They use a range of devices, including their smartphones, to research and to buy goods and services. They demand a seamless experience and value the ability to buy with a few clicks and as few intervening steps as possible. Mike particularly hates having to remember passwords or to go through authentication screens. They also consider it extremely important to have the benefits of competitive markets and robust consumer protection.

The Hills' simple (but demanding) objectives pose significant challenges for regulators and compliance issues for the operators of the online marketplaces that the Hills use both when they are in the United Kingdom and on their regular visits to France. PSD created a single market in payment services across the European Union and established a common set of rules for the payment services industry. However, on several key issues relating to online marketplaces and e-commerce platforms, EU Member State regulators have reached differing views, casting doubt on operators' compliance measures and leading to concerns that inconsistent regulation might distort competition and adversely affect consumer interests.

For example, PSD defined "payment institutions" and imposed upon them a requirement for authorization, subject to a number of exemptions. Crucially, PSD allowed operators to make their own assessments as to the applicability of the relevant exemptions, possibly weakening the regulation and compounding the problems considered to flow from regulators' differing interpretations.

Online marketplace or e-commerce platform operators have sought to remain outside the PSD authorization regime, arguing that processing sale and purchase transactions between consumers and various third-party vendors does not amount to the provision of regulated payment services requiring authorization as a payment institution. Typically, an e-commerce platform will take payment from consumers and then forward those payments to the third-party vendors—having first taken out the commission due to the platform operator. That approach both confers a cash flow advantage on the operator and, arguably, helps to provide the seamless experience that consumers value.

The first line of argument is that the operator's activities do not include the provision of payment services, and specifically that receipt of the purchase price from the buyer and forwarding it to the vendor does not amount to "money remittance." Alternatively, if that activity were found to constitute money remittance, then operators argued that it formed only a minor and ancillary element of the service so that a requirement for authorization as a payment institution would be disproportionate.

Germany's financial regulator, the Federal Financial Supervisory Authority (BaFin), rejected those arguments. BaFin also considered that there would be a "money remittance" service where the operator took on a more active role, acquiring goods from the third-party vendors and then taking payment directly from the consumers. BaFin considered that on an economic analysis, payment still flowed in substance from the consumer to the third-party vendor.

Faced with that regulatory response, e-commerce platform operators are forced to focus more closely on the scope of the available exemptions, arguing that even if their activities amounted to money remittance, they ought to be considered exempt as commercial agents under article 3(b) of PSD, which creates an exemption for "payment transactions from the payer and the payee through a commercial agent authorised to negotiate or conclude the sale or purchase of goods or services on behalf of the payer or payee."

On implementation in the United Kingdom, this text of article 3(b) was carried on a "copy-and-paste" basis into the PSRs as part of an approach adopted by the UK government to reduce the risk of over-implementation or "gold plating" of EU directives. However, the "copy-and-paste" approach did not result in a consistent interpretation and application of the article 3(b) commercial agents exemption across the European Union. In some EU Member States, including the United Kingdom and the Republic of Ireland, the words "on behalf of the payer or payee" have been interpreted in a way that allows an online marketplace operator to claim exemption if it is authorized to act for both payer and payee. In others, with Germany's BaFin once again taking the lead, those words have been read more restrictively, applying only where the operator acts as commercial agent for either the payer or the payee.

BaFin issued a general ruling that e-commerce platforms cannot benefit from the commercial agent exception. In 2014, the French Prudential and Resolution Authority (ACPR) followed suit and contacted all e-commerce platforms in France that were handling payments for their customers to inform them that they were conducting regulated payment services. As a result, platforms in Germany and France must either apply for authorization as a payment institution or cooperate with a licensed bank or payment institution.

PSD2 adopts the narrower interpretation favored by BaFin and ACPR. Consequently, under PSD2, the commercial agent exemption will generally be available only when a commercial agent acts on behalf of either the payer or the payee. If a commercial agent acts for both sides, the exemption is likely to be available only where the agent does not possess or control client funds at any time.

PSD2 emphasizes the need for harmonization of rules across the European Union. Differing interpretations under PSD have potentially distorted competition, with the operators of online marketplaces or e-commerce platforms being required in some EU Member States to incur greater compliance costs than in others.

Recital (11) to PSD2 also highlights a consumer protection concern that had previously arisen under PSD. Under the more liberal interpretations of PSD, it has been possible for operators to claim exemption where they have been acting as an intermediary without having any actual authority or "real margin" to negotiate. PSD2 clarifies that this was not the purpose of the exception. To qualify for the new commercial agent exception, the agent must negotiate or enter into a contract based on an explicit agreement with the payer (buyer) or the payee (seller) and must act on behalf and in the interests of one of these parties.

Taken together, the effect of PSD2 is to "level up" compliance requirements to match those adopted by BaFin and ACPR, bringing many more online marketplace or e-commerce platforms into the authorization regime.

It is also possible that this "leveling up" will not wait for Member State implementation of PSD2, the deadline for which is January 13, 2018. That is because the narrower interpretation of the commercial agents exemption has already been available to regulators under PSD. PSD2 is intended to bring consistency to Member States' treatment of the exemption, but harmony has not yet been achieved. BaFin and ACPR remain fixed in their view that even under PSD the commercial agents exemption does not apply to online marketplaces or e-commerce platforms. Consequently, there is considerable pressure on regulators across the European Union to adopt the narrower interpretation without waiting for PSD2 implementation.

For online marketplace operators, the question now seems to be whether it is possible to avoid the need for authorization by entering into a partnership or some other form of collaboration with a licensed bank or payment institution. If so, they must also consider whether the commercial terms of any such arrangement would provide a sufficient cost saving when balanced against the reporting and other compliance measures required following authorization to justify a decision to remain outside the PSD2 authorization regime.

6. Consumer Protection Concerns, Including Privacy and Data Protection

Mike and Jenny Hill travel frequently between the United Kingdom and France, and they also visit Austria and Germany about once a year. Many of their online purchases are made from amazon.co.uk, but when travelling, they often buy from other Amazon sites, including amazon.de. In *VKI v. Amazon*,[18] the European Court of Justice (ECJ) held that a contractual standard term that chose a supplier's Member State law as the governing law, rather than the consumer's, was unfair towards consumers. The case concerned Amazon EU Sarl, a company incorporated in Luxembourg but conducting sales with Austrian consumers remotely through the website amazon.de. Amazon had no registered office or branch in Austria. The standard terms stated that the contractual governing law was that of Luxembourg. Verein fur Konsumenteninformation (VKI), a consumer protection body, applied to the Austrian court for an injunction to prevent the use of these standard terms. The Austrian Supreme Court referred to the ECJ for a preliminary ruling on the application of the Rome I Regulation[19] and the Rome II Regulation[20] where an injunction action is brought against the use of contractual terms by an entity established in one Member State that, during the course of e-commerce activity, concludes contracts with consumers who are resident in different Member States.

The ECJ held that the law applicable where injunction action is brought against the use of unfair contractual terms between Member States should be that of the country where the interests of consumers are, or are likely to be, affected—in this case, Austria. The ECJ also held that the law applicable to an assessment of a specific

---

18. Case C-191/15, VKI v. Amazon.
19. Regulation EC 593/2008.
20. Regulation EC 864/2007.

contractual term should be determined in accordance with Rome I, whether that assessment is made due to an individual or collective action.

The ECJ also had to consider whether the governing law clause was unfair within the meaning of the Unfair Terms in Consumer Contracts Directive.[21] It concluded that where a contract has not been individually negotiated, a governing law term is unfair insofar as it gives the consumer the incorrect impression that only the law of the supplier Member State governs the contract and does not inform the consumer that under Rome I, he or she also has the benefit of the mandatory provisions of law that would apply in the absence of a governing law term, which is an issue for the national court to determine.

Article 6(2) and article 4 of Rome I provide that law applicable to an obligation arising from tort is the law of the country in which the damage occurs, in this case Austria rather than Luxembourg. This part of the *VKI v. Amazon* decision requires companies to consider redrafting governing law clauses so that they clearly inform consumers that they have the benefit of the mandatory consumer protections in their country of residence.

E-payments and online market places necessarily involve the transmission, storage, and processing of data. Consequently, the Hills' online purchases and payments trigger a range of regulatory and compliance obligations on the part of the payment service providers and merchants.

The European Union's General Data Protection Regulation (GDPR) is scheduled to come into operation on May 25, 2018. As an EU regulation, it has direct effect in EU Member States without requiring implementing legislation at Member State-level. The GDPR replaces the Data Protection Directive 95/46/EC and is intended to override existing legislation enacted to implement that directive within Member States. In the United Kingdom, the relevant implementing legislation was the Data Protection Act 1998 (DPA).

The result of the United Kingdom's referendum of June 23, 2016, which produced a narrow majority in favor of "Brexit," has inevitably created a degree of uncertainty concerning the GDPR's application to the United Kingdom. Much depends on the precise mechanisms used to effect Brexit, and on the outcome of negotiations to determine the scope and nature of the United Kingdom's future relationship with the European Union. However, at the time of writing, the best advice to businesses operating within the United Kingdom is to continue to prepare for GDPR because

1. on most likely timetables for Brexit, which assume a two-year period from the UK government's formal request to leave the European Union under article 50 of the Lisbon Treaty, the GDPR will come into operation and be directly applicable to the United Kingdom before Brexit occurs, and

---

21. EU Directive 93/13.

2. the continuing need for UK businesses to transfer data to and from the European Union requires the United Kingdom to retain or to implement data protection laws that meet the European Union's test of "adequacy."

It is clear that "adequacy" does not require laws to be identical with those of the European Union. For example, data transfers between the European Union and the United States benefit from the Privacy Shield agreed during 2016 to replace the previous Safe Harbor arrangement. However, it is highly likely that the United Kingdom will either elect to adopt the GDPR or that it will implement a very similar legislative regime.

On any reasonably foreseeable basis, payment and online merchant services will have to include data protection as a crucial element of their compliance procedures. As part of that process, it will be essential to consider the interaction between the GDPR and other laws and regulatory obligations. For example, anti-money laundering (AML) and counter-terrorism financing rules such as the European Union's Third AML Directive require customer due diligence (CDD) measures. Those measures include the creation of customer profiles and the retention of customer data for at least five years after the business relationship ends. Those duties must be reconciled with key elements of the GDPR including:

- Pseudonymization, defined by article 4 as "the processing of personal data in such a manner that the personal data can no longer be attributed to a specific data subject without the use of additional information, provided that such additional information is kept separately and is subject to technical and organisational measures to ensure that the personal data are not attributed to an identified or identifiable natural person"
- The "right to be forgotten" provided for by article 17
- Restrictions on "profiling" under article 21

Compliance policies and decisions must also take into account the GDPR principles of "data minimization," "privacy by default," and "privacy by design." Those concepts may be difficult in practice to reconcile with other regulatory obligations relating to fraud, money laundering, and terrorist funding. They may also sit uncomfortably with the collection and processing of data, for example through the application of sophisticated predictive analytics, to gain insights into consumer behavior and purchasing patterns.

Allocating responsibility for data processing and compliance is and will remain a key element in any joint venture or partnership relating to payment or online merchant services. For example, some protection may be afforded to online merchants by solutions such as point-to-point encryption (P2PE), under which merchants are able to encrypt data at the point of sale. Payment data is transmitted to a secure payment gateway for processing. For the merchant, the result is that it never receives consumer card data or other sensitive financial information.

While P2PE offers a degree of insulation to online merchants, it potentially involves the loss of opportunities to gain actionable insights into consumer behavior.

To address that issue, payment service providers may be able to offer approaches such as "tokenization," which assigns a unique alphanumeric code or "token" that can be returned to the online merchant, in place of actual account data. Stripped of data that might allow identification of individuals, tokens have no value to hackers and so do not represent a lure for cybercrime. However, they still allow analysis of customer behavior and the identification of commercial opportunities.

From a commercial perspective, the allocation of risk and responsibility for data protection and other regulatory compliance between merchants and payment service providers goes directly to the price of those payment services, and must therefore play a significant role in commercial negotiations and contract terms between those market players. Given that they are likely to be better-resourced and (perhaps) better-informed than online merchants, it is likely that payment service providers will take on, for a price, a significant share of the compliance burden as initiatives such as the GDPR and the European Union's Digital Single Market agenda develop over the next few years.

7. Cyber Liability Issues

The risk of being the victim of a cyberattack is now greater than ever, as the Hills found out when they were affected by the cyberattack on their bank. The National Crime Agency estimated that there were 2.1 million victims of cybercrime in the United Kingdom in 2015, which probably underestimates the actual incidence because much cybercrime goes unreported. Organizations holding financial data are a prize target. Gaining direct access to a person's accounts through a cyberattack is relatively rare. The more common target is to gain sufficient information about a person through a cyberattack to allow that individual to be scammed into giving up more information. This tactic, known as phishing or spear phishing, is ultimately aimed at persuading individuals into giving up sensitive information, such as credit card numbers or passwords to accounts. It is just one way that a loss of what first appears to be benign information can grow into a serious breach of security.

Hacking has been a known problem for decades. Since 1990, the Computer Misuse Act in the United Kingdom has made hacking a criminal offense. In the regulated financial services sector, regulators have been promoting better information security for a long time and the DPA has required holders of personal data take adequate measures to keep it secure since 1998. However, it was not until April 2010, when the information commissioner was given the power to levy penalties of up to £500,000 and publically report on breaches of the DPA, that cybersecurity became a high-profile public topic. That attention will only grow with the GDPR, which brings with it fines of up to 4 percent of worldwide turnover for serious compliance lapses.

Away from regulated areas, public concern about identity theft and online fraud is now a material factor in deciding where consumers place their trust. It is likely that organizations with poor security track records will be avoided. In an industry based on consumer trust, payment services providers are highly susceptible to brand damage and resulting commercial harm arising from loss of a consumer's personal details.

Consumers are also more likely to seek compensation and bring legal claims than ever before. The GDPR (and the DPA before it) gives individuals the personal right to bring a claim under the GDPR for noncompliance, in addition to any regulatory action. Until recently, compensation in the United Kingdom was only payable where an individual could point to a tangible financial loss. Since *Vidal-Hall v. Google*[22] in 2015, it is now possible to bring a claim for distress damages only, which brings the UK regime in line with the original Data Protection Directive 95/46/EC—a stance that will continue under the GDPR, at least in the short term.

PSD2 also seeks to address security concerns. It requires prospective payment institutions to provide a security document, including a detailed risk assessment describing the measures taken to protect consumers from fraud and from the unlawful use of sensitive and personal data. Under PSD2, all payment service providers are required to establish a framework to manage operational and security risks, including incident management procedures. At least annually, they must report on:

- Updated operational and security risk assessments
- The adequacy of the control and mitigation measures deployed
- Statistical data on fraud relating to different means of payment

Central to PSD2 are the concepts of "strong customer authentication" and secure communication. Strong customer authentication is required when a payer:

- Accesses its payment account online
- Initiates an e-payment transaction
- Carries out any action through a remote channel that may imply a risk of payment fraud or other abuses

In the absence of strong customer authentication, a payer will be liable for a disputed transaction only where the payer has acted fraudulently.

PSD2 is also expected to lead to the emergence and expansion of "payment initiation services" and "account information services" where customers' payment accounts are accessible online. Their objective would be to make payments easier and to help customers manage their (potentially many) accounts. Key features might include comparison services to ensure that payments are directed towards the best deal. While such services go beyond payment and financial services, PSD2 seeks to incorporate them within its consumer protection provisions by ensuring that enhanced security requirements, including the use of strong customer authentication, apply.

The European Union also recently passed the Network and Information Security (NIS) Directive. The NIS Directive compels a minimum level of IT and security on organizations operating in key sectors that are critical for the secure running of

---

22. Vidal-Hall v. Google, [2015] EWCA Civ 311.

society and economies. This expands to certain aspects of the banking sector and may well affect payment service providers, if not directly at least indirectly in terms of more stringent security standards being flowed down through contracts.

Merchants and payment service providers need to give careful thought to mitigating their potential cyber liability. Claimant law firms and litigation funders are waking up to the possibility that large cyberattacks can be a lucrative basis for class actions against deep-pocketed corporations and state agencies. A greater focus on internal information governance is imperative. Data asset registers, information security auditing, and incident response plans should be the norm, but are still often under-developed. Their absence is often the root cause of security incidents and a catalyst for more aggressive enforcement action by regulators.

The UK insurance market is also responding to these pressures with more and better tailored cyber-risk coverage. Coverage is available for both first-party business interruption losses and also against third-party claims. It is not yet clear whether insurance against regulatory penalties (such as the potential 4 percent of turnover penalties under the GDPR) will be permitted. This market is, however, relatively immature in the United Kingdom. There is little in the way of standardized coverage and brokers are grappling with properly scoping the breadth and depth of coverage that is needed. Nevertheless, cyber-risk insurance is likely to become commonplace in future years.

III. CONCLUSION

A few years ago, the connected consumers we have described here would have been difficult to find. Today, these common behaviors are posing new challenges for regulators in the complex interactions of policy goals that include consumer protection, market liberalization, and maintaining competition.

The payment services regulatory environment is actively encouraging new market entrants through providing an appropriate framework by which these entrants can leverage new technologies to deliver their services. However, as commercial actors embrace the use of a wider range of payment services and incorporate them as part of their "omnichannel" environments, there is an increasing risk that regulatory compliance burdens may give disproportionate advantages to the larger retailers and potentially reduce the number of smaller competitors, so leading to an overall reduction in consumer choice.

Chapter 11

Access to Payments and Credit in the Age of Big Data

Nizan Geslevich Packin and Yafit Lev-Aretz[1]

I. DATA ANALYTICS: BIG DATA PLATFORMS AND FINANCIAL SERVICES

A. Description

Propelled by the constantly decreasing costs of information storage and delivery, coupled with a growing ability to instantly capture, manage, process, and analyze unstructured data, big data is nothing short of a revolution. Databases are now created and updated instantly as information is collected online from transactions, web-data trails, e-mail exchanges, videos, photos, search queries, health records, and social networking activities. Furthermore, as the physical world becomes an Internet of Things[2] that is increasingly connected to data networks, more information will be available as data will be communicated through embedded sensors and collected from appliances, machinery, train tracks, shipping containers, power stations, and more. The idea behind big data is fairly simple: "[a]t its core,

---

1. Nizan Geslevich Packin is an assistant professor of law at City University of New York; Yafit Lev-Aretz is a fellow at New York University Information Law Institute.

2. *See*, *e.g.*, Michael Chui, Markus Löffler & Roger Roberts, *The Internet of Things*, McKinsey Q, Mar. 2010, http://www.mckinsey.com/insights/high_tech_telecoms_internet/the_internet_of_things. For more on the connection, see, e.g., Howard Baldwin, *A Match Made Somewhere: Big Data and the Internet of Things*, Forbes, Nov. 24, 2014, http://www.forbes.com/sites/howardbaldwin/2014/11/24/a-match-made-somewhere-big-data-and-the-internet-of-things/; Gil Press, *It's Official: The Internet of Things Takes Over Big Data as the Most Hyped Technology*, Forbes, Aug. 18, 2014, http://www.forbes.com/sites/gilpress/2014/08/18/its-official-the-internet-of-things-takes-over-big-data-as-the-most-hyped-technology/.

big data is about prediction."[3] When enough details about the past are collected and intelligently analyzed, unforeseen links and correlations surface than can lead to extremely accurate predictions about the future.[4] Although these connections can be as serendipitous as a direct correlation between customers' purchases of chrome-skull car accessories and their creditworthiness,[5] their predictive utility has led to widespread adoption in most fields. Indeed, big data insights are being utilized to predict shopping patterns, flu outbreak forecasts, and even smart predictive analysis of students' grades and performances.[6] Big data has also been used to help predict when employees might be getting ready to quit, or to identify potential heart disease to better treat patients.[7]

Big data underpins the new Internet economy, with tech giants like Amazon, Google, Apple, and Facebook leading the front by collecting, analyzing, using, and even selling data.[8] But it is not just these giant technology companies that capitalize on big data and build their business models around it. All sorts of businesses apply sophisticated data analytics to very large data sets, enabling them to predict the behavior of the parties they deal with much more accurately than ever before. Elsewhere, we termed businesses of this sort that enter the financial services landscape "big data and social netbanks."[9] In particular, using big data, companies can infer information about individuals and businesses that would otherwise not be known from plainly reviewing the underlying data. In recent years, the discovery and use of this type of often-personal information, as well as improvements in technology, have led nonbank lenders and

---

3. Viktor Mayer-Schönberger & Kenneth Cukier, Big Data: A Revolution That Will Transform How We Live, Work, and Think 11–12 (2013).

4. *See* Jonas Lerman, *Big Data and Its Exclusions*, 66 Stan. L. Rev. Online 55, 57 (2013), http://www.stanfordlawreview.org/online/privacy-and-big-data/big-data-and-its-exclusions.

5. Charles Duhigg, *What Does Your Credit-Card Company Know About You?*, N.Y. Times, May 12, 2009, http://www.nytimes.com/2009/05/17/magazine/17credit-t.html.

6. Jon Marcus, *Here's the New Way Colleges Are Predicting Student Grades*, Time, Dec. 10, 2014, http://time.com/3621228/college-data-tracking-graduation-rates/.

7. *See* Elahe Izadi, *Tweets Can Better Predict Heart Disease Rates Than Income, Smoking, and Diabetes, Study Finds*, Wash. Post, Jan. 21, 2015, http://www.washingtonpost.com/news/to-your-health/wp/2015/01/21/tweets-can-better-predict-heart-disease-rates-than-income-smoking-and-diabetes-study-finds/.

8. *See* Phil Simon, Too Big to Ignore: The Business Case for Big Data 98–100 (2013); *see also* Dorie Clark, *Four Things You Need to Know in the Big Data Era*, Forbes, Aug. 8, 2013, http://www.forbes.com/sites/dorieclark/2013/08/08/four-things-you-need-to-know-in-the-big-data-era/#795c581d2e86.

9. *See* Nizan Geslevich Packin & Yafit Lev-Aretz, *Big Data and Social Netbanks: Are You Ready to Replace Your Bank?*, 53 Hous. L. Rev. 1211 (2016) [hereinafter *Big Data and Social Netbanks*] (defining "big data and social netbanks" as big data companies and social networks offering bank-like services to their users The big data tech sector includes massively scaled companies that collect and analyze great amounts of information generated from exchanges over their networks. Due to their enormous user base and advanced technological capabilities, the data these companies use ascends to new heights, streams in quicker, and springs from an expanding ambit of sources and formats. Carefully gleaned insights unlock new understandings of consumer behavior that guide and inform business strategy in three aspects: (1) improving the service these platforms provide to their users, for example, better search results or a more accurate recommendation set for future purchases; (2) monetizing the data by facilitating targeted marketing of products and services, particularly customized for individual users; and (3) selling the raw unstructured data to interested parties to analyze, employ, and even sell for various purposes. Also making use of big data, social networks offer users a platform to build social relationships based on shared interests, activities, backgrounds, or real-life connections. Social networks merge big data with personal data and use that fusion for even more refined insights.

financial service providers to offer access to finance in a faster and more efficient manner for both consumers and businesses.[10] For example, data-driven algorithms help expedite credit assessments and can drastically reduce costs.[11] Therefore, more and more nonbanks leverage technology and capitalize on the exposure to a broad audience provided by the Internet in order to reach additional market segments.

Nonbanks in general, and especially online platforms that match borrowers and lenders (commonly known as online marketplace lenders), have been able to significantly reduce their operational costs through virtual business models. The mobile revolution has enabled them to provide loans to borrowers who might not otherwise have received capital, especially in the years following the financial crisis.[12] As a result, financially underserved populations that historically could not, opted not to, or simply did not know how to use banks for a variety of reasons, started to enjoy the use of bank-like services. In other words, the financially underserved population is more likely to use the services of online marketplace lenders than traditional financial service providers.

The unbanked, who are individuals with no official relationship with a bank, and the underbanked, who are individuals maintaining some form of formal connection with a traditional bank but chiefly relying on fringe financial institutions like payday lenders or payroll cards for their financial needs,[13] are two populations that have attracted significant global attention. According to a 2012 report by the World Bank's Global Financial Inclusion Database, three-quarters of the world's poor do not have a bank account for a variety of reasons, such as poverty, costs, travel distances, and other difficulties associated with opening an account.[14] In the United States, the situation is not quite as bad, yet approximately 10.5 percent of

---

10. Referred to as "nonbanks," such entities offer a variety of financial functions. *See* Peggy Twohig & Steve Antonakes, *The CFPB Launches Its Nonbank Supervision Program*, CFPB, Jan. 5, 2012 ("There are currently thousands of nonbank businesses that offer consumer financial products and services, and consumers interact with them all the time. . . . While banks, thrifts, and credit unions historically have been examined by various federal regulators, nonbanks generally have not."), http://www.consumerfinance .gov/blog/the-cfpb-launches-its-nonbank-supervision-program/. In general, nonbanks are commonly viewed as the mirror image of banks—entities providing financial services that do not include the legal power to receive deposits. *See* Arthur E. Wilmarth, Jr., *Why Fed Has Failed to Cope with the Nonbank Bank Dilemma*, Am. Banker, June 29, 1984, http://www.highbeam.com/doc/1G1-3327326.html; Davis W. Turner, *Nonbank Banks: Congressional Options*, 39 Vand. L. Rev. 1735, 1743–57 (1986) (describing the response to nonbank banks and the interpretations of the Bank Holding Company Act's definition of banks).

11. *See* Nizan Geslevich Packin & Yafit Lev-Aretz, *On Social Credit and the Right to Be Unnetworked*, Colum. Bus. L. Rev. 339 (2016) [hereinafter *On Social Credit*].

12. Nima Ghamsari, *How Technology Is Closing the Financial Accessibility Gap*, Forbes, May 18, 2017, https://www.forbes.com/sites/forbesrealestatecouncil/2017/05/18/how-technology-is-closing-the -financial-accessibility-gap/#72b5c27838e2.

13. *See* U.S. Postal Service Office of Inspector General, Providing Non-Bank Financial Services for the Underserved 2 (Jan. 27, 2014) (RARC-WP-14-007), *available at* https://www.uspsoig.gov/sites/default/files /document-library-files/2015/rarc-wp-14-007_0.pdf.

14. *See* Matthew B. Gross, Jeanne M. Hogarth & Maximilian D. Schmeiser, *Use of Financial Services by the Unbanked and Underbanked and the Potential for Mobile Financial Services Adoption*, 98 Fed. Res. Bull. 1 (2012), *available at* http://www.federalreserve.gov/pubs/bulletin/2012/pdf/mobile_financial_ser- vices_201209.pdf; *see also* Asli Demirguc-Kunt & Leora Klapper, World Bank Development Research Group, Measuring Financial Inclusion: The Global Findex Database 11–18 (Working Paper No. 6025, Apr. 2012), *available at* https://elibrary.worldbank.org/doi/abs/10.1596/1813-9450-6025.

the American population is still considered to be unbanked and approximately 17 percent is considered to be underbanked.[15] Therefore, many American households operate at least partially outside of the financial mainstream framework.[16] Similarly, Millennials, who are members of the generation born from 1980 onward and brought up using digital technology and mass media, have been indicating a clear preference for using tech-driven alternatives over traditional bank services.[17]

Because of the constantly rising use of mobile devices and the development of new technologies that enable mobile financial transactions, big data platforms and social networks can now enter the financial services market and offer products that better cater to these underserved populations. The underserved community makes significant use of mobile phones and smartphones:[18] 69 percent of the unbanked have access to a mobile phone, 49 percent of which are smartphones; and 88 percent of the underbanked use mobile phones, 64 percent of which are smartphones.[19] Some of this mobile use is directly targeting financial activities: almost 40 percent of the underbanked with mobile phones reported using mobile banking in 2013.[20] This means that mobile technology has not only revolutionized access to broadband connectivity,[21] but it has also enabled access to financial services for the underserved community by traditional banks and by new online nonbanks.[22]

---

15. Board of Governors of the Federal Reserve System, Consumers and Mobile Financial Services 2014, at 5 (Mar. 2014), *available at* http://www.federalreserve.gov/econresdata/consumers-and-mobile-financial-services-report-201403.pdf.

16. *Id.*

17. *See* Scratch, Viacom Media Network, The Millennial Disruption Index (2013), *available at* http://www.millennialdisruptionindex.com/wp-content/uploads/2014/02/MDI_Final.pdf; Shane Ferro, *33% of Millennials Don't Think They'll Need a Bank Five Years from Now*, Bus. Insider, Mar. 20, 2015,http://www.businessinsider.com/millennials-dont-think-they-will-need-a-bank-2015-3 Footnotes that American Millennials increasingly regard banks as irrelevant and on a brink of disruption. Half of those surveyed believe start-ups will overhaul the way banks work and that innovation will come from outside the banking industry. Importantly, 73 percent would reportedly be more excited to have their financial services provided by Google, Amazon, Apple, PayPal, or Square than by their own mainstream banks.).

18. *See* Board of Governors of the Federal Reserve System, *supra* note 15, at 5.

19. *Id.*

20. *Id.*

21. *See* Simon Kemp, *Social, Digital & Mobile Worldwide in 2014*, We Are Social, Jan. 9, 2014 ("With reference to the continued growth in internet penetration, it seems clear that mobile connections will account for the vast majority of new sign-ups in the coming months. . . . [T]he distribution of mobile penetration matches much more closely to the distribution of the world's population, meaning most people around the world now have a realistic opportunity to access the internet."), http://wearesocial.net/blog/2014/01/social-digital-mobile-worldwide-2014/.

22. Many more technology advancements are still in development as major tech companies seek to expand Internet access to underserved populations. For example, Google is pursuing "Project Loon," a network of balloons traveling on the edge of space with the mission of providing Internet access to rural and remote areas. *See* Project Loon, *Homepage*, https://x.company/loon/ (last visited June 17, 2017). Likewise, Facebook and several phone companies announced in August 2013 the launch of internet.org, a global partnership to make Internet access available to those around the world who lack broadband connectivity. *See Technology Leaders Launch Partnership to Make Internet Access Available to All*, Facebook, Aug. 21, 2013, http://newsroom.fb.com/news/2013/08/technology-leaders-launch-partnership-to-make-internet-access-available-to-all/. Both companies have also acquired drone start-ups to promote their Internet delivery projects. *See* Josh Constine, *Facebook Will Deliver Internet via Drones with "Connectivity Lab" Project Powered by Acqhires from Ascenta*, TechCrunch, Mar. 27, 2014, http://techcrunch.com/2014/03/27/facebook-drones/; Darrell Etherington, *Google Acquires Titan Aerospace, the Drone Company Pursued by Facebook*, TechCrunch, Apr. 14, 2014, http://techcrunch.com/2014/04/14/google-acquires-titan-aerospace-the-drone-company-pursued-by-facebook/.

However, although broadening access to mainstream financial services for underserved populations is a widely supported goal, it also carries many possible risks[23] and potentially unintended consequences, as further described below.

B. Regulatory Coordination

As described above, under the current financial architecture, more and more financial services and products are provided outside of the traditional banking system.[24] Historically, regulators in the United States used laws such as the GlassSteagall Act in order to better monitor and operate the financial industry. But in recent years, a growing number of business entities that are not established under the banking laws and cannot legally accept deposits started to perform more of the functions associated with banks.[25] These nonbank entities offer financial products and services, but unlike banks, thrifts, and credit unions,[26] which have always been required to comply with federal regulations, most nonbanks have not faced this regulation until recently.[27] This different treatment given to the various financial service providers is the result of the longheld view that the legal power to receive deposits is the essence of a "bank." Therefore, entities that are not "banks," even though they offer most of the services that banks offer, are less strictly regulated. Many nonbanks have built their entire business models on this notion in an attempt to be subject to less regulation than traditional financial institutions.

Despite the large number of technology companies performing financial services and their massive pool of subscribers, regulation of online nonbanks still consists of a hodgepodge of state and federal statutes and regulations. Such laws include the federal Bank Secrecy Act (BSA) as modified in 2001 by the USA PATRIOT Act;[28] state money transmitter laws, which typically have a consumer protection purpose but

---

23. *See* U.S. Department of the Treasury, Opportunities and Challenges in Online Marketplace Lending 12–13 (May 10, 2016) (Although "the majority of consumer loans are made to prime and near-prime borrowers, newer entrants have started to move down the credit spectrum and target sub-prime borrowers. Some online marketplace lenders are serving non-prime consumers, some offering rates up to 36 percent to borrowers with FICO scores as low as 580. Some online marketplace lenders are accepting applicants without FICO scores."), *available at* https://www.treasury.gov/connect/blog/Documents/Opportunities_and_Challenges_in_Online_Marketplace_Lending_white_paper.pdf.

24. *See generally* Steven L. Schwarcz, *Regulating Shadows: Financial Regulation and Responsibility Failure*, 70 Wash. & Lee L. Rev. 1781 (2013) (describing that most corporate financing, no longer depends on bank loans but is raised through special purpose entities, money market mutual funds, securities lenders, hedge funds, and investment banks).

25. Exemplifiers include Western Union, https://www.westernunion.com/us/en/home.html (last visited June 17, 2017), and PayPal, https://www.paypal.com/home (last visited June 17, 2017).

26. U.S. depository institutions include commercial banks, thrifts (including savings and loan associations and savings banks that focus on deposits and home mortgage originations), and credit unions. *See* Connecticut Department of Banking, *ABC's of Banking—Lesson Two: Banks, Thrifts, and Credit Unions—What's the Difference?*, http://www.ct.gov/dob/cwp/view.asp?a=2235&q=297886 (last visited June 17, 2017).

27. For a discussion on how the DoddFrank Act sought to ensure that consumers get the benefit of federal consumer financial laws on a consistent basis, see *Big Data and Social Netbanks, supra* note 9, pt. III.A.1.

28. 31 U.S.C. § 5311 (2012). Recent amendments to the regulations implementing the registration requirements of the BSA have adopted the term "money services business" in place of the term "money transmitting business" to identify those businesses subject to the registration requirements. *Id.*

also require compliance with anti-money laundering (AML) rules;[29] Regulation E[30] implementing the Electronic Fund Transfer Act (EFTA);[31] the Truth in Lending Act (TILA)[32] and Regulation Z, which implements the act;[33] the Credit Card Accountability Responsibility and Disclosure (CARD) Act of 2009;[34] the Equal Credit Opportunity Act (ECOA) and Regulation B[35] implementing the act, which apply to all the business entities that extend credit;[36] the GrammLeachBliley (GLB) Act,[37] which governs the privacy of customer information held by a financial institution; and the Fair Credit Reporting Act (FCRA),[38] which is based on the notion that the banking system is dependent upon fair and accurate credit reporting.

In addition, there is a troubling regulatory overlap in connection with the supervision and monitoring of nonbanks by multiple government agencies. Seeking to ensure that consumers get the benefit of federal consumer financial laws on a consistent basis, title X of the DoddFrank Wall Street Reform and Consumer Protection Act[39] established the Consumer Financial Protection Bureau (CFPB) on July 21, 2010. Under the DoddFrank Act, the CFPB has supervisory authority over nonbank covered persons[40] providing three main types of consumer financial products or services: (1) mortgage loans, specifically the origination, brokerage, or servicing of consumer loans secured by real estate, and related loan adjustment or foreclosure relief services; (2) private student or education-related loans; and (3) payday loans.[41]

---

29. *See, e.g.*, M. MacRae Robinson, *Easing the Burden on Mobile Payments: Resolving Current Deficiencies in Money Transmitter Regulations*, 18 N.C. BANKING INST. 553, 564–66 (2014). Unfortunately, there is no national standard for defining which type of money transmission requires licensing, and most regulators choose to take an expansive view of their authority without publishing that interpretation anywhere. As a result, it is harder for businesses to comply with state money transmitter licensing requirements. *See id.*

30. 12 C.F.R. pt. 1005 (2016).

31. *Id.* § 205.3 (2016).

32. 15 U.S.C. §§ 1601–1667f (2012).

33. 12 C.F.R. pt. 1026 (2016).

34. Pub. L. No. 11124, 123 Stat. 1734.

35. 15 U.S.C. §§ 1691–1691f (2012); 12 C.F.R. pt. 1002 (2016).

36. *See* CONSUMER FINANCIAL PROTECTION BUREAU, EQUAL CREDIT OPPORTUNITY ACT (ECOA) VALUATIONS RULE (2014), *available at* http://files.consumerfinance.gov/f/201401_cfpb_compliance-guide_ecoa.pdf.

37. Pub. L. No. 106102, 113 Stat. 1338 (1999).

38. 15 U.S.C. §§ 1681–1681x (2012)

39. Pub. L. No. 111203, tit. X, 124 Stat. 1376, 1955 (2010) (codified as amended in scattered sections of 12 U.S.C.).

40. Covered persons include: "(A) any person that engages in offering or providing a consumer financial product or service; and (B) any affiliate of a person described in . . . (A) if such affiliate acts as a service provider to such person." 12 U.S.C. § 5481(6) (2012).

41. *Id.* § 5514(a)(1)(A), (D), (E). The CFPB also has the authority to supervise any nonbank covered person that it has "reasonable cause to determine, by order, after notice to the covered person and a reasonable opportunity . . . to respond, . . . is engaging, or has engaged, in conduct that poses risks to consumers with regard to the offering or provision of consumer financial products or services." *Id.* § 5514(a)(1)(C); *see also* 12 C.F.R. pt. 1091 (2016) (prescribing procedures for making determinations under 12 U.S.C. § 5514(a)(1)(C)). In addition, the CFPB has supervisory authority over very large depository institutions and credit unions and their affiliates. 12 U.S.C. § 5515(a). Moreover, the CFPB has certain authority relating to the supervision of other depository institutions and credit unions. *Id.* § 5516(c)(1), (e). *See also CFPB Supervision Report Highlights Risky Practices in Nonbank Markets*, CFPB, May 22, 2014, http://www.consumerfinance.gov/newsroom/cfpb-supervision-report-highlights-risky-practices-in-nonbank-markets/.

The CFPB also has supervisory authority over "larger participant[s] of a market for other consumer financial products or services," as it defines them through rulemaking.[42] The CFPB defines a nonbank entity that it seeks to supervise as "a company that offers consumer financial products or services, but does not have a bank, thrift, or credit union charter and does not take deposits."[43] The CFPB is tasked with doing so for purposes of: (1) evaluating compliance with federal consumer financial law; (2) gaining information about such persons' undertakings and compliance systems or procedures; and (3) identifying and assessing risks to consumers and consumer financial markets.[44]

Based on its rulemaking agenda, the CFPB is now focused on nonbanks and entities that offer online banklike services, including services provided to underserved populations.[45] But the CFPB is not the only regulator to cover those financial activities. Specifically, overlap results from the fact that several bodies, such as the Federal Trade Commission (FTC) and the Financial Crimes Enforcement Network (FinCEN), could also claim an interest in policing online nonbanks and mobile payments.[46] Likewise, other authorities also arguably have stakes in the regulation of online nonbanks and mobile payments, including: (1) the Federal Communications Commission (FCC), which is the main federal agency that regulates interstate and international communications;[47] (2) state public utilities commissions, which regulate the utilities that provide essential services;[48] (3) the prudential banking regulators; (4) the U.S. Securities and Exchange Commission (SEC); (5) the U.S. Department of Justice; and even (6) the U.S. Department of Homeland Security.[49]

Overlapping jurisdiction among several regulators is troubling mostly because of the uncertainty it creates. First, when dealing with online/mobile platforms offering banklike services, it is not clear if existing banking regulators, such as the Federal Reserve, the Federal Deposit Insurance Corp. (FDIC), the Office of the Comptroller of the Currency (OCC), or even the National Credit Union Administration (NCUA),[50]

---

42. 12 U.S.C. § 5514(a)(1)(B), (a)(2); *see also id.* § 5481(5) (defining "consumer financial product or service").

43. *Explainer: What Is a Nonbank, and What Makes One "Larger?,"* CFPB, June 23, 2011, http://www.consumerfinance.gov/blog/explainer-what-is-a-nonbank-and-what-makes-one-larger/.

44. 12 U.S.C. § 5514(b)(1).

45. *See* Charles Washburn, Jr., *Let's Get Mobile: The CFPB Turns Focus to Mobile Banking*, JD Supra, July 8, 2014, http://www.jdsupra.com/legalnews/lets-get-mobile-the-cfpb-turns-focus-t-26103/.

46. *See* Benjamin Seeger, *Mobile Payments: Is Plastic Becoming Obsolete?*, Cairncross & Hempelmann, Jan. 25, 2013, https://www.cairncross.com/blog/eat-drink-shop-stay/industry-events/mobile-payments-is-plastic-becoming-obsolete.

47. FCC, *What We Do*, http://www.fcc.gov/what-we-do (last visited June 17, 2017).

48. Such services include energy, telecommunications, water, and transportation utilities. For more on the work of a nonprofit organization dedicated to representing state public service commissions who regulate utilities, *see* National Association of Regulatory Utility Commissioners, *About NARUC*, https://www.naruc.org/about-naruc/about-naruc/ (last visited June 17, 2017).

49. U.S. Government Accountability Office, Virtual Currencies: Emerging Regulatory, Law Enforcement, and Consumer Protection Challenges 11, 19–20 (2014) (GAO-14-496), *available at* http://www.gao.gov/assets/670/663678.pdf.

50. NCUA is an independent federal agency that charters and supervises federal credit unions and insures savings in federal and most state-chartered credit unions. *See* NCUA, *Leadership*, https://www.ncua.gov/about/leadership/Pages/default.aspx (last visited June 17, 2016).

should dominate the regulatory environment. Second, state financial services regulators also play a significant role affecting financial services and activities, but it is not clear how to best coordinate this role with federal regulation. Third, both the CFPB and the FTC[51] currently assume consumer protection responsibility for non-bank financial services offered online. For example, according to the EFTA and Regulation E, the CFPB has authority to regulate both consumers and financial institutions engaged in electronic funds transfers in order to protect against fraudulent and unauthorized transactions.[52] Additionally, the CFPB acts as a backstop to state-level consumer protection by providing that any state regulation or agreement between the consumer and the financial institution that caps consumer liability for a lesser amount will govern.[53] The FTC also has jurisdiction over entities operating in the online banklike services and payments environment, and it shares responsibility with the CFPB for enforcing regulations against Internet platforms to protect consumers.[54]

C. Implications of Big Data in Developing New Ways to Monetize Payment Practices

Big data and social netbanks,[55] as well as major marketplace lending platforms, are relatively new creatures in the financial services market. As such, they raise special concerns that call for specifically tailored regulation. Major financial institutions have complained about the impact of this novel, technologically sophisticated, and unregulated subindustry;[56] regulators that examine emerging alternative payment methods have also called for scrutiny.[57] Financial services practices driven by big

---

51. The FTC protects consumers from fraudulent and deceptive practices through enforcement of the Unfair and Deceptive Trade Act. *See* Federal Trade Commission Act, 15 U.S.C. § 45(a) (2012) (establishing power to regulate unfair or deceptive practices); *id.* § 57a(a) (bestowing authority upon the FTC to establish rules and policies). As part of its efforts concerning online practices, it helped create comprehensive privacy programs to protect consumers' private information. *See* FTC, PAPER, PLASTIC . . . OR MOBILE?: AN FTC WORKSHOP ON MOBILE PAYMENTS 6 (2013), *available at* https://www.ftc.gov/sites/default/files/documents/reports/paper-plastic-or-mobile-ftc-workshop-mobile-payments/p0124908_mobile_payments_workshop_report_02-28-13.pdf.

52. The Dodd-Frank Act transferred rulemaking authority under the EFTA from the Board of Governors of the Federal Reserve System to the CFPB. The Dodd-Frank Act also amended the EFTA and created a new system of consumer protections for remittance transfers sent by consumers in the United States to individuals and businesses in foreign countries. Dodd-Frank Act §§ 1002(12)(C), 1024(b)–(c), and 1025(b)–(c); 12 U.S.C. §§ 5481(12)(C), 5514(b)–(c), and 5515(b)–(c). 15 U.S.C. § 1693 is intended to protect individual consumers engaging in electronic funds transfers (EFTs) and remittance transfers. EFTs include transfers of funds that are conducted by mobile payment businesses. 12 C.F.R. § 1005.3(b) (2016).

53. *See* 12 C.F.R. § 1005.6(b)(6) (2013).

54. 12 U.S.C. § 5581(b)(5)(C) (2012).

55. For an examination of such new financial entities and their characteristics, see generally *Big Data and Social Netbanks, supra* note 9, where we also discuss the special concerns they raise.

56. *See, e.g.*, Penny Crosman, *How Banks Can Win Back "Mind Share" from PayPal, Google, Amazon*, AM. BANKER, May 30, 2014, https://www.americanbanker.com/news/how-banks-can-win-back-mind-share-from-paypal-google-amazon.

57. *See, e.g.*, Eniola Akindemowo, *Contract, Deposit, or E-Value? Reconsidering Stored Value Products for a Modernized Payments Framework*, 7 DEPAUL BUS. & COM. L.J. 275, 295–96 (2009) (discussing the FDIC's recently expressed opinion that stored-value products are access devices and as such are very similar to traditional payment mechanisms and might need to be assessed for regulation under the FDIC if the funds underlying them are ultimately deposited in a financial institution).

data present distinctive new impacts, behaviors, and implications, which are discussed below.

1. Enhanced Access to Financial Services via Social Networks

Big data companies and social networks enjoy a significantly larger user base than traditional banks. The competitive advantage is evident not only in the number of users but also in their diversified financial capabilities: some make use of the traditional banking system while others do not have or only have very limited access to traditional banking services, either due to their geographic locations or because low-status socioeconomic backgrounds make it virtually impossible for them to interact with traditional financial entities. As explained above, easy access to bank-like services via big data platforms or social network accounts is likely to bring many in the financially underserved community into the financial services market, and that is a positive thing. However, social netbanks could consequently dominate the financially underserved community, and, due to network effects and high switching costs, cause consumers to become their captive audience, preventing them from leaving even if they wish to do so.

2. Privacy Concerns

As the most common revenue source for big data companies and social networks has thus far been advertising, big data and social networks constantly attempt to aggregate diverse information about their users, their acquaintances and relatives, marital status, jobs, shopping preferences, political positions, and more. By so doing, those platforms have dramatically increased the ability to personalize advertising content, inter alia, by capitalizing on big data analytics.[58] Users consent to the information collection either impliedly, by using the platforms to post and disclose personal information, or explicitly, by accepting the terms of service.

Big data and its derivative uses are currently one of the most attention-grabbing and relevant privacy challenges.[59] By increasing the amount and scope of personally identifiable information, business firms could cause unintended intrusions into a person's life.[60] Due to the nature of big data analytics, it is virtually impossible to predict when an algorithm could expose personally identifiable information.[61] But even if prediction of such algorithmic consequence were achievable, it is not clear

---

58. *See* Catherine Tucker, Time Warner Cable Research Program on Digital Communications, Social Networks, Personalized Advertising, and Perceptions of Privacy Control (2011), *available at* http://209.59.135.49/pdf/TWC_Tucker_v3a.pdf.

59. *See* Lior Jacob Strahilevitz, *Toward a Positive Theory of Privacy Law*, 126 Harv. L. Rev. 2010, 2021 (2013).

60. *See* Kate Crawford & Jason Schultz, *Big Data and Due Process: Toward a Framework to Redress Predictive Privacy Harms*, 55 B.C. L. Rev. 93, 98–101 (2014).

61. *See id.* at 98–100. For example, Target sent baby-related coupons to a pregnant teenager, who at the time did not disclose her pregnancy to her parents. *See* Charles Duhigg, *How Companies Learn Your Secrets*, N.Y. Times, Feb. 16, 2012, http://www.nytimes.com/2012/02/19/magazine/shopping-habits.html?pagewanted=1&_r=1&hp.

that an appropriate privacy safeguard could be implemented since a few pieces of information can often suffice to identify a specific person even when names and other details are stripped from the data sets.[62]

Big data also has the quality of perpetuating what we may have wanted to bury in the past. Indeed, "big data may mean that we are forever prisoners of our previous actions, which can be used against us in systems that presume to predict our future behavior."[63] In China, for example, big data and social networks offering social net-banking services have already been leveraging such data and adopting it into their lending systems.[64] The use of online personal information to optimize financial services, especially against the backdrop of no regulation, has generated tremendous criticism[65] and has been blamed for interfering with the "right to be forgotten."[66]

3. Cybersecurity Challenges

Recent years have witnessed massive data breaches at big nonbanks and retail businesses.[67] Banks have also identified cybercriminals as one of their major threats and have significantly invested in developing ways to successfully fight cybercrime.[68] And while big data platforms have thus far generally kept their users' information safe, security-related risks could increase considerably once those data-driven businesses begin occupying the financial services industry. To use the words of a senior banker:

> Think about this: If we're down the road two or three years, and three-fourths of the banks and three-fourths of the merchants are on Apple Pay or whatever system. . . . If you're a smart terrorist, what better way to get in to disrupt the financial condition of the United States of America than go to one of their back rooms.[69]

---

62. *See* Natasha Singer, *With a Few Bits of Data, Researchers Identify "Anonymous" People*, N.Y. Times, Jan. 29, 2015, http://bits.blogs.nytimes.com/2015/01/29/with-a-few-bits-of-data-researchers-identify -anonymous-people/.

63. *See* Eleanor Boxham, *Big Banks Are Riskier than Ever, Says FDIC Vice Chair*, Fortune, May 20, 2014, http://fortune.com/2014/05/20/big-banks-are-riskier-than-ever-says-fdic-vice-chair/.

64. *See Big Data and Social Netbanks, supra* note 9, at 21–22.

65. *See* Mayer-Schönberger & Cukier, *supra* note 3, at 195.

66. *See* Alessandro Mantelero, *The EU Proposal for a General Data Protection Regulation and the Roots of the "Right to be Forgotten,"* 29(3) Computer L. & Sec. Rev. 231 (2013); Alexander Tsesis, *The Right to Erasure: Privacy, Data Brokers, and the Indefinite Retention of Data*, 49 Wake Forest L. Rev. 433 (2014) (while businesses have valid reasons to use information in their day-to-day operations, a statutorily defined expiration period is needed to preserve the data subjects' dignity and autonomy rights).

67. *See* B. Dan Berger, *One Year after Target Breach, Consumers Vulnerable as Ever*, Am. Banker, Dec. 19, 2014, https://www.americanbanker.com/opinion/one-year-after-target-breach-consumers-vulnerable-as-ever.

68. As B. Dan Berger wrote:

> Unlike retailers, financial institutions maintain rigorous internal protections to ward off criminal attacks. They are required by federal law—specifically, the *Gramm-Leach-Bliley Act*—and by regulation to protect this information and to notify consumers when a breach occurs that may put them at risk. By contrast, retailers are not subject to any federal laws or regulations on consumer financial data protection and breach notification.

Id.

69. Kristin Broughton, *Apple Pay a Systemic Risk? Banker Warns about Nonbank Players*, Am. Banker, Nov. 21, 2014, http://www.americanbanker.com/news/bank-technology/apple-pay-a-systemic-risk-banker -warns-about-nonbank-players-1071357-1.html.

4. Interpersonal Connections' Effects

A consumer's decision-making process includes five vital steps: need recognition, information search, valuation, decision, and post-purchase evaluation.[70] In any of the steps, personal recommendations have always played a central role.[71] Unlike the past, when word of mouth did not travel very far, sharing experiences, reviews, information, advice, warnings, and tips on social media,[72] transforms that same word of mouth with the power to reach millions of consumers.[73] These social displays successfully exert peer influence on others to follow suit: studies have shown that 72 percent of consumers trust online reviews as much as personal recommendations[74] and that 78 percent of consumers are influenced by posts made by companies on social media.[75]

Those social recommendations are important and legitimate. However, they are prone to manipulation, such as by attempting to fabricate reviews and gain online trendsetters' influence.[76] While the risk of manipulation is endemic to the online environment, manipulation in the financial context could have far reaching consequences and significant harms of the kind that the legal system has traditionally addressed. Regulators should consider setting ex ante rules to minimize manipulations and penalize manipulative conduct to generate deterrence.

Another potential abuse of interpersonal connections has to do with big data and social netbanks' ability to influence users' views and desires. The most-cited example for this power is Facebook's highly criticized[77] "manipulation study," in which Facebook manipulated the news feeds of 689,003 users to assess the effects on their

---

70. *See* Angela Hausman, *Consumer Decision Making Process and Social Media*, Hausman & Associates, Feb. 20, 2014, http://www.hausmanmarketingletter.com/social-media-drives-consumer-decision-making-process/.

71. *See* IBM Software, Grasping the Power of Social Networking for Financial Services: Seizing the Opportunity, Maintaining Regulatory Compliance (Nov. 2012), *available at* http://www.smcapture.com/documents/Power%20of%20Social%20Networking%20for%20Financial%20Services.pdf.

72. *See* Lukas P. Forbes & Eve M. Vespoli, *Does Social Media Influence Consumer Buying Behavior? An Investigation of Recommendations and Purchases*, 11(2) J. Bus. & Econ. Res. 107, 110–11 (2013).

73. *See id.* at 108, discussing Facebook and Twitter as social media tools.

74. *See* Myles Anderson, *Study: 72% of Consumers Trust Online Reviews as Much as Personal Recommendations*, Search Engine Land, Mar. 12, 2012, http://searchengineland.com/study-72-of-consumers-trust-online-reviews-as-much-as-personal-recommendations-114152.

75. *See* Steve Olenski, *Are Brands Wielding More Influence in Social Media Than We Thought?*, Forbes, May 7, 2012, http://www.forbes.com/sites/marketshare/2012/05/07/are-brands-wielding-more-influence-in-social-media-than-we-thought/.

76. *See, e.g.*, *Social Media: A New Tool for Terror Fundraising*, CNN, June 19, 2014 (reporting how significant social media is to terror fundraising, and stating that Twitter, Facebook, and messaging site WhatsApp are crucial tools), http://outfront.blogs.cnn.com/2014/06/19/social-media-a-new-tool-for-terror-fundraising/; Harriet Taylor, *Most Young Terrorist Recruitment Is Linked to Social Media, Said DOJ Official*, CNBC, Oct. 5, 2016 (pointing out that "ISIS [is] so adept in its use of social media for propaganda and recruitment, that most cases of domestic terrorism can now be traced to social media platforms."), http://www.cnbc.com/2016/10/05/most-young-terrorist-recruitment-is-linked-to-social-media-said-doj-official.html.

77. *See* Gregory S. McNeal, *Controversy over Facebook Emotional Manipulation Study Grows as Timeline Becomes More Clear*, Forbes, June 30, 2014, https://www.forbes.com/sites/gregorymcneal/2014/06/30/controversy-over-facebook-emotional-manipulation-study-grows-as-timeline-becomes-more-clear/#1e3e8159caa1.

emotions.[78] Because big data companies and social networks allow many to voice their opinions and thoughts to a vast audience, the way individuals develop their viewpoints has been transformed.[79] The power to present the public with manipulated information in the context of big data and social netbanks is unprecedented.

5. Social Shaming

The rise of shadow credit systems that make use of big data and social information to gauge creditworthiness bears many risks. Social shaming, which stems from the ability of the lender to publicly announce the deficiencies in one's financial actions and status, is one such consequence that is especially relevant in the context of big data and social netbanks. Imagine, for example, that Google's terms of service, to which consumers would consent in return for improved loan terms, stipulate that when a borrower's name is searched, an indication of his or her loan status (e.g., paid in full, payment pending, past due) would appear first on the results page. While the social repercussions of such labeling may be destructive for the financially underserved community and possibly for others as well, this may sound like an entirely reasonable price to pay for a loan.

6. Cyberbullying

Cyberbullying, which already poses a major threat to safety,[80] could be significantly boosted and dangerously transformed with the rise of big data and social netbanks. Cyberbullying necessitates the immense exposure and effortless access of a social platform to be effective. Hence, if social networks become widely used by social netbanks, cyberbullying and online sexual solicitation[81] could also become financial-oriented: effective abuses of social netbanks by their users could result in cases of financial extortion, exploitation, and even assault. The independence and unsupervised nature of social networks makes them extremely popular with children and teens. But those features that attract a younger audience also make social networks a dangerous place for children and teens.[82] Social networks give minors the liberty to engage in hurtful behaviors, such as cyberbullying and cyber threats. With the ability to blackmail, financially extort, or exploit others, which is made easier because of online financial services, cyber violence could get a lot

---

78. *See* Adam D.I. Kramer, Jamie E. Guillory & Jeffrey T. Hancock, *Experimental Evidence of Massive-Scale Emotional Contagion through Social Networks*, 111(24) Proc. Nat'l Acad. Sci. 8788 (2014), http://www.pnas.org/content/111/24/8788.full.

79. *See* Clay Shirky, *The Political Power of Social Media*, 90 Foreign Aff. 28, 28–29 (2011).

80. *See* Press Association, *Number of Children Who Are Victims of Cyberbullying Doubles in a Year*, Guardian, Nov. 13, 2014, https://www.theguardian.com/society/2014/nov/14/35pc-children-teenagers-victims-cyberbullying-fears-grooming-tinder-snapchat.

81. *See, e.g.,* Susan Duncan, *My Space Is Also Their Space: Ideas for Keeping Children Safe from Sexual Predators on Social Networking Sites*, 96 Ky. L.J. 527 (2007).

82. For more on cyberbullying, see Organization for Economic Cooperation and Development Council, The Protection of Children Online: Report on Risks Faced by Children Online and Policies to Protect Them 29–33 (2012), *available at* http://www.oecd.org/sti/ieconomy/childrenonline_with_cover.pdf.

more serious, even if eventually minimized or better managed due to market forces, consumer protection-led calls for action, and improved cybersecurity measures.

7. Legal Capacity of Minors

The number of children using the Internet is constantly rising and the age at which they start surfing the web is constantly dropping.[83] As a result, targeting children as consumers for online products and services has become increasingly common.[84] The growing number of commercial transactions online to which children are a party present potential conflicts with the legal capacity doctrine of contract law. With a few exceptions, contract law allows minors to void contracts, because the law views them as lacking full legal capacity until they reach the age of majority.[85] Effortless access to spending on online or mobile services can also result in significant bills for parents, or alternatively costs for businesses that fail to verify the age of their customers. Because they are inexperienced and lack the skills to fully understand online transactions, children may not receive adequate value or find themselves tied into unwanted subscriptions.

8. Competition with Banks

Social netbanks are likely to promote their rapid growth at the expense of the banking industry's traditional players, which are subject to more burdensome regulation.[86] These advantages, mainly in terms of data storage and data management or

---

83. *See id.* (Ninety-three percent of American children had access to the Internet in 2007; in 2006 in Japan, 65 percent of children aged 10–14 and 90 percent of teenagers aged 15–19 had access to the Internet; in 2008, 93–94 percent of children aged 6–17 had access to the Internet in Finland, Iceland, and the Netherlands; and in 2008, 99 percent of UK children aged 12–15 used the Internet, as did 93 percent of children aged 8–11 and 75 percent of children aged 5–7.). *Id.* at 8–9.

84. For example, a 2010 British study found that two-thirds of children were financially active online, spending £448 million a year. Moreover, according to the same study, children were spending close to £64 million a year online without their parents' knowledge. *See* Jill Insley, *Financially Active Children Put Parents at Risk of Online Fraud*, Guardian, Dec. 10, 2010, https://www.theguardian.com/money/2010/dec/10 /children-parents-risk-online-fraud.

85. *See, e.g.*, Cheryl B. Preston, *CyberInfants*, 39 Pepp. L. Rev. 225, 231–32 (2012).

86. A social network uses "digital technologies to deliver better or entirely new ways of meeting customer needs, often bypassing regulation and re-defining a given industry in the process." *See* Karl Flinders, *Why Google Could Become the Amazon of Banking*, ComputerWeekly, July 30, 2014, http://www .computerweekly.com/news/2240225801/Could-Google-become-to-retail-banking-what-Amazon-is-to-high -street-retail. Accordingly, big data's or social netbanks' future lies in the integration and leverage of the firm's other products to create new customer value that goes beyond payments. "It will be by integrating digital assets such as its search engine, Google Maps, Gmail, Google Play, and Google Now that Google could redefine financial services. Thanks to these capabilities, Google is well positioned to disrupt four interlinked areas, disintermediating incumbents in the process." *Id.* Meanwhile, trying to minimize their access-related disadvantage, traditional banks have successfully pushed regulators to create guidelines to enable them to use social media in a variety of ways. Such methods include "marketing, providing incentives, facilitating applications for new accounts, inviting feedback from the public, and engaging with existing and potential customers, for example, by receiving and responding to complaints, or providing loan pricing." Federal Financial Institutions Examination Council, Social Media: Consumer Compliance Risk Management Guidance (Dec. 11, 2013), *available at* https://www.ffiec.gov/press/PDF/2013_Dec%20Final% 20SMG%20attached%20to%2011Dec13%20press%20release.pdf.

brokering, have already placed small and midsize banks in an inferior position to big data and social netbanks in many respects.[87] Traditional players have already begun to understand the unique attributes and advantages of big data and social netbanks in the financial services markets. Capitalizing on their massive user base, big data and social netbanks enjoy access to troves of self-collected proprietary personal data about their consumers (and their consumers' networks). This access, when coupled with cutting-edge analytics technologies to draw useful insights from the data, provides an unprecedented advantage that is virtually impossible for non-technologically sophisticated competitors to obtain.[88] Consequently, those players have requested that the Federal Reserve or the CFPB actively monitor nonbank payment companies, and, in particular, start studying modern online payment services and social media outlets for the purpose of regulating them in the near future.[89] The Community Banks Council also added that nonbanks are not only subject to less regulation, but are also significantly less risk-averse than traditional community banks because the negative fallout associated with their failure is entirely different.[90] The current regulatory framework, under which non-traditional financial service providers are not incentivized to meet consumers' expectations of banking entities because they are not held to the same high regulatory standards, might lead to an unfair outcome, which might also pose yet-to-be-explored risks.[91] Therefore, traditional banking institutions have argued that leveling the playing field for nonbanks would make the competition between traditional banks and the new tech-driven competitors fairer and improve services for consumers.

---

87. Big data and social netbanks platforms can utilize the enhanced access to their services as well as their special expertise to manage or broker data and promote peripheral bank services' capabilities. For example, similarly to Amazon, which partners with individual retailers to connect them with customers, offering transactional services, product comparison, distribution, and user reviews, Google Plus could offer similar services in retail banking, becoming a middleman across the sector. Flinders, *supra* note 86 ("since the launch of Google Checkout (which recently merged with Google Wallet) in 2006, Google has been acquiring, partnering and investing in firms in areas of financial services, such as payments, comparison and loyalty cards.").

88. According to several senior bankers, "[i]f those folks want to play in the financial services area, and in the payment system, they might well be deemed a SIFI"—a systemically important financial institution—"and let them understand what real regulation is." Chris Larsen, *Bank Payment Systems Still Operate Like CompuServe and AOL*, Am. Banker, July 29, 2014, https://www.americanbanker.com/opinion/bank-payment-systems-still-operate-like-compuserve-and-aol.

89. "We told the board that if they wait to act until they complete a study, it will be too late." Matthew Doffing, *Community Bankers Report to Fed on QM Rule and Tech-Competitors for Payment*, CFPB J., Jan. 23, 2014, http://cfpbjournal.com/issue/cfpb-journal/article/community-bankers-report-to-fed-on-qm-rule-and-tech-competitors-for-payment.

90. *Id.*

91. *Id.*

9. Conspicuous Disclosure and Informed Consent

Banks and other financial institutions[92] have long been required to disclose relevant transaction-related information to their customers.[93] After the 2008 financial crisis, the significance of increased and conspicuous disclosure has been further realized as critical for the safe functioning of financial markets. This understanding resulted in sections 115(f) and 165(d) of the Dodd-Frank Act, which grant the Financial Stability Oversight Council (FSOC) and the Federal Reserve Board broad authority to require additional periodic public disclosures of banks and nonbank-yet-financial companies to "support market evaluation of the risk profile, capital adequacy, and risk management capabilities thereof."[94]

Consumers, regulators, and courts have begun to implement the notion that big data and social netbanks, as well as marketplace lending platforms, should not be exempted from the duty to properly disclose all relevant information, policies, and terms. In a recent lawsuit against PayPal in Europe, a German consumer association argued against PayPal's practices of holding users' funds and demanded increased transparency in the terms and conditions.[95] In the United States, the CFPB has recently finalized new disclosure rules for remittance payments under

---

92. For example, the regulation of money market funds is also premised on disclosure. *See, e.g.*, Jonathan R. Macey, Reducing Systemic Risk: The Role of Money Market Mutual Funds as Substitutes for Federally Insured Bank Deposits (Yale Law & Economics Research Paper No. 422, 2012) (stating that "comprehensive disclosure requirements permit an investor to accurately assess the potential risk of an investment and then make an informed decision."), *available at* http://ssrn.com/abstract=1735008.

93. *See, e.g.*, Ruth Plato-Shinar, *The Bank's Duty of Disclosure—Towards a New Model*, 27 Banking & Fin. L. Rev. 427, 433 (2013) (The duty of disclosure, in its narrow meaning, imposes an obligation on the bank to disclose to the customer any significant information that is essential, required, vital, or necessary for the customer to reach a decision about performing a banking transaction.). One such major disclosure requirement can be found in Regulation DD, Truth in Savings, 12 C.F.R. § 230, which requires depository institutions to disclose the terms of deposit accounts to consumers, as well as subsequent and periodic updates, so that the consumers can make informed decisions. Among other things, in particular, section 230.3 states that "[d]epository institutions shall make the disclosures required . . . clearly and conspicuously, in writing, and in a form the consumer may keep" and "[t]he disclosures shall reflect the terms of the legal obligation of the account agreement between the consumer and the depository institution." The section also provides rules for quoting rates.

94. 12 U.S.C. § 5325(f) (authorizing FSOC). And while this regulation was meant to cover a very small and selective group of entities such as banks and major financial service providers, like the insurance giant AIG, for example, the list of the covered entities is not a closed list. Similarly, an attempt to enhance market discipline in the global context has been proposed for the Basel Accords of the Basel Committee on Banking Supervision on Mar. 25, 2009. *See* European Commission, Commission Services Staff Working Document: Possible Changes to the CRD (2010), http://ec.europa.eu/internal_market/bank/docs/regcapital/consutbesec_en.pdf.

95. eBay Inc., SEC Form 10-Q, at 47 (Mar. 31, 2014), https://www.sec.gov/Archives/edgar/data/1065088/000106508814000060/ebay10-qq12014.htm.

Regulation E, mandated by the Dodd-Frank Act.[96] Following the same rationale, the CFPB also ordered PayPal to afford its potential and existing customers additional disclosures, error resolution privileges, and cancellation rights.[97] Lastly, focusing on mortgage loans under Regulations X and Z, the Real Estate Settlement Procedures Act (RESPA) and the TILA, the CFPB has also issued a new TILA-RESPA Integrated Disclosure Rule, which lists disclosure requirements to which consumers are entitled in the course of a loan application.[98]

Disclosure is not a panacea, as most consumers do not bother reading guidelines, policies, and terms of service.[99] Reasons for not reading range from lack of interest and trouble in making sense of the legal jargon to the time-consuming nature of those documents and the nonexistent bargaining power of those who need to read them.[100] Furthermore, when many consumers enjoy the same product or service pursuant to similar terms, those consumers are incentivized not to read because they feel reassured that the terms must be reasonable.[101]

The difficulty with fictional consent[102] is exacerbated where the service providers are virtual entities, such as big data and social netbanks, because consumers cannot interact in person or physically get information or assistance as they have traditionally done with banks. Online providers of services also retain the right to modify their terms at any time, a practice that if adopted by big data and social

---

96. *See* 12 C.F.R. pt. 1090, and the final rule at http://files.consumerfinance.gov/f/201409_cfpb
_final-rule_larger-participant-rule-international-money-transfer-market.pdf. The rule subjects any non-bank international money transfer provider that provides more than one million international money transfers annually to the CFPB's supervisory authority, effective Dec. 1, 2014. Upon approval, the CFPB's estimate was that the rule would bring new oversight to about 25 of the largest providers in the market. Providers that were not considered "larger participants" could still be subject to the CFPB's supervisory authority if the CFPB has reasonable cause to determine that they pose risks to consumers. *See* Fact Sheet, CFPB, Consumer Financial Protection Bureau Finalizes Rule to Oversee Larger Nonbank International Money Transfer Providers (Sept. 12, 2014), *available at* http://files.consumerfinance.gov/f/201409
_cfpb_fact-sheet_larger-participant-rule-international-money-transfer-market.pdf.

97. *See* CFPB v. PayPal, Inc. et al., No. 1:15-cv-01426 (D. Md. May 20, 2015), http://files.consumer finance.gov/f/201505_cfpb_consent-order-paypal.pdf.

98. *See, inter alia*, 12 C.F.R. pts. 1024 and 1026, and the final rule at http://files.consumerfinance .gov/f/201501_cfpb_final-rule_trid.pdf.

99. This notion is generally supported by a few empirical studies, anecdotal evidence, and the reported personal record of legal scholars and judges. *See generally* Omri Ben-Shahar, *The Myth of the "Opportunity to Read" in Contract Law*, 5 EUR. REV. CONT. L. 1 (2009).

100. *See* Robert A. Hillman, *Online Boilerplate: Would Mandatory Website Disclosure of E-Standard Terms Backfire?*, 104 MICH. L. REV. 837, 840–41 (2006); Margaret Jane Radin, *Boilerplate Today: The Rise of Modularity and the Waning of Consent*, 104 MICH. L. REV. 1223, 1231 (2006).

101. *See* Ben-Shahar, *supra* note 99, at 2.

102. Radin, *supra* note 100, at 1231, states:

Consent is fictional when the terms are filed somewhere we cannot access, as in airline tariffs. Consent is fictional when almost all of us click on-screen boxes affirming that we have read and understood things we have not read and would not understand if we did. Consent is fictional on websites whose terms of service state that just by browsing the site, whether or not one ever clicks on the terms, one has agreed to whatever the terms say, now or as they may be changed in the future. Consent is fictional when the contract ends, as one I saw recently did, with "By reading the above you have agreed to it."

netbanks, would not only work against users' best interests, but also be against common perceptions of contract law principles and bank disclosure duties.[103]

II. SHADOW CREDIT REPORTING AND ALTERNATIVE CREDIT METRICS

A. Description

Traditionally, a credit score has been a numerical expression based on a statistical formula that evaluates an individual's financial health and creditworthiness at a given point in time.[104] First devising its formula in the 1950s, the Fair Isaac Corp. (FICO) has since established itself as an industry standard for consumer credit of all kinds.[105] The three major credit bureaus, Equifax, TransUnion, and Experian, rely on the FICO formula as a benchmark for their own calculations, as each agency applies its own individual model.[106] The three major bureaus also developed VantageScore, which has proven to be prevailing in the credit-card underwriting and certain personal-financial applications industries.[107]

The development of innovative data analytics tools allows traditional credit score suppliers to improve the efficiency of their scoring methods by embracing nontraditional credit criteria to enhance access to financial services. Closely following these developments, FICO has recently decided to incorporate into its legacy scoring system forms of alternative data,[108] including property and public records and even telecommunications and utility bills.[109] Moreover, lenders have reportedly been shifting from credit scoring to "credit analytics" by closely tracking as many of the transactions consumers are involved in as they can, and tailoring their credit offers to consumers accordingly.[110] One credit card issuer found a peculiar yet compelling correlation between a purchase of felt pads for furniture and an

---

103. *See* Patricia Sánchez Abril, *Private Ordering: A Contractual Approach to Online Interpersonal Privacy*, 45 Wake Forest L. Rev. 689, 693–94, 705 (2010).

104. See Hussein A. Abdou & John Pointon, *Credit Scoring, Statistical Techniques and Evaluation Criteria: A Review of the Literature*, 18 Intelligent Sys. Acct. Fin. & Mgmt. 59, 62 (2011), for the different definitions of credit scoring.

105. *See* Nate Cullerton, *Behavioral Credit Scoring*, 101 Geo. L.J. 807, 810 (2013).

106. *See* Kurt Eggert, *The Great Collapse: How Securitization Caused the Subprime Meltdown*, 41 Conn. L. Rev. 1257, 1270 (2009) (noting that the three separate credit agencies can produce varying scores due to their distinct models).

107. *See* Terry Clemans, *Foreword*, 46 Suffolk U. L. Rev. 761, 782 (2013) (describing the creation of VantageScore and its competition). *But see* Ian O'Neill, *Disparate Impact, Federal/State Tension, and the Use of Credit Scores by Insurance Companies*, 19 Loy. Consumer L. Rev. 151, 152–53, 172–73 (2007) (arguing that the lack of one credit model was "largely eviscerated" by the development of VantageScore).

108. *See* AnnaMaria Andriotis, *FICO Announces New Credit Score Based on Alternative Data*, Wall St. J., Apr. 2, 2015, https://www.wsj.com/articles/fico-announces-new-credit-score-based-on-alternative -data-1427989748.

109. *See id.* (noting that as a result of these alternative scoring mechanisms, "of the approximately 53 million Americans who don't have enough credit data to generate traditional FICO scores, about 15 million can be scored").

110. *See* Frank Pasquale, *Redescribing Health Privacy: The Importance of Information Policy*, 14 Hous. J. Health L. & Pol'y 95, 109 (2014).

excellent credit risk.[111] Using big data capabilities, most credit card issuers have also devised models for detection of higher risk, such as charges for marriage counseling that may indicate future financial hurdles and could result in a higher credit risk.[112] The crystal-ball features of big data have made it tremendously appealing for lenders and attracted additional players into the lending industry. For instance, as we show in the remainder of this section, new finance start-ups capitalize on big data's predictive power to create alternative, more accurate credit-scoring models.[113]

The pervasive use of smartphones has generated massive amounts of data that lenders enthusiastically harvest for financial ranking purposes.[114] Lenders also collect and use data produced by non-smartphone mobile phone users, which has proven to offer outstanding predictive value. Factors such as adhesion to airtime limits, voice usage, length of calls, and location are determinative of financial trustworthiness in the developing world.[115] The extensive use of smartphones also contributed to digitization of the credit application process as customers can now explore their credit opportunities online or through a mobile application (app) and apply for credit with the vast majority of technology-centered lending companies.[116]

The exclusion of many creditworthy borrowers who lack credit histories from the mainstream credit system is at the heart of the data-driven lending market. Unlike traditional methods that make allowances for a limited number of scoring indicators, algorithms mine big data to correlate countless potential credit factors based on an individual's attributes and behavior, such as how an applicant clicks through web pages or files a loan application.[117] Some lenders merge credit bureau data with their own data-fueled model, while others employ an independent risk model to establish credit pointers.[118] Some lenders go as far as harnessing data

---

111. Strahilevitz, *supra* note 59, at 2021. *See also If There's Privacy in the Digital Age, It Has a New Definition*, NPR, Mar. 3, 2014, http://www.npr.org/sections/alltechconsidered/2014/03/03/285334820 /if-theres-privacy-in-the-digital-age-it-has-a-new-definition, and Duhigg, *supra* note 5 ("People who bought carbon-monoxide monitors for their homes or those little felt pads that stop chair legs from scratching the floor almost never missed payments.").

112. Duhigg, *supra* note 5.

113. *See* Steve Lohr, *Banking Start-Ups Adopt New Tools for Lending*, N.Y. Times, Jan. 18, 2015, http:// www.nytimes.com/2015/01/19/technology/banking-start-ups-adopt-new-tools-for-lending.html.

114. *On Social Credit*, *supra* note 11, at 355–64.

115. *See* Evgeny Morozov, *Your Social Networking Credit Score*, Slate, Jan. 30, 2013 (analysis of data by ZestFinance, a start-up lender, revealed that applicants who fill out online forms in proper case rather than upper case or lower case only, are likely to be more reliable payers), http://www.slate.com /articles/technology/future_tense/2013/01/wonga_lenddo_lendup_big_data_and_social_networking _banking.html.

116. *See generally On Social Credit*, *supra* note 11.

117. *See* Tracy Alloway, *Big Data: Credit Where Credit's Due*, Fin. Times, Feb. 2, 2015. *See also* Lohr, *supra* note 113.

118. *See* Robinson & Yu, Knowing the Score: New Data, Underwriting, and Marketing in the Consumer Credit Marketplace 12–14 (Oct. 29, 2014), *available at* https://www.teamupturn.com/static/files/Knowing_the _Score_Oct_2014_v1_1.pdf.

derived from the Internet of Things[119] to better appreciate their borrowers' financial standing.[120] Some lenders have built their credit-scoring algorithms around behavioral data gleaned from social media and social networking information.[121] For example, in addition to other indicators, lenders analyze an individual's education, career path, and strength of social ties,[122] and some financial technology (fintech) lending companies have begun using online social data to authenticate factual information in loan applications and further confirm trustworthiness.[123]

B. Social and Policy Issues

The rise of shadow credit systems that are based on big data as a better risk-prediction tool has a number of important social and policy implications. First, the collection and use of information about individuals often involves potential and actual privacy harms. Second, alternative models that focus on new, innovative criteria based on individuals' online footprints can result in undesired and unintended financial as well as social consequences. Third, the new credit systems are based on algorithmic decision-making processes that have been criticized for their opacity, arbitrary results, and discriminatory impact on minorities.

1. Privacy

The utilization of personal and social information for credit-scoring purposes poses two levels of privacy challenges. At the direct level, shadow credit systems have an obvious impact on the loan seeker's privacy when they collect and analyze data about an applicant's family, friendships, jobs, shopping habits, political views, and more. Some applications of big data anonymize the information they collect; yet, anonymization has been proven to be somewhat of a failed technological

---

119. Video: FTC Commissioner Julie Brill, Keynote Address at the Silicon Flatirons Conference: The New Frontiers of Privacy Harm (Jan. 17, 2014) ("On the Internet of Things, consumers are going to start having devices, whether it's their car, or some other tool that they have, that's connected and sending information to a number of different entities, and the consumer might not even realize that they have a connected device or that the thing that they're using is collecting information about them."), https://www.youtube.com/watch?v=VXEyKGw8wXg&index=3&list=PLTAvlPZGMUXNfrXy3VzpDtiPiyJjCjyKt

120. See Scott R. Peppet, *Regulating the Internet of Things: First Steps Toward Managing Discrimination, Privacy, Security, and Consent*, 93 Tex. L. Rev. 85, 123 (2014) ("For example, Safaricom, Kenya's largest cell-phone operator, studies its mobile phone users to establish their trustworthiness. Based on how often its customers top up their airtime, for example, it may then decide to extend them credit."). See also Alloway, *supra* note 117 ("The use of wearable technologies, which can track everything from exercise habits to heart rate, is also opening up another realm of information for data-hungry lenders.").

121. *On Social Credit, supra* note 11, at 106.

122. See Evelyn M. Rusli, *Bad Credit? Start Tweeting*, Wall St. J., Apr. 1, 2013, https://www.wsj.com/articles/SB10001424127887324883604578396852612756398.

123. See Morozov, *supra* note 115; Tom Groenfeldt, *Lenddo Creates Credit Scores Using Social Media*, Digitalist Mag., Feb. 5, 2015, http://www.digitalistmag.com/financial-management/lenddo-creates-credit-scores-using-social-media-02155945.

exercise.[124] The services of those who use social intelligence for financial ranking (such as Lenddo, Neo, Earnest, SoFi, Hello Soda) depend upon personal identification.[125] Some shadow credit industry players would go as far as requiring the applicant's login information and then scanning the individual's entire activity, including not only visible online footprints but also private exchanges.[126]

At the direct level of interaction between the loan applicant and the credit provider, accessing the consumer's private information is justified by the consumer's consent. This is a simple barter: trading private pieces of information about one's life for more attractive credit terms. Providing private information in exchange for products or services has been a foundational business concept in various industries and markets. The behavioral advertising business model exemplifies such an exchange: personal information collected and used for targeted advertising purposes acts as currency to pay for products and services.[127] Experts have argued against this presumably consensual model, stating that consumers cannot reasonably appraise their disutility from the tradeoff and the harm associated with the data collection.[128] Unlike a traditional retail transaction, "payment" made with consumer information proceeds beyond the point of purchase and interferes with consumers' appreciation of the harm to their privacy.[129]

Those arguments, however, do not fully apply to emerging shadow credit models. Alternative credit-scoring calculations require close interaction between the candidate and the service: an applicant must fill out an application, learn about different products, and ultimately choose the best-fitting one. The application process generates an active, voluntary, and well-informed decision to disclose personal information, unlike the one presented by the behavioral advertising model. Furthermore, business models that facilitate mutually agreed upon disclosures in return for a financial benefit have successfully spread in other markets as well. A recent illustration of this model is Progressive's Snapshot program,[130] which is intended to create a voluntary monitoring system. Drivers enrolled in the program receive a personalized insurance rate based on their safe driving habits as recorded by

124. *See, e.g.*, Arvind Narayanan & Vitaly Shmatikov, *De-anonymizing Social Networks*, Proc. 30th IEEE Symp. on Security & Privacy 173, 175 (2009) (showing that a third of the users who can be verified to have accounts on both Twitter, a popular microblogging service, and Flickr, an online photo-sharing site, can be reidentified in the anonymous Twitter graph with only a 12 percent error rate), http://www.cs.utexas.edu/~shmat/shmat_oak09.pdf; Scott Allan Morrison, *Scary New Ways the Internet Profiles You*, Daily Beast, Feb. 8, 2016 ("No site or network is entirely safe, and numerous researchers have already demonstrated how incredibly easy it is to 'reidentify' or 'deanonymize' individuals hidden in anonymized data."), http://www.thedailybeast.com/articles/2016/02/08/scary-new-ways-the-internet-profiles-you.html.

125. *See On Social Credit, supra* note 11, at 360–65.

126. At some point, Lenddo, for example, checked messages for shared slang or wording that suggests affinity. *See Stat Oil*, Economist, Feb. 9, 2013, *available at* http://www.economist.com/news/finance-and-economics/21571468-lenders-are-turning-social-media-assess-borrowers-stat-oil.

127. *See* Katherine J. Strandburg, *Free Fall: The Online Market's Consumer Preference Disconnect*, 2013 U. Chi. Legal F. 95, 100 (2013).

128. *See id.* at 107.

129. *See id.* at 130–31.

130. *See* Progressive, *Snapshot*, https://www.progressive.com/auto/snapshot/ (last visited June 17, 2017).

a small box plugged into their vehicles.[131] The Snapshot program seems to have gained traction with more than 2.5 million enrolled drivers who voluntarily disclose information about their driving patterns to get better premium rates.[132]

Many consumers view authorization of information collection and use of the information in return for a financial benefit as a fair and reasonable trade.[133] A 2016 Pew Research Center study confirmed that for the right deal, a majority of consumers would be willing to share personal information.[134] Thus, the privacy challenge at the direct level of interaction, while it may facially seem significant, is commonly justified on freedom of contract grounds.

Conversely, those facing the greatest privacy risk in the wake of shadow credit systems are third parties, whose presence is intertwined with the loan seeker's actions. Those who interact with the applicant online may not have consented to have their data stored and analyzed by others.

The derivative privacy harm potentially imposed on third parties correlates with the degree of disclosure and invasiveness that the applicant legally accepted. In the most extreme cases, the applicant's consent translates into granting full access to review, analyze, and store all relevant information found on the applicant's private online accounts, including information that third parties may not have intended to convey to others.[135] In less extreme cases, shadow credit score providers mine and research publicly available information, oftentimes without the knowledge or express consent of third parties, but within the parameters of disclosed privacy settings. Once information makes its way online, goes the claim, it becomes public knowledge and is not subject to privacy protections.

Using and storing publicly accessible information about third parties nevertheless presents significant concerns. First, although the applicant is the target of the credit inquiry, the collected data could potentially be kept and cross-referenced to make future determinations as to a third party without his knowledge. Second, some shadow credit-scoring methods are predicated on personal identification. Creditors can make fairly accurate inferences about the identity of third parties with the help

---

131. *See* Progressive, *Frequently Asked Questions About Snapshot*, https://www.progressive.com/auto /snapshot-common-questions/ (last visited June 17, 2017).

132. *See* Press Release, Progressive, Safer Drivers Pay Less for Car Insurance with Snapshot Pay as You Drive Insurance Program from Progressive (May 20, 2015), *available at* http://www.marketwatch .com/story/safer-drivers-pay-less-for-car-insurance-with-snapshot-pay-as-you-drive-insurance-program -from-progressive-2015-05-20.

133. *See* Scott R. Peppet, *Unraveling Privacy: The Personal Prospectus and the Threat of a Full-Disclosure Future*, 105 Nw. U. L. Rev. 1153, 1157 (2011) ("Even with control over her personal information, he argued, an individual will often find it in her self-interest to disclose such information to others for economic gain. If she can credibly signal to a health insurer that she does not smoke, she will pay lower premiums. If she can convince her employer that she is diligent, she will receive greater pay.").

134. *See* Lee Rainie & Maeve Duggan, *Privacy and Information Sharing*, Pew Res. Center, Jan. 14, 2016, http://www.pewinternet.org/2016/01/14/privacy-and-information-sharing/. An earlier study found similar views among European consumers. *See* Nicola Jentzsch et al., European Union Agency for Network and Information Security, Study on Monetising Privacy: An Economic Model for Pricing Personal Information 1 (2012), *available at* https://www.enisa.europa.eu/activities/identity-and-trust/library/deliverables/monetising-privacy.

135. *See On Social Credit, supra* note 11, at 34.

of advanced big data analytics,[136] thereby increasing the risk of privacy harms to third parties who did not otherwise disclose their identities. Finally, some argue that the public/private dichotomy should not guide a decision about a person's financial future. Instead, subject to a reasonableness check within contextual norms, the expectations of an individual whose privacy interest may be harmed should be used as the barometer of privacy violation claims.[137]

2. Social Polarization

Many consumer advocates find fault with the form of algorithmic profiling used by shadow credit systems, blaming it for threatening open society by chilling democratic speech.[138] By indexing people into prescribed sets, algorithmic systems risk dividing society into echo chambers of like-minded individuals.[139] Following similar logic, we argue that an extensive use of shadow credit systems, and especially of social credit models, could trigger social polarization.[140] When credit is reviewed on a social basis, individuals are motivated to perfect their online image for a better creditworthiness grade.[141] Rational users may seek to remove financially hazardous links, such as friends who went bankrupt, lost their jobs, or live in a poor neighborhood, while strengthening beneficial social ties with individuals possessing sound careers and good financial standing. Such online social cleanup is economically wise from the individual user's perspective. However, artificial acts of restructuring bear the potential for broad social ramifications, including the possibility of online social polarization where the level of financial risk catalogs users as follows:

> Those from disadvantaged backgrounds would interact only with users who, likewise, have not been able to break free of the cycle of poverty; ivy league alumni would only allow themselves to be associated with similarly elite peers; an executive wishing to virtually follow an organization committed to helping poor families is likely to avoid creating a traceable connection between herself and the

---

136. For example, researchers were able to predict the characteristics of a group of Facebook users by analyzing their "likes." *See* Zeynep Tufekci, *Algorithmic Harms Beyond Facebook and Google: Emergent Challenges of Computational Agency*, 13 Colo. Tech. L.J. 203, 210 (2015).

137. *See generally* Helen Nissenbaum, Privacy in Context (2010) (describing the importance of social contexts and context-relative informational norms when considering the right to privacy; contextual integrity theory helps determine if the introduction of a new practice or technology into a given social context breaches governing informational norms); Helen Nissenbaum, *Privacy as Contextual Integrity*, 79 Wash. L. Rev. 119, 138 (2004) (arguing that the contextual integrity theory rejects the traditional distinction of public versus private information, and distinguishes between two classes of informational norms: norms of appropriateness, which determine if a specific piece of information is appropriate for disclosure in a given context, and norms of flow or distribution).

138. *See generally* Eli Pariser, The Filter Bubble: What the Internet Is Hiding from You (2011); Joseph Turow, The Daily You: How the New Advertising Industry Is Defining Your Identity and Your Worth (2011); Omer Tene & Jules Polonetsky, *Big Data for All: Privacy and User Control in the Age of Analytics*, 11 Nw. J. Tech. & Intell. Prop. 239, 252 (2013).

139. *See* Tene & Polonetsky, *supra* note 138, at 252.

140. For the possibility of network fragmentation and its effect on the accuracy of social credit systems, see Yanhao Wei et al., *Credit Scoring with Social Network Data*, 35 Marketing Sci. 234, 235 (2014), http://papers.ssrn.com/sol3/papers.cfm?abstract_id=2475265.

141. *See generally On Social Credit*, *supra* note 11, secs. III.B and V.

unfortunate, and for similar reasons may be reluctant to "like" the business page for her best friend's debt refinancing company.[142]

Individuals commonly build online relationships with their likes, but even so, existing social circles do not necessarily reflect a strict allocation based on financial risk.[143] Connections online are also formed on grounds that could join people from entirely different economic classes,[144] such as a shared taste in music or a favorite online game.[145] Social networks also function as a dynamic information source (e.g., consuming news), as a reciprocal communication means for individuals and businesses (e.g., following Target on Instagram), and as matchmaker for individuals with similar interests (e.g., networking platform MeetUp, where users form online circles around shared interests and then "meet up" offline). Users also capitalize on social networking to maintain connections as they move between offline communities and preserve early-life connections, notwithstanding the expected decline in the number of similarity points.[146] The social consequences of shadow credit systems are likely to extend beyond virtual realms, because online social networks merge online and offline behavior.[147] If financial health and possible risk indicators regularly guide online socialization, reflections of the practice would quickly surface in real life, too. Offline connections that lack online counterparts are more costly to maintain, especially when not supported by geographical proximity.

The emerging shadow credit models and the potentially resulting social segregation risk a number of adverse consequences. First, online social polarization is likely to drive a decrease in the resources accrued through relationships among people, referred to as social capital.[148] Individuals benefit from the resources of their networks, including helpful information, personal ties, or communal organizations.[149]

---

142. *Id.* sec. V.A.
143. *See* Miller McPherson et al., *Birds of a Feather: Homophily in Social Networks*, 27 Ann. Rev. Soc. 415, 416 (2001).
144. *See id.* at 1143. *See also* Daria J. Kuss & Mark D. Griffiths, *Online Social Networking and Addiction—A Review of the Psychological Literature*, Int'l J. Envtl. Res. Pub. Health 2528, 2531 (2011).
145. *See* Sabine Trepte et al., *The Social Side of Gaming: How Playing Online Computer Games Creates Online and Offline Social Support*, 28 Computers Hum. Behav. 832, 832 (2012) ("The results complement existing research by showing that online gaming may result in strong social ties, if gamers engage in online activities that continue beyond the game and extend these with offline activities.").
146. *See* Nicole B. Ellison et al., *The Benefits of Facebook "Friends": Social Capital and College Students' Use of Online Social Network Sites*, 12 J. Computer-Mediated Comm. 1143, 1144 (2007).
147. *See, e.g.*, Nicole Ellison et al., *With a Little Help from My Friends: Social Network Sites and Social Capital, in* A Networked Self: Identity, Community, and Culture on Social Network Sites (Zizi Papacharissi ed., 2011); Charles Steinfield et al., *Online Social Networks Sites and the Concept of Social Capital, in* Frontiers in New Media Research 115 (Francis L.F. Lee et al. eds., 2012); Ellison et al., *supra* note 146, at 1150; Adalbert Mayer & Steven L. Puller, *The Old Boy (and Girl) Network: Social Network Formation on University Campuses*, 92 J. Pub. Econ. 329, 346 (2008).
148. *See* Pierre Bourdieu & Loïc J. D. Wacquant, An Invitation to Reflexive Sociology 119 (1992) (expanding the concept of "capital," which was traditionally related only to economics, to include social, cultural, and symbolic resources, and defining social capital as "the sum of the resources, actual or virtual, that accrue to an individual or a group by virtue of possessing a durable network of more or less institutionalized relationships of mutual acquaintance and recognition").
149. *See* Pamela Paxton, *Is Social Capital Declining in the United States? A Multiple Indicator Assessment*, 105 Am. J. Soc. 88, 92 (1999).

Greater social capital has been found to spawn a variety of positive social outcomes, including improved well-being,[150] decreased crime rates, and better-functioning financial markets.[151] As shadow credit systems risk a drop in social capital, the afore-mentioned benefits may give way to greater social disorder, lower participation in civic undertakings, and even growing distrust among network peers.[152]

Moreover, online social networks have also enhanced access to a variety of financial resources through the ability to turn social capital into economic capi-tal.[153] Social capital also correlates with social mobility, which affects the distribu-tion of economic wellbeing over time.[154] Studies show that economic wellbeing can be passed on to the next generation in the form of higher earnings and that a major share of the variation between families at the tenth and ninetieth income percentiles continues into the next generation.[155] Social capital impacts therefore could affect these prospects for social mobility as an unintended consequence.[156] These complex interactions make it difficult to assess the ultimate economic and social impact of behavioral changes affecting social networks.

3. Financial Risks

Since marketplace lenders are not typically subject to traditional banking regula-tions, there are no capital requirements imposed on them or the participating inves-tors or private lenders that provide them with capital. Without adequate capital reserves to weather difficult financial circumstances, marketplace lending has a potential to create new risks that deserve the attention of regulators.[157] The current

---

150. *See* John A. Bargh & Katelyn Y.A. McKenna, *The Internet and Social Life*, 55 Ann. Rev. Psychol. 573 (2004).

151. *See* Paul S. Adler & Seok-Woo Kwon, *Social Capital: Prospects for a New Concept*, 27 Acad. Mgmt. Rev. 17, 29–30 (2002).

152. *See* Ellison et al., *supra* note 146, at 1145.

153. A similar argument was made in the context of traditional (offline) social networks by Pierre Bourdieu. *See* Pierre Bourdieu, *The Forms of Capital*, in Sociology of Economic Life 69, 103 (Mark Granovetter & Richard Swedberg eds., 2001).

154. *See, e.g.*, Jere R. Behrman, *Social Mobility: Concepts and Measurement*, in New Markets, New Oppor-tunities? Economic and Social Mobility in a Changing World 69, 70 (Nancy Birdsall & Carol Graham eds., 2000); Gary S. Fields, *Income Mobility: Concepts and Measures*, in New Markets, New Opportunities? Economic and Social Mobility in a Changing World 101 (Nancy Birdsall & Carol Graham eds., 2000).

155. *See* Pablo A. Mitnik et al., *New Estimates of Intergenerational Mobility Using Administrative Data* 70–72 (2015), https://www.irs.gov/pub/irs-soi/15rpintergenmobility.pdf.

156. *See* Xavier de Souza Briggs, Harvard University Kennedy School of Government, Bridging Networks, Social Capital, and Racial Segregation in America 34 (Working Paper No. RWP02-011, Jan. 2003), *available at* https://research.hks.harvard.edu/publications/getFile.aspx?Id=35; *see also* Silvia Domínguez & Celeste Watkins, *Creating Networks for Survival and Mobility: Social Capital among African-American and Latin-American Low-Income Mothers*, 50 Soc. Probs. 1 (2003).

157. *See, e.g.*, Brayden McCarthy, *Regulation Could Be a Blessing in Disguise for Online Lenders*, Am. Banker, Aug. 4, 2015, http://www.americanbanker.com/bankthink/regulation-could-be-a-blessing -in-disguise-for-online-lenders-1075841-1.html; Todd Baker, *Marketplace Lenders Are a Systemic Risk*, Am. Banker, Aug. 17, 2015, http://www.americanbanker.com/bankthink/marketplace-lenders-are-a-systemic -risk-1076047-1.html; Michael Kang, *The Risks and Rewards of Marketplace Lending*, NATO Ass'n Can., Mar. 23, 2016, http://natoassociation.ca/the-risks-and-rewards-of-marketplace-lending/; John Gapper, *Cracks Are Appearing in Fintech Lenders—Marketplace Is Vulnerable to the Credit Cycle Rather Than Floating in a Brave New World*, Fin. Times, May 11, 2016.

lack of protection and accountability from regulatory oversight,[158] along with a growing significance of marketplace lenders in consumer credit markets, may present new sources of systemic risk should there be an economic slowdown.[159] However, the nature and extent of these risks are contested, as some disagree that marketplace lending can cause such undesired and unintended financial consequences and advocate for the financial advantages and soundness of this industry.[160]

4. Black Box Decision Making

It is now well established that credit bureaus commonly employ "black box techniques," engaging in crucial, yet secretive, decision making when it comes to their methods for data mining and analysis.[161] Because of the complexity of existing credit-scoring models and the opacity around them, those systems are enigmatic even to sophisticated borrowers.[162] Scored individuals may find it challenging to engage in optimal credit behaviors, as it is not always easy to find correlations between certain acts and higher or lower creditworthiness.[163] The information asymmetry does not stop at the consumers' end. In fact, existing credit-scoring models also baffle regulators, who often lack the ability to fully comprehend, challenge, or audit them.[164]

In addition to the heightened opacity of credit-scoring systems, those systems are also commonly criticized for generating arbitrary and inconsistent results. One study shows that 20 percent of consumers are likely to have a score that is "meaningfully" different from the score used by a lender to make a credit decision.[165] Thus, trustworthy consumers could end up being sanctioned[166] or suffer from de facto discriminatory lending practices,[167] with some fearing far-reaching consequences from these errors.[168]

Critics argue that credit scoring has a disparate impact on traditionally disadvantaged classes because there are common factors among minority groups that

---

158. *See, e.g.*, Thaya Brook Knight, *Marketplace Lending: Regulation Ahead?*, CATO INST., Mar. 14, 2016, http://www.cato.org/blog/marketplace-lending-regulation-ahead.

159. *See* McCarthy, *supra* note 157; Baker, *supra* note 157; Kang, *supra* note 157; Gapper, *supra* note 157.

160. *See, e.g.*, Mike Cagney, *How Marketplace Lenders Will Save Financial Services*, AM. BANKER, Aug. 19, 2015, http://www.americanbanker.com/bankthink/how-marketplace-lenders-will-save-financial-services-1076174-1.html.

161. *See* FRANK PASQUALE, THE BLACK BOX SOCIETY 22 (2015).

162. *See* Danielle Keats Citron & Frank Pasquale, *The Scored Society: Due Process for Automated Predictions*, 89 WASH. L. REV. 1, 10 (2014).

163. *See id.* at 11.

164. *See id.*

165. *See* CONSUMER FINANCIAL PROTECTION BUREAU, *supra* note 36, at 7 (analyzing 200,000 credit files from the three major credit bureaus, TransUnion, Equifax, and Experian).

166. *Id.*

167. *See* Cassandra Jones Havard, *"On The Take": The Black Box of Credit Scoring and Mortgage Discrimination*, 20 B.U. PUB. INT. L.J. 241, 245 (2011).

168. *See* Brenda Reddix-Smalls, *Credit Scoring and Trade Secrecy: An Algorithmic Quagmire or How the Lack of Transparency in Complex Financial Models Scuttled the Finance Market*, 12 U.C. DAVIS BUS. L.J. 87, 95, 118 (2011).

mirror higher rates of denial than approval for credit.[169] Minorities, for example, are more likely to have their mortgage applications denied.[170] The utilization of big data in shadow credit systems presents new challenges in assessing the causes of disparate impacts on minorities that are already endemic to existing credit-scoring systems.

When discussing algorithmic decision-making processes that involve "black box techniques," four main concerns are commonly voiced: (1) the dignity of the data may be compromised if the data used is inaccurate or inappropriate; (2) the algorithmic modeling may be biased or limited; (3) human oversight is insufficient as machine learning increasingly eats into human control over algorithmic decision making; and (4) algorithmic processes and their uses are oftentimes opaque.[171] These four concerns are addressed further below.

Data-Related Concerns. Errors, outages, and losses in large data sets can generate inaccuracies that are augmented when multiple data sets are merged.[172] The choice of data to collect could be tainted by widespread biases, and consequently maintain those preconceptions.[173] Data sets also suffer limitations, such as the ability to manipulate them effectively and at a low cost[174] and the discovery of false correlations, in which the statistical significance reinforces the assumption of meaningful connection between the variables even though no such meaningful connection exists.[175]

Algorithmic Design Issues. Similarly to data collection, which is at risk of transforming cultural clichés and stereotypes into empirically certifiable data sets,[176] algorithmic design is also prone to the computerized laundering of such stereotypes. Even when the creator of an algorithm adheres to legal and moral standards, the algorithm may still be affected by bias, generate illegitimate discrimination, or perpetuate an existing discriminatory practice.[177] Data about zip codes, for example, while facially objective, is notoriously known to signal race.[178]

---

169. *See* Citron & Pasquale, *supra* note 162, at 13–16.

170. *See* Skylar Olsen, *A House Divided—How Race Colors the Path to Homeownership*, Zillow, Jan. 15, 2014, http://www.zillow.com/research/minority-mortgage-access-6127/.

171. *See On Social Credit, supra* note 11, at 407.

172. *See* Danah Boyd & Kate Crawford, *Critical Questions for Big Data: Provocations for a Cultural, Technological, and Scholarly Phenomenon*, 15 Info. Comm. & Soc'y 662, 668 (2012).

173. *See* Solon Barocas & Andrew D. Selbst, *Big Data's Disparate Impact*, 104 Cal. L. Rev. 671 (2016), http://papers.ssrn.com/sol3/papers.cfm?abstract_id=2477899.

174. *See* Rick Swedloff, *Risk Classification's Big Data (r)evolution*, 21 Conn. Ins. L.J. 339, 355 (2015); Boyd & Crawford, *supra* note 172, at 668.

175. *See* Boyd & Crawford, *supra* note 172, at 669. *See also* Gary Marcus & Ernest Davis, *Eight (No, Nine!) Problems with Big Data*, N.Y. Times, Apr. 6, 2014, http://www.nytimes.com/2014/04/07/opinion/eight-no-nine-problems-with-big-data.html?_r=0.

176. *See* Michael Schrage, *Big Data's Dangerous New Era of Discrimination*, Harv. Bus. Rev., Jan. 29, 2014, https://hbr.org/2014/01/big-datas-dangerous-new-era-of-discrimination/.

177. *See* Danah Boyd & Kate Crawford, Six Provocations for Big Data, Presented to the Oxford Internet Institute's a Decade in Internet Time: Symposium on the Dynamics of the Internet and Society (Sept. 21, 2011), http://softwarestudies.com/cultural_analytics/Six_Provocations_for_Big_Data.pdf.

178. *See* Tene & Polonetsky, *supra* note 138, at 985.

The Blackest Black Box of Machine Learning. Data is used to identify correlations and improve performance over time by internalizing those trends into the analyzing system, also known as "unsupervised machine learning."[179] The learned statistical patterns are general and not specifically associated with some state or outcome.[180] Thus, even if variables like race and gender are hidden in the observed factors, the learning algorithm is likely to uncover them, add them to its analysis, and later justify facially objective but de facto biased decisions against members of minority groups.[181]

Lack of Transparency. Notwithstanding the harmful potential of data-driven decision making, their specifics remain secret.[182] Technically, it is oftentimes impossible to learn how the analyzing algorithm operates because there is an intellectual property interest in the code.[183] It is also hard to review such systems because information about the mined data, the targeted correlations, and the factors to be quantified and calculated for credit profiling purposes remain opaque. When secrecy veils unacceptable decision-making processes, both oversight and accountability are frustrated because those evaluative methods would not be exposed until adverse repercussions surface, and, even then, it would be hard to point to the exact harmful course.

---

179. *See* Peter Flach, Machine Learning: The Art and Science of Algorithms That Make Sense of Data 3 (2012); Committee on the Analysis of Massive Data et al., Frontiers in Massive Data Analysis 66–69 (2013).

180. *See* Committee on the Analysis of Massive Data et al., *supra* note 179, at 101–02.

181. *See* Lauren Kirchner, *When Big Data Becomes Bad Data*, Pac. Standard, Sept. 9, 2015, http://www .psmag.com/nature-and-technology/when-big-data-becomes-bad-data.

182. *See, e.g.*, Danielle Keats Citron, *Technological Due Process*, 85 Wash. U. L. Rev. 1249, 1308–09 (2008); Lucas D. Introna & Helen Nissenbaum, *Shaping the Web: Why the Politics of Search Engines Matters*, 16 Info. Soc'y 169, 172 (2000); Frank Pasquale, *Restoring Transparency to Automated Authority*, 9 J. Telecomm. & High Tech. L. 235, 244–45 (2011); Daniel J. Steinbock, *Data Matching, Data Mining, and Due Process*, 40 Ga. L. Rev. 1, 45 (2005).

183. *See* Jeremy Kun, *Beware! Big Data Is Not Free of Discrimination*, Soc. Sci. Space, Aug. 13, 2015, http://www.socialsciencespace.com/2015/08/beware-big-data-is-not-free-of-discrimination/.

Chapter 12

Toward the Internet of Value

The Internet of Things and the Future of Payment Systems

Jessie Cheng[1]

I. A WORLD OF INTERCONNECTED OBJECTS

Nearly everywhere today, headlines proclaim an "Internet of Things." But what is this digital transformation, and where is it leading us?

The phrase broadly refers to an interconnected network of everyday objects, made "smart" through built-in sensors and network connectivity that allow them to collect, send, and receive information in a fully automated way.[2] In practical terms, the Internet of Things involves a transformation of everyday physical objects into smart objects able to react to and communicate with the world around them in an efficient and frictionless way. Picture lighting and blinds that automatically respond to changing conditions outside or refrigerators that order new milk when a carton goes bad. These smart objects streamline day-to-day chores and remove human decision making.

---

1. Jessie Cheng is currently deputy general counsel at Ripple and vice chair of the Payments Subcommittee of the American Bar Association Business Law Section's Uniform Commercial Code Committee. Previously, she was counsel in the legal group of the Federal Reserve Bank of New York and, prior to that, an associate at the law firm Wachtell, Lipton, Rosen & Katz.

2. *See, e.g.*, FTC Staff Report, Internet of Things: Privacy & Security in a Connected World 1 (2015), *available at* https://www.ftc.gov/system/files/documents/reports/federal-trade-commission-staff-report -november-2013-workshop-entitled-internet-things-privacy/150127iotrpt.pdf; European Commission, Directorate-General of Communications Networks, Content & Technology, Definition of a Research and Innovation Policy Leveraging Cloud Computing and IoT Combination 18 (2014).

The interconnected ecosystem of the Internet of Things is not limited to consumer applications. Industrial applications of the Internet of Things include interconnected business-to-business systems for tracking inventory, equipment functionality, and operating efficiency. Radio-frequency identification (RFID) technology can already be used to identify and track objects wirelessly. Just recently, General Electric opened what it calls a "digital foundries" around the world.[3] Factory floors will likely see a continued transition toward sophisticated computer-controlled production and automation, with smart machines communicating with each other and their industrial surroundings.

Taking the Internet of Things one step further, smart objects in the physical world can also have the ability to synthesize information and deliver analysis to individuals in real time. As the costs of adding sensors, microchips, and Internet connectivity to products decrease, data can be further transformed into more easily distillable value. The Internet of Things has the potential to fundamentally transform business operations and our day-to-day lives. These technological strides and new transformations on the horizon will also challenge existing payment systems and the current legal framework.

II. THE LIMITATIONS OF TODAY'S PAYMENT NETWORKS

The Internet of Things has the potential to fundamentally transform the way payments are made. Evident today is a movement away from the conventional payment mechanisms of cash and plastic cards, edged out by what would once have been considered the most unlikely objects. A smart watch, like the Apple Watch, can be used to initiate contactless payments through cell phone-stored financial information. A pair of smart glasses, like the Google Glass, could potentially also deliver a swift shopping experience.

Beyond easing the mundane burdens of the modern consumer, the payment capabilities enabled by the Internet of Things can also significantly expand access to financial services for people in the world's poorest regions, empowering the financially underserved to become more involved in the global financial system. Individuals without access to traditional bank accounts can instead use their smart objects, such as smartphones, to hold value and make payments.[4]

The transformative potential of the Internet of Things, however, is limited by today's inefficient, fragmented, and costly payments infrastructure. The Internet of Things enables communication between objects—a seamless exchange of information—but lacking is a built-in streamlined exchange of value.

---

3. *See, e.g.*, Tomas Kellner, *New "Digital Foundry" in Paris Expands GE's Global Software Footprint*, GE Rep., June 13, 2016.

4. *See, e.g.*, Gabriel Demombynes & Aaron Thegeya, World Bank, Kenya's Mobile Revolution and the Promise of Mobile Savings (2012); Ignacio Mas & Dan Radcliffe, Bill & Melinda Gates Foundation, Mobile Payments Go Viral: M-PESA in Kenya (2010).

For example, imagine using a smart medicine cabinet. It might automatically detect when the medicine runs low and seamlessly initiate a payment for refill using stored financial information. This saves you time and effort: no need to drive to the pharmacy, no hassle trying to figure out how to pay with various spending accounts and health plans, and a lower risk of running out of medicine—everything can be done remotely, in real time. However, the Internet of Things empowers you in this way only if you have a method of payment at hand that the smart medicine cabinet and the pharmacy accept.

But what if you do not have access to a credit card or a bank account? Or, what if you are paying for an ailing family member located abroad? Your payment method may not be interoperable with the local pharmacy there, or your U.S. bank may decline to process the transaction. And even if there happens to be compatibility, the risk of unpredictable time delays and opaque foreign exchange rates, service fees, and lifting fees remains.

Payments flow relatively freely along domestic rails within a country, particularly when the payor and payee happen to have accounts with the same bank or within the same network. Payment across networks, however, is riddled with inefficiencies and frictions. Today's payment networks are siloed, and even where connections between payment networks do exist, they are likely slow and expensive. To open up the interconnectedness of the global economy to its full potential, the Internet of Things cannot be left to run on the fragmented rails of today's existing payment systems. Rather, it must be underpinned by the Internet of Value—interoperability across the world's payment systems, allowing payments to move as seamlessly as other information.

III. TOWARD A WORLD OF INTERCONNECTED PAYMENT NETWORKS

The evolution in payments toward global interconnectedness will build upon the technological advances in communication and transportation throughout history that have linked geographically remote commercial counterparties and created the foundation for international transactions. More recently, developments in computing have automated routine and complex procedures for payments processing. Electronic networks allow for faster and more secure communication. However, financial institutions and payment systems continue to operate in silos. Seamless, global interconnectivity has not yet been achieved and some cross-border business processes still rely on manual or only semi-automated procedures. The technologies underpinning the Internet of Value can potentially cure these inefficiencies and frictions, as well as serve as the platform for future innovations that may seem like a pipe dream today.

But this future world is perhaps nearer than we think. Remember, the Internet itself is not one single network or system—it is a network of networks, enabled by open protocols like Transmission Control Protocol/Internet Protocol (TCP/IP) for sending information across independent telecommunications networks. It is easy to communicate over the Internet with anyone around the world in real time, regardless of what provider they happen to use. The power of the Internet comes from this open connectivity. The same can be done for payments.

Technologies such as the Interledger Protocol (ILP) represent the beginning of the Internet of Value, in which exchanging value will be as streamlined as exchanging information today on the Internet. ILP and technologies like it create connections between the many banks and payment systems around the world—from domestic payment systems and the books of correspondent banks, to digital wallets, blockchains, and beyond. It does so through an open, universal protocol.[5] Through this technology, payments around the world can be made efficiently and inexpensively. The global payments interconnectivity that results from this technology will transform the payments landscape, and this Internet of Value will serve as the foundation for the Internet of Things.

Financial institutions will likely continue to play a key role in the Internet of Value, but taking full advantage of its transformative potential will require that they, too, evolve. Many are already pursuing key features of interoperability and real-time payments across currencies. Financial institutions that embrace the potential of ILP and technologies like it will create new services for customers—and avoid being left behind as other payment service providers adapt to and benefit from innovation-fueled changes.

More broadly, participants in the Internet of Things will reshape the payments industry as a whole and drive forward a transformation in how the world transacts—a fourth industrial revolution. As the number and diversity of smart objects increase, more and more quotidian objects will be converted into independent payment-initiation devices. These smart objects will automatically detect the need for a purchase—such as ordering replacement parts directly from foreign manufacturers—and seamlessly initiate payment on behalf of their consumer or institutional owners. Smart objects may also trigger a payment transaction in the other direction, to their owners—such as by submitting insurance claims directly from a remote factory floor. Within an increasingly integrated global economy, these payment capabilities will translate into greater transaction volumes for retail (that is, low-value) cross-border transfers. Even micropayments (one-time payments of tiny amounts) may quickly become a reality as individuals and companies enable objects to make automated payment decisions on their behalf.

IV. LEGAL AND POLICY CONSIDERATIONS FOR AN INTERCONNECTED WORLD

The Internet of Things, underpinned by the Internet of Value, will drive an evolution in the global payments industry. However, the industry must grapple with

---

5. For more information about the ILP, see the white paper *A Protocol for Interledger Payments* by Stefan Thomas and Evan Schwartz, *available at* https://interledger.org/interledger.pdf.

fundamental issues plaguing payment systems today. Ensuring security and privacy, as well as managing identity and financial information across multiple devices and locations, will be challenging. Nevertheless, rapid innovation in smart objects and the transformative potential of the Internet of Things will likely lead to new solutions. The real challenge may well be in future-proofing—developing a legal framework that can continue to be applied in the future, even where the technology and its applications evolve.

A. Identity and Access Controls

Identity and access controls enforce gatekeeping policies with respect to smart objects and the information they contain. They can also control the transfer of information over networks to which the smart object is connected. Together, these measures ensure the integrity and security of information at the time it enters a smart object or network, while it resides on the device and in the network, and while it is in transit within the network.

A system of connected smart objects capable of executing payment transactions raises new challenges for identity and access management. The number and type of smart objects in a particular individual's or institution's possession may be ever-changing. Conversely, there may be multiple users, each with their own payment methods, granted access to a given smart object—and who those users are at a given moment in time may also be in flux. Thus, there is no longer a static, one-to-one relationship between users and smart objects. Conventional controls and management systems that mainly focus on individuals—such as user identifications (IDs)—may be ineffective in capturing the new complex relationships between smart objects and their users. In this way, today's identity and access management solutions are stuck in a pre-Internet past. They depend on the same user ID and password gatekeeping used to secure static information stored on unconnected personal computers and isolated system folders. They were not, therefore, built with interoperability in mind. As a result, users are left to cope with a panoply of user IDs and corresponding passwords, ever-growing in number and required complexity, simply to do business and stay in touch with the rest of the world. And some users, overcome by password fatigue, may simply flout the advice of security experts—they may use essentially the same user ID and password for many similar smart objects or rely on easily crackable remembered words, creating security vulnerabilities to increasingly sophisticated fraudsters.

Applying conventional identity and access management solutions to the multitude of smart objects populating the Internet of Things would exacerbate these already existing security problems, as well as reinforce the fragmentation and inefficiencies of today's payment systems. Without interoperability, users must redundantly establish separate identities for each smart object they use, and then keep track of them all. They may be called on to prove their identity by, say, submitting a copy of a passport or utility bill—which provides more data than may be necessary, creating yet more security problems.

However, the Internet of Things itself may transform identity and access management. Interoperability can be achieved through common standards for how smart objects connect and communicate with each other. When smart objects can speak to each other in a common language, their identity and access controls can efficiently coordinate and seamlessly recognize a given user without a slew of cumbersome user IDs and accompanying passwords. Accommodating the great diversity of smart objects—varying in their manifold uses as well as sophistication—though, will be a challenge. Nevertheless, many unpredictable applications may arise once smart objects speak the same language—we are, after all, still witnessing the solutions human ingenuity and creativity can discover once empowered by the Internet.

B. Authentication and Authorization

The gatekeeping role played by identity and access control policies discussed above allow only certain individuals through to access a smart object and the information it contains, and keep all others out. How does one establish that one is in fact among those certain individuals that should be permitted through—that one is in fact the authorized user that one purports to be? One approach is to provide some piece of information that only the rightful user ought to know (such as a personal identification number (PIN) or password). Another is to use some object that only the rightful user possesses (such as a debit card or token device). A third approach is to rely on something that the rightful user simply is (a physical characteristic such as fingerprints and iris patterns). These approaches can be used individually or in some combination (called multifactor authentication) to form a set of authentication and authorization procedures.

These approaches to the problem of authentication and authorization offer varying degrees of robustness and convenience. The "something you know" approach is common and relatively inexpensive to implement, but it is subject to well-known weaknesses. Passwords can be cracked, particularly if they are jotted down on Post-it notes left lying around for all to see. The "something you are" approaches have been sprouting up fast and continue to capture the imagination. One day, we could sign on to a smart object using a fingerprint scanner and authorize a money transfer with a spy thriller-esque eye scan. However, such biometric hardware is expensive, systems generally lack compatibility, and the technology is still maturing. Moreover, biometrics are not secret and cannot be changed or invalidated once compromised or intercepted—and the risk of interception may be particularly high where arrays of smart objects are relaying biometrics over an open network.

There is great variation, too, within these categories of authentication approaches. The "something you have" approach, for example, can use static or dynamic data authentication. Credit and debit cards with magnetic stripes use static data authentication: they store sensitive payment data that is unchanging. Whoever knows your card number, expiry date, and so forth can use that information over and over again to make fraudulent purchases. Credit and debit cards with a Europay, MasterCard, and Visa (EMV) chip, on the other hand, use dynamic data authentication. This means every time you use an EMV card for payment, the microchip generates a code that is unique to that transaction, and that code is used to authenticate and authorize that particular transaction. The EMV chip itself is difficult to counterfeit. Even if a fraudster were to steal card information from one of your transactions, the stolen transaction code created in that instance would not be usable again and the fraudster's transaction would simply be denied. In short, dynamic data authorization makes it harder for fraudsters to profit from what they steal.

Dynamic data authentication is not limited to physical credit and debit cards. Consumers today can load their financial information onto smartphone-based payment systems that use this more secure method to authenticate transactions. However, even these systems are not iron clad. One weak spot is at the point of enrollment, when financial information is first loaded onto the smartphone. That is, clever fraudsters can take stolen financial information and load it onto their own device. In case any red flags are raised and the bank phones up to request more information from the enrollee (a "something you know" approach), the fraudster may be equipped with just enough information about the victim to pass the test. It is only after financial information is loaded onto a smartphone that the risk of misuse is vastly reduced.

The problems of fraudulent or unauthorized charges are further compounded for consumers if the Internet of Things is left to run on the fragmented and disparate rails of today's existing payment systems. Different payment methods come with different statutory consumer protections. For example, the strongest level of statutory protection for unauthorized charges generally applies to credit card transactions, capping consumer liability at $50.[6] A $50 ceiling also applies to debit card transactions, but unauthorized charges must be reported within two business days; the ceiling can increase to a $500 cap or unlimited liability if the consumer fails to timely report the unauthorized charge.[7] Other payment methods may lack these consumer protections. Because smart objects can be linked to a wide variety of payment rails—various types of cards, bank accounts, and even virtual currency wallets—consumers are left with a complicated patchwork of consumer protections, in some places robust but in others threadbare. Can the average user be expected to manage and mitigate this nuanced variation across an array of smart objects on an ongoing basis?

Until the Internet of Value arrives, the smart objects of the Internet of Things must be cobbled together with today's traditional payment rails, and the chain will only be as strong as the weakest link. As financial transactions have moved from cash to checks to the electronic transfers of today, sophisticated fraudsters have

---

6. 15 U.S.C. § 1643; 12 C.F.R. § 1026.12.
7. 15 U.S.C. § 1693g; 12 C.F.R. § 1005.6.

followed. And as more consumers use payments-enabled smart objects, more points are open to attack. Even worse, an attack on one interconnected smart object could potentially provide a gateway for a fraudster to gain access to a trove of other payment capabilities and stored financial information.

C. Privacy and Security

One of the paradoxes of modern life is that we cherish our privacy, our right to be left alone, yet we obligingly hand off our personal data and financial information in day-to-day interactions. We may take cybersecurity seriously and diligently observe online precautions, but we gladly surrender our credit card information and personal details to retail websites, for example. However inwardly conflicted we may be, our expectations around privacy are evolving. It is harder these days to shut out an increasingly connected and ubiquitous online world. Already, many aspects of our lives today—shopping, fitness, banking, gaming, entertainment, and social connections—are captured on our Internet-connected smartphones. As the amount of information collected and transmitted by smart objects continues to increase at an unprecedented rate, the Internet of Things will likely raise novel privacy and security concerns.

Of course, the technology-neutral privacy and security concerns familiar to us today remain front and center. Take, for example, the complaint brought by the Federal Trade Commission (FTC) against TRENDnet, Inc., settled in September 2013.[8] According to the complaint, TRENDnet, an electronics company, sold video-monitoring cameras that provide live video feeds over the Internet. It had marketed these cameras to consumers as home security and baby monitoring devices, allegedly claiming in its product descriptions that these cameras were "secure." However, the cameras' faulty software apparently allowed hackers to access the live video feeds of hundreds of consumers unbeknownst to them and view their private lives and the interiors of their homes. Concluding that TRENDnet had "failed to provide reasonable security to prevent unauthorized access to the live feeds" from its cameras, the FTC brought its enforcement action using its general consumer protection enforcement powers under section 5 of the FTC Act regarding "unfair or deceptive acts or practices."[9] As the TRENDnet action illustrates, the FTC views unfair and deceptive trade practices in the context of information security as falling within the ambit of its authority, and it will likely play a key role in the interconnected system of the Internet of Things.

The result is that manufacturers of traditional household devices, now made smart and Internet-connected, must become experts in consumer privacy and security matters to which they may previously never have given a second thought. In addition to the FTC Act, state-level prohibitions against unfair, deceptive, or abusive acts and practices (UDAAP) may also be important—state attorneys general

8. *In the Matter* of TRENDnet, Inc., FTC File No. 1223090.
9. 15 U.S.C. § 45(a).

may interpret the scope of these UDAAP laws as the FTC has interpreted its section 5 authority. Beyond these general consumer protection laws, other sectoral laws may also come into play. In particular, the Gramm-Leach-Bliley Act,[10] the California Financial Information Privacy Act,[11] and similar laws that protect the privacy of personal financial information will raise important legal considerations for smart objects capable of initiating payments through stored financial information.

Missing from this bevy of legislation, however, are any privacy and information security laws dedicated specifically to the smart objects that make up the Internet of Things. Any targeted regulation of this nascent space must strike a balance between fostering innovation and growth that enrich our lives, on the one hand, with protecting consumer privacy and the use of sensitive personal information, on the other. Indeed, a number of panelists speaking before the U.S. Senate Committee on Commerce, Science, and Transportation at a February 11, 2015, hearing on this issue urged Congress not to rush to regulate the Internet of Things.[12] In its January 2015 report, "Internet of Things: Privacy & Security in a Connected World," the FTC concluded that there is "great potential for innovation" in this uncharted space, and any Internet of Things-specific legislation would be "premature" at this early stage.[13] However, recognizing the increasing need to manage ongoing data security threats—as well as the potential for smart objects to amplify those threats—the FTC reiterated its previous recommendation to enact broad-based federal privacy legislation that is "strong, flexible, and technology-neutral." Its report also offers concrete steps that smart object developers can take to enhance and protect consumer privacy and security, applying to the core principles and recommendations the FTC has featured in other reports (reasonable security, data minimization, privacy notices, and consumer choice as to collection of personal data).

These privacy and security concerns have gained traction in the European Union as well. An independent EU advisory body called the Article 29 Working Party on Data Protection released a 2014 opinion stressing that the existing EU data protection legal framework is fully applicable to the Internet of Things.[14] In particular, the opinion highlighted individual autonomy and consent, with users remaining "in complete control of their personal data throughout the product lifecycle," and with consent being "fully informed, freely given, and specific."

The contrasts that exist between the FTC's 2015 guidance and the Article 29 Working Party's 2014 opinion perhaps reflect the cultural and political differences between the United States and the European Union regarding online privacy. The United States has generally viewed personal data protection largely through the lens of consumer protection, whereas the European Union sees it as a fundamental

---

10. *Id.* § 6801 *et seq.*

11. Cal. Fin. Code § 4050 *et seq.*

12. *The Connected World: Examining the Internet of Things: Hearing before the Senate Comm. on Commerce, Science, and Transportation* (Feb. 11, 2015). Further information is available at http://www.commerce.senate.gov/public/index.cfm/2015/2/the-connected-world-examining-the-internet-of-things.

13. FTC Staff Report, *supra* note 2, at 47–54.

14. Op. 8/2014 on Recent Developments on the Internet of Things (Sept. 16, 2014).

right of EU citizens. Although the Article 29 Working Party's opinion contributes to unifying the application of the EU data protection framework to the Internet of Things across the continent, still lacking today is any formal and coordinated global effort toward harmonization. The resulting fragmentation of the Internet along national lines may become more apparent and problematic as the interconnected system of the Internet of Things draws even more personal data into the Internet's borderless space.

V. THE NEXT TRANSFORMATION

Already today, one's connection to the Internet is no longer limited to a box that sits on a basement desk. An increasing number and diversity of objects are being equipped with sensors, Internet connectivity, and data analytics capabilities. These smart objects have the potential to fundamentally transform business operations and our day-to-day lives, and they are already beginning to form the backbone of the Internet of Things.

However, to open up the interconnectedness of the global economy to its full potential, the Internet of Things cannot be left to run on the fragmented rails of today's existing payment systems. A lack of global interoperability results in inefficiencies and frictions, further compounded as more smart objects initiate transactions over the Internet's borderless space. Cobbling the Internet of Things with today's fragmented payments infrastructure may introduce new risks and vulnerabilities. Rather, the Internet of Things must be underpinned by the Internet of Value—interoperability across the world's disparate payment networks. The resulting global payments interconnectivity will transform the way businesses operate and the way people relate to the world around them, as well as serve as the platform for future innovations that may seem like a pipe dream today.

Chapter

Structure and Purpose of Payment Systems

Regulation in a World of Emerging Technology

George M. Williams jr

I. INTRODUCTION: FUNDAMENTAL CHARACTERISTICS OF PAYMENT SYSTEMS

The term "payment system" suggests in common parlance a focus on the operational mechanism of a complex device aimed at transferring money, generally involving a variety of technical means for completing such transactions. Although these connotations match the understanding of the term in other legal systems,[1] the legal study of payment systems in the United States generally has a broader scope.[2] While a narrow understanding of the term obscures in many ways the function and purpose of payment systems in their present form(s), a broader, more flexible approach allows us to explore a richer and ultimately more complex set of relationships within human society that accompanies intangible transfers of value in recognized, generalized forms.

Historical studies and current macroprudential considerations make it plausible to treat payment systems as any regular (i.e., structured and repetitive) arrangements for the transfer of intangible valuables or of intangible tokens representing

---

1. For example, the Payment Systems Directive of the European Union, Directive 2007/64/EC of the European Parliament and of the Council of 13 November 2007 on Payment Services in the Internal Market Amending Directives 97/7/EC, 2002/65/EC, 2005/60/EC, and 2006/48/EC, and Repealing Directive 97/5/EC, excludes a number of businesses, including payments based on checks, from the scope of its coverage.

2. As one example among many, see James Steven Rogers, The End of Negotiable Instruments—Bringing Payment Systems Law Out of the Past (2012). See also David Mills et al., Federal Reserve Board, Distributed Ledger Technology in Payments, Clearing, and Settlement (Dec. 2016) (2016-095).

297

such valuables. From this perspective, money, regardless of its physical form, is itself a payment system, because it does not function by itself but only within a set of tacit or governmental arrangements governing the manner in which the applicable monetary tokens can function. In other words, the tokens are not, by themselves, anything. They cannot even be tokens unless they are tokens of something, which is the socially regulated system of monetary units. Analyzing similarities and differences between money and systems that transfer money and other valuables (including money-like valuables) allows us to identify salient characteristics and possible areas of future development. Studying the social, economic, and technical aspects of those systems also allows us to adapt them to their intended purposes as circumstances change.

Payment systems can also usefully be considered in light of their role in the broader context of the entire economy, or at least of the financial system that supports the economy. An evaluation from this perspective may allow the development of a deeper understanding of the nature, function, and purpose of payment systems and of the ways they are regulated. For example, payment systems may be seen as one of the ways in which different parts of the economic system net out their relationships with one another, or as a way in which an economic system measures or regulates its own performance. Indeed, payment systems, together with closely associated legal frameworks involving debt and addressing the time value of money, appear to be the nucleus from which all of our current financial institutions have sprung, with each type of institution becoming subject to its own special set of laws and regulations that have been adapted to the more specific functions and structures necessary to accommodate the type of asset being traded or transferred and the technological capabilities of the relevant time period. Complexity abounds within this constantly evolving system, in which change is a constant feature.

Conversely, it can be argued that the typical characterization of money as serving as a means of payment, a store of value, and a unit of account implicitly contains or perhaps presupposes the notion of an economic system. Being a means of payment is senseless unless the notion of trade, exchange, or obligation already (or at least also) exists. Serving as a unit of account expresses the notion of exchange in a different way, by establishing a measure of what is exchanged and a means of determining whether an obligation has been satisfied; and being a store of value permits the continuation of exchange over more than one short time period.

II. PAYMENT SYSTEMS: THE EMERGENCE OF INTANGIBLE MARKERS

Payment systems, and sometimes entire new financial institutions, emerge when a particular type of exchange activity creates value beyond that created for the original participants, this value being the satisfaction of a need for a regularized and trustworthy service generally useful to at least a meaningful segi. To people living in a society controlled by a powerful individual rule might include the calculation and collection of taxes along with some the manner in which recurring market transactions are conducted. The ments establish or maintain agreement about the nature and amount abstract tokens that can be transferred for particular purposes. This abstractness allows the accumulation of uniform exchange value, rather than the accumulation of miscellaneous collections of disparate objects. This kind of social value and the circumstances under which it can arise appear to be responsible for many of the salient and recurrent characteristics of payment systems and other financial institutions.[3]

We currently have a number of systems for the transfer of different types of intangibles. Listing some of them will by itself constitute a hint as to their similarities and differences. Physical money is transmitted by hand and by way of other nonelectronic media with the understanding that it can, without further transfer or conversion, be used immediately, without transformation into some other form. Banks, automated clearing houses, and money transfer businesses effect the transfer of money domestically and internationally by accepting or delivering cash and by debiting and crediting bank accounts. Credit cards also function by means of an extensive linked system of information about the holders and issuers of the cards and the merchants who will be paid when the cards are used, which is closely linked to banking systems.

The indirect holding system for securities that is governed in substantial part by article 8 of the Uniform Commercial Code and some parallel federal regulations transfers interests in securities by debiting and crediting securities accounts maintained by banks, securities broker-dealers, Federal Reserve Banks, and the Depository Trust Company. Many of these securities represent interests of various kinds in real property. The Mortgage Electronic Registration Systems, Inc. (MERS® System) maintains and transfers interests in mortgage notes electronically. Various kinds of peer-to-peer lending arrangements, securitization structures, and trading desks that arrange for the transfer of interests in loans increasingly resemble payment systems whose "currency" is loans, although that analogy is a bit extreme. A number of systems for the creation, holding, and transfer of virtual currencies function in part as payment systems.

These varied arrangements in some ways reflect and in other ways modify or develop transfer techniques that are attested for earlier periods in history. For example, the crediting and debiting of measures of grain within the same closed

---

3. Here it is useful to note Martin Shubik's trilogy, THE THEORY OF MONEY AND FINANCIAL INSTITUTIONS (MIT Press, 1999–2010), which uses game theoretical notions in an effort to derive money and financial institutions from first principles. Something acts like money if it can be directly exchanged for every other commodity. What might be called the fitness of money has the advantage of not having to be treated as an asset or liability in any system of double entry accounting, another foundational device for payment systems and banks, as well as commercial enterprises, in the sense that it is not itself treated as having a value that fluctuates.

system of a government granary, as in Sumeria, appears to constitute a transfer of something resembling units of account. The transfer of rights to special, immovable objects has also functioned as a kind of payment.[4] Generally speaking, however, the kinds of social arrangements that closely resemble what we think of as payment systems appear to have arisen out of efforts to solve certain kinds of difficulties or develop a particular form of functionality. Among the difficulties to be resolved or functionalities to be developed, the following seem recurrent:

- Protecting (safeguarding) stores of valuables that may ultimately be transmitted and that at the very least serve as (incipient) units of account
- Transmitting value quickly over long distances
- Protecting the integrity of whatever is being used as a store of value and a means of payment
- Ensuring that any payments are made by and to the correct persons (i.e., finding ways to prevent fraudulent orders and incorrect deliveries)
- Conveniently carrying out transactions of widely different magnitudes and frequencies

These difficulties seem to be inherent in the logic of payment instruments and systems, but that perspective develops through long periods of technical, intellectual, and social experience, as opposed to pure insight. The changes we see more recently are variations on these themes made possible by new technical capabilities rather than by completely new fundamentals.

Solutions to these difficulties have varied over time based on the level of technology, the effectiveness of government, and the inventiveness of participants. For example, in addition to gathering wealth for the ruler, temple granaries in Sumeria may also have served as devices for the protection of the grain stored there, standard measures of which served as units of obligation and payment. The initial development of varying instruments of payment and their transmission may not be unrelated to the fact that at the same time computational techniques were being worked out and propagated that allowed rulers and others to determine how much labor or goods was owed upon the partial completion of a task or upon the combining of different tasks. Being able to pay or receive odd, partial, or nonstandard amounts required the corresponding development of payment instruments that could be delivered in such amounts, and the amounts themselves were meaningless unless they could be calculated and associated with some other measure that was

---

4. For example, rai stones, circular disks carved from limestone quarried on Palau and Guam and used as a form of currency on Yap. The oral history of ownership is crucial. *See* Wikipedia, *Rai Stones*, https://en.wikipedia.org/wiki/Rai_stones (last visited May 8, 2017), and the various references cited there. The website of the Deutsche Bundesbank also contains some interesting information. *See* Deutsche Bundesbank, *Stone Money*, https://www.Bundesbank.de/Redaktion/EN/Standardartikel/Bundesbank /Coin_and_banknote_collection/stone_money.html (last visited May 21, 2017). The Bundesbank apparently has a rai stone in its collection of money. It does not seem too far-fetched to note some similarity between such stones and the transfer of rights between customers by a securities intermediary acting with respect to immobilized securities (security entitlements).

treated as creating or constituting an equivalence.[5] In other words, the deve
of payment systems has more or less from the beginning been associated
tendency to ever greater calculation and abstraction.

This gradual abstraction of value from grain to bullion to coinage to bills of
exchange and beyond restructured each of the difficulties to be resolved and functionalities to be developed that were mentioned above.

- The stores of valuables to be transmitted and serve as (incipient) units of
  account were reduced in bulk by the use of metals, then coinage, and then
  paper or book entries
- Lighter or purely intangible values can be transmitted quickly over long
  distances, or may not even need to be transmitted at all, except notionally
- Protecting the integrity of whatever is being used as a store of value
  becomes a more focused and technical activity
- The increasing abstractness and distance of payments requires more sub-
  tle and bureaucratic ways of ensuring that any payments are made by and
  to the correct persons, ranging from enclosing markers inside clay balls
  in Sumeria and, at a later time in Europe, by tearing bills of exchange and
  then matching torn halves when delivery was made, to encryption
- The gradual reduction of payment to the transmission of coins, paper, and
  book entries very much simplified the execution of transactions of widely
  different magnitudes and frequencies

These abstractions and the changes they induced, reflected, or made possible
can be conceived of as the gradual decontextualization of payment to a nominal,
neutral, transferable unit of account with a moderately long shelf life. Holding such
units amounts to holding the rights to a certain volume or amount of generalized
power to purchase or exchange. The function of a payment system is to decontextu-
alize these units away from the notion of physical exchange or distance and establish who (as between sender, recipient, transferring vehicle, and strangers) retains
or obtains rights to these purchase or exchange rights. That is, payment systems
currently reflect at least two processes or levels of abstraction or generalization.

III. STABILIZING AND STANDARDIZING SYSTEMS

The notion that payment is the nucleus of the economy as a whole plays two different roles. As the core of the system, payment naturally attracts the attention of
the state or the ruler, both as a matter of self-interest (such as receiving the desired

---

5. This would appear to be (part of) the message of Norman Biggs, Quite Right: The Story of Mathemat-
ics, Measurement, and Money (2016). See also William N. Goetzmann, Money Changes Everything: How Finance Made
Civilization Possible (2016), which also has a somewhat more detailed discussion of early Mesopotamian
money and finance.

amount of taxes) and as a matter of ensuring that payment functions as anticipated for the benefit of all who participate in such activities, including the operator or regulator of the system. In addition, as the nucleus leads to the creation of other institutions and itself becomes a specialized subpart of a larger system, both it and the institutions it spawns become the focus both of more specialized rules relating to the perceived narrowness of their respective (sub)functions and to rules that link these narrow functions to the broader public good. As mentioned in the discussion of macroprudential supervision in Part V below, this then ultimately engenders a new level of generalization that attempts to deal with the interactions of the systems as an entirety, rather than studying, regulating, and operating each system (and participant in the system) as a single, more or less isolated entity.

Accomplishing such results required (and continues to require) certain cognitive skills or predilections and coordinated social effort, whether on the part of ad hoc groups, governments (or rulers and their staffs), or mixtures of the two. Although the exact historical steps by which means of payment were created are difficult, and perhaps impossible, to establish in detail, there is substantial evidence that, whatever else has gone on, governmental involvement has typically been instrumental in ensuring the functionality and trustworthiness of the applicable system. For example, Christine Desan, in *Making Money*,[6] demonstrates the importance of the governmental framework in England to the establishment of a monetary system, with the requirement to pay taxes in coin being one of the central aspects of that framework. In many monetary systems, even simple matters such as the availability of small-denomination coinage (which was typically a matter of governmental decision making with regard to the operation of mints) can have a large effect on the level of economic activity and financial well-being of the less well-off members of society.

Alain Bresson, in *The Making of the Ancient Greek Economy*,[7] shows something similar regarding the use of prescribed coinage by certain Greek city-states in the Classical era. According to Bresson, the use of coins as a means of payment in virtue of their denomination, rather than the weight and type of metal of which they were composed, depended on the demands of the governments, the way in which the governments operated and financed their activities, and the level of equality among participants in the economic system.[8]

---

6. CHRISTINE DESAN, MAKING MONEY (2014). Desan also discusses the importance of being a unit of account at numerous places in her book. This issue was of day-to-day importance when the coinage available for payment stemmed from multiple mints or rulers and a common means of comparison was essential. The use of fiat money hides this aspect of money to some extent, but it reappears when transferring money that is not legal tender where it is currently deemed to be located or when an internationally active company must decide which unit of account to use in keeping its books. From that perspective, the transfer of money that is not legal tender takes on some of the characteristics of commodity transfers, even though a bank-centric payment system is typically used.

7. ALAIN BRESSON, THE MAKING OF THE ANCIENT GREEK ECONOMY 260–85 (2016).

8. There is interesting information about early Greek entrepreneurs who provided small coins (at interest) for use during the business day in David M. Schaps, *War and Peace, Imitation and Innovation, Backwardness and Development: The Beginnings of Coinage in Ancient Greece and Lydia, in* EXPLAINING MONETARY AND FINANCIAL INNOVATION: A HISTORICAL ANALYSIS 41 (Peter Bernholz & Roland Vaubel eds., Springer 2014).

Frederic C. Lane and Reinhold C. Mueller, in volume 1 of *Money and Banking in Medieval and Renaissance Venice,*[9] and Mueller alone in volume 2,[10] provide a thorough discussion of the intrinsic role of government in the authorization and supervision of the Venetian monetary system. Among other things, persons engaged in money collection and transmission were required to make their accounts public annually, in an effort to maintain trust in the main actors in the system. Emily Kadens has shown[11] that systems thought to be built or based upon trust in the creditworthiness of individuals in fact appear to rely upon the credibility of the credit systems themselves (i.e., on the degree to which the systems reliably produce certain outcomes supporting creditors).

The development of systems based on denomination rather than substance (including the Roman-law contract type known as the *mutuum*, pursuant to which like measures of the relevant commodity were paid, rather than like market values) and the creation of concepts such as negotiability and finality of payment were also crucial to the creation of our conception of what a payment system is or should be.

Establishing and testing the maintenance of the standards thought to be crucial to the maintenance of the type of payment system being operated can require the development of special skills. In a system that depends for its operation on the maintenance of a specific metallic composition, weights, and minting quality, it can prove advantageous to have an expert in charge of the process. For example, Isaac Newton served as master of the Royal Mint in England from 1700 to 1727.[12] The development of a Western system of paper money was accompanied by the acquisition and institutionalization of skills relating to printing, paper, ink, and other methods of maintaining the integrity of the currency,[13] and the passage from bills of exchange to checking led to changes in regulatory, jurisprudential, and practical skills in order to undergird the effectiveness and soundness of the flows of funds effectuated by these techniques.[14]

IV. MODERN TRANSITIONS: TECHNOLOGICAL AND LEGAL CHANGES

In the past 60 or 70 years, changes in communications and computational technology have widened the scope of payment systems and the ways users and regulators think about them. Without such changes, it is difficult to conceive of

---

9. FREDERIC C. LANE & REINHOLD C. MUELLER, 1 MONEY AND BANKING IN MEDIEVAL AND RENAISSANCE VENICE (1985). *See also* JACQUES LE GOFF, MONEY AND THE MIDDLE AGES (2012) (translation of the French edition published by Perrin in 2010).

10. REINHOLD C. MUELLER, 2 MONEY AND BANKING IN MEDIEVAL AND RENAISSANCE VENICE (1997).

11. Emily Kadens, *Pre-Modern Credit Networks and the Limits of Reputation*, 100 IOWA L. REV. 2429 (2015).

12. *See, e.g.*, BIGGS, *supra* note 5, at 96–97.

13. This is apparent from the efforts undertaken in most countries to reduce counterfeiting. For some of the early history of paper money, see GOETZMANN, *supra* note 5, at 144–202.

14. *See* ROGERS, *supra* note 2, and the works cited therein.

the kinds of credit and debit cards that currently exist, of the process by which checks are now cleared and truncated, or of mobile payment and banking applications.

Credit card systems illustrate the fundamental dependence of payment systems on technology, the way new legal issues arise out of changes in underlying facts, and the creation of new social concerns in response to the ways in which new systems are used. The payment systems that accompanied the development of credit, and then debit, cards required the creation, at various levels, of a set of procedures (instantiated in telecommunications and computing hardware and software—along with humans at the beginning) for generating and evaluating sale and customer information. The different levels involved included merchants, banks, and the enabling organizations whose structure and processing capabilities make cards work. The information gathered and the ability to communicate and compare it with stored information made it possible to check the validity of the card being used, the identity and credit status of the user, the amount of credit available under the card, and the participation of the relevant merchant in the membership group of those who had agreed to accept the card on particular terms. The availability of this information on a trustworthy and rapid basis allowed a generalization of the department store charge card and the traveler's letter of credit, which had narrower uses and a less-developed technological infrastructure.[15] The card itself became a device that authorized the activity of the entire informational and transfer system, unlike a check, for example, which was itself an order but not confirmation of the creditworthiness of the payor. In connection with a card transaction, the order was separate from the device.

The entities associated in various ways with the particular brands of credit and debit cards (such as the merchants who have agreed to accept the cards, the banks that issue them, and the card users themselves) are subject to—and sometimes beneficiaries of—laws and regulations. These legal provisions deal with matters such as responsibility for unauthorized card use, the bankruptcy of the cardholder, the manner in which cardholders are solicited, the use to which a bank or other card issuer can put information obtained from its cardholders or about their accounts, and the ability of merchants to recoup from their customers some of the fees the merchants are charged when a transaction occurs.[16] In addition, the wide use of cards has generated social concern about both debt and the extensive amounts of personal data that are often made available or sold.

To use the terminology (mentioned earlier) of payments systems as ways of establishing rights to rights in a manner that renders distance largely irrelevant, credit and debit cards represent a generalized mechanism for both determining

---

15. Department store charge cards were essentially mechanical extensions of store credit; traveler's letters of credit may have made credit available outside the issuing bank's country of origin but were not accepted everywhere by everyone and did not come with simple or automatic means of verification.

16. Prepaid cards are subject to a somewhat different regulatory scheme. *See* Chapter 3.

which rights exist (i.e., the creditworthiness of the card holder) and effecting an enforceable transfer of some of those rights from the place such rights are stored to another storage point. The manner in which the transferable rights are first made available for potential transfer is one of the factors enabling excessive indebtedness, which came to be perceived as a social issue requiring some consideration, and the means of transfer themselves and the ease with which they could be misused generated a different set of concerns (e.g., establishing responsibility for theft or fraudulent misuse). The mere existence of credit cards also created new kinds of businesses (such as merchant processors) and financial accounting concerns (such as the proper treatment of purchases of credit card portfolios).

Checks provide another example of technological changes impacting usage and regulation. As the manner in which checks are cleared has changed on account of technologies such as optical scanning, the expectations of bank customers have also changed. Articles 3, 4, and 4A of the Uniform Commercial Code as well as Federal Reserve Regulation J on check collection and Fedwire and Regulation CC on check collection and funds availability apply in this context. As noted by James Steven Rogers, the technology and practices behind clearing and customer expectation have also rendered portions of article 3 outmoded,[17] something that is not particularly surprising given the way in which the regulation of payment systems interacts with perceived social needs and practices and technological capability. However, the lesson Rogers draws from this obsolescence is particularly interesting in light of other current developments. Rather than suggesting a narrow adjustment to clarify the workings of the system, he suggests that modern practices relating to the use of checks and promissory notes require a fundamental reconceptualization: "[T]he fundamental principle of loss allocation is not negligence. Rather, it is that the risk of unavoidable loss should be borne by the providers of the payment system not by the users of the system."[18]

This view reflects the social concern for protecting the confidence of users of the payment system in the reliability of the system as a whole, something that is typically accomplished by protecting the users from some of the consequences of the way in which the system and its participants operate. Other ways of protecting that confidence (or trust) include having a regulator correct failures in the system or having a trusted operator who takes responsibility for the system's functioning.

---

17. The notion of negotiability is particularly associated with paper-based transactions. Rogers treats this as a result of the fact that checks (and ordinary promissory notes) themselves are only infrequently transferred, even though the value they represent is transmitted by the systems that have substantially replaced a paper-based mechanism. Note that this requires attention to be paid to two different notions of transfer, one relating to the vehicle and the other to the value being conveyed. More importantly, Rogers's insights derive from the ways in which payment systems have adapted in practice to the needs of the users, providers, and regulators. They do not derive from technical legal analysis alone. Instead, they reflect a general concern for the way in which payment systems now work as ways of effectively transferring rights to rights.

18. ROGERS, *supra* note 2, at 166.

Concern for protecting the system and its users also drives studies of the ways in which the various parts of the system function best.[19] A risk allocation of the type suggested by Rogers can raise perplexing issues in a system that by design has neither a trusted provider nor a regulator in the first place, as is at least arguably the case in certain systems that generate and transfer cryptocurrencies, such as Bitcoin. Although there are now institutions for the storage and subsequent transfer of Bitcoins, such as those established under New York State's so-called BitLicense regulation,[20] by their very nature Bitcoins or similar computational (distributed ledger or blockchain) technologies represent the claim that the nature of the system itself establishes and justifies the desired trust or confidence and therefore do not require either a centralized, trusted provider or government regulation or supervision. In other words, the computational structure and incentives of Bitcoin are intended to establish and maintain the trust that in other systems is provided by a regulator or certified operator.[21] In a system without a provider, no one would stand ready to compensate users for unavoidable losses. In Bitcoin systems these losses have so far largely arisen from apparent outside attacks on the system rather than from failures of the system to act as programmed. Other potential sources of loss or failure include carelessness with the private keys that authorize and protect transactions.[22]

Under the New York BitLicense regulations, a licensee must satisfy capital requirements that are set forth in a general manner that refers to the licensee's assets and exposures, liabilities, business volume, leverage, liquidity, product line and other licenses (e.g., other banking or insurance licenses), the existence of other financial protection (such as a trust account or bond), and the price volatility of the virtual currency. Presumably, it will take time to establish what kinds of errors or problems might drive the customer of a licensee to seek compensation, the frequency with which any problems might arise, and the distribution of users between those who prefer to act as individuals and those that make use of intermediaries, whether licensed or not. During that time it will be necessary to evaluate the need for protection and the proper way to identify the types of losses, if any, for which compensation is considered just and practicable, either for the sake of the participants or for the sake of the system's integrity, or both.

---

19. *See, e.g.*, The Future of Payment Systems (Andrew Haldane, Stephen Millard & Victoria Saporta eds., Routledge 2014), and Payment Systems: Design, Governance, and Oversight (Bruce J. Summers ed., Central Banking Publications 2012).

20. N.Y. Comp. Codes R. & Regs. tit. 23, ch. I, pt. 200, Virtual Currencies.

21. For an accessible and fairly thorough discussion of this computational structure and the various incentives, see Arvind Narayanan et al., Bitcoin and Cryptocurrency Technologies: A Comprehensive Introduction (2016). *See also* Anton Badev & Matthew Chen, Federal Reserve Board, Divisions of Research & Statistics and Monetary Affairs, Bitcoin: Technical Background and Data Analysis (Oct. 7, 2014) (2014-104).

22. The case of Greene v. Mizuho Bank, Ltd., 2016 U.S. Dist. LEXIS 114555 (N.D. Ill. Aug. 26, 2016), provides an interesting illustration of how the operation of standard payment systems can interact with the operation of bitcoin storage and transfer when a bank attempts to protect itself from perceived fraud.

Regulators are already considering the use of the distributed ledger systems to support the issuance of legal tender in virtual form.[23] Despite the existence of a distributed ledger in such a case, it is conceivable that the regulator or its appointed agents could be considered the system providers and be responsible for the kind of compensation discussed in Rogers.

V. MACROPRUDENTIAL CONSIDERATIONS

The characterization, functioning, and protection of payment systems and their users also relate to two aspects of such systems mentioned above: their nature as a core of the economy as a whole and the more recent macroprudential focus on payment systems as a potential source of harm to the economy or financial system as a whole if improperly operated or structured. This parallels the shift in concern from the microprudential regulation of single institutions to the macroprudential regulation of those institutions as a system. Microprudential regulation assumes that protecting the safety and soundness of each single institution will protect the system consisting of all of those institutions as they interact with one another and the economy. The parallel shift for payment system regulation is the shift from making each system reasonably error-free, efficient, and fair to making sure that the interactions of all payment systems and their participants do not endanger the rest of the financial system, the economy, or society. Using the terminology of abstraction and generalization mentioned above, macroprudential regulation generalizes from individual payment systems and financial institutions in an effort to determine whether the ensemble of all of these parts behaves in ways that enable a better understanding of how they function and can best be protected from either misuse or systemic risk.

Payment systems as a core of the economy have received attention since the financial crisis of 2007–2008 as a component of the heightened degree of macroprudential regulation and supervision that is represented statutorily by the Dodd-Frank

---

23. *See, e.g.*, Federal Reserve Board Governor Lael Brainard, Speech to the Institute of International Finance Blockchain Roundtable: The Use of Distributed Ledger Technologies in Payment, Clearing, and Settlement (Apr. 14, 2016). The speech also deals with the transfer of electronic tokens representing assets other than money. In addition, the Federal Reserve Board has a more general project that aims to improve payment systems in other respects. In July 2016, the Bank of England released Staff Working Paper No. 605, *The Macroeconomics of Central Bank Issued Digital Currencies*, by John Barrdear and Michael Kumhof. The working paper frames its discussion roughly as follows:

> Digital currency systems can offer a number of *benefits*, such as improved competition, accessibility and resiliency. . . . But such systems also incur additional *costs*. This includes costs related to the storage and synchronization of multiple ledgers, even when all copies can be trusted as accurate and their operators as honest. However much higher costs can arise when participants cannot trust each other to operate correctly. For some systems, these costs can be prohibitively high from a societal perspective.

Id. at 5–6 (italics in original). These issues are discussed in somewhat more detail in Federal Reserve Board, *supra* note 2.

Wall Street Reform and Consumer Protection Act. Examples include regulations[24] dealing with systemically important financial utilities,[25] policies dealing with payment system risk,[26] and the elaboration and heightened enforcement of rules and procedures regarding the prevention of money laundering. Anti-money laundering rules now relate not only to the transmission of legal tender by way of payment systems, but increasingly extend to parallel systems for transmitting value, such as securities brokerages, casinos, real estate sales, and trade financing.[27]

Concern with macroprudential regulation has also led to the study of how interconnected networks of payment, obligation, and liquidity can create or exacerbate systemic risk to the financial system. In effect, this involves the study of how different systems for the transfer of value, including but not limited to payment systems, interact with one another both notionally (in the form of a system of financial obligations, undertakings, relationships, and expectations) and in reality when in fact transfers are required to occur. Studies of this kind take as their object two types of structural relations that occur in and between financial institutions. In addition to spot transactions, two different types of anticipated or contractually structured sets of transactions occur all the time: within an institution, different departments or units arrange to provide funding for one another and the transfer of various kinds of assets among themselves; and the same kinds of interlinked funding and asset transfers take place between institutions. These internal and external relationships typically form complex networks of obligations and expectations.[28] The failure of expected items of value (securities, sources of liquidity) to be available; the failure of the transmission systems to function as designed because of design, operational, or financial inadequacy; and changes in the expectations of system participants can sometimes lead to a financial crisis or at least unexpected volatility. An article published by the Office of Financial Research contains interesting

---

24. Federal Reserve Board, Regulation HH, Financial Market Utilities.

25. These systemically important financial utilities are designated in the United States by the Financial Stability Oversight Council. One of the utilities that have been designated is the Clearing House Payments Company, in its capacity as operator of the Clearing House Interbank Payments System. Other utilities that have been designated engage in the transmission or clearing of other financial instruments, such as foreign currencies, securities, and commodity interests.

26. Board of Governors of the Federal Reserve System, Policy on Payment System Risk, 79 Fed. Reg. 67,326 (Nov. 13, 2014).

27. In THE CURSE OF CASH (2016), Kenneth S. Rogoff argues for the elimination of large bills as a means of reducing money laundering. One of the reasons given for believing that such an elimination would be possible is the extensive use of credit and debit cards, with the caveat that bills of some denomination might be necessary for days in which there is no electricity or electronic communication is not available. All of these considerations reflect a macroprudential evaluation of payment systems.

28. Derivatives can be thought of (in some cases, at least) as carrying these interrelationships farther in two ways: (1) by internalizing an entire network of financial relationships and structuring a payoff based on the contingent results of such relationships, and (2) linking together relationships and parties that otherwise have no external financial connection with one another (or no financial connection of the type characterized in the derivative). This kind of modeling can be thought of as yet another level of abstraction or generalization with respect to financial instruments, devices, and systems. Sometimes derivatives may depend only on the happening of a particular event, but sometimes their operation (and the occurrence—or not of a particular event) can depend on whether entire systems of transfers operate and interact as designed and as expected.

maps of flow relations within and between financial institutions based on information from early stages of the recent financial crisis.[29] The flows within institutions do not appear to differ conceptually from credits and debits within the systems of temples, governments, or bank-like entities at the time money and payment systems began to develop, although they certainly are more numerous and interact with one another in more complex ways. Indeed, within present-day intra- and inter-institutional systems, various types of assets can, by virtue of their interactions with other assets and expectations and the complex functions they serve in the networks created by these expectations and functions, begin to act more and more like money (i.e., become "near money"). This kind of transformation and the complexity of the interconnections out of which it arises typically are used to justify macroprudential regulation, since it is by definition not confined within a single entity.

These networks represent interlinkages of different types of transfer systems, and the ways in which they interact reflect to some degree what would be expected of an activity or object that satisfies the three principal purposes typically accorded to money alone: serving as a means of payment, unit of account, and store of value. The correspondence is weakest with respect to the function of money as a unit of account, but some jurisdictions expressly treat cryptocurrencies as units of account,[30] and some non-currency assets and commodities can easily serve as units of account if they are widely held and easily representable by an intangible token of some kind. As long as the assets are capable of measurement in terms of units (regardless of their market value, as in the case of the Roman *mutuum*), they may easily serve as units of account.[31] Furthermore, as indicated by the current concern with the use of trade goods as a means of circumventing anti-money launder-

---

29. RICHARD BOOKSTABER & DROR Y. KENETT, OFFICE OF FINANCIAL RESEARCH, LOOKING DEEPER, SEEING MORE: A MULTILAYER MAP OF THE FINANCIAL SYSTEM (July 14, 2016) (OFR Brief Series 16-06). The mapped interrelationships deal with short-term funding, assets, and collateral flows.

30. The German Bundesanstalt für Finanzdienstleistungsaufsicht treats virtual currencies as units of account and financial instruments for purposes of applying the regulatory system for which it is responsible.

31. Note that currency amounts wired by banks are treated by recipients as the same as money issued by the government. Some of those amounts represent so-called "inside money," which is created by banks as part of fractional-reserve banking. Although the nondepositor recipient of inside money does not acquire a claim against the transferring bank, the transferred money is no longer available to the bank as a setoff against any failure of the borrower to repay the loan that generated the inside money. In this sense, transfers externalize risk created by banks. For what would appear to be a related notion, see Markus Brunnermeier & Yuliy Sannikov, *The I Theory of Money* 5 (Aug. 8, 2016), *available at* http://scholar.princeton.edu/sites/default/files/markus/files/10r_theory.pdf:

> Like in monetarism (see e.g. Friedman and Schwartz (1963)), an endogenous reduction of the money multiplier (given a fixed monetary base) leads to disinflation in our setting. While inside and outside money have identical risk-return profiles and so are perfect substitutes for individual investors, they are not the same for the economy as a whole. Inside money serves a special function. By creating inside money, intermediaries diversify risks and foster economic growth. Hence, in our setting a monetary intervention should aim to recapitalize undercapitalized borrowers rather than simply increase the money supply across the board. A key characteristic of our approach is that we focus more on the role of money as a store of value instead of the transaction role of money.

ing rules, numerous kinds of assets may in the appropriate circumstances serve as money-substitutes. The kinds of near money that can arise in networks, as discussed above, in effect serve as both means of payment and relatively safe stores of value. In other words, the regular use and acceptability of various kinds of assets in networks of transfer can have at least two indirect effects, namely, creating money substitutes and implicit payment systems. The fact that this happens in networks serves to re-emphasize the role of systems of explicit and implicit transfer (rather than tokens) in creating what we often call money. Given that the classic characteristics of money are to some extent shared by all transfer systems, they can be used, together with other factors, such as technological requirements and type of asset, to classify transfer systems and compare them in terms of how well they fulfill one characteristic or another.[32]

To the extent that payment systems can be treated, as discussed above, as methods for transferring rights to rights (in money) in a way that decontextualizes distance, the same should be true of any method for transferring rights to rights in any other kinds of assets, so long as the rights in the other types of assets can be expressed abstractly and uniquely (encoded, in some sense) in a way that people are willing to consider satisfactory as an indication or representation of such rights. We currently seem reasonably satisfied with the transfer of rights with respect to rights in securities held by intermediaries or on the books of issuers. The rights are "encoded" in part by reference to the names of the securities, the intermediaries, the account holders, and (sometimes) the specific accounts. Distributed ledgers using blockchain technology might encode this information differently. Transfers of real property would likely require the use of different kinds of title registration systems.

---

32. Macroprudential considerations regarding money and its transmission also arise, in other guises, in other areas of the economy. The establishment of the eurozone and the discussions of the weaknesses in the zone's structure revealed by Greece's economic difficulties were and continue to be accompanied by discussions of the concept of an optimum currency area (i.e., the conditions under which a nonuniform political-economic area can successfully function with one unit of legal tender). Although these discussions typically concern labor relations, taxation, redistribution of governmental funds, trade, and similar matters, they can also be understood as relating to the effect of money serving as a unit of account. The notion of a unit of account seems to deal with two different but related aspects of money: serving as a unit of measurement to allow comparisons between assets and liabilities and serving as a unit in which all of the assets and liabilities of businesses and governments in the currency area must be denominated. When these two roles combine with one another, the use of a single currency in a political-economic area will, by virtue of the arithmetic effects, often generate stresses when businesses and governments are subject to substantially different economic conditions. The stresses may be generated by economic and governmental practices and policies, but they play out by virtue of the standard unit of measurement as it is reflected in accounts required by the applicable accounting systems. Such effects do not follow automatically if two systems use different units of account. For two extensive and general discussions of the issues relating to the eurozone, see MARKUS K. BRUNNERMEIER, HAROLD JAMES & JEAN-PIERRE LANDAU, THE EURO AND THE BATTLE OF IDEAS (2016), and JOSEPH E. STIGLITZ, THE EURO: HOW A COMMON CURRENCY THREATENS THE FUTURE OF EUROPE (2016).

VI. POSSIBLE FUTURES

The increase in macroprudential supervision, the possibility that something like blockchain technology (and the distributed network structure associated with it) may become commonplace, and the ways in which communications technologies (including the use of powerful mobile devices) can either enable or implicitly force changes in the practice of transfers suggest that at least two broad types of change are likely: (1) the development of new technical means of abstractly representing assets and effecting their transfer or (more likely) the transfer of rights in the underlying assets, and (2) the creation of a broader conception of transfer for the purposes of study, regulation, and statutory drafting. Dealing both practically and in a supervisory capacity with various flows will become easier and quicker with the development of algorithms that calculate the state-conditional cash flows of financial instruments,[33] and the results of such calculations should make it possible to better visualize and conceptualize the kinds of flows that make up the financial system.[34]

In addition, the multiplication of the means of transfer and the rights being transferred and the likely changes in the types of devices (such as blockchain) that effectuate and document such transfers[35] are likely to suggest and perhaps compel changes in the statutes (such as the Uniform Commercial Code) and regulations (such as those of the Federal Reserve Board) that in effect codify what we expect of such systems. It is not particularly difficult to work through several articles of the Uniform Commercial Code and find numerous spots where changes in detail may need to be carefully worked out, for example in the way security interests can be created and perfected in virtual currencies.[36] It may also be necessary, for example, to establish new definitions of or standards for the finality of certain transfers and the recognition of adverse claims. More speculatively, it may ultimately even make sense to isolate general standards for all kinds of transfers, to be supplemented by specific qualifications for particular asset types, rather than having a separate statute, regulation, or more or less cohesive body of law for each type of transfer.[37]

An even more speculative consideration also suggests itself. The increasing focus on various types of electronic and/or telephonic payment systems and the

---

33. This is one of the principal purposes of the software project referred to as ACTUS, which is being developed by the ACTUS Financial Research Foundation and other individuals and institutions for ultimate release as open-source software. For more information, see http://www.actusrf.org.

34. Visualizing institutional and systemic cash flows in real or near time will likely not only allow financial institutions to be more closely managed (and regulated) but also to suggest either new financial instruments or systems.

35. The dematerialization of securities transfers being a not-yet-distant example of such a change.

36. This is not to suggest that creation and perfection are currently impossible but only that the process can perhaps be simplified and clarified.

37. This might resemble the German practice of creating a general part for certain codes or collections of statutes that contains basic principles that will be utilized throughout the more specific laws or rules.

broadening of notions about the keeping of ledgers can be thought of as potentially creating state of affairs in which people think of the payment system itself as, in some sense, money, rather than as just a means of transmitting value. The multiplying variety of payment systems, the gradual deemphasizing of cash in some countries, and the online direction of various asset management and payment functions all hint at such a possibility. It is difficult to imagine in detail what kind of effects such a conception of money might have, but the role of the regulator or the state might have to be focused more on the system as a whole than it already is, and the roles of financial intermediaries may require some redefinition.

Index

state laws and regulation *(continued)*
  card system under, 28, 33, 36, 37
  contextual commerce under, 155, 156–59, 165
  coordination of, in age of big data, 266
  cryptocurrencies under, 60, 136, 145–47, 306
  escheat requirements, 99–100
  Internet of Things, 294–95
  mobile transactions under, 97, 98–100, 105–6, 111–12, 117–22
  nonbank money transmission under, 16, 47, 48, 49, 50, 58–71, 73, 74, 97, 98–99, 145–47, 156–59
  penalties for violation of, 68–71
  policy questions and considerations, 117–22
  privacy–related, 71, 73, 105–6, 294–95
  security–related, 71, 73, 105–6, 155, 165, 294–95
  stored–value products under, 158–59
  unclaimed property laws, 99–100
statutes of limitation, for ACH system breaches, 9
stored–value products
  contextual commerce, 155, 158–59
  nonbank money transmission, 49, 61–63, 158–59
  open–loop arrangements, 158–59
  state laws and regulations, 158–59
  See also gift cards; prepaid accounts; prepaid cards
store loyalty cards, 87, 240, 248
Stripe, 234
Suspicious Activity Report
  card system, 45
  money laundering prevention, 173, 177, 184, 190
  nonbank money transmission, 56–57
Switzerland
  Financial Market Supervisory Authority, 204–5
  instant/faster payments, 235
  money laundering prevention, 204–5
  SEPA role, 226

Target Corporation, 25
taxation
  money laundering and, 169, 172

payment system structure and purpose, 299, 302
  by regulation, 226
  virtual/cryptocurrencies and, 141, 142–43
Telephone Consumer Protection Act (TCPA), 107–8
telephone transactions
  ACH system, 8, 13–14
  National Do Not Call Registry, 108–9
  nonbank money transmission, 48
  TCPA on, 107–8
  Telemarketer Sales Rule on, 108–9
  telephone–initiated entries in ACH system, 13–14
  See also mobile transactions
terrorist financing prevention
  cryptocurrencies, 144
  European framework, 197–98, 200–202, 255
  federal enforcement, 169
  freezing and confiscation of funds, 201–2
  mobile transactions, 94, 96
  nonbank money transmission, 53, 57
  prepaid access, 183
  sanctions, 192, 197–98, 200–202
third–party senders, in ACH system, 14, 15–16, 101
third–party service providers, in ACH system, 101
TILA. *See* Truth–in–Lending Act
tokenization
  cryptocurrency, 125 (*see also* Bitcoin)
  fees, 85
  fraud and security issues, 86, 256
  mobile transactions, 82–84, 85, 86, 92, 247
  money, 298
Trading with the Enemy Act (TWEA), 196
Trans-European Automated Real-time Gross Settlement Express Transfer (TARGET), 225
transit routing numbers, 6
transparency
  big data and, 273–75, 285
  blockchain technology, 129
  money laundering prevention, 179, 199
  payment processor requirements, 110